Also by Jim Hougan

Spooks
Decadence

SECRET AGENDA

SECRET AGENDA

Watergate, Deep Throat and the CIA

Jim Hougan

Random House New York

Grateful acknowledgment is made to the following for permission to reprint previously
published material:

Harper's magazine: "Mission Impossible" by Eugenio Martinez. Copyright © 1974 by
Harper's magazine. All rights reserved. Reprinted from the October 1974 issue by special
permission.

The New York Times Company: Report from The New York Times News Service,
published in the Baltimore *Sun*, January 26, 1979. Copyright © 1979 by The New York Times
Company. Reprinted by permission.

Putnam Publishing Group: excerpts from *Undercover* by Howard Hunt. Reprinted by
permission of The Putnam Publishing Group. Copyright © 1974 by E. Howard Hunt.

St. Martin's Press, Inc.: excerpts from *Will: The Autobiography of G. Gordon Liddy*. Copyright © 1980 by G. Gordon Liddy. Reprinted by permission of St. Martin's Press, Inc., New
York.

Simon & Schuster, Inc.: excerpts from *Blind Ambition* by John W. Dean. Copyright ©
1976 by John W. Dean. Reprinted by permission of Simon & Schuster, Inc.

Times Books/The New York Times Book Co., Inc.: excerpt from *On Watch: A Memoir*,
by Elmo R. Zumwalt, Jr. Copyright © 1976 by Elmo R. Zumwalt, Jr., Admiral U.S.N.
(Retired). Reprinted by permission of Times Books/The New York Times Book Co., Inc.

Library of Congress Cataloging in Publication Data
Hougan, Jim.
Secret agenda.
Includes index.
1. Watergate Affair, 1972–1974. 2. United States.
Central Intelligence Agency. 3. Intelligence service—
United States. I. Title.
E860.H68 1983   364.1′32′0973   82-42810
ISBN 0-394-51428-9

As Ever: For Carolyn, Daisy and Matt;
For Michael Salzberg;
Necnon Diaboli Advocato: R.D.L.

I had this nagging feeling that the Watergate might turn out like the Reichstag fire. You know, forty years from now will people still be asking did the guy set it and was he a German or was he just a crazy Dutchman?

—Howard Simons,
Washington Post

We witness an attempted coup d'etat of the U.S. government . . . through well-measured steps by a non-elected coalition of power groups.

—Bruce Herschensohn,
Nixon aide

Special thanks should be extended to Robert Fink and Jeffrey Goldberg for their research assistance and patient criticism.

Contents

APPENDIXES

Introduction

In the early morning hours of June 17, 1972, five men were arrested in the Watergate headquarters of the Democratic National Committee (DNC). Wearing business suits and surgical gloves, they were in possession of bugging devices and photographic equipment.

Within twenty-four hours, police and FBI agents established links between the arrested men, the Committee to Re-elect the President (CRP) and the Nixon White House. In the meantime a political cover-up had already begun: evidence was shredded and burned, perjury contemplated, and justice obstructed by some of the most important officials in the U.S. government. Despite this, and despite the administration's efforts to depict the break-in as "a third-rate burglary" unworthy of attention, the story stuck tenaciously to the front pages of liberal newspapers throughout the United States. During that summer and fall, the press, and in particular the *Washington Post*, pursued the issue in an effort to learn the extent and nature of the administration's "dirty tricks," and the identities of those responsible for them.

As the President's reelection neared, it became increasingly difficult for those involved to stonewall the press. An employee of one of the arrested men told the FBI that he had monitored some two hundred telephone calls emanating from the DNC, which, he claimed, had been bugged for the first time in May of 1972. With the guidance of an anonymous source, nicknamed Deep Throat, *Washington Post* reporters rattled the White House with a barrage of front-page articles about secret campaign funds, vicious campaign practices and much more. Soon a Senate select committee was convened to explore the affair, and one of the first witnesses that it heard was a former CIA officer named James McCord. A turncoat in the eyes of his accomplices, McCord was one of the men arrested in the

Watergate. Infuriated by the Nixon administration's handling of the affair, and fearful of receiving a draconian sentence, McCord had written a letter to the judge who presided over the criminal case against the original defendants. In that letter, McCord wrote that perjury had been committed, that there were other conspirators who were yet to be named, and that political pressure had been applied to ensure the silence of those under arrest. McCord promised to tell all, and soon afterward so did White House officials such as John Dean. Finally, after a succession of damaging revelations and the enforced resignation of subordinates, the President was hoisted by his own petard: the existence of a secret White House taping system was revealed and, with it, Nixon's complicity in the cover-up. On August 8, 1974, he announced his resignation as President of the United States.

Public reaction to that announcement was a mixture of jubilation (on the part of Nixon's enemies) and relief (on the part of his friends). For nearly two years the country had been blitzed by the minutiae of Watergate and force-fed the images of increasingly uninteresting men. Was there anyone left who did not consider himself a reluctant expert on the subject? Probably not.

It is against some odds, therefore, that ten years after the affair has been put to rest I offer the reader a new book on what has already been the subject of more than a hundred and fifty books. That I do so is partly the result of an accident. I had intended to write not a book about the Watergate affair but a magazine profile of a private detective named Louis J. Russell. An alcoholic and a womanizer, Russell had been one of the country's foremost "Red hunters" during the 1950s while a top staff member of the House Committee on Un-American Activities (the notorious HUAC). In researching the sordid details of Russell's life, I soon learned of his employment by McCord and, what is more, of his presence at the Watergate break-in on the night of the arrests. In an attempt to understand what he was doing there on that momentous evening, I studied the break-in with more attentiveness than the authorities themselves had displayed a decade earlier. Because the burglars had been caught in the act, the burglary itself had not seemed to warrant intensive investigation. The best efforts of the press, the Senate and subsequently the special prosecutor were therefore applied to questions of political responsibility and culpability in the cover-up. For that reason, many questions about the break-in had been left unanswered—not the least of which was its purpose.

Eventually I was able to answer some of these questions by interviewing men and women whose evidence had been ignored. These were not, for the most part, White House officials or Cabinet members but lowly workers at the DNC, waitresses and maintenance men at the Watergate, landladies, secretaries, cops, neighbors, desk clerks and security guards. The details they provided led to a picture of the Watergate break-in that was far different from what had been transmitted via television at the time.

Besides these interviews, I was able to obtain (through the Freedom of Information Act) literally thousands of pages of FBI documents pertaining to Watergate. These included interviews, laboratory reports, summaries, chronologies, "air-tels," photographs and telephone records. Most of this material—indeed, almost all of it—was never available to the Senate's Ervin committee. An internal memorandum of the FBI states that "[T]he only information we furnish to that Committee is the opportunity to review FD-302s of interviews conducted during the McCord investigation. Such FD-302s must be specified by the name of the person interviewed and are made available only for review, not copying."[1] In effect, the FBI investigation of the Watergate affair was off-limits, except on the most restricted basis, to the very committee that sat in judgment of the Nixon administration. Clearly, the Senate's conclusions—and American history—would have been radically different if the bureau's findings had been shared more freely at the time.

I was the first outsider, then, to get an inside look at the FBI's Watergate investigation, and what I found was startling. The most fundamental premise of the affair has always been that White House spies bugged the Democrats in their headquarters at the Watergate complex—apparently to gain political intelligence. FBI documents, however, and other evidence that was either ignored or overlooked by Senate committees, prosecutors and the press show conclusively that:

· telephones in the Watergate offices of the Democratic National Committee (DNC) were never bugged;

· false evidence (in the form of a crude, defunct bugging device) was planted inside the DNC months after the Watergate arrests, so as to conceal the truth about the affair.

Further investigation showed that:

[1]FBI memo from the legal counsel to the director, December 12, 1973, "Subject: Senate Select Committee on Presidential Campaign Activities; request to interview special agents Arnold L. Parham and Robert L. Wilson."

· G. Gordon Liddy, the ostensible leader of the espionage team, was in actuality a dupe of his subordinates, E. Howard Hunt and James McCord;

· Hunt and McCord were secretly working for the CIA while using the White House as a cover for domestic intelligence operations that (in Hunt's case) included spying upon the administration he had sworn to serve;

· clients of prostitutes in the Columbia Plaza Apartments, hard by the Watergate complex, were the real targets of the bugging operation.

"Watergate," then, was not so much a partisan political scandal as it was, secretly, a sex scandal, the unpredictable outcome of a CIA operation that, in the simplest of terms, tripped on its own shoelaces. There is more, much more, but the point is made: our recent history is a forgery, the by-product of secret agents acting on secret agendas of their own.

What follows in this book does not pretend to be a "definitive" account of the Watergate affair. On the contrary, it is simply an attempt to correct the record insofar as it is possible to do so, and to suggest avenues of further investigation. Inevitably, because evidence has been destroyed and the accounts of witnesses are often in direct conflict with one another, it sometimes happens that issues of apparent importance to the scandal cannot be resolved. We have chief Plumber David Young's word, for example, that the Moorer-Radford spy scandal is of particular importance in understanding the Watergate affair. Unfortunately, however, Young has sworn not to discuss the matter, with the result that our account of the Moorer-Radford matter ends on an inconclusive note. In a similar way, the CIA's intensive surveillance of columnist Jack Anderson, culminating in a meeting at which Anderson and CIA Director Richard Helms both appear to have been spied on, becomes increasingly mysterious—rather than less so—the more one studies it. Why did the agency terminate its surveillance at the very moment that Hunt, Liddy and a supposedly retired CIA physician were meeting to discuss ways of terminating the columnist himself? A third cul-de-sac concerns certain events that occurred in Washington on the night of May 26, 1972, the night of the so-called banquet break-in. The only conclusion that one can fairly reach after studying the evidence is that the subject is important enough for more than one person to lie about it. Finally, there are general questions to which no specific answer suggests itself: e.g., to what extent did conflicts within the U.S. intelligence community, or schisms between American foreign-policy-makers, contribute to President Nixon's downfall? Or were those rivalries no more than trace elements in the poisonous atmosphere in which Nixon's downfall happened to occur?

In the absence of the power to subpoena testimony and evidence —a power not usually available to authors—these questions are unlikely ever to be answered. Still, they must be asked if we are to understand *the dimensions* of the mystery we have come to study. For this reason, then, *Secret Agenda* must occasionally embark upon a puzzle that it does not solve. To ignore such puzzles as the Moorer-Radford affair, or to pretend that they do not exist, would be an act of bad faith.

My hope, then, is that this book will be read as a political detective story, and one, moreover, that will lead to the formation of a new, nonpartisan commission of inquiry. Clearly, the whole truth will become known only through the efforts of such a panel, one armed with subpoena powers and with access to evidence that, until now, has been unavailable—i.e., to the Watergate files of the FBI and the CIA.[2]

---

[2]The author's efforts to obtain access to certain CIA documents pertinent to the Watergate affair have been frustrated by the agency's procrastination. A Freedom of Information Act (FOIA) request filed by this writer with the National Archives was referred to the CIA more than three years ago. Though the agency claims that it has nothing to hide where Watergate is concerned, it has yet to release a single requested document or to cite any FOIA exemptions for having failed to do so.

I

WELL-MEASURED STEPS

1.
Of Hunt and McCord

Of all those who played important roles in the Watergate affair, no two proved more decisive than E. Howard Hunt and James McCord. Here, then, at the very beginning of our reexamination of the scandal it will be useful to look at the careers and personalities of both men, to gain some understanding of the CIA components for which they worked and to take note of the clandestine relationship that existed between them.

Hunt was a GS-15 CIA staff officer in the late fall of 1969 when he approached a fellow alumnus of Brown University, Charles Colson, and asked if there was any possibility that he might come to work for the Nixon White House. Seated with Hunt in the White House cafeteria, Colson demurred, explaining that he himself had only just been appointed to the Nixon team and, as a newcomer, had little influence upon the White House's hiring practices. Despite this, however, Colson tells us that Hunt continued to "pester" him for more than a year in an effort to win a consultancy.

While Howard Hunt has been thoroughly deglamorized, and even trivialized, by his participation in the Watergate affair, his life has been more interesting than many imagine.[1] A war correspondent for *Life* magazine in 1943, he joined the Office of Strategic Services (OSS) that same year, serving in the celebrated 202 Detach-

[1]My brief biography of Hunt relies on the following sources: the résumé that he submitted to the Robert R. Mullen Company in 1970; his entries in *Who's Who* and *Contemporary Authors*; Senator Howard Baker's September 24, 1973, summary of Hunt's career in the CIA; Hunt's autobiography, *Undercover: Memoirs of an American Secret Agent* (New York: Putnam, 1974); and Tad Szulc's biography of Hunt, *Compulsive Spy: The Strange Career of E. Howard Hunt* (New York: Viking Press, 1974). More than one source is necessary in order to reach a consensus of probability about Hunt's years in the CIA, so many are the contradictions and omissions in the various biographies.

ment in Kunming and Shanghai, China.[2] Demobilized at war's end, he applied for and received a Guggenheim fellowship in 1946. With that in hand, he spent a year banging around Mexico, working on a novel, and then traveled to Hollywood to try writing screenplays. Becoming bored with that, he joined U.S. Ambassador Averell Harriman's staff as a press aide in 1948, moving to Paris as part of the Economic Cooperation Administration (ECA). Whether or not this was a cover for actual CIA employment, as journalist Tad Szulc has written, is disputed.[3]

It was while with the ECA that Hunt met Dorothy Wetzel. Bright and attractive, Dorothy had spent the war years in Bern, Switzerland, working for the Treasury Department's Hidden Assets Division (which was responsible for tracking down concealed Nazi assets abroad). At the end of the war she became a technical consultant on a Dick Powell film, *To the Ends of the Earth*, about the international narcotics trade. Shortly afterward, she went to Shanghai and, while there, wed a French marquis. The marriage did not work out, however, and she was already divorced when Hunt was paid $35,000—a fortune at the time—for the film rights to a novel that he had written, *Bimini Run*.[4] Shortly thereafter they were married. According to Hunt, it was then that he joined the CIA.

His first posting appears to have been to Vienna, a mecca for Cold War intriguers. He was then sent to Mexico City (1951–52), after which he became chief of covert operations for the Balkans, a post he held while serving in Washington. In 1954 he participated in planning the invasive coup d'état against Guatemala's left-wing

[2]The detachment was celebrated not only for its work with Chinese guerrillas, but also for the postwar exploits of some of its more notorious members—men such as Hunt, Florida attorney Paul Helliwell, arms dealer Mitchell Livingston WerBell III, Bangkok exporter Willis Bird and the Drug Enforcement Administration's Lucien Conein.

[3]Compare Szulc's *Compulsive Spy*, pp. 63–66, with Hunt's *Undercover*, pp. 53–66. According to Szulc, Dorothy Hunt was a CIA officer and, in fact, may have joined the agency before Hunt himself did. Questioned about this by the Senate's Ervin committee, CIA Director Richard Helms said that in "the dimness of [his] recollection," Mrs. Hunt had been a CIA employee prior to marrying Howard (see the Ervin committee's *Hearings before the Senate Select Committee on Presidential Campaign Activities of 1972*, 93d Cong., 1st sess., May 1973–June 1974, Book 8, p. 3262).

[4]Curiously, the hero of *Bimini Run* is an ex-Marine named "Hank Sturgis." This has naturally led to speculation that Hunt named his two-fisted protagonist after Frank Sturgis, the ex-Marine who participated in the Watergate break-in. This, however, incorrectly implies that Hunt and Sturgis knew each other as early as 1949 (when *Bimini Run* was published). In fact they did not. Sturgis was born Frank Fiorini. When his mother remarried, he took her new last name (Sturgis) as his own. The christening of Hunt's protagonist was only a coincidence.

president, Jacobo Arbenz Guzmán. Only days before the coup was carried out, he was transferred to the CIA's North Asia Command (comprising China, Japan, North and South Korea, Taiwan, Okinawa, Hong Kong and Subic Bay). Based in Tokyo, he was chief of covert operations in that area until 1956, when the agency appointed him chief of station in Montevideo, Uruguay. This post was to last four years, until, in late 1959, Hunt was brought home to assist in planning for what ultimately became the Bay of Pigs invasion. When the invasion failed, he was named to outgoing CIA Director Allen Dulles's personal staff. A year later, after Dulles had been ousted, Hunt was appointed the CIA's first chief of covert actions for the Domestic Operations Division. What this job entailed is unknown, but it certainly included subsidizing news services and books (e.g., Fodor's travel guides) in which the agency had an interest. According to Hunt himself, the new job also involved spying on GOP presidential candidate Barry Goldwater.[5] What is more worrisome, though, is that Hunt is said to have played a continuing role in the CIA's ongoing efforts to assassinate, unseat or harass Fidel Castro in the aftermath of the Bay of Pigs.

It was at about this time that Hunt was asked to serve as deputy chief of station in Madrid, a city he liked and one, moreover, that served the CIA as a staging ground for assassination attempts against Castro.[6] Hunt's appointment, however, was blocked by the former U.S. ambassador to Uruguay, Robert Woodward, who disliked Hunt and who was then ambassador to Spain. Despite this, Hunt went to Madrid (though not to the embassy) in an undercover capacity during 1965, remaining there until 1966. Returning home from this last posting abroad, he worked at the CIA's headquarters in Langley, Virginia, under State Department cover until his retirement in 1970.

These, then, were the outlines of Howard Hunt's career in the CIA, though a simple recitation of facts can hardly convey what it must have been like to work behind the lines in China or to carry out assignments in Vienna during the Cold War.

When Hunt first approached Colson for work in the White House, he was still a part of the CIA. His retirement from the agency would not occur until April 30, 1970, and, considering his

<hr>

[5] Hunt, *Undercover*, p. 133.
[6] Warren Hinckle and William Turner, *The Fish Is Red: The Story of the Secret War Against Castro* (New York: Harper & Row, 1981), pp. 192, 239–42; and Szulc, *Compulsive Spy*, p. 97.

past record, the possibility that this retirement was bogus is quite real. Indeed, this was the *third* time that Hunt had left the Central Intelligence Agency.

The first occasion was in 1960, when he was issued fraudulent retirement papers to facilitate his liaison with anti-Castro exiles. When that invasion was launched, only to founder, Hunt returned to the agency's staff—having never actually left its payroll. Five years later, in 1965, Hunt quit for the second time. The author of more than four dozen pulp thrillers and novels of the occult, Hunt left the agency in furtherance of a counterintelligence scheme that revolved around his literary efforts. The purpose of the scheme, according to government sources familiar with Hunt's curriculum vitae at the agency, was to draw the KGB's attention to books that Hunt was writing under the pseudonym David St. John. These spy novels alluded to actual CIA operations in Southeast Asia and elsewhere, and contained barely disguised portraits of political figures as diverse as Prince Norodom Sihanouk and the late Senator Robert F. Kennedy. It was the CIA's intention that the KGB be led to believe that the books contained security breaches, and toward that end the agency created a phony "flap" that was capped by Hunt's supposedly "forced retirement." In his memoir of his years as a spy, Hunt does not mention the counterintelligence aspects of the David St. John novels, but writes: "I resigned from the CIA [this second time], and was at once rehired as a contract agent, responsible only to [the CIA's Deputy Director for Plans, Thomas] Karamessines."[7]

Leaving aside the precedents established by Hunt's false retirements in 1960 and 1965, the authenticity of his 1970 departure from the CIA should be questioned on yet other grounds. To begin with, Hunt's transition to civilian life was considerably smoothed by the interventions of the CIA director himself, Richard Helms. Not only did Helms see to it that Hunt received large no-interest personal "loans" from a special CIA fund,[8] but the director also went out of his way to write a personal recommendation on Hunt's behalf, urging the Washington-based Robert R. Mullen Company to hire him.[9] Itself a CIA cover, the Mullen Company would become increasingly entangled in the agency's affairs by virtue of its impend-

[7]Hunt, *Undercover*, p. 134.
[8]Ibid., p. 140.
[9]Ibid., p. 141, and Szulc, *Compulsive Spy*, p. 105. Besides Helms, columnist William F. Buckley also recommended Hunt for the job at the Mullen Company.

ing involvement with the Howard Hughes empire and that empire's links to the CIA and Project Jennifer.[10] The Mullen Company, then, was in a poor position to ignore Helms's "recommendation," and, indeed, it did not. Hunt got the job.

The circumstances of Hunt's retirement from the CIA are important. If it can be shown that his departure was merely an operational convenience, useful for the purposes of deniability and, perhaps, infiltration, then it would appear that the CIA—and not the White House—was Hunt's real principal throughout the Watergate affair. And there is much to suggest this.

For example, internal memoranda of the CIA establish that the agency's Central Cover Staff reviewed *and extended* Hunt's top-secret security clearance prior to his retirement, and that, moreover, this was done in anticipation of Hunt's continued "utilization" by the CIA.[11] Other agency memos establish that Hunt's continuing utility was due to many things, including his "access to Colonel White"[12] and Hunt's role in negotiations between the CIA and the Mullen Company.[13]

[10]Project Jennifer was a top-secret CIA/naval task force operation to recover a sunken Soviet submarine and, with it, Soviet naval codes. The mission was to have been carried out under cover of a commercial oceanic mining operation supposedly financed by Howard Hughes. The operation had only just gotten under way when former CIA agent Robert A. Maheu was purged from his high position in the Hughes organization. As a result of that purge, Hughes interests came to be represented in Washington by the GOP-oriented Mullen Company rather than, as formerly, by Lawrence ("Larry") O'Brien, chairman of the Democratic National Committee (DNC) and the ostensible target of the Watergate break-in. (For an account of Project Jennifer, see Roy Varner and Wayne Collier, *A Matter of Risk* [New York: Random House, 1978].)

[11]"Subject: E. Howard Hunt—Utilization by Central Cover Staff," October 14, 1970, memo to Thomas Karamessines, cited in Senator Howard Baker's dissenting appendix to the *Final Report* (June 1974) of the Senate Select Committee on Presidential Campaign Activities of 1972 (the Ervin committee), p. 1121. The FBI "Summary" of the bureau's Watergate investigation refers, on p. 81, to the CIA's "ad hoc" use of Hunt following his retirement from the agency in 1970.

[12]The CIA's interest in Hunt's access to an otherwise unidentified "Colonel White" was revealed by Charles Colson in an interview with the author. Colson's source for that information was notes that he had taken on a Watergate-generated CIA file—a file that he had obtained from presidential counsel J. Fred Buzhardt, Jr. (The file is discussed in later pages.) While Colson did not know who Colonel White might be, two candidates come to mind. The first is Colonel Lawrence K. ("Red") White, then the executive director/comptroller of the CIA. For reasons that will be made apparent in subsequent pages, however, a more likely candidate is Lieutenant Colonel George Hunter White (a.k.a. Morgan Hall), like Hunt a veteran of the Office of Strategic Services (OSS). A retired senior narcotics official and longtime CIA contract agent, White was the CIA's principal operative in domestic intelligence operations involving male and female prostitutes and the testing of drugs upon unwitting subjects. (See John M. Crewdson and Jo Thomas, "Abuses in Testing of Drugs by C.I.A. to Be Panel Focus," *New York Times*, September 20, 1977, p. 1.)

[13]"Subject: Wrap-Up of Agency's Association with Robert R. Mullen and Company" (un-

The intention that Hunt continue to be used by the agency while employed at the White House is easily demonstrated. Not only does Hunt appear to have made timely reports to important CIA officials concerning his approaches to Colson,[14] but he met regularly with top officials of the CIA's operations directorate for more than two years after leaving the agency.[15] While Hunt claims that these meetings were merely lunch and tennis dates, there is reason to wonder: social luncheons are a standard pretext for meetings between agent handlers, case officers and their wards.[16] Such circumstantial evidence, however, is by no means the only reason to believe that Hunt continued to work for the agency after leaving it. On the contrary, the FBI *tells us* that Hunt was used by the CIA on an "ad hoc basis" while he worked at the White House.[17] Similarly, a sworn statement by a worried CIA officer describes how Hunt made frequent, secret reports to CIA Director Richard Helms and others at the agency, using CIA channels on the National Security Council (NSC), while supposedly working exclusively for the Nixon administration.[18]

Moreover, when it came time for Hunt to undertake a series of questionable intelligence operations, ostensibly on behalf of the White House, it was the CIA that provided him with the extensive "technical support" that the missions required.[19] In a similar way, Hunt relied upon veteran CIA contract agents to help carry out these operations, and even applied to the CIA's External Employment Assistance Branch (EEAB) for help in locating men skilled at

---

dated CIA memorandum), and the executive session testimony before the Ervin committee (Senate Select Committee on Presidential Campaign Activities of 1972) of Thomas Karamessines, February 5, 1974. Hunt's negotiations with the Mullen Company on behalf of the CIA are discussed on pages 1121–26 and 1151–52 of the Ervin committee's *Final Report*.

[14]H. R. Haldeman (with Joseph DiMona), *The Ends of Power* (New York: Times Books, 1978), p. 143 (discussing Hunt's contact with Howard Osborn, director of the Office of Security, on July 1, 1971); and the author's interview with Charles Colson (concerning Hunt's contact with CIA Director Helms in January 1971).

[15]Nedzi report (*Inquiry into the Alleged Involvement of the Central Intelligence Agency in the Watergate and Ellsberg Matters, Hearings before the Special Committee on Intelligence of the House Committee on Armed Services*, 94th Cong., 1st sess., May 1973–July 1974), p. 506.

[16]Ibid., pp. 1009–30 (testimony of Louis Vasaly and Lee R. Pennington, Jr.).

[17]FBI memorandum of June 20, 1972, by special agent Arnold L. Parham, p. 26.

[18]"CIA Employee Statement, January 17, 1974," reprinted in *Statement of Information, Hearings before the House Committee on the Judiciary*, 93d Cong., 2d sess., May–June 1974, Book 2 ("Events Following the Watergate Break-In"), pp. 298–99.

[19]This support included false identification, wigs, voice modulators, a gait-altering device, a miniature camera, a tape recorder concealed in an attaché case, darkroom services and the help of the agency's "graphics studio." See the Ervin committee's *Final Report*, pp. 1135–44, and G. Gordon Liddy, *Will: The Autobiography of G. Gordon Liddy* (New York: St. Martin's Press, 1980), pp. 193, 202, 218.

lock-picking, electronic sweeps and entry operations.[20] He used the agency to conduct computer name traces as required,[21] and had a sterile telephone installed in the White House to ensure the secrecy of his regular telephone conversations with unidentified officials at the CIA.[22] To these facts still others might be added, but to do so would only belabor the point: Hunt's retirement from the CIA was dubious in the extreme.

James McCord's own retirement from the CIA is also questionable. On August 31, 1970, four months after Hunt joined the Mullen Company, McCord gave up his federal employment, saying that he needed to earn more money in order to care for his retarded daughter. The difficulty with this explanation is that McCord seems to have made few, if any, plans to supplement the CIA pension due him after nineteen years of service. Although he did manage to work part time as an instructor for a course in industrial security at Montgomery County Junior College, this did little to alleviate the financial burdens that he said afflicted him.

Whatever his reasons for leaving the CIA, his career with the intelligence agency had been a murky one. A former FBI agent, he joined the CIA in 1951 after handling counterespionage assignments for the bureau. His first task with the agency was in a "rearguard" capacity, identifying CIA employees whose left-wing pasts might prove embarrassing should Senator Joseph McCarthy learn of them. As a part of that assignment, McCord came into daily contact with the inner circle of Cold War Red hunters, including two men who would play crucial roles in the Watergate affair: HUAC's Lou Russell and the American Legion's Lee R. Pennington.[23]

For most of the 1950s and early 1960s McCord was attached to the Security Research Staff (SRS), a component of the Office of Security, whose mission was to combat Soviet attempts to penetrate the CIA.[24] Becoming deputy chief of the SRS in about 1960–61,[25] McCord played a disputed (and apparently ancillary) role in the Bay of Pigs invasion.[26] Shortly afterward, he was placed under cover as

[20]Ervin committee's *Final Report*, p. 1141.
[21]Ibid.
[22]FBI interview of David Young, July 3, 1972, conducted by special agents Robert C. Lill and Daniel C. Mahan, FBI serial 139–66, pp. 153–54.
[23]Nedzi report, pp. 1023–31.
[24]Ibid., p. 467.
[25]Ibid., p. 1031.
[26]A profile of McCord, "Man in the News," published in the *New York Times* on March 29,

a civilian employee of the Department of the Army and issued an official passport for an overseas assignment that was to last two years.[27] Already a GS-15 (as he would be at his retirement nine years later), McCord left the United States in October 1961 to take undercover command as the CIA's senior security officer in Europe. Returning to CIA headquarters in late 1963, he became involved with Hunt in an operation code-named "Second Naval Guerilla."[28] In that operation, anti-Castro Cubans, including Bay of Pigs veterans whom Castro had released in return for medical supplies, were trained in guerrilla tactics at bases in the United States, Nicaragua and Costa Rica. The plot is believed to have included Hunt's recommendation that Castro be assassinated prior to a military invasion, but the scheme never reached fruition. In the ensuing years, McCord continued his rise through the clandestine ranks of the U.S. natural security bureaucracy. In 1969 he distinguished himself by the brilliance of his debriefing of American pilots who had returned from Russia after crash-landing there.[29] By then McCord had reached his highest position within the CIA, becoming director of the technical and physical security sections of the Office of Security. In those jobs, McCord's boss was Howard Osborn (coincidentally, a high school classmate and close friend of E. Howard Hunt).[30]

The reputation of the Office of Security tends to be that of a guard service staffed by gumshoes and technicians whose principal tasks are to conduct background investigations, enforce security regulations and protect the agency's property. In reality, however, the

---

1973, states that McCord "is believed to have played a role in the abortive Bay of Pigs invasion of Cuba in 1961." Tad Szulc echoes that view in *Compulsive Spy* (p. 97). General Vernon Walters, however, states in a CIA memorandum of July 6, 1972, that a review of CIA files "provided no indication that [McCord] was involved in Cuban matters and that he was not assigned to the Bay of Pigs operation." Walters then qualifies that statement with the assertion that McCord "might have developed personal acquaintances which are not recorded in official personnel and security records." Those who are familiar with the CIA's ways of doing (and saying) things will realize that Walters' statement does not preclude the possibility that McCord was involved in Cuban matters. All it precludes is the existence of any record to that effect in the CIA's files.

[27]Report of special agent Kenneth J. Haser, FBI serial 139-166-744, pp. 53-54.

[28]See Szulc, *Compulsive Spy*, pp. 96–97, and Hinckle and Turner, *Fish Is Red*, pp. 148–53. The involvement of Hunt and McCord in the Second Naval Guerilla operation is discussed in subsequent pages concerning Cuban exile Enrique Ruiz-Williams and CIA "resettlement" operations with respect to Bay of Pigs veterans.

[29]"Man in the News," *New York Times*, March 29, 1973.

[30]Hunt and Osborn attended Hamburg High School in Hamburg, New York. See J. Anthony Lukas, *Nightmare* (New York: Viking, 1976), p. 91.

Office of Security is far more complex, and even mysterious. Its broad responsibilities—to protect CIA assets, operations and personnel—require it to maintain close liaison with any number of police departments, to operate wherever the agency has "assets," and to maintain more than 1.7 million security files on individuals who are, for one reason or another, legitimately or not, of interest to the CIA.[31] The OS is also responsible for housing and guarding defectors, for helping to establish their bona fides, and for assisting in their debriefing. Similarly, it is the Office of Security that debriefs retiring agency employees and administers the sometimes embarrassing polygraph tests that are a part of the CIA's routine. By no means finally, the inviolability of all classified information within the domain of the CIA is ultimately the responsibility of the OS.

By the very nature of its work, the Office of Security has domestic responsibilities that go far beyond those of any other CIA component. If, for example, a CIA officer falls afoul of the local police, it is the OS that will handle (or manipulate) the matter to ensure that no secrets are compromised. Similarly, if a CIA officer suffers a mental breakdown, it is the OS that will take charge of him, consult its list of approved psychiatrists and, if necessary, bundle the patient off to a CIA sanatorium. And, of course, if a staff member is suspected of leaking secrets, whether to the press or to the enemy (often no distinction is made between the two), it is the Office of Security that will investigate the matter, conduct physical surveillances and, if necessary, break into his home in order to install eavesdropping devices, which the Office of Security will then proceed to monitor.

The OS, in other words, is an action component of the CIA, with hands-on responsibility for some of the agency's most sensitive matters. Accordingly, and unlike most other sections of the CIA, it reports directly to the DCI himself—the Director of Central Intelligence. In effect, the OS is an extension of the director's office in a way that other CIA components are not; and because of this organizational peculiarity, by virtue of which the office is unaccountable to anyone but the DCI, it has served as a vehicle for some of the agency's most questionable operations. It was the OS, for example, that

· conducted the CIA's first "mind control" programs, Bluebird

[31]Rockefeller Report (Report to the President by the Commission on CIA Activities Within the United States [Washington, D.C.: Government Printing Office, June 1975]), pp. 101–15.

and Artichoke, slipping experimental drugs to a series of unwitting "volunteers" (at least one of whom died as a direct result);[32]

· launched an array of Mafia-assisted operations to assassinate Fidel Castro;[33]

· helped to establish deniable proprietaries, or "mission impossible" agencies, such as Robert A. Maheu Associates, to facilitate operations that were in fact unlawful;[34]

· surveilled and infiltrated black and antiwar organizations in the U.S. (from 1962 to 1972);[35]

· carried out an illegal mail-opening project that lasted for more than twenty years;[36] and

· worked as the principal collection agent for the domestic spying project, Operation Chaos, carried out under the nominal auspices of the counterintelligence staff.[37]

At the heart of many of these activities, a tabernacle within the inner sanctum, was the Security Research Staff (SRS), a cadre within the Office of Security. Headed by the late General Paul Gaynor, Watergate spy James McCord's immediate superior for many years, the SRS managed the literally mind-boggling Bluebird and Artichoke programs, and coordinated many of the domestic spying activities associated with Operation Chaos and Project Two.[38] Most important, the SRS was the primary, hands-on counterintelligence unit within the CIA. Its central function was to seek out and expose security risks, as well as to identify Soviet penetration agents not only within the CIA but also in other branches of government. It was, in other words, *the* vehicle for "mole hunting," as much as James Angleton's counterintelligence staff was. This fact, as important as it is obscure, has so far gone unnoticed by writers on the subject of intelligence whose fascination with the glamorous Angleton—a poet, fly-fisherman, orchidologist and pro-

[32]John Marks, *The Search for the Manchurian Candidate* (New York: Times Books, 1979), pp. 21–49.
[33]*Alleged Assassination Plots Involving Foreign Leaders*, an interim report of the Senate Select Committee to Study Governmental Operations with respect to intelligence activities, 94th Cong., 1st sess., November 20, 1975, pp. 74ff.
[34]Ibid.
[35]Rockefeller Report, pp. 101–15.
[36]Ibid.
[37]Ibid., pp. 130–50.
[38]Project Two was an operation that entailed infiltration of the Black Power and antiwar movements in the United States, supposedly for the purpose of training CIA undercover agents for assignments abroad. The operation got under way in 1969 and, apparently, was terminated in 1974. See the Rockefeller Report, pp. 136–39.

fessional spinner of webs—is understandable. Still, his shop was something of an ivory tower, preoccupied with strategic analyses of broad intelligence issues, whereas the OS, and the SRS, were in the alleys and sometimes in the gutter.[39]

In many ways, the SRS was unique. A critical component of the CIA's internal security apparatus, it was effectively immune from scrutiny. Whenever a new employee was hired or an agent induced to work for the CIA, details of that relationship would be forwarded to the Office of Security for background checks and approval. This was a well-known procedure, but what was less known was the fact that this information was also routed to the Security Research Staff, where, as sometimes happened, earlier approvals were vetoed by General Gaynor and his staff. A lifelong counterintelligence specialist, fascinated by the idea of a "Manchurian candidate," General Gaynor was separately provided with this information so that he might compare the names of new personnel and agents with dossiers in his legendary "fag file."[40] The file consisted of details concerning more than three hundred thousand Americans, mostly homosexuals, who had been arrested at one time or another for sexual offenses.[41]

Here we have touched upon a matter that impinges directly on the Watergate affair: the compilation of dossiers on the sexual habits of selected Americans. Supposedly the information in Gaynor's file was used to screen applicants for employment at the agency, and to keep tabs on employees and agents who might become involved in activities that would render them vulnerable to blackmail. But these were not the only purposes to which the file was put, and neither was it the only such file to which the SRS had access. General Gaynor worked closely with the deputy chief of the Washington Police Department, Captain Roy E. Blick. According to every account, the late Captain Blick was sexually obsessed. A source for both J. Edgar Hoover's FBI and the CIA under Allen Dulles and Richard Helms, Captain Blick maintained exhaustive files on the subject of sexual deviance, files that are said to have included the

[39]The five components of the counterintelligence staff were Research and Analysis (concerned with the organizations, assets and operations of Soviet intelligence agencies); Operations (which monitored CIA activities worldwide); Special Operations (the counterintelligence staff's closest analogue to the SRS); World Communism/Special United (which studied political-action plans relating to world Communism); and the Israel unit.
[40]The phrase is not the author's but one used by CIA officers themselves when referring to Gaynor's archive.
[41]Rockefeller Report, p. 249.

names of every prostitute, madam, pimp, homosexual, pederast, sado-masochist, and most points in between, of whatever national- ity, who came to the attention of the police in the country's capital. Inevitably, because of the seizure of "trick books" during police raids, those files also contained the names and sexual preferences of many of the prostitutes' clients, including those of congressmen, diplomats, judges and spooks. According to Blick's subordinates, the captain, not content with mere dossiers, also maintained (presuma- bly at public expense) a "sex museum" in his offices until the time of his death.

"There were all kinds of things, and he loved to show it off: pornographic pictures of every sort, and he even had an automatic fucking machine! Damnedest thing I ever saw," recalls Herndon (Virginia) Police Chief Walter Bishop.

The working relationship between Blick and Gaynor was useful to the CIA in a number of ways. As columnist Jack Anderson has reported, "Through field offices scattered around the country, the Office of Security maintains close ties with state and local police. In each field office, a 'black book' is kept of the males and females who can be safely recruited to entertain the CIA's visitors. The black books contain names, telephone numbers and details, gleaned largely from local vice squads. In Washington, for example, CIA agents paid regular visits to the police department's vice squad to photograph documents. The late Deputy Chief Roy E. Blick, who headed the 'sex squad' for years, kept exhaustive records on 'per- verts' and 'miscreants' around the country. He had a close, back- room relationship with the CIA. . . ."[42]

Among those visitors whom the CIA had occasion to entertain were foreign leaders, agents in transit and defectors. But entertain- ment was by no means the only purpose served by the agency's liaison with local vice squads around the country. Blackmail was another function, and, toward that end, the Office of Security main- tained safehouses—literally, houses or apartments untraceable to the CIA—in a number of American cities. Still other safehouses were dedicated to "science." In New York and San Francisco, for exam-

[42]Jack Anderson and Les Whitten, "The CIA's 'Sex Squad,' " *Washington Post*, June 22, 1976, p. B-13. According to Anderson and Whitten, "the sex operation was supervised (from 1964 to 1974) by security director Howard Osborn." Osborn denied this, however, and General Gaynor's activities (e.g., his maintenance of the so-called fag file) make it apparent that it was he who had direct responsibility for the operation.

ple, CIA agent George White installed prostitutes in lavish apartments outfitted with two-way mirrors, video equipment and microphones concealed in objets d'art, such as Japanese screens. Pitchers of martinis were kept in the refrigerators, and the walls were hung with animal skins, Toulouse-Lautrec prints, and pictures of manacled women being whipped and tortured.[43] The furniture was covered in black velveteen, and CIA operatives—both thoughtful physicians and hardened agents, such as Colonel White—could sit in secret rooms (equipped with chamber pots) and watch the fun through two-way mirrors disguised as oil paintings of ships at sea.[44] The fun consisted of testing exotic drugs on the prostitutes' unwitting clients (considered fair game because they were, at least technically, engaged in an illegal activity). Of particular interest to the agency was the degree to which a drug would

· induce amnesia,

· render a subject unnaturally suggestible,

· stimulate aberrant behavior (so that the victim could be discredited in public),[45]

· alter sexual patterns,

· elicit information,

· or create dependency in a subject.

In short, the CIA was in the behavior modification, or "mind control," business.[46] The extreme sensitivity of such operations, which contravened, among other laws, the Nuremberg Code, made the Office of Security their logical staging ground. Because General Gaynor was the ultimate reference point of all new personnel and agents, and because his shop was one of the most hermetic in the CIA, the SRS was uniquely situated to deploy agents whose exis-

---

[43]John Jacobs, "Turner Cites 149 Drug-Test Projects," *Washington Post*, August 4, 1977, p. 1; John Jacobs, "The Diaries of a CIA Operative," *Washington Post*, September 5, 1977, p. 1.
[44]John M. Crewdson and Jo Thomas, "Abuses in Testing of Drugs by C.I.A. to Be Panel Focus," *New York Times*, September 20, 1977, p. 1.
[45]Some have speculated that Senator Edmund Muskie's emotional outburst in the 1972 New Hampshire primary, an outburst that badly damaged his public image and his campaign for the presidency, was the result of a dirty trick—i.e., of a drug surreptitiously administered. While there is no evidence that this occurred, it would be naïve to dismiss the possibility out of hand. As we will see, G. Gordon Liddy and Howard Hunt plotted to discredit Jack Anderson by exactly this method.
[46]By far the best account of the CIA's "mind-control experiments" is John Marks's *Search for the Manchurian Candidate*. See also George Lardner, Jr., and John Jacobs, "Lengthy Mind-Control Research by CIA Is Detailed," *Washington Post*, August 3, 1977, p. 1; and John M. Crewdson and Jo Thomas, "Files Show Tests for Truth Drug Began in O.S.S.," *New York Times*, September 5, 1977, p. 1.

tence was entirely unknown to the rest of the CIA, and whose operations were therefore both invisible and completely deniable. The relevance of this to the Watergate affair will be made apparent.

But the SRS was by no means the only "hot shop" in which James McCord worked. As a colonel in the Air Force Reserve, McCord served as commander of the Special Analysis Division (SAD) of the Wartime Information Security Program (WISP),[47] which was a creature of the Office of Emergency Preparedness (OEP). In the event of a "national emergency," declared by either the President or the Secretary of Defense, the Office of Wartime Information Security would activate contingency plans for imposing censorship on the press, the mails and all telecommunications (including government communications).[48] In addition, provision existed for the preventive detention of civilian "security risks," who would be placed in military "camps," thereby quashing any effective dissent. The civilians selected for preventive detention were expected to include antiwar activists, trade-union leaders, members of radical political organizations and others identified on the FBI's "custodial detention cards."[49] The peacetime rubric under which these plans were rationalized was the specter of election-year violence. There were reports—in fact unfounded rumors—that the Weather Underground was planning to bomb the polls on Election Day, and that one or both of the national political conventions would end in a bloodbath.[50] The presidential election might, therefore, have to be "postponed" in the interest of public safety. The implementation of WISP might be expected to restore order within a short period of time, during which the incumbent President would remain in office.[51]

[47] Jerry Oppenheimer, "Bug Suspect Quit High Military Job," *Washington Daily News*, June 29, 1972, p. 5.
[48] Department of Defense Directive 5230.7, June 25, 1965, amended May 21, 1971.
[49] "U.S. Government Information Policies and Practices—Problems of Congress in Obtaining Information from the Executive Branch," Part 8 of the *Hearings before the Foreign Operations and Government Information Subcommittee of the House Committee on Government Operations*, 92d Cong., 2d sess., May 12–June 1, 1972. See also Ron Shaffer, "Congress to Probe Army Censor Unit," *Washington Post*, June 21, 1972, and Bob Woodward and Carl Bernstein, "U.S. Censorship Plan Bared," *Washington Post*, October 23, 1972.
[50] Rumors about contingency plans to postpone the elections were first published in the *Staten Island Advance*, a conservative daily newspaper owned by the Newhouse chain. With respect to those rumors, it should be pointed out that it would have been entirely uncharacteristic for the Weather Underground to have targeted the polls (as opposed to the pols) for violence. There was, however, at least one paramilitary group that might have been capable of such violence: the anti-Castro Cubans recruited by E. Howard Hunt and Bernard Barker.
[51] The suspicion that Nixon's men were conspiring to contrive the "national emergency" that

As for McCord's SAD unit, its responsibility was to develop and test computer procedures for handling the federal "watch lists" and "custodial detention" targets, dispensing orders to various military units on the basis of geographical location and functional duties. Toward that end, McCord participated in WISP-connected war games conducted at the government's supersecret Mount Weather facility. Given McCord's background in counterespionage and counterintelligence, he may be said to have been ideally suited for activities of this kind.

These are, of course, only the broad outlines of McCord's intelligence career. More than a decade after his retirement, details of that career remain highly classified, and McCord himself has repeatedly refused to be interviewed on the subject. Some flesh was recently added to this skeletal biography, however, by Enrique ("Harry") Ruiz-Williams, a geologist and veteran of the Bay of Pigs.

Ruiz-Williams was perhaps the leading spokesman for those anti-Castro Cubans who had been imprisoned on the Isle of Pines following the CIA's unsuccessful invasion of Cuba. After the prisoners' negotiated release in December 1962 it was Ruiz-Williams who represented them in talks with the U.S. government. At the time, the Kennedy administration was equally concerned with resettling and controlling the men, while continuing also to mount covert operations against Cuba under the rubric of Second Naval Guerilla. Roughly half of the veterans were inducted into the Army at Fort Jackson, South Carolina, where they were given special military training. The remaining veterans, men such as Watergate burglar Eugenio Martinez, were either "pensioned off" or placed under contract to the CIA.[52]

According to Ruiz-Williams, Hunt and McCord were his han-

---

they were so well prepared to deal with was by no means an exclusive concern of frightened liberals and the more paranoid cadres of the Left. Many right-wing elements (e.g., the John Birch Society) shared those same fears. Thus, ultraconservative writer Gary Allen was moved to describe Executive Order 11490 (in which the President assigned emergency-preparedness functions to various federal agencies) as a "blueprint for tyranny"; see Allen's book, *Nixon's Palace Guard* (Boston: Western Islands, 1971). As will be seen in later pages, these same concerns were shared by members of Nixon's own administration, including Secretary of Defense James Schlesinger and White House caretaker Alexander Haig.

[52]Some of the men who played important roles in the government resettlement operation were Joseph Califano (later attorney for the DNC), who was special assistant to Secretary of the Army Cyrus Vance in 1963; Alexander Butterfield and Alexander Haig (respectively, the custodian of the presidential taping system and deputy to Henry Kissinger), who were military assistants to Califano; and private investigator A. J. Woolston-Smith (whose Watergate role is discussed in later pages).

dlers during the time that he worked as a CIA contract agent with the Second Naval Guerilla operation. Hunt was Ruiz-Williams' liaison to CIA headquarters, while McCord performed the same function with respect to the brigade veterans at Fort Jackson. "I was confused," the Cuban recalls, "[because] both of them said to call [them] Don Eduardo. Both Hunt and McCord." There were, Ruiz-Williams told his interviewers, "dozens of meetings and countless telephone discussions" between himself and the two CIA men, with the meetings taking place in Washington and New York. Hunt, he said, "never opened up to me. He knew I like my martinis, and he'd have a martini with me. But I never trusted him, and he never trusted me."[53]

Ruiz-Williams' recollection of his relationship to Hunt and McCord during the 1960s is interesting for several reasons. First, it confirms James Angleton's assertion that "McCord was an operator, not merely a technician." Second, the anti-Castro agent is right on the money when he confesses that he was confused by the reliance of Hunt and McCord upon the same alias, Don Eduardo (Mr. Edward).[54] That same modus operandi would be a hallmark of the Watergate affair, with Hunt and McCord using the same false identification papers. Indeed, McCord would be arrested and booked under a Hunt alias, "Edward Martin," producing a phony ID on which the birthdate was identical with Howard Hunt's own. But what is most important about Ruiz-Williams' recollection is the news that Hunt and McCord were known to each other as early as 1963. Hunt's testimony is that he did not meet McCord until April 1972, and Gordon Liddy himself was led to understand that it was he who first introduced the two men.[55]

[53]Hinckle and Turner, *Fish Is Red*, pp. 152–54.
[54]A file on Hunt's activities, maintained "outside the normal CIA filing system," was requested from the CIA by the Ervin committee. The CIA's initial response was to claim that the "Mr. Edward file" could not be located and might not exist. Repeated requests from the committee, however, were eventually satisfied when the agency provided it with access to a rather uninteresting dossier concerning Howard Hunt. Minority staff members on the committee speculated that this dossier was a surrogate created in an effort to mollify the committee, and that the authentic "Mr. Edward file" concerned the activities of *both* Hunt and McCord while using the Mr. Edward/Don Eduardo alias. See the *Final Report* of the Ervin committee (Senate Select Committee on Presidential Campaign Activities), pp. 1138, 1163. (As an incidental matter, it should be noted that the identification papers in McCord's possession at the time of his arrest appear to be the only pieces of Watergate evidence to have disappeared from police and prosecution files. The false ID was issued by the CIA to Howard Hunt, and vanished immediately after McCord's fingerprinting by Washington police.)
[55]Nedzi report, pp. 503, 509.

Is Ruiz-Williams mistaken? It appears not. Indeed, the relationship between Hunt and McCord may be even older than the anti-Castro agent knew. Persistent if unconfirmed rumors allege that the two men met each other in 1954–55, when Hunt was covert-action chief of the CIA's North Asia Command. At the time Hunt was responsible for propaganda broadcasts beamed from Taiwan to the Chinese mainland, North Korea and the Soviet Union. McCord is believed to have been one of the technicians working on these broadcasts; so, it is said, was McCord's friend Alfred Wong, the Secret Service agent who would one day take charge of the presidential taping system in the Nixon White House.

More substantive than these rumors, however, is the information given to the FBI by a woman named Miriam Furbershaw. Furbershaw's information came to the attention of the FBI when GOP Congressman Larry Hogan informed the bureau that one of his constituents had news about the activities of James McCord (then under arrest). What the constituent had to say concerned an apartment in Chevy Chase, Maryland, and an unpleasant controversy arising from its rental.

Mrs. Furbershaw was a retired intelligence officer who had worked for decades as chief of research on the Pentagon's Beach Erosion Board.[56] Alert and au courant, though in her seventies, Mrs. Furbershaw is very much "a little old lady," albeit one from the John le Carré Finishing School. Her conversation is studded with the jargon of spooks, with references to "cutouts" and "safehouses" coming easily to her lips. And what she has to say, and what her neighbors confirm, is puzzling indeed.

Two or three years before the Watergate scandal, Mrs. Furbershaw says, she rented her basement apartment to James McCord.[57] At the time, McCord told her that he was a retired CIA officer who had previously worked for Presidents Kennedy and Johnson. He said that he was residing in Baltimore but required a pied-à-terre in Washington—preferably one that would be convenient for his "consulting work" at the Pentagon. McCord was in fact a resident of nearby Rockville, and so far as anyone knows, he does not appear

[56]The business of the Beach Erosion Board is to provide constant surveillance of the world's changing coastlines and collect data of importance to the military's maritime and amphibious operations.
[57]Mrs. Furbershaw is uncertain of the time frame in which McCord was her tenant, and FBI reports contradict one another on the subject.

to have had a consulting contract with the Pentagon. In any event, Mrs. Fubershaw agreed to rent the apartment to him for $100 per month, imposing the conditions that he would neither smoke in his bedroom nor entertain women in the rooms. McCord agreed, adding that he would use the apartment only "intermittently."

According to Mrs. Furbershaw, however, McCord failed to live up to all of her conditions. He paid his rent on time, using crisp $100 bills, but there was more than one occasion on which "young girls" visited during the night. So it was that the fastidious Mrs. Furbershaw decided to evict McCord. In an angry confrontation with her tenant that was carried out in the presence of a young woman said to have been crying hysterically on the bed, McCord's landlady ordered him to leave.

In her interview with the FBI, Mrs. Furbershaw said that McCord had several male visitors while a tenant, and that one of these visitors was E. Howard Hunt. The FBI also reported that "McCord in conversation with Furbershaw, stated that he was engaged in counterintelligence and other phases of military intelligence,"[58] and that "During installation of a separate telephone in McCord's basement apartment, the telephone company installation man commented to Mrs. Furbershaw that there was considerable 'bugging equipment' inside her tenant's apartment."[59]

All in all, a peculiar affair, and not merely because Hunt and McCord would later testify that they did not meet each other for the first time until April of 1972, long after Hunt's visit to the Furbershaw apartment and McCord's eviction. Furbershaw's reminiscence is interesting also because McCord is not supposed to have been in possession of bugging equipment prior to April 1972. Which is to say that Hunt and McCord were engaged in some kind of clandestine operation before the Watergate break-in, and that the operation apparently involved young women and bugging equipment.

The reader may wonder whether this interpretation is a fair one. Might not McCord have rented the Furbershaw apartment to carry on a private dalliance? Probably not. While we can imagine the more playful Hunt and Liddy so engaged, McCord's reputation as a rectitudinous family man seems well deserved. Moreover, while we can imagine a man renting an apartment to carry on an ex-

---

[58]See FBI serial 139-4089-2213, concerning the bureau's interview with Furbershaw on May 25, 1973.
[59]Ibid.

tramarital affair, and while we may even concede that fire-breathing Baptists like McCord occasionally stumble on The Path, there is nothing in McCord's personality to suggest that he is prone to *calculated* sinfulness. It is especially difficult to imagine McCord renting an apartment for the purpose of carrying on a series of separate affairs with different women; if he were that promiscuous (and there is nothing to suggest that he was), the convenience of hotels would have been manifest. Finally, the dreary hypothesis that the Furbershaw apartment was a private rendezvous does not take into account either the mystery of Hunt's presence or the existence of the bugging equipment.

With respect to Mrs. Furbershaw herself, she has never pressed her story on others, much less sought to capitalize on it. She was identified only with great difficulty, and while she does not seek publicity, neither does she waffle when recounting the tale. McCord, she remembers, used his own name when renting the apartment, and she knew him well enough to recognize him when Watergate became a front-page story. Clinching the matter is the confirmation provided by a former neighbor of Mrs. Furbershaw. While this neighbor knows nothing about the circumstances of McCord's eviction from the apartment, she distinctly recalls his presence there as a tenant. She remembers that McCord, leaving the apartment in the morning, would sometimes wave to her in her backyard.

If, as it appears, the apartment was not used for private or personal purposes, it would seem to have been a safehouse of some sort. The payments with new $100 bills, along with the presence of women and bugging equipment, suggest that McCord and Hunt were engaged in an intelligence operation—an operation of which Gordon Liddy, the White House and, ultimately, the Senate were kept in ignorance. And while it is impossible to say with certainty on whose authority this operation may have been conducted, it would be negligent not to recall that, historically, the Office of Security was *the* launching point for domestic operations involving prostitutes, as well as the repository for all data, tape-recordings and photographs collected in the course of such operations. Finally, we may point to an interesting parallel, possibly only a coincidence, between McCord's rental of the Furbershaw apartment and Colonel George White's rental of an apartment in the San Francisco area: in each case, the landlords were active or retired government workers holding high security clearances for reasons that had nothing to do with their tenants' activities.

The mysteries surrounding James McCord are many—so many, in fact, that we may sometimes imagine that there were two of him, just as there were two Don Eduardos. There was the James McCord who worked as an administrator-technician in the Office of Security, and there was the James McCord who was a counterintelligence operative. There is McCord's well-deserved reputation as a Bible-thumper, pious as the day is long, and, in stark contrast to that, McCord's high position within one of the more sordid precincts of the CIA. There is the matter of McCord's early retirement from the agency and, also, of his bland acceptance of what must have been reduced financial circumstances, in blatant contradiction of the very motive that supposedly led him to depart from government. There is his reputation for honesty, but there is also the pattern of deception and concealment that underlies both his work for the CIA and his relationship to men such as Howard Hunt. There is (should we not wonder?) the photograph on the wall of McCord's office at the CRP, a photograph signed by CIA Director Richard Helms and inscribed "To Jim/ With *deep* appreciation."[60] (The emphasis is in the original.) And so it goes, the man and his shadow, tugging at each other until, in the end, there seem to be two men with opposite personalities—one a saint, the other a "sinner."

That so little is known about the man is due in large part to the fact that the Senate and the press, reviling Nixon, wished desperately to believe in the sincerity of Nixon's newfound accuser, and so avoided questioning McCord's bona fides or probing too deeply into his background. Indeed, even in an area as banal as "political leanings," almost nothing has been published about McCord. The official record takes note of the fact that he is (or was) "a registered Republican," but goes no further. And yet, what a Republican! In a secret letter to General Paul Gaynor, McCord explained his concerns in apocalyptic terms: "When the hundreds of dedicated fine men and women of CIA no longer write intelligence summaries and reports with integrity, without fear of political recrimination— when their fine director [Richard Helms] is being summarily discharged in order to make way for a politician who will write or

---

[60]FBI interview of Millicent ("Penny") Gleason, conducted by FBI special agents Charles W. Harvey and Paul Magallanes, July 1, 1972, p. 7.

rewrite intelligence the way the politicians want them [sic] written, instead of the way truth and best judgment dictates, our nation is in the deepest of trouble and freedom itself was never so imperiled. Nazi Germany rose and fell under exactly the same philosophy of governmental operation."[61]

Pretty strong stuff—*Nazi Germany?* What is McCord talking about? Why would the replacement of Richard Helms as director of Central Intelligence imperil our freedom as never before, and pave the way for the coming of a totalitarian (and, by McCord's implication, a fascist) regime? Is this merely rhetoric, or does McCord actually believe what he has written?

The best evidence on the matter is contained in McCord's autobiographical account of the affair, *A Piece of Tape.* In it, he *tells* us: "I believed that the whole future of the nation was at stake. If the Administration could get away with this massive crime of Watergate and its cover up, it would certainly stop at nothing thereafter. The precedent such would set for the nation would be beyond belief, beyond recovery, and a disaster beyond any possible reversal, if it were able to succeed in the cover up."[62]

Again, we must remind ourselves of McCord's subject. What is he talking about? What is this "massive crime" that he so neatly distinguishes from the "cover up"? It is, simply, the bugging (or, more accurately, the reputed bugging) of the DNC. But that McCord should regard electronic eavesdropping as a "massive crime" is incredible, given his past responsibilities at the CIA. It is difficult to understand how a professional "wireman," as McCord has often been described, could regard bugging as anything other than banal. And if McCord felt that bugging the DNC was such a "massive crime," why did he agree to do it in the first place? And even beyond this, what are we to make of McCord's apocalyptic assessment of the cover-up? "Beyond belief, beyond recovery, and a disaster beyond any possible reversal . . ." Isn't it more nearly true to say that the cover-up was an error in political judgment that implicated administration officials in illegalities that might otherwise have been avoided? Why the rhetoric of doom? Does McCord know something that we don't?

Apparently. At least, he thinks he does. In a series of queer

---

[61] The letter was written in January 1973, seven months after McCord's Watergate arrest.
[62] James W. McCord, Jr., *A Piece of Tape* (Rockville, Md.: Washington Media Services, Ltd., 1974), p. 60.

"newsletters," written in the aftermath of Watergate (and virtually uncirculated), McCord put forward a right-wing conspiracy theory that the Rockefeller family was lunging for complete control over the government's critical national security functions, using the Council on Foreign Relations and Henry Kissinger as its surrogates.[63] Supporting his case with mostly irrelevant quotations from the Bible, Shakespeare, Thomas Edison and others, McCord mixed evangelical religion and the politics of conspiracy to give the newsletters a special flavor—a flavor that is also to be found in his book.

Of all the Watergate books, *A Piece of Tape* is easily the strangest (and most difficult to find). It is unbelievably, even pointedly, dull and irrelevant. It tells us virtually nothing about McCord, his work for the CRP or the events leading to the Watergate arrests, but nevertheless manages to be inaccurate or misleading on an astonishing number of matters. Indeed, even the circumstances of the book's preparation and appearance are peculiar: it was written, edited, printed and distributed by McCord himself, despite the fact that he had been offered the services of a ghost-writer and the resources of a major publisher.[64] Why he chose this means of publication is unknown, but it may well be that he feared the close scrutiny that a publisher and ghost-writer would pay to his role in the affair. McCord was prepared to offer his analysis, but not his narrative of what had actually occurred.

Despite this, *A Piece of Tape* is quite revealing and, as psychological evidence of McCord's frame of mind, invaluable. Throughout we are struck by McCord's vindictiveness, by his wrathful piety, by his obsessiveness and by his nearly mystical apprehension of the Watergate affair. The book's title is deliberately ambiguous and constitutes an invitation to the reader to guess at its hidden meaning. As the author points out:

> *A piece of masking tape opened a door that shook a nation to its very foundations.*[65] *A measuring tape that was Watergate plumbed the depths of the most powerful nation in the world. A piece of magnetic tape may impeach*

[63]The *McCord Washington Newsletter*, edited and published by Ruth and James McCord (Rockville, Md.), August–September 1974, Vol. 2, No. 7, p. 3.
[64]Respectively, Eric Norden and Holt, Rinehart & Winston. In addition, Warner Brothers was negotiating for motion picture rights to the book.
[65]McCord is referring here to the masking tape that the burglars used to tape open the locks to doors in the Watergate office building.

the most powerful man in the world.[66] *Is a nation's will and character now being measured with yet another piece of tape in the hands of Him who created all that is?*

Lest we miss the point, McCord goes on to define the word "tape," and does so in such a way as to invite the reader to ponder its meaning in an esoteric, almost cabbalistic, way:

TAPE: to size up; figure out . . . record on magnetic tape . . . measure . . . fasten, bind . . . make secure. Red Tape. Tape measure; a . . . rule for measuring the circumference and diameter.

Finally, McCord takes the plunge and provides us with (we are told) every biblical reference to the word "tape." Because he clearly believes that all these references are swollen with some hidden meaning, they are worth quoting here:

Early in April . . . the hand of the Lord was upon me . . . going nearer I saw a man whose face shone like bronze standing beside the Temple gate, holding in his hand A MEASURING TAPE . . . He said to me, 'Son . . . watch and listen and take to heart everything I show you, for you have been brought here so I can show you many things, and then you are to return to the people of Israel to tell them all you have seen.'
Ezekiel 40:3

After this David subdued . . . the Philistines by conquering Gath, their largest city. He also devastated the land of Moab . . . he divided his victims . . . AS MEASURED WITH A TAPE. . . . He also destroyed the forces of King Hadezer of Zobah in a battle at the Euphrates River. . . .
2 Samuel 8:1–6

If you see some poor man being oppressed by the rich, with miscarriage of justice everywhere throughout the land, don't be surprised! For every official is under orders from higher up, and the higher officials look up to their superiors. And so the matter is lost IN RED TAPE and bureaucracy. And over them all is the King. Oh, for a King who is devoted to his country! Only he can bring order from the chaos.
Ecclesiastes 5:8

[66]"A piece of magnetic tape" refers to the presidential taping system that Nixon employed in the Oval Office, and, perhaps more explicitly, to the notorious "18 ½ -minute gap" in those tapes.

This is hardly what one would expect of the bland and dispassion-
ate "registered Republican" that most people imagine when they
conjure up an image of James McCord. Is there any doubt that
McCord would have us identify him with the biblical David, the
slayer of Goliath, conqueror of Gath and devastator of Moab?
Hardly. Neither can there be any doubt that McCord himself identifies with the biblical figure who, "early in April," found "the hand
of the Lord" upon him.

What, in the end, is to be made of McCord? Accounts in the press
portrayed an ordinary man in extraordinary circumstances. A sympathetic figure, if only because he threatened the tenure of a much
despised President, McCord was spared the intensive scrutiny that
afflicted so many others in the affair. The details of his CIA career
went virtually uninvestigated, as did the ambiguities of his retirement and the loopholes in his testimony. A latter-day Fortinbras, at
once a hero and a seeming bit player, McCord was interesting to the
press only insofar as he would shout "*J'accuse!*" at the Nixon administration. As for the rest—the quasi-mystical incantations about
TAPE and the right-wing conspiracy theories that later emerged in
his "newsletters"—it was best left unexamined lest skeptics begin to
question his motives and objectivity.[67]

But we have gotten ahead of the story. If we are to begin at the
beginning, we must go back to the spring of 1971, when McCord was
living in quiet retirement in Rockville, Maryland. We do not know
if he subscribed to the local newspaper, the *Montgomery County
Sentinel,* but if he did, he may well have seen the byline of a cub
reporter named Bob Woodward. As for Howard Hunt, he had been
retired for nearly a year when, in April, he decided to visit Miami.

---

[67]One wonders how McCord, who took such pleasure giving inflated significance to the word
"tape," overlooked the *Oxford English Dictionary*'s definition of Watergate as, principally, a
Middle English term meaning "to leak." (Thank you, Ron Rosenbaum.)

2.
ODESSA: The Plumbers Get to Work

Howard Hunt's visit to Miami in the spring of 1971 is said to have been made in connection with an advertising account at the Mullen Company.[1] It is apparent, however, that the visit was also timed to coincide with commemorative celebrations marking the tenth anniversary of the Bay of Pigs invasion. The first person that Hunt seems to have contacted upon arriving in Miami was Bernard Barker, a man whom Hunt says he had not seen for nearly ten years.

Nicknamed Macho, Barker was the Havana-born son of an American father and a Cuban mother. He had served in the U.S. Air Force during World War II, had been shot down and interned as a prisoner of war. Returning to Cuba at war's end, he enlisted in the regime of Carlos Prío Socarrás, joining Cuba's secret police (the Bureau of Investigations) as a sergeant. During that time, according to FBI reports, "he became associated in gangster activities" while working also as an FBI informant.[2] In 1960, in anticipation of the Bay of Pigs invasion, the FBI relinquished its control of Barker, turning him over to the CIA.[3]

By then his claim to American citizenship had been revoked as a consequence of his service in a foreign police force (despite his work for the FBI). And although this claim had been reinstated in

[1]Hunt, *Undercover,* pp. 143–44.
[2]FBI teletype, serial 139-4089-70, June 20, 1972.
[3]CIA memorandum, July 6, 1972, for L. Patrick Gray, the then acting director of the FBI, signed by Lieutenant General Vernon Walters, acting director of the CIA, found in *Statement of Information, Hearings before the House Committee on the Judiciary,* 93d Cong., 2d sess., May–June 1974, Book 2, p. 530.

1954, it was not until 1967 that he was finally naturalized as an American citizen.[4]

Barker's 1971 meeting with Hunt was an emotional one. Calling him by his nom de guerre, Eduardo, Barker introduced Hunt to other veterans of the Bay of Pigs, including future Watergate burglar Eugenio Martinez. Nicknamed Musculito, Martinez was a legendary figure in the counterrevolutionary underground. A blue-eyed Cubano, naturalized as an American in 1970, he had driven a supply boat called the Prowler during the Bay of Pigs operation, and had captained more than two hundred clandestine maritime missions against the Castro regime in the years that followed.[5]

According to Martinez, he was skeptical of Hunt's explanation for his visit to Miami that year—and, also, of Hunt's claim to have retired from the CIA. As Martinez has written:

[Hunt] had been the maximum representative of the Kennedy administration to our people in Miami. . . . So when Barker told me that Eduardo was coming to town and that he wanted to meet me, that was like a hope for me. He had chosen to meet us at the Bay of Pigs monument, where we commemorate our dead, on April 16, 1971. . . . I always go to the monument on that day, but that year I had another purpose—to meet Eduardo, the famous Eduardo, in person.

He was different from all the other men I had met in the Company. He looked more like a politician than a man who was fighting for freedom. He was there with his pipe, relaxing in front of the memorial, and Barker introduced me. I then learned his name for the first time— Howard Hunt. . . . We went to a Cuban restaurant for lunch and right away Eduardo told us that he had retired from the CIA in 1971 and was working for Mullen and Company. I knew just what he was saying. I was also officially retired from the Company. Two years before, my case officer had gathered all the men in my Company unit and handed us envelopes with retirement announcements inside. But mine was a blank

---

[4]Barker's claim to U.S. citizenship was reinstated by means of a private congressional bill instigated by attorney Murdoughs Madden—ironically, a member of Edward Bennett Williams' law firm. (What made this ironic was Williams' later role as attorney for the Democratic National Committee and the *Washington Post*.) The bill was introduced in Congress on March 10, 1954, by Senator Harrison Williams of New Jersey, the same Harrison Williams who, twenty-five years later, would be disgraced in the FBI's Abscam sting operation. The signers of Barker's successful petition for naturalization in 1967 were Paul Steiner and Angelo Dundee, the latter a promoter of boxing matches and sometime trainer of Muhammad Ali. (Like Dundee, Barker was also a boxing promoter.) See FBI serial 139-4089-1205, June 28, 1972, p. 59.
[5]FBI serial 139-4089-1205, pp. 62, 170–71.

paper. Afterward, he explained to me that I would stop making my boat missions to Cuba but I would continue my work with the Company. . . . Not even Barker knew that I was still working with the Company. But I was quite certain that day that Eduardo knew.[6]

As Martinez makes clear elsewhere in his memoir about the April 1971 visit, Hunt's purpose was recruitment. " 'What is Manolo doing?' . . . 'What is Roman doing?' . . . He said he wanted to meet with the old people. It was a good sign. We did not think he had come to Miami for nothing."[7] It was in this way, then, that Hunt obtained his agents for secret operations that, as it happened, were as yet undreamed of by the Nixon administration, which would supposedly conceive of, and sponsor, them. As Hunt's friend from the Brown Alumni Association, Charles Colson, put it in an interview with this writer: "Hunt's visit to Barker [in April 1971] was, pure and simple, a get-ready-for-action call. You'd have to be an idiot to think otherwise." Leaning forward in his chair with a look of anger and perplexity, Colson added: "But there wasn't any action anticipated. Not then. The Pentagon Papers hadn't been published. The Plumbers were months away. So, you tell me: how did Hunt know [in April] that he'd need the Cubans?"

Indeed, it was almost two months later, on June 13, 1971, that the *New York Times* began to publish excerpts from the 46-volume Defense Department archive that reporters dubbed the Pentagon Papers. President Nixon's first reaction, we are told, was relatively low-keyed because, while the documents told a great deal about America's involvement in Vietnam, virtually all of it concerned the past administrations of Democratic Presidents John F. Kennedy and Lyndon B. Johnson.[8]

Soon, however, Nixon was persuaded that a catastrophe had taken place. His National Security Adviser, Henry Kissinger, argued that publication of the Papers was a serious blow to the integrity and conduct of U.S. foreign policy, which, he insisted, depended on secrecy for success. Kissinger then went on to smear Daniel Ellsberg, who had leaked the Papers, saying that he was "a sexual pervert, [that he had] shot Vietnamese from helicopters in Vietnam, used drugs, [and] had sexual relations with his wife in

[6]Eugenio Martinez, "Mission Impossible," *Harper's*, October 1974, p. 51.
[7]Ibid., p. 52.
[8]Lukas, *Nightmare*, p. 68.

front of their children." Finally, Kissinger added that Ellsberg was "the most dangerous man in America today" and that he "must be stopped at all costs."[9]

The concern about Ellsberg—the Papers that he had leaked and his familiarity with still other national security secrets—was exacerbated by the specter of an alleged Soviet plot. According to an FBI report that was itself predicated upon the information of one Victor M. Lessiovski (a.k.a. Fedora), some five thousand to six thousand uncensored pages of the Pentagon Papers had been delivered to the Soviet embassy on June 17.[10] Those pages were said to include coded cable traffic and information that would jeopardize not only U.S. foreign policy but U.S. intelligence operations and the lives of American soldiers as well. CIA Director Richard Helms was skeptical, however. As he explained to White House officials, "I doubt very much if we will get to see if it is a true report but, quite honestly, we know the fellow [Fedora] who has been giving us these reports and we have our doubts about them."[11] Indeed, that was something of an understatement.

For years the CIA and the FBI had been quarreling over the bona fides of a succession of Soviet-bloc defectors. Depending upon which defector, or set of defectors, one believed, the CIA and the FBI were or were not home to American "defectors-in-place"— moles, in other words, or double agents working secretly on behalf of the Soviet Union. One of the central figures in the dispute was Lessiovski, a KGB officer who was then a special assistant to U Thant, secretary general of the United Nations.[12] Code-named Fedora by the FBI, Lessiovski pretended to serve as a double agent for the United States by providing FBI Director J. Edgar Hoover and

[9]Seymour M. Hersh, *The Price of Power: Kissinger in the Nixon White House* (New York: Summit Books, 1983), p. 385. In this passage, Hersh is quoting Charles Colson's recollection of what Kissinger said to Nixon about Ellsberg.

[10]David Young memorandum of conversation, July 21, 1971, in *Statement of Information Submitted on Behalf of President Nixon, Hearings before the Committee on the Judiciary*, 93d Cong., 2d sess., Book 4 ("White House Surveillance Activities"), May–June 1974, pp. 104–7.

[11]Ibid.

[12]David J. Garrow, *The FBI and Martin Luther King, Jr.* (New York: Norton, 1981). Garrow was the first writer to publicly identify Fedora as Lessiovski. Readers interested in counterintelligence issues may want to read the following books and articles: Edward J. Epstein, *Legend: The Secret World of Lee Harvey Oswald* (New York: McGraw-Hill, 1978); Anthony Summers, *Conspiracy* (New York: McGraw-Hill, 1980); Henry Hurt, *Shadrin: The Spy Who Never Came Back* (New York: McGraw-Hill, 1981); David C. Martin, *Wilderness of Mirrors* (New York: Harper & Row, 1980); Seymour M. Hersh, "The Angleton Story," *New York Times Magazine*, June 25, 1978; Edward J. Epstein, "The Spy War," *New York Times Magazine*, September 28, 1980; and David Ignatius, "Spy Wars," *Wall Street Journal*, October 4, 1979.

three U.S. presidents with (dis)information that was later determined to have been "cooked" in Moscow.[13]

The issue of Lessiovski's legitimacy was anything but academic. On the contrary, it went to the heart of America's national security. According to a biography of Richard Helms, the former CIA director asked his friend *Washington Post* editor Ben Bradlee if he knew what had worried him most as director of the CIA. Bradlee thought about it, and confessed that he did not know.

"The CIA is the only intelligence service in the Western world," Helms is quoted as having said, "which has never been penetrated by the KGB. . . . That's what I worried about."[14] What Helms was implying, of course, was that the CIA's unique virginity was too good to be true—contrary to what Lessiovski/Fedora had to say.

Indeed, so worrisome was this matter, and so high were the stakes that it implied, that it seems to have contributed to a historic split between the FBI and the CIA—a freeze in relations between the two agencies that was at its coldest point when the Pentagon Papers began to be published. From the winter of 1970 to the fall of 1972 the FBI and the CIA were almost entirely without communication with each other.[15] The seriousness of that breakdown in communications becomes apparent when one considers the division of labor that existed (and exists) between the FBI and the CIA. The former is responsible for all counterespionage operations within the United States, while the latter is primarily concerned with intelligence activities of an extraterritorial kind. In the 1970–72 period, however, the CIA's counterintelligence staff, headed by James Jesus Angleton, was of the firm opinion that the FBI's counterespionage operations were being manipulated by a Soviet dispatch (Victor

---

[13]It would be interesting to analyze Lessiovski's disinformation over the years in order to learn what it was that the Soviet Union wanted us to believe. (The CIA and FBI have no doubt made such an analysis, but it has never been made public.) Certainly, Lessiovski wished us to believe that neither the FBI nor the CIA had ever been successfully penetrated by Soviet agents or American defectors-in-place. A second role of Lessiovski's seems to have been that of an agent provocateur—that is, he took every opportunity to contribute to the political polarization afflicting the United States during the 1960s. Toward that end, he disseminated false information to the effect that Ellsberg and Dr. Martin Luther King were Soviet agents or dupes, and that the antiwar movement was under the direct influence of spooks in the Kremlin and Havana. Undoubtedly, that disinformation contributed directly to the FBI's harassment of Dr. King, and to such illegal domestic intelligence operations as the CIA's Operation Chaos.

[14]Thomas Powers, *The Man Who Kept the Secrets: Richard Helms and the CIA* (New York: Knopf, 1979), p. 53.

[15]Nedzi report, p. 192. While the Fedora issue contributed enormously to the deterioration in relations between the FBI and the CIA, the direct cause of the communications freeze was the CIA's unwillingness to inform the bureau of the identity of one of its sources.

Lessiovski). Under ordinary circumstances this would have been terrible enough, but the agency might at least have been able to assess the damage that was being done. Because of the breakdown in communications between the two agencies, however, the CIA found itself completely in the dark, and it can only have feared the worst.

Charles Colson, then special counsel to the President, knew nothing of these issues when he supported Henry Kissinger's insistence, against Richard Helms's advice, that a hard line should be taken toward Daniel Ellsberg. Colson likened Ellsberg to Alger Hiss (a comparison calculated to ingratiate him with Nixon), and pointed out in memoranda to Haldeman that Ellsberg might be used to "discredit the New Left." If, for instance, Ellsberg could be shown (by whatever means) to be disreputable, America's antiwar faction would be discredited because of his close association with it.

The arguments of Kissinger and Colson, which won support from others in the administration, prevailed. The result was a decision to assign certain White House personnel to study the subject of "leaks," revise existing classification procedures and coordinate a campaign against Daniel Ellsberg. These personnel would eventually become the White House Special Investigations Unit, or the Plumbers. At the time, however, it was not anticipated that their activities would require the commission of felonies. While the plans to discredit Ellsberg were politically cynical, they were not necessarily criminal, and the broad purposes of the Special Investigations Unit were, at least in concept, legitimate.

While the unit would not formally exist until July 24, its eventual chief was brought to the White House on July 1.[16] This was David Young, a thirty-two-year-old Oxford scholar and a protégé of Nelson Rockefeller's. Prior to his new employment, he had been Henry Kissinger's appointments secretary on the National Security Council.

On the same day that Young arrived at the White House, Howard Hunt received a telephone call from Colson. According to Hunt, he "was unprepared for Colson's call and for the intensive grilling concerning [Hunt's] views of Ellsberg and the publication of the Pentagon Papers . . ."[17] As he had done the previous January, when

---

[16]Young was the administration's third choice to head the Special Investigations Unit. Both Richard Allen (later National Security Adviser to President Ronald Reagan) and Patrick Buchanan, a White House speechwriter for Nixon, declined the job.
[17]Hunt, *Undercover*, p. 146.

he had approached Colson to offer his services to the White House, Hunt notified the CIA of his most recent contact.[18]

Five days later, "On Monday, July 6," Hunt writes, "Colson called me again and asked me to come to the White House. He had been thinking over our conversation, he told me, and the need for someone with my background on the White House staff.

" 'I've got a full-time job,' I reminded Colson, 'but if you can work it out with Bob Bennett, I'll be glad to help.' "[19]

If Colson could work it out with Bob Bennett? Clearly, Hunt is being disingenuous. As we have seen, Hunt had spoken to Colson about a job at the White House more than a year before, and, according to Colson, the CIA man had been pestering him ever since. Indeed, Colson tells us that Hunt and Bennett had offered their services gratis only six months before; obviously, then, Hunt had no reason to doubt Bennett's cooperation. For his own reasons, Hunt wishes to appear a reluctant bride, and to conceal his repeated attempts to inveigle his way into the White House.

In the event, the pro forma approval of Hunt's employment came on July 7, when Colson introduced Hunt to John Ehrlichman. At that meeting, with Ehrlichman's bags already packed for a trip to the Western White House that same afternoon, Hunt was asked about his relationship to the CIA. He replied that he "had retired a year before and had been working in private industry ever since."[20] It was Ehrlichman's impression that Hunt had not been in contact with the CIA for more than a year.

On the evening of the following day, July 8, after Ehrlichman had decamped for San Clemente, California, with the top echelon of the Nixon administration, Hunt arranged for an interview with former CIA operative Lucien Conein. A familiar of Ho Chi Minh, Conein was well acquainted with the back alleys of both Hanoi and Saigon. He had served for more than a decade in Vietnam and was familiar with many of the circumstances surrounding the 1963 assassination of South Vietnam's president, Ngo Dinh Diem. Hunt and Colson hoped that Conein could provide information that would implicate former President John F. Kennedy in the coup that had toppled Diem. Accordingly, they met with Conein in the vacant offices of John Ehrlichman, swapping "war stories" and drinking more than was good for them. To record the en-

---

[18]Interviews with Colson and H. R. Haldeman. See also Haldeman, *Ends of Power*, p. 143.
[19]Hunt, *Undercover*, p. 148.
[20]Ibid. pp. 148–49.

counter, Hunt took the precaution of having the Secret Service install a clandestine taping system in the room.

As for Ehrlichman, he was oblivious to the way in which his office was being used. Joan Hall, Colson's secretary, was sworn to secrecy by Hunt and her boss about the use to which Ehrlichman's office had been put in his absence. Not that it mattered much in the end. The tape recorder, installed in the cushions of a couch, failed to operate because, we are told, Conein sat on it throughout the interview.

In the meantime, John Ehrlichman *did or did not* telephone General Robert E. Cushman, Jr., deputy director of the CIA, to ask that the agency provide assistance to Hunt in his "security" work.[21] Whether it was Ehrlichman who requested that liaison or whether it was unilaterally established by the CIA, it was actually Hunt who called Cushman's office in mid-July to request an appointment. The person he spoke with was Carl Wagner, Cushman's special assistant, and an acquaintance of Hunt's since their tour of duty with the CIA's North Asia Command during the 1950s. Wagner set up the appointment for July 22.

On that day Hunt rode to the agency's Langley headquarters in a chauffeured White House limousine. Despite the ostentation of this arrival, he took the precaution of ascending to General Cushman's office in a private elevator reserved for the CIA's top echelon and most secretive visitors. Greeting Cushman, he suggested that Wagner leave them alone, which Wagner did even as the general activated a hidden tape recorder in the room.[22]

Why Cushman took this precaution with Hunt, an old friend and former office-mate, is uncertain.[23] While it is true that Cushman did not know what Hunt was seeking—in fact Hunt was there to obtain a disguise for an interview with Clifton DeMotte, a man purported to have explosive information about the Chappaquiddick scandal—the resort to secret taping suggests a certain mistrust. Whatever the reason for the taping, however, the transcript shows that the two men talked together for twelve minutes, with only a part of their conversation devoted to the subject at hand. As Hunt put it at the

---

[21]The issue of Ehrlichman's alleged request for CIA assistance to Hunt is discussed in Appendix III: "Ehrlichman vs. Cushman."

[22]A transcript of the July 22 meeting between Cushman and Hunt is published as an appendix to the Nedzi report, pp. 1125–31.

[23]Hunt and Cushman had shared an office together in CIA's Clandestine Division during the spring of 1950. See Lukas, *Nightmare*, p. 80.

time, "I've been charged with quite a highly sensitive mission by the White House to visit and elicit information from an individual whose ideology we aren't entirely sure of, and for that purpose they asked me to come over here and see if you could get me two things: flash alias documentation, which wouldn't have to be backstopped at all, and some degree of physical disguise for a one-time op—in and out."[24] Cushman readily agreed to the request, though it must be said that Hunt exaggerated the mysteriousness of his "mission," namely, to interview a gossip in Providence, Rhode Island.

One wonders who it was that Hunt made reference to when he said that "they asked me to come over here. . . ." Certainly not to John Ehrlichman, because he was still in California, and so far as anyone knows, he had never heard of Clifton DeMotte. The suggestion that Hunt should interview DeMotte had actually come from Hunt's boss at the Mullen Company, Robert Bennett, and that suggestion had been approved by Colson. It was not an operation of the Special Investigations Unit because, on July 22, that unit did not yet exist. As for the "ideology" of DeMotte, the issue was a canard. DeMotte had worked for the Kennedys in a previous electoral compaign, and he was now offering gossip about Chappaquiddick in hopes of receiving an appointment in the Nixon administration. He was an opportunist, not a Sandinista, and the disguise that Hunt sought can only be described as unnecessary. After all, had DeMotte wished, he could have traced Hunt—under whatever alias he might use—back to Robert Bennett.

However peculiar the disguise may have been, Hunt obtained it on the following day, July 23. In a Wisconsin Avenue safehouse near the National Cathedral, Hunt met with Steve Greenwood, a technician in the CIA's Technical Services Division (TSD). There he was given a brown toupee (others would later describe it as a red wig), and a pair of spectacles whose lenses, while thick and owlish, were clear. A dental cast was made of his palate for the purpose of handcrafting a speech-alteration device that would change the tone of Hunt's voice. While Greenwood shaped the device (it would introduce a lisp to Hunt's speech), the White House spy signed for the "pocket litter" that the TSD man provided. This consisted of alias identification made out in the name of Edward J. Warren, and among other things, it identified "Mr. Warren" as a member in good standing of the Hot Rod Club of America. In addition, Hunt re-

[24]Nedzi report, p 1125.

ceived a gait-altering device that gave him a convincing limp.[25]

It was on the following day, July 24, that the White House Special Investigations Unit was finally convened for the first time. President Nixon, while in San Clemente, had approved its creation on the basis of discussions with Haldeman and Ehrlichman, after reading a memorandum on the subject that David Young and Egil ("Bud") Krogh had written. Like Young, Krogh was in his thirties, a former Navy communications officer who had come to Washington from Ehrlichman's Seattle law firm, having previously worked for the Stanford Research Institute. Besides heading the Plumbers, he was executive director of the Cabinet Committee on International Narcotics Control.

The Special Investigations Unit came to be called the Plumbers because of a private joke of David Young's. Assigned to "stop leaks," Young had had a placard affixed to his office door: DAVID R. YOUNG/ PLUMBER. That office was in Room 16, in the basement of the Old Executive Office Building. It consisted of four rooms, and was equipped with a KYX scrambler. The scrambler was a telephone secured with a combination lock, and its code was changed daily by Secret Service agents using magnetic IBM cards. The virtue of the scrambler was that it enabled those using it to speak without fear that their conversations would be understood by potential eavesdroppers. On the debit side, conversations could take place only with parties having identical equipment and codes. This meant that the Plumbers were able to talk freely with certain military installations and some components of the U.S. intelligence community. According to one of the Plumbers, "We used [the scrambler] mostly to talk to the CIA at Langley. It sounded as if we were speaking to each other from opposite ends of a long drainpipe."[26] This was the comment of no less a communicator than G. Gordon Liddy, the former FBI agent who would one day become "the silent man of Watergate" and, subsequently, the debating partner of LSD evangelist Dr. Timothy Leary.

Liddy had come to the Plumbers unit from the Treasury Department on July 19. While a T-man he had managed to alienate virtually everyone by the politically embarrassing public stand that he

[25]Lisping, limping, seemingly half blind and bewigged, "Mr. Warren" must have seemed a peculiar hot-rodder indeed. Despite the bizarre trappings, the creator of the disguise, Steve Greenwood, received a special award from the CIA for inventing it.
[26]Liddy, *Will*, p. 147.

had taken on the subject of gun control—in essence, that there shouldn't be any. He had worked with Egil Krogh on narcotics matters, impressing him with his forcefulness, analytical clarity and diligence.

Immediately, Liddy imposed his peculiar imagination on the Plumbers, creating a "sensitivity indicator to distinguish our product from that of the agencies we were coordinating and other White House sources. Our *o*rganization had been *d*irected to *e*liminate *s*ubversion of the *s*ecrets of the *a*dministration, so I created an acronym using the initial letter of those descriptive words [italic added].[27]

"[The acronym] appealed to me because when I organize, I am inclined to think in German terms and the acronym was also used by a World War II German veterans organization belonged to by some acquaintances of mine, *Organisation Der Emerlingen Schutz Staffel Angehorigen:* ODESSA. On the blackboard, in German for clarity and added security, I diagrammed the new ODESSA organization. The only exception to the German was the use, common in the Nixon White House, of the Greek letter and mathematical symbol, pi, as a symbol for the President."[28]

It is easy to imagine Liddy's irritation with the fact that no one had had the wit to designate the President as *der Führer*, thereby spoiling the homogeneity of Liddy's Teutonic approach. But there is something even odder here than meets the eye. ODESSA was the code name for the "underground railroad" that helped Nazi war criminals flee retribution at the end of World War II. To describe ODESSA as a "German veterans organization" is about as accurate as referring to Auschwitz as a housing project for European minorities. When Liddy writes that some acquaintances of his belong to that organization, he is not merely tweaking us with his apparent affection for things Nazist but almost inviting federal authorities to question him on the subject. (Whereupon Liddy would presumably refuse to answer.) So, also, Liddy tweaks us when he brags of taking his children to see the Nazi propaganda epic *Triumph of the Will*, and, even, of arranging for that film to be screened in the White House itself.[29] Similarly, he goes out of his way to compare (approvingly) FBI Director J. Edgar Hoover and Adolf Hitler, writing that

[27]Ibid., p. 147.
[28]Ibid., pp. 147–48.
[29]Ibid., pp. 156–57.

he was moved to join the FBI (in 1957) because he regarded it as "an elite corps, America's protective echelon, its Schutzstaffel."[30] One might go on, citing Liddy's preoccupation with "the family gene pool" and similar matters, but in the end, Liddy's affection for the Nazi style seems no more relevant than James McCord's avowed hatred of it.[31] The actions of both men throughout the Watergate affair are more easily explained in terms of operational dictates— orders—than political beliefs.

Seldom has there been an institution as peculiar as the White House Special Investigations Unit. Formed in partial response to the disinformation of a Soviet double agent, it was under the command of a Christian Scientist considered so rectitudinous that his associates dubbed him Evil Krogh in the same spirit that 300-pound bruisers tend to be nicknamed Tiny. The unit's co-commander, David Young, was a Kissinger spin-off widely regarded as an emissary of the Rockefeller family. Under these two were G. Gordon Thunderbolt and his soon-to-be sidekick, E. Howard Hunt, a supposedly retired CIA agent whose superheated imagination had produced a pulp oeuvre as enormous as it was bizarre. By putting Liddy and Hunt together, the White House ignored the likelihood that the fantasy lives of these two agents would reach a critical mass. But as exotic as this milieu was in its own right, its liaison agent from the CIA was equally interesting. This was John Paisley. According to a memorandum of the Special Investigations Unit, Paisley was responsible for conducting the overall "leak analysis" with which the Plumbers would be concerned. As the memorandum quoted below makes clear, this was far more than a mere liaison matter. In effect, Paisley and the OS were placed in charge of programming the Plumbers' entire investigation.

THE WHITE HOUSE

WASHINGTON

August 9, 1971

MEMORANDUM FOR THE RECORD

SUBJECT: Meeting with Howard Osborn and Mr. Paisley at CIA Headquarters, 3:00 P.M., August 9, 1971

[30] Ibid., p. 59.
[31] Ibid., pp. 34, 54–55.

I met with Howard Osborn and a Mr. Paisley to review what it was that we wanted CIA to do in connection with their files on leaks from January, 1969, to the present.

I reviewed the need for us to gain a data base on all leaks at least since January of 1969. It was decided that Mr. Paisley would get this done by next Monday, August 16, 1971, utilizing the running file which the USIB Subcommittee has maintained on leaks.[32]

The specific questions, at least as a starter, which Paisley will attempt to answer, are as follows:

(1) Frequency of leaks associated with particular writers.

(2) The gravity of leaks.

(3) The relationship between leaks and, for example, the likelihood of a SALT agreement.

(4) The frequency with which particular bureaucracies are involved.

(5) Comparison of the frequency and gravity of leaks in this Administration with the frequency and gravity of leaks in previous Administrations.

(6) The recurrence of particular motives.

(7) The use of Congress as a vehicle to leak.

(8) Comparison of leaks which occur overseas with those which occur at home.

(9) Estimate of proportion of leaks which are pro-Administration with those which are anti-Administration.

(10) Estimate of number of leaks which are deliberately planted by the Administration.

(11) Estimate of number of leaks which come from one source in comparison with leaks which are pieced together from several sources.

(12) Comparison of number of leaks which put out essentially correct information with comparison of number of leaks which put out essentially incorrect information.

(13) Breakdown of subject areas which seem to have the heaviest concentration of leaks.

(14) Breakdown of level of officials leaking.

The above questions should be reviewed with Paisley within the next two days. It should also be made clear that there must be given definitions in this study.

The New York Times exhibit and *The Washington Post* exhibit will also be made available to CIA in order to feed it into their data base, and we

[32]USIB: United States Intelligence Board.

should also get State Department's leak file and Defense Department's leak file.

David Young[33]

According to Marianne Paisley, John Paisley's wife, meetings between Paisley, Osborn and the Plumbers were frequent during the ensuing months, and occurred at both the Paisleys' home and at the Office of Security in the CIA's Langley headquarters.

Despite this, the Senate, the press and the federal prosecutors proved uninterested in Paisley's connection to the affair. The assumption seemed to be that he was one of the agency's "gray men," an anonymous figure whose career had been spent behind the scenes within the country's most secretive bureaucracy. It was not until September of 1978, when a body bobbed to the surface in Chesapeake Bay, that Paisley became fascinating in a public sort of way. By then, of course, Paisley himself was no longer available for questioning, though no one could be sure whether he had gone to heaven, hell or Moscow.[34]

[33]*Statement of Information Submitted on Behalf of President Nixon, Hearings before the Committee on the Judiciary,* 93d Cong., 2d sess., Book 4 ("White House Surveillance Activities"), May–June 1974.
[34]See Appendix I, "Some Notes on Paisley."

3.
The Unplumbed Depths of Daniel Ellsberg

In a July 28, 1971, memorandum to Charles Colson, Howard Hunt proposed that the CIA perform "a covert psychological assessment/evaluation" of Daniel Ellsberg. The memo urged the collection of all derogatory information on Ellsberg, including the "files from his psychiatric analyst."

The CIA was expert in the preparation of such profiles; its staff physicians and psychiatrists regularly analyzed the personalities and habits of foreign leaders as diverse as Menachem Begin and Hafez Assad. To apply this expertise to an American citizen was, of course, something else again, but the CIA complied. On July 29, after discussing the matter with CIA Director Richard Helms, Howard Osborn instructed the CIA's Office of Medical Services to create an Ellsberg profile.

On August 10 the profile was completed, and two days later it was submitted to the Plumbers at a meeting in Room 16 attended by Hunt, Liddy, David Young and physicians from the CIA. The profile consisted of a single-spaced, one-and-a-half-page typewritten commentary, which suggested that Ellsberg had a problem with authority figures, probably suffered from mid-life crisis and, in leaking the Pentagon's documents, may well have acted upon motives of a patriotic kind. The Plumbers' reaction to these psychiatric bromides was disappointment and irritation. While the doctors protested that it was impossible to prepare an in-depth psychiatric study without more detailed information about Ellsberg's personality, Hunt was skeptical. "I had seen the Agency produce [such profiles] on Mossadegh, Castro, world leaders on whom we had much less information than we had presented to the Central Intelligence

Agency, [information] which comprehended almost the totality of the FBI reports on Dr. Ellsberg."[1] Nevertheless, the Plumbers agreed to acquire further information about Ellsberg, and the CIA promised to try harder once that information had been obtained.

It hardly mattered that the findings were unsatisfactory because the decision had already been reached to burglarize the offices of Ellsberg's psychiatrist, Dr. Lewis J. Fielding. On August 11 the Plumbers had been given written approval by John Ehrlichman to conduct a "covert operation" to obtain Ellsberg's psychiatric dossier, provided that the operation was "done under [the] assurance that it is not traceable."[2]

Toward that end, Hunt set out to obtain further assistance from the CIA. On August 18 he requested that a particular secretary in the CIA's Paris station, a woman with whom Hunt had worked before and whom he admired, be brought home to work in Room 16. The request was denied. Two days later, on August 20, Hunt went to the safehouse on Wisconsin Avenue. There he met with the CIA's Cleo Gephart, a TSD technician, and was issued a tape recorder concealed in a typewriter case. In the meantime Gordon Liddy had expressed admiration for the espionage paraphernalia that Hunt had been collecting, and urged his colleague to make arrangements for him to be similarly outfitted. Accordingly, on August 25, Hunt and Liddy went to yet another safehouse in the District of Columbia. This was a spare efficiency apartment in the new Southwest section. Introduced to Steve Greenwood, Liddy was given alias documentation that identified him as "George Leonard," a resident of Kansas. A 35-mm Tessina camera, concealed in a tobacco pouch, was also provided, as were the inevitable wig, a gait-altering device, a set of false teeth with a missing incisor and a pair of thick glasses to match Hunt's own. (Liddy approvingly points out that the frames were of West German manufacture.)[3]

So equipped, "Mr. Leonard" and "Mr. Warren" departed for Los Angeles that afternoon, there to conduct a feasibility study for the proposed break-in. That evening the two men entered the building in which Dr. Fielding had his office. Fielding himself had left earlier,

---

[1]Nedzi report, p. 497. See also the testimony in those hearings (pp. 25-37) of Dr. John R. Tietjen, director of Medical Services for the CIA, and Dr. Bernard M. Malloy.
[2]August 11, 1971, memo from Egil Krogh and David Young, "Pentagon Papers Project—Status Report," to John Ehrlichman (reprinted in the Nedzi report, pp. 397-98).
[3]Liddy, *Will*, p. 162.

but a cleaning lady was at work in the hall. Conversing with her in Spanish, Hunt said that he and his friend were physicians who wished to leave a message for Dr. Fielding. On that pretext, Liddy was allowed to enter the doctor's office and, using the Tessina, photographed its interior while Hunt remained outside, chatting with the cleaning lady. Their reconnaissance completed, the two men returned to Washington on the "red-eye," arriving at Dulles Airport at 6:00 A.M. on August 26. Notified in advance of their arrival, Steve Greenwood met them in the airport lounge. He was given the Tessina camera, containing the film that Liddy had exposed, and the roll of film from Hunt's personal camera, a Minolta. Greenwood promised to have the film developed at the CIA and prints made of each frame.[4]

This the CIA did on August 27, making a separate set of prints for its own files. The images were from Hunt's Minolta, and showed Liddy standing in a parking lot beside the office building. A Volvo was in the background, its license plate visible, and there was a name printed on the wall above the vehicle: DR. LEWIS J. FIELDING. That afternoon the prints were given to Hunt, though what happened to the negatives is a matter of dispute. Hunt claims that the CIA retained them, while the CIA insists that they were handed over to Hunt with the prints. Whatever the truth may be, the photography mission was less than a complete success: the entry into Dr. Fielding's office accomplished nothing because, according to the CIA, the Tessina camera had failed to work properly. Liddy, then, got nothing for his efforts.

It is a peculiar business. The reconnaissance was not only poorly executed and dangerous for Hunt and Liddy to personally carry out, but it does not seem to have served any useful end.[5] After all, one does not usually commit a crime, as Hunt and Liddy did, in order to "case" the scene of that crime's intended repetition a week later. Why, then, did they do it? Probably "because it was there." They had the funds for airfare, the allurements of California beckoned, and even more important, they were eager to become opera-

[4]Ibid., pp. 163–64.
[5]One wonders what would have happened if Dr. Fielding's office had been equipped with alarms. One wonders, also, about Liddy's explanation as to why the reconnaissance was important—i.e., to see if Dr. Fielding's filing cabinets had locks and, if so, what kind. Because, of course, neither Hunt nor Liddy was expert at lock-picking, and they had already resolved to employ torsion wrenches and crowbars in the break-in.

tional. They were, after all, anything but reluctant spies. On the contrary, they were narcissists in love with the romance of espionage, as both Hunt's penchant for unnecessary disguise and Liddy's affection for Germanic cryptonyms suggest.

Whatever the reason for the recon, it got results, though not, perhaps, the ones that Hunt and Liddy intended. To begin with, Egil Krogh was appalled to learn that his subordinates were planning to personally burglarize Dr. Fielding's office. He wanted surrogates used so that, whatever happened, the White House would not appear to be directly involved should anything go wrong. Accordingly, Hunt contacted Bernard Barker in Miami, telling him that a secret mission was in the offing and that men would be needed.

A second result of the reconnaissance was that it caused eyebrows to be raised within the CIA itself. One of the TSD technicians who examined the photos said that he found them "intriguing," and realized that they had been taken in Southern California. A second CIA officer, after contemplating the photo of "Mr. Leonard" in the parking lot, concluded that the pictures were obviously "casing" photos.[6]

Whether or not these conclusions were reported to the CIA's top echelon is unknown. What is known is that, on August 27, even as the photos were being handed over to Hunt, General Cushman called John Ehrlichman to say that the CIA would no longer provide assistance to Howard Hunt. According to Ehrlichman, the call came as a surprise to him because, until Cushman pronounced an end to the CIA's generosity, Ehrlichman had not known that any such assistance had been extended. Still, the call seemed routine to Ehrlichman, and he did not question Cushman about the decision. Ehrlichman received as many as a dozen calls a month from bureaucrats complaining that members of the White House were making excessive demands. He knew exactly how to handle such complaints: in essence, do nothing. Either the problem would solve itself by going away, or someone would "squawk" that a particular agency was being obstructive. In that way, Ehrlichman believed, he would learn who it was that had asked the CIA to assist Hunt: it would be whoever squawked.[7] (No one did.)

[6]Lukas, *Nightmare*, p. 102. See also the testimony of General Cushman in the Nedzi report, pp. 2–24, and the written statement of the then DCI, James R. Schlesinger, pp. 166–68.
[7]Ehrlichman's account of the CIA's cutoff of aid to Hunt is contained in his statement to the House Committee on Armed Services, published in the Nedzi report, pp. 331–42.

According to the CIA, the decision to cut off Hunt had nothing to do with the photographs that he had taken.[8] Rather, the decision was reached because Hunt's demands had become excessive, and because he had introduced a stranger (the mysterious "Mr. Leonard") to the relationship. A note documenting this was written by General Cushman to CIA Director Helms on August 31, 1971, recording his call to Ehrlichman. In the note, Cushman remarks, "I indicated Hunt was becoming a pain in the neck. John said he would restrain Hunt."[9] In fact John Ehrlichman did not contact Hunt about Cushman's call (or anything else, for that matter).

There is in all of this—in Cushman's call to Ehrlichman and in his note to Helms—a suggestion that someone may have been "papering the record" in the interests of plausible denial. Cushman's note, for example, is an informal one, scrawled on a routing slip with the indication that Hunt should receive a copy. That seems implausible, however, in view of Cushman's curt phraseology about Hunt's becoming "a pain in the neck." What is more to the point, though, is the fact that the CIA did *not* end its assistance to Hunt and Liddy on August 27. On the contrary, Ehrlichman was simply told that it had. As Liddy himself has written, "Hunt and I continued to call on and receive CIA assistance well into 1972."[10]

[8]"Preliminary CIA Comments on Senator Baker's Revised Staff Report, 'CIA Investigation,'" pp. 1161–65 of the Ervin committee's *Final Report*, June 1974.
[9]Nedzi report, p. 9.
[10]Liddy, *Will*, p. 162. The nature of the assistance given to Hunt and Liddy long after the supposed CIA "cutoff" is discussed in later chapters. A passage from Liddy's book is worth quoting, however. It was written in the context of preparations being made to burglarize Dr. Fielding's office. Because Liddy was to serve as a guard on that operation, he considered arming himself. As he writes (*Will*, p. 165), "A gun would be too noisy without a silencer, and none of mine, including a sterile CIA 9-mm assassination piece I now owned, was threaded to receive one, so I brought to the office a folding Browning knife—deadly and quiet." What is bothersome about the passage is Liddy's reference to the gun, and his clear suggestion that it had only recently been provided to him by the CIA. What makes this suggestion explicit is his use of the word "now" in the phrase "[a] CIA 9-mm assassination piece I now owned . . ." Had Liddy used the phrase "then owned," or words to that effect, his meaning might have been different—i.e., it would have suggested that he no longer had the weapon. So, also, had Liddy simply omitted the word "now" from the passage, his meaning would have been otherwise: the sentence would then convey no more than that he owned an assassination pistol at the time of the Fielding break-in. By including the word "now" in the passage, Liddy deliberately implies that the gun was newly acquired. From whom? The implication could not be clearer: from the CIA. For that is how he describes the weapon: a "sterile assassination pistol . . . issued by the CIA." While it is true that Liddy does not say that the gun *was issued to him* by the CIA, the context of the passage and its sense makes it difficult to conclude otherwise. (A photograph of the weapon, incidentally, is reproduced in *Will*.)

With the "reconnaissance" of Dr. Fielding's office accomplished, the plan to burglarize it would be put in action. Assembling in Los Angeles on Labor Day weekend, the team consisted of Hunt, Liddy and three Cubans—Bernard Barker, Eugenio Martinez and Felipe De Diego. The group was, to say the least, well equipped. Liddy had acquired a de facto Minox "attack kit," including an automatic "C" camera, mini-tripod, copying stand, flash unit, waist-level finder and darkroom equipment. In addition, he brought along his personal 35-mm camera, a Retina "of German manufacture." To this was added a Polaroid camera, surgical gloves, a glass cutter, a crowbar, black plastic with which to cover the windows of Dr. Fielding's office, four walkie-talkies and a length of nylon line with which the burglars might rappel from the second-floor office should their presence be discovered. The purpose of the Polaroid was, ostensibly, to make certain that the break-in would go undetected—that is, the interior of the office and its files would be photographed with the Polaroid upon entry so that the burglars might later return everything to the condition and place in which they found it.[11]

I use the word "ostensibly" because the presence of the glass cutter and crowbar suggests that a certain indelicacy was anticipated, as, indeed, does the absence of a locksmith. For how were the burglars to enter the offices? Did they assume that the door to the building and the door to Dr. Fielding's own office would be left unlocked?

In the event, Hunt and Liddy remained outside while the Cubans smashed the window on the ground floor and used the crowbar to pry open the front door to the psychiatrist's office. Once inside, Barker showed his compatriots a slip of paper on which Liddy had written the name E-L-L-S-B-E-R-G. A search for the file then began. Filing cabinets were ripped open and their contents pillaged. With so much damage done to the windows, the filing cabinets and the office door, there could be no question of returning things to their original order. So the break-in team disturbed the office even further, scattering files and pills across the floor in the hope that the police would conclude that the burglary had been perpetrated by drug addicts. To prove that they had searched the office thoroughly, Barker took Polaroid photographs

---

[11]With respect to the Fielding break-in, my account relies on the following sources: Ervin committee *Hearings*, Book 1, pp. 357–58, 375–76, 492, 504–5, and Book 9, pp. 3674–77; Martinez, "Mission Impossible," pp. 52–53; Hunt, *Undercover*, pp. 169–74; and Liddy, *Will*, pp. 166–68.

of the wreckage—which, of course, was exactly the opposite reason that the Polaroid had been brought along in the first place.

This vandalism accomplished, the team returned to their hotel and shared a bottle of champagne with Hunt and Liddy. According to Barker, the "celebration" was a muted one because the entry team had failed to locate the Ellsberg file.

Surely, this goes beyond mere "bungling." There is a playfulness to the affair. On the one hand, there is the apparent care demonstrated by the deployment of surgical gloves, the precaution represented by the Polaroid camera and, of course, the careful reconnaissance of ten days before. On the other hand (or, rather, *in* it) is the crowbar that was put to such flamboyant use.

What is more significant, however, is the question of "the take" from the Fielding burglary or, rather, the supposed lack of it. According to De Diego, in direct contradiction of Barker and Martinez, the Ellsberg file was in fact located and photographed.[12] De Diego testified that he held the file in his hands, turning its pages, while Martinez photographed it with the Minox.[13] It is difficult to understand how there can be any disagreement on the issue. Either the file was found or it was not. Either the mission was a success, as the champagne celebration suggests, or it was a failure.

Dr. Fielding's comments on the subject make it clear that De Diego is telling the truth. According to the psychiatrist, his notes on the Ellsberg case were indeed in his office at the time of the break-in. Moreover, Fielding adds, the burglars had obviously found them: the notes were lying on the floor when he arrived at his office on the morning after the burglary and, he said, the pages had clearly been "fingered."

The issue of what was and what was not photographed revolves around the two cameras, the Polaroid and the Minox. The former produced on-the-spot snapshots of the wreckage that had been made of Fielding's office and, according to Hunt and Martinez, at least one picture of Ellsberg's name in a pop-up telephone directory. According to Martinez, these photos were necessary to prove that the break-in had occurred, and, in fact, they were given to Egil Krogh and David Young upon Hunt's return to Washington. When John

---

[12]Martinez, "Mission Impossible," pp. 52–53, and Barker's testimony in the Ervin committee *Hearings*, Book 1, pp. 357–58, 375–76.
[13]*The Watergate Hearings: Break-in and Cover-up*, edited by the staff of the *New York Times* (New York: Bantam Books, 1973), p. 69.

Ehrlichman saw the pictures, he was "appalled" by the destruction wrought in what was supposed to have been a "covert" operation.

But what of the film in the Minox?—the film that De Diego claims contained images of Dr. Fielding's notes on Ellsberg's analysis. Following the break-in, the Minox was given to Hunt in Liddy's presence with the information that it had not been used. To Liddy's knowledge, therefore, the film was never developed, and its fate remains unknown.

If De Diego is telling the truth, however, the Nixon White House was as much a "victim" of the Fielding break-in as were the doctor and his patient because the White House was apparently deprived of the fruits of the felony that it had financed. Of this we may be glad, but on reflection, the double cross implied by De Diego raises serious questions. The Fielding break-in, after all, had been rationalized on national security grounds. Indeed, Hunt and Liddy believed that the KGB was a beneficiary of the Ellsberg leak.[14] Like Hunt, Martinez was a patriot and a professional; it is inconceivable that either man would have sabotaged a secret mission alleged to be in the national interest. On whose authority, then, did they act? Who had the clout to persuade Hunt that the take from the Fielding break-in should be diverted, and to whom was it to be diverted?

To answer those questions, attention should be paid to the fact that, at the time of the break-in, the CIA's Office of Security was profoundly worried about Daniel Ellsberg, and not merely because of the Pentagon Papers. In a 1981 interview with a former staff member of the Ervin committee, I was shown copies of documents —FBI reports, newspaper clips and memoranda from various government agencies—that the Plumbers had provided to the CIA ten years earlier. These documents all concerned Daniel Ellsberg, and they had been provided to the agency as background material for its psychological study. Looking them over, I was struck not so much by what they had to say about Ellsberg but, rather, by the marginal notations, circled phrases and exclamation points that crowded the pages whenever Ellsberg's relationship to a writer named Frances Fitzgerald was mentioned. My source said that the notes had been written by analysts assigned to the CIA's Office of Medical Services and Office of Security. Their concern—indeed, what seems to have been their panic—stemmed from the fact that

[14]Nedzi report, pp. 494–95.

Fitzgerald, the talented author of *Fire in the Lake*, was the daughter of the late Desmond Fitzgerald, a former deputy director of the CIA. Indeed, Des Fitzgerald was a legendary figure within the agency, and one of the original "Knights Templar."[15] He had been involved in some of the agency's most sensitive and controversial operations, including attempts to assassinate Fidel Castro.[16] The CIA saw his liberal daughter's friendship with Ellsberg as a threat, and worried that it might lead to the exposure of operations that the CIA hoped would remain state secrets. Neither Howard Hunt's pal Howard Osborn nor anyone else could be certain of the extent to which "Frankie" Fitzgerald's father had confided in her about his past, nor the extent to which she may have confided in Ellsberg about her father's career. To the Office of Security the prospect was real that the Pentagon Papers might be succeeded by a second leak, and that this second leak would hit the CIA directly. The agency, then, was as concerned about Daniel Ellsberg as was the White House itself.

To know that the CIA and, in particular, the Office of Security were worried by Ellsberg does not prove that the Minox film (exposed in the Fielding break-in) ended up in the agency's files. But that hypothesis seems very likely in view of the fact that Howard Hunt was regularly and secretly sending packages to the CIA from the White House—this, according to the so-called "Mr. X Affidavit," a sworn statement whose exotic sobriquet was earned by virtue of the fact that its author, Rob Roy Ratliff, was a covert employee of the CIA whose identity the agency wished to protect. The state-

[15]The Knights Templar were members of a Catholic military order founded during the Crusades. Those CIA officers who were close to William Donovan, the Catholic chief of the wartime Office of Strategic Services (OSS), were jokingly referred to as Donovan's Knights Templar, perhaps because they, like their ancient predecessors, were a mysterious and tightly knit group dedicated to a "sacred cause."

[16]Des Fitzgerald's involvement in efforts to murder Fidel Castro was revealed in the Church committee hearings (*Alleged Assassination Plots Involving Foreign Leaders*, an interim report of the Senate Select Committee to Study Governmental Operations with Respect to Intelligence Activities, 94th Cong., 1st sess., November 20, 1975, pp. 85ff.). Fitzgerald had been chief of the CIA's Task Force W, responsible for covert operations (including assassination attempts) against Cuba in 1963. In a tragic irony, Fitzgerald was meeting with Rolando Cubela, a.k.a. AM/LASH, in Europe on November 22, 1963, the very day of President John F. Kennedy's assassination. The purpose of the meeting with Cubela, in which Fitzgerald apparently posed as a senior U.S. senator, was to give the Cuban agent a weapon disguised as a fountain pen, with which Cubela was to murder Castro. (See Anthony Summers, *Conspiracy* [New York: McGraw-Hill, 1980], pp. 349–52. Summers interviewed Cubela in a Cuban jail; Cubela's account of the plots contradicted the testimony that several CIA officials had given to the Senate.)

ment was written more than six months after Ratliff visited the home of the then CIA director, James Schlesinger. Ratliff had gone to Schlesinger's home in May 1973 to warn him of a potential embarrassment—i.e., that Howard Hunt, while a consultant at the White House, maintained a secret relationship to the CIA. According to Ratliff's statement:

> My secretary . . . and I frequently speculated about the possible involvement of Howard Hunt and the Watergate affair, and the possible involvement of the Agency. I was aware that Hunt had frequently transmitted sealed envelopes via our office to the Agency. We had receipts for these envelopes, but were unaware of the contents. However, . . . [my predecessor] told me that he had opened one of the packages one day to see what Hunt was sending to the Agency. He said that the envelope . . . appeared to contain "gossip" information about an unknown person—he assumed that it had something to do with a psychological study of that person. [My secretary] subsequently confirmed this information.
>
> . . . As the news of the Watergate and Hunt's involvement spread, we —at a date unknown—decided that it was not prudent nor necessary to retain the receipts for envelopes which we had transmitted from him to the CIA, and we destroyed these receipts.[17]

In a 1982 telephone interview with this writer, the CIA man commented publicly on his statement for the first time. Ratliff said that he had been assigned as a CIA liaison to the National Security Council (NSC) in the Executive Office Building. Hunt's packages were routinely received and hand-carried to the CIA until shortly before the Watergate arrests in mid-June 1972. Ratliff, who came to the White House in early 1972, did not know when this practice began, but he believed that it dated back to the beginning of Hunt's consultancy at the White House. As to the contents of the packages, Ratliff said that they contained "gossip" material about different people. Asked if Daniel Ellsberg was among those mentioned in the materials, Ratliff replied that, to his knowledge, Ellsberg was *not* mentioned and the gossip did not concern him; the gossip concerned White House officials and others in the administration. Asked if tape-recordings or film cassettes were included in the pack-

[17]"CIA Employee Statement, January 17, 1974," reprinted in *Statement of Information, Hearings before the House Committee on the Judiciary*, 93d Cong., 2d sess., Book 2 ("Events Following the Watergate Break-In"), May–June, 1974, pp. 298–99.

ages, Ratliff said that he did not know. He was told, however, that his report to Schlesinger had revealed the tip of what turned out to be an iceberg.

According to a former staff member of the Judiciary Committee, to which Ratliff's statement was submitted, the gossip was "almost entirely of a sexual nature. It was very graphic. Some of it concerned people who worked in the White House."

It is unfortunate that Ratliff's statement has been bowdlerized at the CIA's request. Its obscurity (until now) is probably attributable in large measure to the deletions imposed upon it for what we are told are national security reasons. Ratliff's name, and those of his colleagues, have been deleted from the public version of the statement. So, too, the names of those CIA officials who received Hunt's packages have also been deleted. However, according to a source with access to Ratliff's uncensored statement, the recipients of Hunt's gossip were two: CIA Director Helms, to whom at least some of the packages were addressed, and psychologists and psychiatrists assigned to the agency's Medical Services staff. It was this information that led Ratliff to the conclusion that psychological profiles of American citizens were being prepared by physicians at the CIA. In his statement, Ratliff expressed ignorance of whether Richard Helms had authorized the creation of such profiles, and he would not rule out the possibility that Hunt and the agency's shrinks were operating "free lance" or on their own. Nevertheless, Ratliff wrote, he found it "hard to believe that an individual of the Agency would become involved in something like this without some approval from higher authority within the Agency. . . ."[18]

To these details Charles Colson would add one other. In a 1980 interview with this writer, Colson read aloud from notes that he had taken years before when, for a time, he was in possession of what he calls "the CIA's Watergate file."[19] And according to Col-

---

[18]Ibid., pp. 298–99.

[19]This was a file that consisted of CIA documents relating to the Watergate affair. The file had been put together by the Office of Security, and then provided to the CIA inspector general's office. At the request of the President's counsel, J. Fred Buzhardt, the file was made available to the White House. According to Colson, Buzhardt permitted him to copy the file. A Freedom of Information Act (FOIA) request for this same file was made by the author in 1981, but, to date, the agency has failed to declassify a single page. While Charles Colson is no longer in possession of his copy of the file (he says that he was made to surrender it to the special prosecutor's office), his notes appear to be reliable. In several instances of which the author is aware, Colson's notes include accurate quotations from CIA documents that the author has seen elsewhere but that, nevertheless, remain classified.

son's notes on that file, Hunt's White House packages contained tape-recordings *as well as* written information.

Lieutenant General Vernon Walters, deputy director of the CIA, was clearly mistaken, then, when he told the House Armed Services Committee that "We [at the CIA] had had no contact whatsoever with Mr. Hunt subsequent to 31 August 1971." This statement was immediately amended by CIA Director James Schlesinger, who told the committee: "There were additional contacts by Agency personnel with Mr. Hunt after that date, Mr. Chairman. Those contacts were all associated with the preparation of the Ellsberg profile."[20] This testimony, given to Congress some nine days after Ratliff had gone to Schlesinger with news of Hunt's courier system, was also mistaken. As Ratliff told this writer, the contents of those of Hunt's packages of which Ratliff himself had knowledge did *not* concern Daniel Ellsberg. Hunt, moreover, continued to send his secret packages to the CIA long after the Ellsberg profile had been abandoned, and way beyond the alleged cutoff of CIA assistance at the end of August 1971.

Given the destination of these packages, it must be obvious that psychological profiles were being prepared on Americans other than Daniel Ellsberg. Whether this activity was, as Ratliff feared, "free lance"—that is, an unsanctioned operation—or whether it had the approval of the CIA's top echelon is uncertain. But the purpose of such profiles is quite clear: to predict or to affect the behavior of the person who is profiled. There was, of course, nothing new in this: the agency had been applying the same expertise to foreign leaders for more than a decade. What *was* new, however, was the application of this discipline to *Americans*. Whether free-lance or sanctioned, the prospect of such an operation can only seem Orwellian—and yet it was hardly inconceivable. In his recent biography of Henry Kissinger, Seymour Hersh wrote that "Sometime in 1969, a group of academics [from Duke University] . . . came to a NSC staff meeting to discuss a new technique in parapsychology, constructing abstract models of the personalities of world leaders. Theoretically, the verbal models—or machines, as the academics called them—could be used to simulate and predict the behavior of . . . [foreign leaders]. Lack of relevant data, the scientists explained, prevented them from building certain machines—there was nothing, for instance, on Leonid Brezhnev of

[20]Nedzi report, p. 57.

the Soviet Union. . . . At this point, [NSC staffer Roger] Morris exclaimed, 'Look, it isn't the unpredictability of foreign government that concerns us as much as it is the unpredictability of American government. If you could build us a Nixon machine, it'd be better.' To Morris' surprise, nobody laughed. In fact, no one said anything at all."[21]

In light of the Ratliff statement, it is clear that the notion of a "Nixon machine"—or, for that matter, a "Kissinger machine" or even *a bipartisan collection of machines*—was on minds other than the jesting Roger Morris'.[22] And one of the first steps toward making the notion of such a machine a reality was to infiltrate Howard Hunt into the White House, where he could gather the information or "gossip" needed to create such "machines."

The sensitivity of Hunt's assignment, carried out under cover of the very people on whom he was spying, is indicated by the degree to which he and the agency went to conceal their ongoing relationship in the wake of his "retirement." Here is Hunt's testimony on the matter:

MR. NEDZI: Upon retirement were you ever given the understanding that you may be called upon in the future to provide certain services for the Agency?

MR. HUNT: No, sir.

MR. NEDZI: What form did your contact with your former colleagues take?

MR. HUNT: I saw them very infrequently. I was located downtown, I would see them occasionally on Pennsylvania Avenue, walking into restaurants or stores.

MR. NEDZI: At the time you were hired [by the White House] was there any kind of suggestion that your duties would involve continuing contact with the CIA?

MR. HUNT: Oh, no, sir.[23]

---

[21]Hersh, *Price of Power*, pp. 115–16.

[22]In fact, such machines were more than notional. The field of psychological assessment had been of special interest to former CIA Director Allen Dulles (whose wife had been a longtime patient of Carl Jung). For more than a decade, Dulles supported research in the field, using CIA funds to patronize the Society for the Investigation of Human Ecology and the Human Ecology Fund. In 1965 a firm called Psychological Assessments Associates, Inc., was established with headquarters in Washington, D.C. Founded by two retired CIA psychologists, the firm's main source of funding was the CIA. See Laurence Stern, "Behind Psychological Assessments' Door, a CIA Operation," *Washington Post*, June 21, 1974, p. A3.

[23]Nedzi report, pp. 506–7.

To reconcile Hunt's testimony with the facts is an impossible task. *Of course* there was an "understanding" about his providing continuing services to the agency. As we have seen in those pages where Hunt's retirement is discussed, the CIA had a memorandum to that effect in its own files, and FBI reports take note of the fact that Hunt continued to be used by the CIA on what the bureau described as an "ad hoc basis." He was the middleman in cover negotiations between the CIA and the Mullen Company; he relied upon the agency for technical support that he and Liddy required; and, according to David Young, he had "a private line (installed in his office) for operatives and CIA contacts to reach him directly. . . . As far as [Young] was concerned, Hunt's former associates at CIA and individuals furnishing information in connection with the international drug problems [sic] were the only ones who knew to call him on this line."[24] The CIA, of course, claims that its contacts with Hunt were terminated in late August 1971, but the truth is that Hunt remained in frequent clandestine contact with the agency until his arrest in mid-1972. The envelopes described by Rob Roy Ratliff are evidence of this, and so also are Hunt's regular "tennis dates" and luncheons with ranking CIA officers. In mid-October 1971, for example, Hunt sat down to lunch with Thomas Karamessines, the CIA's deputy director of Plans. The purpose of their meeting, we are told, was to discuss the Mullen Company's cover. But, as former *New York Times* reporter J. Anthony Lukas has written, that explanation is implausible.[25] Karamessines was too high-ranking to concern himself with the details of cover arrangements involving only a few CIA agents (as was the case at Mullen). In any event, such arrangements were not the responsibility of

---

[24]Interview of David R. Young by special agents Robert E. Lill and Daniel C. Mahan, July 3, 1972, FBI serial 139-166. The telephone to which Young made reference was listed in the name of Kathleen A. Chenow, Young's secretary, and it was billed to her home rather than to the White House. According to Young, this procedure was used so that Hunt's secretive conversations would bypass the White House switchboard. This, Young believed, was desirable so that those people calling Hunt would not realize that he was employed by the White House. In this, however, Young appears to have been mistaken. Hunt bragged of his White House employment to both his contacts at the CIA and Bernard Barker (according to Kathy Chenow, the most frequent caller on the phone). The real reason for the billing procedure involving Chenow, then, seems to have been to mask the callers from the White House rather than vice versa. (See FBI serial 139-4089-1745, interview of Kathleen A. Chnow [sic], conducted July 3, 1972, by Robert C. Lill and Daniel C. Mahan.) Hunt's telephone, listed in Chenow's name, should not be confused with a second unusual telephone in the Plumbers' office—the one armed with a KYX scrambler that, Liddy tells us, was used "mostly" for conversations with the CIA (*Will*, p. 147).
[25]Lukas, *Nightmare*, p. 102.

Karamessines but that of the Central Cover Staff. The real purpose of Karamessines' meeting with Hunt is unknown, therefore, but it seems pertinent to recall that in 1965 it was to Karamessines that Hunt reported during his time of false retirement. Karamessines, in other words, was Howard Hunt's case officer.

At an even later date, according to Gordon Liddy, Hunt relied upon the CIA's graphics section to prepare the infamous Gemstone charts.[26] This was in December 1971 or January 1972, and contrary to what one might conclude from the testimony of former CIA Director James Schlesinger, those charts had nothing to do with Daniel Ellsberg. Neither, for that matter, did Hunt's even later contact with the CIA's External Employment Assistance Branch (EEAB)—on which occasion he sought a locksmith and a wireman to burglarize and surveil Las Vegas publisher Herman ("Hank") Greenspun (who was rumored to have information damaging to Senator Muskie). Finally—and sufficiently, to my mind—we have Gordon Liddy's word that Hunt went to the CIA as late as March 1972 to obtain a series of vicious political caricatures of Senator Edward Kennedy—this, seven months after the supposed termination of the agency's assistance to him.[27]

What all these clandestine contacts add up to is the clear implication that the CIA was Howard Hunt's real principal during his time of employment at the White House. Once this is understood, the possibility suggests itself that several of Hunt's White House operations, publicly described as failures, were actually successful. The Fielding break-in is a good example: both Felipe De Diego and Dr. Fielding himself believe that the notes on Daniel Ellsberg's psyche were photographed during the burglary. If, as we may believe, the CIA was Hunt's real principal, then the disappearance of the loot—the Minox film on which the Ellsberg dossier was allegedly recorded—is hardly mysterious. It would have been given to the CIA by Hunt, and denied to the White House under the pretext that the dossier had not been found in Dr. Fielding's office.

Indeed, this is the pattern that would define virtually all of the

[26]The Gemstone charts, which will be discussed later, were diagrammatic illustrations of Gordon Liddy's intended political intelligence operations.
[27]Liddy, *Will*, p. 218. The creation of the Kennedy cartoons was a clear violation of the CIA's charter, and it is of at least passing interest that (as with so many other revelations in Liddy's book) it was never investigated.

activities that Hunt carried out on the alleged behalf of the White
House. As we will see, within a few months of being hired by the
Nixon forces, he would establish a record of near-perfect imperfec-
tion:

· the Conein interview (in which the subject sat on the tape
recorder);

· the DeMotte interview (in which the subject had nothing of
interest to say);

· the Fielding break-in (in which the object of the search was
never found).

Hunt was 0-for-3 and before the affair would be over, his streak
would run to 0-for-9—or so we are told. He would, by virtue of this
immaculate incompetence, come to be seen as a kind of clown—a
spook whose operations inevitably backfired. Thus, the press—
while condemning those who dismissed the Watergate break-in as
a mere "caper" or "third-rate burglary"—would nevertheless be
quick to pronounce the burglars "bunglers." Just as the Nixon
forces wished that we would dismiss the break-in with a laugh, so
did liberal Democrats and the press intend that we should dismiss
the burglars with a grin. This was so, in large part, because Nixon's
enemies wished to make a morality play of the affair. Necessarily,
this entailed a simple story with the President at its center. Close
scrutiny of the burglars (and of the burglaries themselves) was to be
avoided because such scrutiny raised questions about their loyalty
to President Nixon. This, in turn, obscured the issue of presidential
guilt and, in doing so, threatened Nixon's ouster. In a sense, therefore, the Democrats and the press were as much opponents of a full
investigation of the Watergate affair as was the White House itself.
Both sides had reason to fear the truth.

4.

Total Surveillance

It was in September 1971, shortly after Hunt's failure in California, that White House investigator Jack Caulfield was told to find someone suitable for handling technical security matters for the Committee to Re-elect the President (CRP). A much decorated veteran of New York City's police department, Caulfield had spent most of his career on the Big Apple's "Red Squad." New to Washington, he was at a loss as to whom he should recommend. Accordingly, he turned for advice to Alfred Wong, Secret Service chief of the technical services division in the White House.

To Wong, Caulfield passed along the criteria that he had been given: the CRP candidate should be a retired Secret Service agent, a resident of Washington and a skilled security man whose loyalty to President Nixon had been demonstrated in the past. According to Caulfield, in an interview with the author, Wong reported back to him that after "an exhaustive search" he was unable to find anyone who met those criteria. (In retrospect, this must seem odd: there are, after all, literally hundreds of former Secret Service agents living in the Washington area, some of whom would certainly have fit the bill.) In the event, Wong recommended his longtime friend, James McCord, glossing over the fact that the Rockville resident had never worked for the Secret Service. Moreover, as evidence of his friend's loyalty to President Nixon, Wong had nothing to show but that McCord was a registered Republican. Caulfield remembers his irritation at Wong's deviation from the criteria, but under pressure to hire someone he agreed to McCord. On October 1, therefore, McCord began part-time work at the Committee to Re-Elect the President.

Despite the fact that McCord was to guard the inner workings of Nixon's most strategic campaign entity, he himself was never subjected to a background investigation by any of the President's men. Had there been such an investigation, reasons to hesitate over his appointment might have surfaced. While McCord had his champions at the CIA, there were others who fretted over his eccentricities.

One of those who fretted was William McMahon, a technical security expert who had worked for McCord at the CIA and, subsequently, for the Secret Service detachment at the White House. As McMahon told me, this latter unit was effectively "infiltrated" by McCord and the CIA at the inception of Nixon's first term in office. "McCord was 'lending' CIA technicians to Wong," McMahon explained, "to handle assignments at the White House. Supposedly, Wong was understaffed, but I don't think so. I held [Wong's] job myself [at a later date], and we had all the people we needed without having to go to the agency. I don't know what they were up to, but the fact of the matter is, you had these guys from the Office of Security working in the White House under Secret Service cover."

That the CIA should have infiltrated the White House is a startling idea, but McMahon is by no means its only adherent. As H. R. Haldeman has written: "Were there CIA 'plants' in the White House? On July 10, 1975, Chairman Lucien Nedzi of the House of Representatives Intelligence Committee released an Inspector-General's Report in which the CIA admitted there was a 'practice of detailing CIA employees to the White House and various government agencies.' The IG Report revealed there were CIA agents in 'intimate components of the Office of the President.' Domestic CIA plants are bad enough, but in 'intimate components' of the Office of the President'?"[1] Haldeman then goes on to speculate about the identities of the CIA men in the White House. His main suspect is Alexander Butterfield, the former Air Force officer whose White House responsibilities included overall supervision of the presidential taping system. That system consisted of some two dozen room microphones and telephone taps that Wong's Secret Service detachment had installed in the White House and at Camp David; voice-activated by the Presidential Locator System or manually by Butterfield, the microphones and taps fed into a set of concealed Sony tape recorders.[2] Haldeman's suspicions about But-

[1]Haldeman, *Ends of Power*, pp. 109–10.
[2]Among the rooms bugged were the Oval Office, the Cabinet Room, the President's office in the Executive Office Building, the Lincoln Sitting Room and the Aspen Lodge at Camp David. The Presidential Locator System was a device by means of which the President's aides

terfield—who denies that he was a CIA asset—were shared by Rose Mary Woods, President Nixon's personal secretary. Together they criticize Butterfield for voluntarily revealing the existence of the taping system; they point with suspicion to Butterfield's early service as a military aide to GOP nemesis Joseph Califano, and make much of the fact that the circumstances of Butterfield's White House appointment are disputed.[3]

Haldeman and Woods are not alone in their suspicions of Butterfield, or in their concern over the Inspector General's report. If Bill McMahon is correct, McCord's seconding of CIA personnel in undercover assignments at the White House amounted to the calculated infiltration of a uniquely sensitive Secret Service unit: the staff responsible for maintaining and servicing the presidential taping system, and for storing its product. Moreover, unless *both* Haldeman and McMahon are mistaken—about Butterfield's secret allegiance and McCord's loan of personnel to Wong—then the CIA would seem to have had unrivaled access to the President's private conversations and thoughts. Charles Colson, among others, believes that this is precisely what occurred. "The CIA had tapes of everything relating to the White House," Colson told me. "And they destroyed them two days after [Senator Mike] Mansfield asked them to save all of their tapes."[4]

Even if we leave aside the information and suspicions of Haldeman, Woods, Colson and McMahon, it is nevertheless clear that

---

were kept informed of his whereabouts in the White House; as he moved from room to room, lights on the device, corresponding to particular rooms, would wink on and off.

[3] Haldeman, *Ends of Power*, pp. 109, 205. The disputed circumstances concerning Butterfield's appointment are these: both Butterfield and Haldeman insist that it was the other who made the first approach with respect to working at the White House. Butterfield says that Haldeman, a college chum, telephoned him to ask if he would serve as his deputy. Haldeman contradicts this, saying that his call to Butterfield was in response to a letter that Butterfield had written to him, asking for a White House appointment. Butterfield does not recall having written such a letter. A second element in the dispute is Butterfield's insistence that he had to resign from the Air Force in order to take the job at the White House. Haldeman says that this resignation, which terminated a promising military career, was entirely unnecessary. The suspicion is that the resignation was part of a protocol concerning cover arrangements between the CIA and the Air Force.

[4] The CIA denies Colson's allegation, insisting that it was never in possession of such tapes. And, in fact, Colson is incorrect when he claims that Senator Mansfield ordered the agency to preserve "all" of its tapes: Mansfield's order referred only to materials that were relevant to Watergate. (The CIA's reaction to Mansfield's order is discussed in more detail in later chapters.) Whatever the truth may be, Colson's allegations against the CIA were sincerely made. So convinced was he that the agency had the "White House tapes" in its possession that he plotted with a private detective, Gordon Novel, to erase them before they could be made public. An impossible scheme, it entailed the use of a "de-Gaussing gun" deployed across the Potomac.

the White House was the focal point of an extraordinary degree of clandestine surveillance during the Nixon years. In May 1969, for example, Henry Kissinger initiated an extensive wiretapping program, serviced by the FBI under the oversight of Kissinger's deputy, Alexander Haig, against prominent journalists, members of the National Security Council (NSC), and the Pentagon. In all, seventeen taps, augmented by at least four cases of physical surveillance, were carried out during the next twenty-two months. The program was finally terminated at the insistence of FBI Director J. Edgar Hoover. The last of the taps was ordered removed in February 1971, coincidentally the same month that the presidential taping system became operational in the White House.[5]

To the Kissinger taps, the President's tapes and Howard Hunt's Pony Express service to the doctors at Langley should be added still other intrusions upon the secrecy of the administration. Besides the "dead key" mechanisms in common use at the CIA, White House and NSC, there are persistent rumors that President Nixon was bugged (without his consent).[6] David Young is alleged, on good authority, to have told his Watergate attorney, Anthony Lapham, that the Plumbers had bugged the President. Asked about this, Lapham said that while he would not deny the report, neither would he confirm it. "I just can't talk about it at all," he said.[7]

Young's rumored admission is hardly unique, however. Veteran journalist Tad Szulc has described how a painter with the General Services Administration (GSA) placed an eavesdropping device in the Oval Office. The device, he said, was a miniature laser about the size of a thumbnail and paper-thin. The painter, a Hungarian refugee who owed his presence in the United States to the CIA, and who himself was a sometime CIA helpmate, allegedly painted the device on the wall in the course of an otherwise routine re-

[5]With respect to the Kissinger taps, see Tad Szulc, *The Illusion of Peace: A Diplomatic History of the Nixon Years* (New York: Viking Press, 1978), pp. 181ff.; Roger Morris, *Haig: The General's Progress* (New York: Playboy Press, 1982), pp. 153–67; and Hersh, *Price of Power*, pp. 83–97, 193–94, and 318–26.
[6]Dead keys permit one to monitor and record telephone calls and conferences without the awareness of the participants.
[7]After representing Young, Lapham was appointed general counsel to the CIA. He has since returned to private practice. My attempts to contact Young for comment on the bugging allegation were unsuccessful.

modeling. The bug, according to Szulc, was discovered by the Secret Service, several months after it had been emplaced, and removed.[8]

Szulc's article was published to little effect. The nature of the eavesdropping device raised technical questions about its operation: how, for example, could a laser device work beneath a coat of paint and in an office whose windows consist of bulletproof plastic lamination that is several inches thick? The painter denied the story, the Secret Service refused to comment upon it, and the CIA said nothing. A respected reporter, Szulc stuck by his story when questioned by the Senate Intelligence Committee. But he would not reveal his source, and so the matter ended.

One might be inclined to dismiss such reports with a shrug because, after all, they cannot be confirmed. But the leitmotif of bugging is so prevalent in the Watergate affair that it would be naïve to reject such reports out of hand. Indeed, as Nixon's memoirs make clear, he himself suspected that he was the victim of electronic eavesdropping. Kissinger, too, fretted about ensuring the secrecy of White House communications. In fact, the President's National Security Adviser was so concerned about the privacy of his communications, and the leaks bursting around him, that he rejected the usual communications channels available to his office. Rather than relying upon White House, State Department or CIA channels, Kissinger approached Admiral Thomas Moorer, then Chief of Naval Operations, and requested a medium that neither the CIA nor any other intelligence service could penetrate. Moorer accommodated the request by giving Kissinger access to the supersensitive SR-1 channel used by the Navy's top-secret spy unit, Task Force 157.[9]

Created by Moorer in 1965–66, TF-157 was at first staffed by only a few agents. Before long, however, it had grown to more than a hundred full-time operatives and support personnel worldwide. While its operations remain classified, it is clear that its principal target was the Soviet Navy. It monitored nuclear weapons shipments aboard Soviet vessels passing through nautical "choke points" such as the Strait of Magellan; eavesdropped on Soviet communications at sea; recruited agents with access to Soviet-bloc port facilities;

[8]Tad Szulc, "The Spy Among Us," *Penthouse*, July 1975, p. 44.
[9]Bob Woodward, "Pentagon to Abolish Secret Spy Unit," *Washington Post*, May 18, 1977.

acquired new Soviet weaponry and defense systems for analysis and evaluation; and, generally, gathered intelligence in the ports and souks of countries as far apart as Argentina and Pakistan.[10] All of these operations were conducted with great secrecy, of course, with TF-157 agents assigned to a network of commercial covers, many of which had been established for the Navy by a corrupt former CIA agent named Edwin P. Wilson.[11]

A veteran of the CIA's Office of Security, Wilson is said to have been tasked by the agency with the responsibility of making secret reports on the activities and assets of TF-157.[12] While we do not know the details of those reports, it would be surprising, given the CIA's interest in Henry Kissinger, if Wilson was not specifically directed to obtain information concerning the SR-1 channel. And, in fact, according to a former senior analyst at the agency, the CIA mounted an aggressive operation to identify and crack a communications channel that can only have been SR-1 while using the pretext (among its own agents and analysts) that the sought-after channel was a new and uniquely sophisticated vehicle for *Soviet* naval communications. That this search was ultimately successful was suggested, the analyst said, by the formation of a special analysis group to study communications transcripts that were alleged to have been obtained from Soviet sources in Eastern Europe but, as it happened, were far more concerned with Kissinger and the White House than with the Soviet Union.

The atmosphere of the Nixon administration has been described by many (including Nixon himself) as "paranoid." That it was so was due to many things, not least of which was the sense of siege at the White House—a perception nurtured by seemingly constant antiwar riots, mass demonstrations and the revolutionary rhetoric of the young. But the administration's paranoia had other causes as well. Not only was the intelligence community a house divided, and hence a wellspring of mutual suspicions, but even within the individual agencies sides had been taken and the loyalty of patriots

[10]*Raymond Acosta, et al.* v. *Office of Personnel Management*, no. DC08318010060, United States of America Before the Merit Systems Protection Board; Joe Trento, "FBI Probing Ex-Spy's Role in Task Force," *Sunday News Journal* (Wilmington, Del.), October 5, 1980, p. 1; and Bob Woodward, "Pentagon to Abolish Secret Spy Unit." Further information concerning TF-157's activities was obtained by the author in interviews with former task force operatives.
[11]Wilson has become notorious in the aftermath of his conviction on charges that included gunrunning and attempted murder.
[12]Trento, "FBI Probing Ex-Spy's Role in Task Force."

questioned. Indeed, James Jesus Angleton, founder and longtime chief of the CIA's counterintelligence staff, was himself the target of a lengthy, top-secret report—compiled by one of his subordinates —suggesting that Angleton was a Soviet penetration agent, or "mole."[13] If that prospect was a daunting one for the United States, so also was the suspicion directed against Henry Kissinger. Allegations against Kissinger's loyalty had festered in the CIA's files for more than a decade prior to his appointment as the President's National Security Adviser. At least one Soviet-bloc defector, Michael Goleniewski, insisted that Kissinger had been recruited by the Soviets in the aftermath of World War II, when he had served with the Army counterintelligence corps in occupied Germany.[14] According to Goleniewski, Kissinger was given the code name Colonel Boar. A peculiar story, it took an even stranger twist in 1964, when the People's Republic of China went out of its way in an effort to discredit the allegation—which, perhaps predictably, had the opposite effect in some precincts of the U.S. intelligence community. Eventually, no less a figure than Angleton himself would pronounce Kissinger "objectively, a Soviet agent," while others would question not merely the wisdom of Kissinger's decisions but the motives that lay behind them.[15] They would whisper, half-jokingly, about "Colonel Boar," while pointing to Kissinger's diminution of the CIA's influence on the National Security Council, and his embarrassing disregard for the agency's raison d'être: the NIEs, or National Intelligence Estimates, whose importance Kissinger had drastically reduced. They would question the search for what Kissinger called "détente," its "linkage" to the SALT talks, and his role in each. They would condemn Kissinger for negotiating a rapprochement with the People's Republic of China at the expense of the Taiwanese government. America's ignominious reverses in Vietnam would be blamed in part on Kissinger's perplexing refusal to inform the American military, in a timely way, of the cease-fire date agreed upon with the North Vietnamese. They would worry,

[13]The report was prepared by Clare Petty, who resigned from the CIA upon presenting it in late 1974 to the then CIA director, William Colby.

[14]Goleniewski's own bona fides may be questioned. While he has been described in the *New York Times* as "the most productive agent in the history of the C.I.A.," he himself claims to be the heir to Czar Nicholas of Russia. (See Edward Jay Epstein, "The Spy War," *New York Times Magazine*, September 28, 1980.)

[15]Daniel Schorr, "The Conspiracy to Create Traitors," *Washington Post*, October 12, 1980.

also, over Kissinger's modus operandi, his overweening secrecy and occasional deception of his own allies.

Kissinger was not, of course, the only Cabinet member whose integrity or loyalty came under assault. Nor, indeed, were the suspicions and name-calling a one-way street. On the contrary, Kissinger and members of his staff freely slandered those with whom they disagreed. Thus Kissinger described Nixon as "a madman" and a secret "drunk," Secretary of State William Rogers as "a fag," Secretary of Defense Melvin Laird as a "crook" and "a traitor," and CBS News reporter Marvin Kalb as "an agent of the Romanian government."[16]

What is relevant here is not the validity or invalidity of these judgments but the fact that these and similar smears were broadcast and that a certain atmosphere resulted—one of mutual suspicion and clandestine concern. Admiral Elmo Zumwalt, formerly chief of naval operations, describes the atmosphere well as he explains his reasons for resigning office:

> I refused [to remain in the Nixon Administration] because by then I had become so sure that certain continuing national policies and procedures were *inimical to the security of the United States* that I no longer wanted to be associated in any capacity with an Administration responsible for them. . . . [Emphasis added.]
> . . . I refer to the deliberate, systematic and, unfortunately, extremely successful efforts of the President, Henry Kissinger, and a few subordinate members of their inner circle to conceal, sometimes by simple silence, more often by articulate deceit, their real policies about the most critical matters of national security: the strategic arms limitation talks (SALT) and various other of the aspects of "detente," the relations between the United States and its allies in Europe, the resolution of the war in southeast Asia, the facts about America's military strength and readiness. Their concealment and deceit was practiced against the public, the press, the Congress, the allies, and even most of the officials within the executive branch who had a statutory responsibility to provide advice about matters of national security.
> What is important to record is the inextricable relationship the Nixon Administration's perversion of the policy-making process bore to its ignoble outlook. Its contempt for the patriotism and intelligence of the American people, for the Constitutional authority of the Congress, and for the judgement of its own officials and experts *reflected Henry Kiss-*

[16]Hersh, *Price of Power*, pp. 90, 93, 109.

inger's world view: that the dynamics of history are on the side of the Soviet Union; that before long the USSR will be the only superpower on earth and the United States will be an also-ran; that a principal reason this will happen is that Americans have neither the stamina nor the will to do the hard things they would have to do to prevent it from happening; *that the duty of policy-makers, therefore, is at all costs to conceal from the people their probable fate and proceed as cleverly and rapidly as may be to make the best possible deal with the Soviet Union while there is still time to make any deal.* [17] [Emphasis added.]

This, then, was the atmosphere of paranoia that pervaded the White House when Howard Hunt joined the Plumbers and, three months later, James McCord signed on as security director for the Committee to Re-elect the President (CRP). Beset by leaks as massive as the Pentagon Papers, and besieged by critics on both the Right and the Left, the Nixon administration conducted its affairs amid the suspicions of a feuding intelligence community, at least part of which was convinced that the administration's chief foreign-policy-maker, Henry Kissinger, was "objectively" (and perhaps "subjectively") a Soviet agent. It was in this context that Kissinger became the focal point of a bizarre espionage operation, whose discovery, six months before the Watergate arrests, crystallized the administration's fears.[18]

This was the Moorer-Radford affair, and while it remains a conundrum more than a decade after it was officially put to rest, it is important to discuss it for two reasons: first, it constitutes the military counterpart to Howard Hunt's spying on the White House. And secondly, when the time comes at the end of this book to examine the question of Deep Throat's identity, the Moorer-Radford affair will add special resonance to our deliberations.

In essence, the affair concerned leaks to newspaper columnist Jack Anderson and the attendant discovery that "a military spy ring" was operating inside the White House and the NSC. The seriousness with which the affair was taken is suggested by the metaphor that was most often applied to it: *Seven Days in May.* Because the affair concerned military spying upon the civilian command structure, it was perhaps predictable that the press would

[17]Elmo R. Zumwalt, Jr., *On Watch* (New York: Quadrangle Books, 1976), p. xiv.
[18]While the operation was first investigated in December 1971, it was not revealed to the public until nearly two years had passed.

compare it to the popular novel by Fletcher Knebel and Charles W. Bailey II about a military takeover of the U.S. government. Newspapers throughout the country referred to it in that way, as did *Time* magazine.[19] Senator Harold Hughes, in urging a congressional investigation of the matter, used the same metaphor in the *Congressional Record*.[20] W. Donald Stewart of the Defense Investigative Service concurred, and made it clear that he did not think the metaphor a hyperbole. Stewart, who was the Pentagon's chief investigator of the affair, asked this writer: "Did you see that film *Seven Days in May?* That's what we were dealing with, and the Senate whitewashed it. [Admiral Thomas] Moorer [chairman of the Joint Chiefs of Staff] should have been court-martialed."

Admiral Robert O. Welander, a key figure in the scandal, bridled at such comparisons: "I have been characterized in the media as a 'military spy,' " Welander complained, "and accused of all manner of illicit and nefarious activities with insinuations that could not be more repugnant to me as a professional military officer. Such reckless allegations regarding me as an individual are one thing . . . , but to see my work on the National Security Council staff cast in the light of an organized plot by the military of this country against its foreign policy and national security interests—some type of military takeover—or some sinister effort to subvert civilian control is the grossest and most irresponsible distortion of fact."[21]

That hearings into the Moorer-Radford affair were held in early 1974 was something of an accident. While interviewing witnesses in connection with its investigation of the Watergate affair, the Senate learned that in late 1971 David Young and the Plumbers had investigated a "military spy ring" within the National Security Council (NSC). Shocked by this news, which carried with it the implication that the Plumbers had indeed been concerned with matters of legitimate national security interest, the Senate convened hearings under the auspices of the Committee on Armed Services.

In all, five witnesses were called. Henry Kissinger testified first. Next came Admiral Thomas Moorer, then chairman of the Joint Chiefs of Staff (JCS). Moorer was succeeded by Yeoman Charles

[19]"An Excessive Need to Know," *Time,* January 28, 1974.
[20]*Congressional Record,* February 5, 1974, p. 2113.
[21]Moorer-Radford *Hearings (Transmittal of Documents from the National Security Council to the Chairman of the Joint Chiefs of Staff, Hearings before the Senate Committee on Armed Services,* 93d Cong., 2d sess.), February–March, 1974, Part II, p. 117.

Radford, an aide to Admiral Welander. Welander testified next; during the period in question, May–December 1971, he had been assistant for national security affairs to JCS Chairman Moorer while serving also as liaison officer to the NSC.[22] The last witness was Fred Buzhardt, then general counsel to the Department of Defense.

The story that emerged may be summarized in the following way. In December 1971 Jack Anderson wrote a series of newspaper columns concerning the deployment of American warships in the Indian Ocean. Appearing in the midst of the India-Pakistan war, the columns raised the specter of American military involvement on a second Asian front. And because Anderson chose to quote verbatim and at length from top-secret memoranda intended for Henry Kissinger, it was apparent that there had been a breach in national security.

Within twenty-four hours of the second such column's appearance, Yeoman Radford was arrested on information provided to the Pentagon by Admiral Welander, Radford's own commanding officer and immediate supervisor.[23] According to Welander, Anderson had obviously had access to three secret memoranda. The first two of these memoranda, written for the record, concerned meetings of the Washington Special Action Group (WSAG, a crisis-management unit created by Nixon). The third memo had been written by Welander himself, and its distribution had been extremely limited: only he, Radford, Kissinger, and Alexander Haig were supposed to have seen it. Contemplating the three memos together, Welander estimated that "maybe 50 [people] would have access to one document, maybe 50 to the other, but I would bet not more than 10 would have access to both. But of those 10, who would have had access to my memorandum, which was rather unique? . . . [T]he only person who could have had all three was either me or Radford," Welander testified.[24]

Because Welander himself had not leaked the information to Anderson, or so he claimed, the admiral concluded that Radford must have done so—and the yeoman was turned in.

The matter might have ended there, with Radford taking the blame for the leak, had not the yeoman, while denying responsibility for the Anderson columns, confessed to even more shocking activi-

[22]Ibid., pp. 114–19.
[23]Jack Anderson, "U.S., Soviet Vessels in Bay of Bengal," *Washington Post*, December 14, 1971.
[24]Moorer-Radford *Hearings*, Part II, p. 148.

ties than those of which he stood accused. In the course of a hostile interrogation by the Pentagon's Donald Stewart, Radford "broke down," saying that he had routinely stolen top-secret documents from the attaché cases and burn bags of Henry Kissinger and Alexander Haig.[25] He had accomplished this, he said, in the course of his ordinary duties and while accompanying Kissinger and Haig on missions abroad. The stolen information, he testified, was given by him to Admiral Welander, who, in turn, transmitted it directly or through middlemen to Admiral Moorer; perhaps a thousand documents were involved.[26] Having admitted to this, Radford insisted that he had never leaked information of any kind to Jack Anderson or to any other reporter. Nevertheless, the yeoman acknowledged that he was in fact "casually" acquainted with Anderson.[27]

Such were the rough outlines of the story when it finally came to the public's attention in 1974. No one was prosecuted in the case (much to the outrage of Donald Stewart and others). Radford was quietly transferred to a reserve naval recruiting station in Salem, Oregon, wiretapped by the FBI and told to hold his peace.[28] Welander was given a seagoing command, and Moorer seems not to have been affected.

As for the Senate hearings, critical witnesses, such as Donald Stewart, David Young, Alexander Haig, and a clutch of NSC and Pentagon staffers, were never called to testify—this, to the articulated irritation of senators such as Harold Hughes (Dem.–Iowa) and, in Stewart's case, to the annoyance of the would-be witness himself. The reports of Young and Stewart were unavailable. Records of interrogations were "lost." And while the results of poly-

---

[25] The "hostility" of the interrogation is made clear by the following testimony:
SENATOR HUGHES: Did they use the rubber hose on you?
YEOMAN RADFORD: No, but I would not have been surprised. He [Donald Stewart] was almost hysterical. . . . His eyes were bloodshot and he looked like he was mad.
SENATOR HUGHES: Were you physically threatened in any way?
YEOMAN RADFORD: No, he did not lay his hands on me in any way. He pounded the desk. He made motions like I supposed he would leap across the desk at me at any moment. . . .
SENATOR HUGHES: You broke down and cried?
YEOMAN RADFORD: Yes, sir.
From the Moorer-Radford *Hearings*, Part II, p. 104. Radford's theft of documents from Kissinger and Haig are discussed throughout the *Hearings*, but see pages 100–1 and 104–5.
[26] Ibid., pp. 58–59.
[27] Ibid., pp. 70–71.
[28] With respect to Radford's transfer and wiretapping, see FBI Memorandum from T. J. Smith to E. S. Miller, June 14, 1973, "Subject: Charles Edward Radford II, Sensitive Coverage for the White House, COVE-ESPIONAGE."

graph tests given to Radford, Welander and others were provided to the Committee on Armed Services, they were useless: no records had been kept of the questions, so the answers were meaningless.

In the end, the senators threw up their hands, asserting that perjury had certainly been committed by at least one of their five witnesses, but they could not tell by whom. There was much more to the affair, the Senate agreed, but the Senate could not get to the bottom of it—not, at least, so long as the powerful Senator John Stennis chaired the Committee on Armed Services.

Reading the transcript of the hearings places a strain on one's credulity, so many are the contradictions, omissions and anomalies. It is odd, for instance, that Radford should have accompanied Haig to Southeast Asia in 1971, and odder still that the yeoman should have traveled with Kissinger on the first and last legs of his secret trip to China, because, after all, Yeoman Radford was assigned to a Pentagon office under Admiral Welander, and not to Kissinger's NSC staff.[29] Questioned about this in 1974, Welander agreed that Radford's special assignment came at Haig's specific request. But the reasons for that request seem spurious. According to Welander, Radford was asked to accompany Kissinger to the negotiations in Paris because, it was felt, a male stenographer could also "run errands" and handle baggage—which a female stenographer could not do.[30] In any event, the entourages were said to be "all-male."

The implausibility of these explanations is attested to by the skepticism with which they were greeted by Pentagon investigators. According to a senior Senate staffer who was privy to the details of Radford's interrogation, "There was an obsessive line of questioning that had to do with homosexuality. I got the impression that, well, maybe they felt this would explain the kid's assignment to the NSC traveling staff."[31]

Nor was this the only peculiarity of the affair. For example, Admiral Moorer was supposedly the ultimate consumer of Radford's "collection efforts." What was odd about this was that Admiral Moorer later insisted that he had access to the same material through conventional channels.[32] Kissinger trusted him. Moorer

[29]Moorer-Radford *Hearings*, Part I, pp. 50, 54, and Part II, p. 159.
[30]Ibid., Part II, pp. 159–160.
[31]No evidence was found to suggest that any of those involved in the Moorer-Radford affair were anything other than heterosexual.
[32]Moorer-Radford *Hearings*, pp. 5, 149.

knew of Kissinger's China trip when even the CIA did not, and as we have seen, it was Moorer who provided Kissinger with the secret communications channel, SR-1, on which Kissinger came to rely. Why, then, would Moorer have had Radford steal information that Moorer was already receiving on a routine, legitimate basis? To make certain that Kissinger was not holding out on him? Perhaps, but the risk would seem to have outweighed the gains.

There are other problems with the Senate's study of the affair. If we are to accept the prevailing wisdom, itself but a guess in the dark, we must believe that Radford provided Anderson with a copy of the Welander memorandum, knowing that only two copies existed, and that therefore he would necessarily be a suspect in any leak investigation that might result. We must also believe that Radford and Anderson were then so bold as to dine in public with each other at the Empress, a Chinese restaurant of which Anderson was a part owner, and did so, moreover, on the very eve of the incriminating column's publication.

To believe all that, however, is to underestimate the intelligence of both the columnist *and* the yeoman. Which is what the Senate and the Pentagon appear to have done. The press was told, incorrectly, that Anderson and Radford were family friends of long standing, and that they and their families attended "the Mormon church" together.[33] The dinner at the Empress and a subsequent meeting that followed on the heels of Radford's arrest were considered strong evidence of the men's collusion. Finally, it was pointed out, no further leaks occurred in the wake of Radford's interrogation, which suggested to some that Radford must have been Anderson's source.

But that reasoning is fallacious. The administration's investigation was intense and, in the end, came to include conspicuous CIA surveillance of the columnist. Under those circumstances only the most careless leaker—whether Radford or someone else—would have continued to supply Anderson with information. Moreover, it is simply untrue to assert that Radford was a long-standing friend of Jack Anderson's. He had once met Anderson's elderly parents while stationed in India. With respect to the columnist himself, Radford had shaken his hand on only one occasion prior to Decem-

[33]"An Excessive Need to Know," *Time*, January 28, 1974.

ber 1971. This was at an Anderson family reunion in late 1970, to which Radford had been invited by the columnist's parents. As for the ill-timed dinner at the Empress, Radford told me, "Jack just called up, and asked if I'd have dinner with him. As far as I'm concerned, it was purely social. There wasn't any particular reason for it." Why, then, did Radford bother to go? "Because he was Jack Anderson. He was famous. Why shouldn't I go? Who wouldn't have?"

So, too, while Anderson and Radford were both members of the Mormon Church, this is no more relevant than if they had been Catholics. They belonged to different wards (the Mormon equivalent of parishes), and had never knowingly attended worship together.[34] As for the meeting between the columnist and the yeoman following the fateful column's publication, it was so improbable that the Senate had no idea what to make of it, and chose not to dwell upon it. According to Radford, this meeting was also at Anderson's initiative, and it came as a surprise. Radford was asleep in bed when late at night the celebrated columnist appeared, very much unexpectedly, in Radford's bedroom.[35] There the nonplussed naval stenographer and the syndicated reporter chatted briefly, with Anderson commiserating over Radford's having been wrongly identified as his source. Anderson then departed the house, leaving the yeoman perplexed between the sheets.

What was Anderson doing? While protesting, on the one hand, that Radford was not his source, he seems to have done everything possible to make it appear as if Radford had been leaking to him. Why did Anderson, knowing full well that the morning paper would contain WSAG and NSC secrets to which Radford was one of the few men who had been privy, ask Radford to dine with him in public? Why, when Radford was the prime suspect in the leak investigation that followed, did Anderson go late at night to Radford's house, knowing that the yeoman must be under surveillance, and that, in any case, he would be questioned on a polygraph about any and all meetings he had ever had with Anderson? To this writer, at least, it seems apparent that Anderson, an acknowledged master at protecting the identities of his sources, was setting up Radford as a fall guy—almost certainly in an effort to protect his real source.

[34]Moorer-Radford *Hearings*, Part III, p. 24.
[35]Ibid., Part III, pp. 36–37.

According to Radford, the spying on the NSC began under Admiral Welander's late predecessor, Admiral Rembrandt Robinson.[36] When Welander took over the liaison office between the NSC and the Joint Chiefs of Staff, Radford recalled, "[H]e indicated to me that he knew what I had done for Admiral Robinson. . . . He indicated he wanted me to do the same type of thing [for him]. . . . He said, I understand that you have gone on these trips and brought back information of interest, and he asked me if I would do the same thing for him."

> SENATOR HUGHES: Did you bring back additional information and turn it over to [Admiral Welander]?
> RADFORD: Yes.
> SENATOR HUGHES: He knew it was material you had gathered clandestinely?
> RADFORD: Yes, sir.
> SENATOR HUGHES: He made no—he did not reprimand you for that at all?
> RADFORD: No, sir. He was rather pleased.[37]

The information that Radford acquired on behalf of Admiral Welander included Eyes Only messages addressed to President Nixon, Dr. Kissinger and General Haig.[38] As Radford testified, these messages were sometimes filched and copied from the senders' briefcases or were rescued from various burn bags. To indicate their extreme sensitivity, Radford testified that the documents included "the transcription of a conversation I saw, between Dr. Kissinger and [Chinese Premier] Chou En Lai"—easily one of the most sensitive documents generated during the Nixon administration.[39] That Welander knew the documents were taken by "irregular" means was clear to Radford. The yeoman did not "sanitize" any of the materials he had obtained. "It was delivered in pure form," he told the Senate. Moreover, "[O]n a number of occasions, [Admiral Welander] asked me how I got it, or where I got it . . . and I told him."[40] For his part, Welander admitted that he passed along Radford's intelligence to JCS Chairman Moorer. This, he said, included "a

---

[36]Admiral Robinson was killed in a May 1972 helicopter crash in Tonkin Bay.
[37]Moorer-Radford *Hearings,* Part II, pp. 60–61.
[38]Ibid., Part II, p. 74.
[39]Ibid., p. 69.
[40]Ibid., p. 65.

collection of tissue copies and rough drafts of staff reports, memoranda of conversations, and outgoing cables." Questioned about this, Welander admitted, "I did think it odd that [Radford] would mail some of it back from New Delhi, and that so much of it was crumpled discards and partial drafts."[41] Despite this, Welander said, it did not occur to him that these documents had been "pilfered," or he'd have put a stop to it.

Radford denies that. As the yeoman told the Senate, "I was approached about going on a trip with Dr. Henry Kissinger in July, 1971, and . . . Admiral Welander told me that he would be interested in anything that 'I could get my hands on.' I remember something specifically, something about diplomatic dealings with China, and that anything I could gather in this area would be of particular interest to him. He cautioned me to be careful and don't get caught. He said, 'Don't take any chances.' I brought back copies of everything that I could. Upon giving the information to Admiral Welander . . . , he said that I did a great piece of work, and that I should never tell anybody what I had done. This is the first time that I ever saw him seem worried. I remember this clearly because of his manifest concern."[42]

But if, as Radford insists, Welander had guilty knowledge of Radford's activities, why did the admiral expose the yeoman? Subjecting Radford to the scrutiny of the Pentagon and the Plumbers risked revealing Radford's clandestine activities on Welander's own behalf—which, indeed, is exactly what happened. The affair, then, seems to make little sense. On the one hand, we have a newspaper columnist who goes out of his way to suggest that Radford is his source, even as he goes through the motions of denying precisely that. On the other hand, we have an admiral who exposes his own spy within the NSC, with the predictable result that the admiral, too, is embarrassed. Radford, then, may be excused for answering affirmatively when Senator Stuart Symington asked, "Have you ever felt you were being singled out as the fall guy in this situation?"[43]

The identity of Anderson's source is not an issue that is ever likely to be resolved. The process of elimination used by Admiral Welander to identify Yeoman Radford is by no means a conclusive one.

[41]Ibid., p. 129.
[42]Ibid., p. 16.
[43]Ibid., p. 35.

The Pentagon memoranda concerning the WSAG meetings may have had limited distribution, but they were hardly unique; there were other memos written by other people about those same meetings, and it may have been these that Anderson acquired. And while Welander's own memorandum had even narrower limits of distribution, that proves little: Xerox machines are to Washington as barnacles are to a wooden hull, and anyone on the staffs of the designated recipients might have copied Welander's memorandum. So much, at least, we must assume in the absence of any public questioning of Haig or his staff.

But there are other issues in the affair that are at least as important as the identity of Anderson's source. In the hearings, for example, a frustrated Senator Harold Hughes suggested that since Admiral Moorer had no need of Radford's purloined secrets, those secrets may perhaps have been routed to Moorer as an operational precaution—that is, Hughes suggested, perhaps the secrets were stolen on behalf of some as yet unidentified party, with the originals being sent to Moorer as a precaution in the event that the operation should one day be exposed. "I am . . . try[ing] to determine," Hughes said, "whether or not [Radford] might have been pilfering information and as a cover, giving it to the Pentagon while he was really giving copies to someone else."[44] As to who this unidentified party might have been, one cannot say. But certainly, in view of the CIA's concern about Kissinger, the agency's seeming curiosity about the SR-1 communications channel, and Hunt's secret reports from the White House to Langley headquarters, the agency must be regarded as a likely suspect. It was spying upon the White House and so, according to Radford, was he.

When I interviewed Radford years after these events had been, if not laid to rest, at least anesthetized by the passage of time, the onetime naval spook confessed to me that his spying activities were even more complex than has yet been told. Besides the raids on the attaché cases of Kissinger and Haig, and the retrieval of crumpled carbon copies from the NSC's burn bags, the yeoman had a source of his own within the Office of the President; and this source, according to Radford, provided him with gossip and classified data about the White House. The Pentagon's Donald Stewart confirms this, saying that this information was elicited from Radford during

[44]Ibid., Part I, p. 62.

interrogation. Like Radford, however, Stewart refuses to identify the White House source, confirming only that he continued to serve at the highest echelons of government as late as 1981. Asked jokingly if Radford's source might have been "Deep Throat," Stewart didn't bat an eye; "He could have been," the investigator said. And Radford agrees: "I never thought of it," he told me, "but . . . possibly." In Stewart's opinion, Radford should have been court-martialed (along with Moorer and Welander) and his source prosecuted under the espionage laws. To Stewart, the affair was a conspiracy from conception to cover-up.

Radford, too, hints at some terrible conspiracy, asserting that Kissinger's foreign policy was "catastrophic" by design. According to the yeoman, his spying activities were part of an effort to combat a conspiracy that was supposedly conceived by "the Rockefeller family," perfected by the Council on Foreign Relations (CFR), and implemented by Henry Kissinger.[45] The purpose of this alleged conspiracy, according to Radford, was to win the Soviets' cooperation in guaranteeing the Rockefellers' "continued domination" over the world's currencies—in exchange for which, Radford insists, Kissinger was to construct a foreign policy that would ensure eventual Soviet hegemony and a one-world government. This, at least, is what Radford claims he was told by those who commanded him to spy on the President's national security adviser.

While the validity of Radford's conspiracy theory is not worth commenting upon, it is useful to know where the idea originated. In essence, it is a construct of America's extreme right wing, reminiscent of nothing so much as the beliefs of John Birch Society founder Robert Welch. In 1966 Welch published an article in *American Opinion* that, according to George X. Johnson, a critic of such theories, told how "the Insiders had established the Federal Reserve System, plotted World Wars I and II, and invented the graduated income tax to rob the middle class. Meanwhile the Insiders sheltered their own wealth with tax-exempt organizations such as the Ford and Rockefeller foundations, which were also used to fund social programs to mollify the masses. Welch told how the Insiders started the United Nations as a forerunner to one-world government. . . . Members of the social, educational, economic, and political elite

[45]It is at least ironic, in view of Radford's allegations, that his commanding officer, Admiral Welander, had been attached to the CFR for a year prior to taking command of the Pentagon-NSC liaison office. (See Moorer-Radford *Hearings*, Part II, p. 114.)

were using communism 'to impose their rule ever more rigidly and tyrannically, *from the top down.* . . .' "[46] Unless Radford was recruited under a false flag, therefore, it seems that his actions were motivated by an extreme-right-wing analysis that saw Henry Kissinger's foreign policy as the cutting edge of a supposed Communist conspiracy.

According to Radford, this analysis, or conspiracy theory, was confided to him by Admiral Welander, who attributed it to Admiral Moorer. In my interview with Moorer, the former chairman of the Joint Chiefs of Staff made it clear that what with the war in Vietnam and the antiwar protesters at home, the times had been perilous indeed. "The country was in a state of total chaos—anarchy," he said. "No one could be trusted. Anything might have happened." But Moorer said he did not share the right wing's antipathy toward Kissinger, whatever Radford may have been told. "The dislike of Kissinger came down to one word: détente—détente with the Soviet Union. I saw Henry three or four times a week. [Zumwalt and others] saw him much less often. So we looked at things a little differently."

In the end, despite its having been Moorer's "watch" and despite his having received "the take," one tends to believe him because, when all is said and done, he did not have a motive for spying on Kissinger. For this reason, then, Moorer would seem to have been as much a victim in the affair as Kissinger himself, as much a fall guy as Radford.

[46]George Johnson, *Architects of Fear* (Los Angeles: J. P. Tarcher, 1983), pp. 133–34.

5.
The Prescient
Investigator

Even while the Pentagon and the Plumbers were secretly investigating the Moorer-Radford affair, FBI Director J. Edgar Hoover made a peculiar remark to newspaper columnist Andrew Tully. "By God," Hoover said, "he's [Nixon's] got some former CIA men working for him that I'd kick out of my office. Someday, that bunch will serve him up a fine mess."[1]

When finally reported, more than a year later, the remark caused many to nod with the satisfaction that one feels at the fulfillment of a prophecy. Published when the Senate Watergate hearings were at a rolling boil, Hoover's comment seemed self-explanatory. No one seems to have asked the obvious: To whom was Hoover referring? Possibly to White House consultant E. Howard Hunt, but beyond Hunt, the trail ends. McCord had started work as a full-time employee of the Committee to Re-elect the President (CRP) on January 1, 1972, and it is unlikely that he would have come to Hoover's attention so soon—especially in his capacity as security director for the then quiescent CRP. Nor could Hoover have meant the Cubans. They were not all "former CIA men," and they did not work for the President.[2] What is more, they had handled only one assignment for Hunt (the Fielding break-in), and there is no reason to suppose that Hoover was ever privy to that operation. The matter, then, remains a mystery, inviting speculation that Nixon may have had other former CIA men working for him who have yet to be identified. About all

[1]Tully's interview with Hoover was not published until July 19, 1973.
[2]As we have seen, only Martinez and Barker had a prior relationship to the CIA, the former as a contract agent and the latter as an informant.

that one can positively say on the subject is that Hoover somehow anticipated the scandal that was to follow upon his death.

But Hoover was not the only seer in the Watergate affair. On the contrary, the prescience of one A. J. Woolston-Smith went far beyond the FBI director's prediction of "a fine mess."

Woolston-Smith, known to his friends as Wooly, is an expatriate New Zealander. Suave, cynical and gently sardonic, he is a spook from the old school with a preference for pipes, three-piece suits and unblended Scotch whisky. For more than thirty years prior to Watergate, he lived and worked in New York City, retaining both his New Zealand passport and connections to the British intelligence services. Like others who came to play peculiar roles in the Watergate affair, he had worked with Robert A. Maheu Associates (RAMA) during the 1960s. Forming his own research and investigative agencies, Science Security Associates and the Confidential Investigations Bureau, Woolston-Smith traveled worldwide on behalf of clients whose problems ranged from marital infidelity to multinational pharmaceutical conspiracies involving electronic eavesdropping and industrial espionage. At the same time, Woolston-Smith provided occasional assistance to what he calls the Cigar Institute of America.[3] His New York offices, for example, were used as "a clearinghouse" in the previously mentioned resettlement operation involving Cuban veterans of the Bay of Pigs.[4] Aside from his work for the CIA, Woolston-Smith labored also for a handful of law firms, principally that of Dickstein, Shapiro & Galligan (later Colson & Shapiro). It was on the recommendation of this firm that "Wooly" came to perform occasional services for William Haddad, a quite prominent Democrat who, in his capacity as publisher of the now defunct *Manhattan Tribune*, fancied himself a muckraker.

In December 1971 Woolston-Smith told Haddad that the GOP's New York–based November Group was up to no good. Actually, the November Group was a collection of (mostly) advertising executives who supported President Nixon's reelection and who had banded together to plan a media strategy for the coming campaign.

[3]Woolston-Smith's reference to the CIA as the Cigar Institute of America is a historical allusion to the fact that British intelligence operations in Burma were formerly conducted under cover of the Imperial Tobacco Company.
[4]With reference to the resettlement program, it is of interest that the operation involved the creation of Radio Free Cuba and the Cuban Freedom Committee, each of which was launched under the covert auspices of the Robert R. Mullen Company.

G. Gordon Liddy was the Group's incorporator, its secretary and one of its three directors. James McCord was in charge of the Group's security.[5]

Leaving aside for the moment the question of Woolston-Smith's sources and methods, his concern about the November Group soon yielded enough information to alarm his confidant William Haddad. On March 23, 1972, therefore, Haddad wrote to Larry O'Brien, chairman of the Democratic National Committee, to say that "sophisticated surveillance techniques" were being used against the Democrats. Intrigued, O'Brien sent a memo to John Stewart, the DNC's director of communications, on March 30, telling him to follow up on Haddad's communiqué. Nearly a month later, on April 26, Stewart met in New York with Wooly, Haddad and others. At that meeting, Wooly recalls, Haddad took the floor and told Stewart of a plan to burglarize and bug the DNC, adding that McCord and Liddy were somehow involved, and that the operation would be carried out with the help of men from Miami's Little Havana community. The information that Haddad had received from Woolston-Smith, however, was not completely accurate. Wrongly, he informed Stewart that the operation was to be carried out under the auspices of the November Group, and said that the operation's purpose was to prove that Castro agents had contributed illicitly to the Democrats' campaign coffers. Near the end of the meeting, Woolston-Smith produced a bugging device, or what appeared to be a bugging device, and demonstrated how the eavesdropping installation would work.

On April 28 Haddad wrote to Stewart:

> I talked to Woolston-Smith. Yes, he does have good information; and, yes, he did want to cover expenses for producing it in an acceptable way. He explains that he wasn't looking for payment for his services, but to cover what looked like necessary expenses to tie down his theory with factual presentations (like checks, etc.).
>
> Instead of pursuing this with money, I decided to see what a good

<hr>

[5]It is not known precisely when McCord assumed responsibility for the November Group's security. He worked part time for the RNC and CRP in the fall and early winter of 1971, becoming security director of those organizations in early January 1972. Prior to that time John Ragan handled security for the RNC and November Group. Ragan was an ex-FBI agent with ties to the International Telephone & Telegraph Corporation (ITT) and, in the opinion of Woolston-Smith, to the CIA as well. Ragan played a role in the Kissinger wiretaps, also: it was he who bugged columnist Joseph Kraft.

investigative reporting operation could do with it now. So I went ahead along those lines. If they draw a blank, I'll be back to you on how to proceed, and I'll keep you informed.

My own journalistic judgement is that the story is true and explosive. It would be nice for a third party to uncover it, but if they fail due to the type of inside work required, I would move back to Woolston-Smith.[6]

As Haddad later testified, he provided Jack Anderson with his "entire file" on the subject. Indeed, Haddad said that he mailed the file to the columnist on *two* occasions. According to Haddad, Anderson claimed to have lost the file, and so he had sent a second copy to him. For his part, Anderson replied that the so-called file consisted of a single, rather "sloppy" letter that was vague in content and in error on the subject of the November Group's alleged involvement. Haddad denied this, saying that Anderson was "mistaken" about the extent of the file.

What is undisputed is the fact that Anderson's investigation yielded no public result. To many Senate investigators, and to many of Anderson's fellow reporters as well, this was more than a little surprising in view of the columnist's extraordinary sources within the intelligence community, his unconcealed disapproval of the Nixon administration, and the size and quality of his investigative staff. Moreover, as skeptics in the Senate and the press took pains to point out, Anderson was almost ideally situated to uncover the story. Not only were the syndicated columnist and James McCord both employers of the same down-at-the-heels private detective, a man named Lou Russell, but Anderson was a close friend of Frank Sturgis. As early as 1960 the adventurer had been the reporter's houseguest when they collaborated on magazine articles about plans to overthrow Fidel Castro.[7] Additionally, Anderson's acquaintance with Sturgis had been renewed relatively recently. In the summer of 1971 Anderson had met with Sturgis and Bernard Barker in Miami. At that meeting the Miami men had told Anderson that they were "back in business" with the legendary "Eduardo," the CIA officer (Howard Hunt) for whom Barker had worked during the Bay of Pigs operation.[8]

[6]Haddad provided a copy of his April 28 letter to the Senate Select Committee on Presidential Campaign Activities (the Ervin committee).
[7]See Jack Anderson, "Soldiers of Fortune," *Parade*, June 12, 1960, and Frank Fiorini (a.k.a. Frank Sturgis) "as told to" Jack Anderson, "We Will Finish the Job," *Parade*, May 14, 1961.
[8]Unpublished version of the Baker Report, Section II, p. 1, and Section III, p. 7. The Baker

For these reasons, the Senate's minority staff made it a point to question those involved in the Woolston-Smith–Haddad matter. Anderson's failure to uncover the story was incredible to them, especially in view of the timeliness of certain events. The columnist's meeting with Barker and Sturgis, for example, was contemporaneous with Hunt's hiring at the White House, and followed directly on the heels of Hunt's reacquaintance with the Cubans in April of 1971. Similarly, Woolston-Smith's information could not have been more up to date. He had learned in December 1971 of the administration's plans to mount an espionage operation against its rivals—plans that, according to Gordon Liddy, were not discussed until after Liddy's appointment to the CRP on December 6. As for the specific targeting of the DNC, Woolston-Smith informed John Stewart of the fact at their April 26 meeting in New York; and yet, it was only "in late April" that Liddy himself was apprised that the DNC was to be bugged.

That Woolston-Smith's information was more than a lucky guess is certain: the choice of the DNC as a target of electronic eavesdropping remains perplexing even to this date. While it is true that the Democrats' Larry O'Brien was a controversial figure in his own right, his political importance seemed in eclipse. In any event, he had moved his offices, and most of his files, to Florida by the time that the break-in took place. What, then, was there to overhear on his telephone, and what was to be gained by burglarizing the few files of his that remained? The sheer improbability of choosing the DNC as a target would seem to rule out the possibility that Woolston-Smith arrived at his information by guesswork or deduction.

The issue of the Democrats' prior knowledge of the break-in raises a number of questions: Who was Woolston-Smith's source? Why did the Democrats, forewarned, fail to take precautions? How could Anderson have stumbled so badly? And not least of all, why did the burglars pick on the DNC?

The probable source of Woolston-Smith's information was a

Report is published as an appendix to the *Final Report* prepared by the Ervin committee. This published version, however, does not contain two important sections that were originally part of the Baker Report. According to Howard Liebengood, formerly an aide to Senator Howard Baker, an agreement was reached between Senators Ervin and Baker immediately prior to the publication of the committee's *Final Report* on the Watergate affair. In return for deletions from the *Final Report* of material concerning President Nixon and Bebe Rebozo, Baker agreed to delete from his own report sections concerning "prior knowledge," Woolston-Smith, and the relationships and contacts between Jack Anderson and the Cubans. The above references, therefore, are not to be found in the Ervin committee's *Final Report*.

grapevine that had its roots in Manhattan and in the suburbs of northern Virginia. Woolston-Smith's secretary, Toni Shimon, was the daughter of a Runyonesque former Washington police detective named Joseph Shimon. A convicted wiretapper in his own right, Shimon was a partner of one John Leon in a detective agency named Allied Investigators Inc. One of the investigators with whom Shimon and Leon were allied on a part-time basis was Louis James Russell. In December 1971 Russell was working for General Security Services, Inc. (GSS), the private guard service under contract to protect the Watergate offices in which the DNC was located. At that time he was also moonlighting at Allied Investigators and looking for work that was better paid than either job. Apparently he found it because, in March, he quit GSS to join McCord Associates. There he worked for a time as a night guard at the CRP (while continuing to moonlight for Allied and free-lancing as a tipster for Jack Anderson). A garrulous man whose experience at GSS raises the suspicion that he was an "inside man" for McCord, Russell may well have bragged to Leon and Shimon about the Republicans' plans to bug the Democrats. That would have been entirely in character for Russell, and from Leon and Shimon it was only one step to the latter's daughter and her boss, A. J. Woolston-Smith.

According to Wooly, in his conversations with Haddad the motive behind the impending break-in was for the Republican spooks to gather evidence of supposed Fidelista donations to the Democrats' campaign coffers. In reality, of course, this had little or nothing to do with the break-in. It was a "false flag" that Hunt waved in front of the Cubans in order to recruit them. In my interview with Judge John Sirica's probation officer for the Cubans, Frank Saunders, he said: "The Cubans were duped. They were told that an assassination team was waiting in Spain, and that it would be sent to kill Castro if and when they broke into the Democrats' headquarters." Saunders said, "The whole thing comes down to criminal intent. You see, they [the Cubans] really believed it was a national security matter. I tried to tell Sirica this, and he threatened to fire me. He told me never to discuss the issue again. Then he changed his mind, and said that I should put it all down on paper, seal the paper and put it in a bank vault 'in case anything happened to me.' I was scared. I was afraid I'd lost my pension, and from what the Judge said and the way that he acted, I was afraid for my life, too.

I guess I should have been braver, and said something. But I didn't." The Cubans, then, were duped by Hunt into believing that they were part of a CIA operation that would culminate in Castro's demise. This was ridiculous, as Hunt knew—there was no assassination team waiting in Spain.

The more closely one examines the Woolston-Smith affair, the more likely one is to conclude (wrongly) that the Watergate arrests were the result of a Democratic trap. H. R. Haldeman subscribes to that theory, and has written about it in his book. There are many who find Anderson's inability to crack the story absurd, given the leads and sources that he had, and not a few regard the Democrats' apparent diffidence as unbelievable. They point out that the Democrats seem to have gone out of their way to minimize the affair's significance. In a civil deposition, for example, John Stewart apparently changed the date of the April 26 meeting with Woolston-Smith to June 20, three days after the Watergate arrests, noting on the deposition that this change was made to "conform to the facts." Obviously, had Woolston-Smith not confided in the Democrats until June 20, his information would have had no significance whatsoever. Asked about this, Stewart later agreed that the New York meeting had indeed occurred in April.

Similarly, Watergate skeptics point with suspicion to Stewart's inability to recollect more than one or two conversations with Woolston-Smith, whereas Wooly himself estimates that he and Stewart spoke *twice a week* on the subject. Indeed, according to Woolston-Smith, Stewart's interest in the subject was "hot—right up to, and after, the break-in."

As for Larry O'Brien, skeptics are unconvinced by his assertion that while the information was taken seriously, there was nothing to be done about it. The DNC did not have the money to perform a countermeasures sweep of its telephones or to add extra security at its headquarters. The explanation seems specious to many because, at the very least, O'Brien or Stewart might have notified General Security Services, Inc., of the eavesdropping threat— which, both admit, they failed to do even after GSS guards reported an attempted break-in during the month of May. As for the costs of countermeasures, the DNC was in an excellent position to protect the integrity of its telephone conversations. At least one security specialist offered to provide that service gratis, only to be turned down.[9] The Democrats, moreover, counted S. Harrison Dogole among their financial supporters. Indeed, Dogole was one of those men whose social status would be enhanced by his inclusion on the Enemies List. And as it happens, he was the proprietor of Globe Security Systems, Inc., the fourth largest private security agency in the United States. Certainly Dogole could have been counted on to provide a specialist to sweep the DNC's telephones. But he was never asked to do so.

The Democratic-trap theory is by no means inherently implausible. Since the target was apparently not worth the effort necessary to protect it, the Democrats would have been clever to give Liddy and Company the rope needed to hang themselves. As for Anderson, it is easy to imagine his going along with such a scheme; after all, the proof of the crime would be in the pudding, and until the crime had been committed, anything that he might write about its planning would have been deniable and open to partisan attack.

In the end, however, I do not believe the trap theory to be a valid one, because if the Democrats had been lying in wait for McCord and the Cubans, they would surely have brought about their arrest prior to June 17. What makes this assumption a certainty is the fact that the June 17 break-in represented the *fourth* assault on the Democrats' offices and the second occasion on which the offices were actually entered. Had a trap been in the works, the Democrats would have sprung it in May. They had no way of knowing that McCord and the Cubans would return to the DNC in June.

[9]This was Clyde Wallace, the proprietor of the Spy Shop in Washington, D.C., whose customers, ironically, included James McCord.

6.

Project Mudhen

In mid-January 1972, even as Woolston-Smith conferred with Bill Haddad about the administration's plans to bug the Democrats, Howard Osborn, director of the CIA's Office of Security, ordered an investigation of Jack Anderson.

As a part of this operation, code-named Project Mudhen, the backgrounds and "behavioral patterns" of Anderson and his associates became the subject of study by General Gaynor's Security Research Staff. A month later, with Gaynor's spadework done, Osborn ordered that the columnist be placed under intensive surveillance. On February 15 sixteen agents, using eight cars, were dispatched to shadow the reporter and three of his colleagues. Photographic equipment was installed in an "observation nest" across the street from Anderson's office, with every visitor to be filmed and identified. For security reasons, cryptonyms were assigned: the surveillance team became Sugar; Anderson (a teetotaler) was dubbed Brandy; secretary Opal Ginn was designated Sherry; legman Joseph Spear was rechristened Champagne; while Brit Hume was stuck with the inglorious sobriquet Eggnog.

Four years later Anderson brought suit against Richard Nixon, CIA Director Richard Helms and others, charging that his privacy had been invaded in the course of a political conspiracy to destroy his professional reputation.[1] In its defense the CIA argued that the Anderson surveillance was dictated by national security considerations, and, specifically, that beginning in December 1971 the columnist had begun publishing classified information, including information that derived from documents originating at the CIA.

---

[1]Anderson's suit, seeking $22 million in damages, was ultimately dismissed when the columnist declined to identify his sources in court. See *Anderson* v. *Nixon, et al.*, CA 76-1794, U.S. District Court for District of Columbia.

An insufficient defense (in the opinion of presiding Judge Gerhard Gesell), it contained at least an element of truth. As Richard Helms's biographer has written, "In a memo to Kissinger on October 4, 1972, Helms cited seventy-three Anderson columns based on secret intelligence documents, forty from the CIA on subjects ranging from the health of Lon Nol of Cambodia to the CIA's relationship with the Bureau of Narcotics and Dangerous Drugs, and thirty-three from the Washington Special Action Group (WSAG), a subcommittee of the National Security Council."[2]

What weakened the CIA's defense is the fact that, however problematic Jack Anderson's actions may have been, the CIA's charter prohibits domestic surveillance of American citizens who are not themselves employed by the agency. Mudhen was, purely and simply, an illegal operation.

It was also an untimely one. The leaks to which Richard Helms referred had for the most part been resolved to the satisfaction of the intelligence community. Rightly or wrongly, Yeoman Charles Radford had been identified as Anderson's source within the National Security Council. Coincidentally or not, Anderson's access to—or, at least, his publication of—national security secrets dwindled precipitously thereafter. The Office of Security's decision to place Anderson under surveillance in February is therefore peculiar because the problem appeared to have been solved.

If the project was perplexing because of its untimeliness, it was interesting also for the fact that it was redundant and wholly uncoordinated with other agencies. As the columnist himself has noted, "The Pentagon, according to its former security chief, W. Donald Stewart, conducted at least 11 separate investigations of us, sparing no expense. The FBI secretly grabbed our telephone records, and the Internal Revenue Service conducted a penetrating, year-long audit of my finances."[3] To which it might be added that Anderson was also the subject of a White House–inspired investigation by International Intelligence Incorporated (Intertel), and an ad hoc investigation by McCord Associates. It appears, then, that Anderson was the target of a conspiracy whose origins rested with White House concerns about leaks. And yet the matter is subtler.

[2]Thomas Powers, *The Man Who Kept the Secrets: Richard Helms & the CIA* (New York: Knopf, 1979), p. 263.
[3]Anderson's column, "Washington Merry-Go-Round," *Washington Post*, September 9, 1977, p. D15.

While some such conspiracy no doubt existed, Project Mudhen (and the CIA) were not a part of it: Mudhen was a CIA operation whose "product" was consumed by the Office of Security, and only by the Office of Security. No reports were made to the White House, and there is no evidence that the White House or any other federal agency was aware of the operation.[4] What, then, was the CIA doing? The surveillance was so intense and involved so many agents that the risk of exposure was enormous, as the Office of Security soon realized when Anderson's children began to photograph the funny men sitting in cars outside their home. It was, in other words, the sort of operation that would have been anathema to the usually cautious Richard Helms. How, then, is one to explain its illegality, dangers and untimeliness?

The evidence suggests that Project Mudhen was instituted for some purpose other than identifying leakers. A CIA memorandum for the chief of the Security Research Staff, General Paul Gaynor, cites an irresponsible article published in the *Washington Observer Newsletter*.[5] The memo to General Gaynor pretends to implicate Jack Anderson in an alleged Mafia conspiracy "to attack conservative organizations, Members of Congress and high public officials who want to crack down on Communists, rioters and assorted left-wingers."[6] According to the article or memo—the latter paraphrases the former in such a way as to seem an advocate of the article's thesis —the supposed conspiracy has been masterminded by the publisher of "a pornographic sheet called National Enquirer," Generoso Pope, Jr. He, we are told, is a former CIA officer who joined forces with "[Drew] Pearson and the Anti-Defamation League, who [sic] assigned its top spy, Sanford Griffith, to work with the smear conspiracy. This alliance between the Mafia and the ADL is not new —allegedly the family-owned tax-dodging Generoso Pope Foundation aids Jewish charities and Zionist funds, and is suspected of being a secret conduit for CIA funds."[7] The memo then goes on to report the findings of the Office of Security with respect to the Bell-McClure Syndicate, the North American Newspaper Alliance

[4]There was a single exception to this—that is, the Air Force was informally notified by a CIA officer of a contact between Anderson and a Pentagon employee. The observation was characterized by the CIA as the product of a chance encounter.
[5]July 1, 1969.
[6]CIA memorandum for chief, Security Research Staff, "Subject: Jackson Northman Anderson," January 17, 1972.
[7]This memorandum is Exhibit V in *Anderson* v. *Nixon, et al.*

and World Wide Features, Inc.—alleged keystones in a supposed liberal-Zionist-Mafia conspiracy to "muscle in on newspaper syndication on a global basis."

The contents of the memo are obviously claptrap, and it is remarkable (and worrisome) that the Office of Security would take them seriously enough to include them as part of its background study on Anderson. Drafted on January 17, 1972, the memo may well have contributed to the CIA's decision to place Anderson under surveillance.

The memo presages James McCord's own investigation of the columnist (conducted in the spring of 1972). Indeed, the tone and contents of the memo are so compatible with McCord's own view of the columnist's supposed place in the scheme of things that it would not be surprising if it turned out that he was a principal source for the memo. And as it happens, McCord was an acknowledged source for both the *Washington Observer Newsletter* (quoted in the memo) and the equally right-wing and anti-Semitic Liberty Lobby (with which the *Newsletter* was associated). We have an inkling of McCord's attitude toward Anderson from a book proposal that the spy drafted in the aftermath of his arrest and conviction.[8] In that proposal there is a section of inspired paranoia entitled "Jack Anderson—the Man Who Brought You the Eagleton Case." In that section, McCord smears the columnist and his associates by a process of innuendo, lumping them together with Meyer Lansky, the Mafia, the Israeli defense industry and alleged business swindles, and basing all evidence on guilt by association.

Which is not to say that Anderson is above reproach. On the contrary, he is an enigmatic figure, both in and out of the Watergate context. The CIA's interest in the columnist dated back to 1960, and ultraconservatives of the McCarthy stripe have long regarded him with suspicion, questioning his loyalty to the United States and attacking him in print and in the courts.[9] So, too, some liberals view Anderson with a measure of suspicion, citing his nearly blinkered support of the Taiwanese, South Korean and Israeli governments. Still others have criticized his business associations.[10]

[8]Nedzi report, pp. 838–43 ("Counter-Espionage Agent for the Republicans," by James McCord).
[9]With respect to the CIA's long-standing interest in Anderson, there is an agency memorandum from (DELETED) to the deputy chief, Security Resarch Staff, "Subject: Anderson, Jackson (Jack) Northman," March 14, 1960.
[10]In 1976, for example, the columnist's connections to a clutch of South Koreans became a subject of public controversy. On November 22 of that year Anderson reluctantly announced

Certainly Anderson is, and always has been, a man of parts—and a lint trap for the suspicions of partisans from both the Right and the Left. And while it is not surprising that the CIA should have been interested in the columnist, it is surprising that the agency undertook to place him under intense surveillance at the time that it did.

Those who carried out the surveillance received orders directly from Howard Osborn; and while these agents find it "incomprehensible" that Osborn would have initiated Mudhen on his own, the fact remains that there is nothing to suggest otherwise. Not that we would expect the prudent Helms to have authorized such an operation in writing; that was not his way. Still, it is also true that Helms seems to have regarded the columnist with a level-headedness that the Office of Security clearly lacked.

More than a month after the Office of Security had placed Anderson under surveillance, Helms arranged a luncheon with the columnist for March 17, 1972. The Office of Security's concern about the impending luncheon is made absolutely clear in a CIA memo written at the time:

---

his intention to resign as chairman of the executive committee of the Diplomat National Bank, and to resign as well from the bank's board of directors. The bank was controversial because 46 percent of its stock (the controlling interest) was owned by Tong Sun Park, a millionaire agent of the Korean Central Intelligence Agency (KCIA), and surrogates of South Korean evangelist Sun Myung Moon. In Senate hearings the bank was subsequently identified as "a window," or conduit, for KCIA operational funds in the United States. Anderson further announced that he intended to relinquish his interest in the Empress chain of Chinese restaurants. At the same time, the columnist's association with karate entrepreneur Jhoon Rhee ("Nobody bodda me!") was also criticized. With Anderson, Rhee was a director of the Diplomat National Bank and a partner in the World Blackbelt League. Both Rhee and Tong Sun Park were subpoenaed as witnesses in the Senate's "Koreagate" hearings, an inquiry into the programmatic bribery of U.S. officials, journalists and others as part of an operation by the KCIA to influence the course of U.S. foreign policy. Questioned about these business relationships by *Washington Post* reporter Scott Armstrong, Anderson suggested that Armstrong was acting as a mouthpiece for the Central Intelligence Agency and, in effect, smearing him. But criticism of Anderson's personal and business relationships has by no means been confined to his association with the Diplomat National Bank, the Moonies and a group of KCIA agents. He has been criticized by his own staff for his association with wheeler-dealers such as I. Irving Davidson. A lobbyist and arms merchant, Davidson is a man of unsavory reputation. Targeted by the Justice Department's Organized Crime and Racketeering Strike Force, the lobbyist has represented institutions as repressive (and/or corrupt) as Somoza's Nicaragua, Papa Doc's Haiti, the Indonesian National Army and the Israeli arms industry. Despite this, or perhaps because of it, Anderson and Davidson shared offices together for nine years. (See *Korean Influence Inquiry, Executive Session Hearings before the Senate Select Committee on Ethics,* 95th Cong., 2d sess., March–April 1978, Vols. I and II, and, in particular, Exhibit 273 in those hearings, entitled "1976 KCIA Plan for Operations in the United States." See also Scott Armstrong, "Columnist to Quit Role with Bank," *Washington Post,* November 22, 1976, p. 1.)

1. On 14 March 1972, the Director of Security advised that on 17 March 1972, the Director will lunch with BRANDY. This meeting will take place at the Montpelier Room Restaurant of the Madison Hotel, Washington, D.C. The Director has further advised that the purpose of the confrontation will be to attempt to dissuade BRANDY from publishing certain sensitive classified material in his forthcoming book. It is of particular significance that this luncheon appointment was made at the request of the Director and, obviously, the arrangements concerning the locale were facilitated by BRANDY.

2. It was pointed out to the Director of Security that the Director should be apprised of the possibility that BRANDY may seek audio coverage of the meeting. This conclusion can be based on the following factors:

a. Recent [CIA] coverage at the Empress Restaurant, Washington, D.C. revealed BRANDY in possession of portable recording equipment;

b. There is a distinct possibility that BRANDY may utilize the services of one (DELETED)[11]

c. Positive information that BRANDY has recently visited the U.S. Recording Company, such firm being a known supplier of sophisticated audio equipment; . . .

d. The fact that BRANDY may well have viable contacts or relationships with the staff of the Madison Hotel and, indeed, might be leasing permanent space at that establishment which could be utilized as an audio listening post.

3. On 15 March 1972, the Director of Security advised that he had briefed the Director regarding the above considerations, but that the latter is still intent on going through with the proposed luncheon meeting.

4. It was proposed to the Director of Security that certain limited [CIA] coverage should be effected in the Montpelier Room during the meeting between BRANDY and the Director. Two (2) teams of two (2) agents each will also lunch at the restaurant and maintain general . . . observations particularly on the possibility of any audio or photographic coverage of the Director while he is in BRANDY's presence. If such a contingency is discovered before the Director's arrival at the restaurant, Headquarters should be immediately notified. . . . In the event such developments arise while the Director is in the establishment, *no action should be taken by SUGAR team members* excepting the notification, at the earliest opportunity, to (DELETED) supervisory personnel. At no time should the Director be made aware of SUGAR coverage

---

[11]The deleted section appears to refer to one of two men: private investigator Richard Bast, who sometimes worked with Anderson, or Martin Kaiser, a former supplier of sophisticated audio equipment to the FBI.

within the restaurant although it should be noted that he is agreeable to our intended operation. . . .[12] [Emphasis in original memorandum.]

It is a queer business. The book that gave rise to Director Helms's concern was *The Anderson Papers*, written with George Clifford and published by Random House more than a year after the strange luncheon was held. A contract for the book had been signed on February 2, 1972, and Anderson's subject was to have been the making of U.S. foreign policy under Henry Kissinger. Ultimately, however, the book became a kind of behind-the-scenes report on Anderson's investigative triumphs (such as the one concerning ITT lobbyist Dita Beard) and pratfalls (Senator Thomas Eagleton).

But what makes the circumstances of the luncheon seem queer is not so much the alacrity with which Helms reacted to Anderson's contract with Random House as the surveillance within the surveillance. The Office of Security's explanation for placing the CIA director under (temporary) surveillance seems strained.

That Anderson might have "wired himself" for the luncheon was, of course, a possibility, however remote. But what difference would it have made? Helms, and other CIA executives, breakfasted routinely with reporters, briefing them on "background" with respect to any number of sensitive issues. There would have been nothing improper about the CIA director's urging the columnist to restrain himself in areas affecting national security, and so it is difficult to understand the Office of Security's alarm at the prospect of the meeting. Moreover, the question arises as to what good it did to place the meeting under surveillance. As the CIA memo itself emphasizes, *"no action should be taken. . . . At no time should the Director be made aware . . ."* If the concern was that Anderson might be tape-recording Helms for later publication, of what use was the surveillance if the agents were enjoined from warning the director that eavesdropping was in progress? Would it not have been a simple matter to interrupt the luncheon on a pretext? Helms might easily have been equipped with a "beeper," and if eavesdropping was detected, he might have excused himself to make a phone call, and away from the table, he could have been warned. The surveillance, then, served no clear purpose. What's more, one can only

[12]The memorandum, dated March 15, 1972, and entitled "Project Mudhen, #577 681," is Exhibit B in *Anderson v. Nixon, et al.*

wonder at the memo's instruction that *the director* should not be made aware of the surveillance. It would have made more sense to say that *the columnist* should not be made aware of the surveillance —but there it is. It is the director's awareness with which the Office of Security is concerned.

Finally, the Office of Security must have known that had Anderson, ignoring promises of confidentiality, wished to report upon the luncheon, tape-recordings would have been superfluous. A respected columnist, he routinely published the contents of interviews, relying on his own notes and recollection.

The Office of Security's explanation for surveilling the luncheon is implausible. On the one hand, its ongoing surveillance of Anderson, which involved so many agents, was of the hostile sort—a surveillance so intense as to be obvious, and therefore intimidating to its subject. On the other hand, OS memoranda are explicit about the fact that the CIA's own director was not to know that he was being watched. It is fair, then, to say that the Office of Security placed the luncheon under surveillance not to protect Helms but to find out what was said.

Within a week of the meeting in the Montpelier Room, Howard Hunt and Gordon Liddy discussed ways to murder Jack Anderson.[13] Liddy reports that Hunt introduced him to Dr. Edward Gunn, a supposedly retired CIA physician for whom Hunt claimed an unusual expertise: the unconventional application of medical and chemical knowledge. Lunching in the Hay-Adams Hotel with Hunt and Dr. Gunn, Liddy privately doubted that the doctor had ever retired from the CIA. To say that he had was simply a way of distancing the physician from his secretive employers in Langley— a standard precaution. Hunt, after all, had used Liddy's nom de guerre, George Leonard, in introducing him to Dr. Gunn. And given the dark purpose of the meeting—to find some way to *stop* Jack Anderson—the use of aliases and avowals of false retirements was understandable. Seated in the Hay-Adams, very nearly in the

[13]In his autobiography (*Will*, p. 207), Liddy describes the meeting at which Anderson's assassination was plotted. Erroneously, he writes that the session took place "on a brisk February day." Brisk it may have been, but February it was not. As Liddy's own text makes clear, the meeting took place after Thomas Gregory was recruited (February 20) and placed in Senator Edmund Muskie's camp (March 1); after Hunt had journeyed to meet with Dita Beard in Denver (March 15); and shortly before Jeb Magruder discussed the Gemstone plan with John Mitchell for the last time (March 30). In testimony before the Senate, Hunt placed the meeting as having occurred on or about March 24, 1972.

shadow of the White House, Liddy wondered on whose behalf Hunt was acting. It must, he thought, be Chuck Colson. To Liddy's knowledge, Colson was Hunt's only "principal.[14]

To Liddy's knowledge. But, as we have seen, Hunt did not tell Liddy everything; on the contrary, he concealed any number of matters from his co-conspirator. And with respect to Hunt's "principals," Liddy was certainly in the dark. On the one hand, Charles Colson was indeed Hunt's most visible principal, but there was an invisible principal as well: the CIA's Office of Security. The question of principals is an important one because, after all, it would be useful to know just who it was that suggested to Hunt that he plan to "neutralize" the columnist. According to Hunt, the suggestion was Charles Colson's. According to Colson, the idea was Hunt's, and it was "harebrained." It was predictable, of course, that Colson would deny responsibility for making the suggestion. But we should keep in mind a third possibility: that it was the Office of Security which suggested to Hunt that Anderson should be "stopped."

Several plans were considered.[15] The initial conception was to surreptitiously administer a massive dose of LSD to the columnist, the expectation being that Anderson would behave so erratically that his sanity would come into question and, with it, his credibility. Reportedly, Dr. Gunn dismissed this plan on the grounds that the effects of LSD are unpredictable. To the apparent "relief" of Hunt and Dr. Gunn, Liddy then took the bull by the horns: if drugs were an unreliable preventative, why not cure the problem by assassinating the man? All agreed that this was rather easier to accomplish and, of course, totally effective. Various methods were discussed until, finally, it was decided that the target should be made to seem the victim of a fatal mugging. Following their meeting with Dr. Gunn, Hunt and Liddy then discussed who should be assigned to carry out the killing. The Cubans seemed a logical choice, but Hunt raised an objection: What if his "principal" thought the Cubans

---

[14]Liddy, *Will*, pp. 207–8.

[15]In fairness to Dr. Gunn, Liddy points out that Jack Anderson's name was never mentioned in connection with the plot. The conversation, for the protection of the conspirators, was conducted in a hypothetical way. Nevertheless, Liddy is convinced that the good doctor "guessed" that Anderson was the target because, when discussing the feasibility of a vehicular "accident," Dr. Gunn suggested a site near Anderson's home and on his way to work. At the end of the conversation, Liddy gave Dr. Gunn a $100 bill "to protect Dr. Gunn's image as 'retired.' " Liddy, then, is among those who seem to believe that the CIA knew of the plot to murder Anderson. Indeed, he seems to believe that the plot had the CIA's approval, or else Dr. Gunn would not have been so forthcoming at the meeting.

untrustworthy? What if he wanted someone else to handle the job?

In that case, Liddy said, he'd take care of it himself.[16]

Hunt's hypothetical reservation about the Cubans is striking. Why did Hunt imagine that his "principal," whether Colson or the Office of Security, would object to using the Cubans to assassinate Jack Anderson? If anything, they would have seemed ideal for the job—except, perhaps, for the fact that Sturgis and Barker, at least, were friendly with the columnist. Hunt may have feared that this friendship might get in the way of their "professionalism." But to have had this concern, Hunt would necessarily have had to know of that friendship. And if he knew of the friendship, why would he have picked Jack Anderson's pals to burglarize Dr. Fielding's office and the DNC? Why, moreover, having raised his hypothetical objection to the Cubans, did Hunt seem to accept Liddy's offer to accomplish the deed? If Charles Colson was in fact Hunt's "principal," he would presumably have disdained the idea of using the CRP's general counsel to mug and murder a prominent columnist. Whatever else Colson may have been, however dangerous he may have been, no one has ever accused him of being as stupid as that. If, on the other hand, the Office of Security was Hunt's secret principal, Liddy's association with the CRP would not have been an obstacle to his use as an assassin.

If the scheme to neutralize Jack Anderson did originate in the Office of Security, then some of the more perplexing aspects of Project Mudhen begin to make sense. Anderson's "behavioral patterns"—his movements to and from work and the home, the whereabouts of his associates at particular times—would have been of unique value to anyone plotting his assassination. Was there a time and place when, on a regular basis, he was uniquely susceptible to the sort of mugging that Liddy planned? Did he have a dog, and if so, did he walk him alone at night? Was the columnist a jogger, and if so, where did he jog, when and with whom? Learning such details would take a while, but the Office of Security had the time, the personnel and the inclination to do so. Its surveillance of Anderson lasted from February 15 through early April. The termination of that surveillance, on the heels of the meeting with Dr. Gunn, seems ominous in retrospect, because, obviously, if there had been a CIA plot to kill Anderson, or if the CIA was for some reason abetting

[16]Liddy, *Will*, pp. 209–10.

such a plot, it would have been foolish to keep the columnist under surveillance at the time of the actual murder. The termination of the CIA surveillance, along with its timing, smacks of an accommodation.

One final matter ought to be noted here. This is that Hunt neglected to inform Liddy that Dr. Gunn was an associate of James McCord's.[17] He could not tell Liddy this because, at the time, Hunt was still concealing from Liddy the fact that he even knew McCord. So Liddy was given the impression that Gunn was a CIA officer whose "retirement" was merely an operational pretext. Ignorant of Dr. Gunn's relationship to McCord, Liddy was oblivious also to McCord's own interest in Anderson. Liddy was never told that shortly after his meeting with Dr. Gunn, McCord conducted his own investigation of the columnist, using Lou Russell as his informant, and that the results of this investigation were delivered by hand to the Office of Security.

As Liddy was kept in ignorance of so much, it is hard to conclude other than that he was a dupe—a dupe, moreover, who may have come within an ace of being a patsy. That he did not become a patsy (at least, not a patsy in a murder case) was apparently due to a change in priorities dictated by Jeb Magruder's activation of the Gemstone plan.

[17]FBI serial 139-4089-1340 makes reference to an LEAA grant application prepared by McCord, who identified himself as the director of the Institute for Protection and Safety Studies. Included as a part of the grant application submitted by McCord was Dr. Gunn's résumé.

7.
The Tickler

In a conversation with President Nixon, John Dean would one day wonder: "How did it all start? Where did it start? It started with an instruction to me from Bob Haldeman to see if we couldn't set up a perfectly legitimate campaign intelligence operation over at the Re-Election Committee."[1]

In an effort to accommodate Haldeman, Dean asked his aide Jack Caulfield to come up with a proposal. A veteran spook with dreams of glory, Caulfield concocted Operation Sandwedge, suggesting the creation of "a Republican Intertel," a private intelligence agency for GOP clients and one, moreover, that would have a "black bag" capability. Because Caulfield lacked the polish and contacts required of someone to head such a firm, the plan was rejected. Nevertheless, Dean continued to be "tickled" by Haldeman's staff assistant, Gordon Strachan, who repeatedly inquired as to whether Dean had found an alternative to Caulfield. It was under this pressure from Haldeman's aide that Dean approached the Plumbers' Bud Krogh to ask if David Young would be available to handle campaign intelligence. Krogh demurred, recommending G. Gordon Liddy instead.[2] Shortly afterwards, Liddy and Dean conferred, and as Liddy recalls, Dean "was serious as cancer."[3] According to Liddy, Dean said that a $1 million fund would be made available for campaign intelligence. Liddy accepted the offer; the post of general counsel to the CRP would serve as his cover for clandestine operations.

[1] *The White House Transcripts*, the full text of the recorded presidential conversations submitted by Richard Nixon to the Committee on the Judiciary of the House of Representatives, edited by Gerald Gold and the staff of the *New York Times* (New York: Bantam, 1974), Appendix 6, p. 134 (conversation of March 21, 1973).
[2] John Dean, *Blind Ambition* (New York: Simon & Schuster, 1976), pp. 66–71.
[3] Liddy, *Will*, p. 181.

Before any operations could be undertaken, however, a plan had to be drawn up and approved. Accordingly, Liddy sat down to map out the Gemstone plan. At a January 27 meeting in the Attorney General's office, Liddy made his million-dollar pitch with the help of flow charts drawn up for him by the CIA's graphics studio.[4] Present at the meeting with Liddy were John Mitchell, John Dean and Jeb Magruder. The plan that Liddy presented contained the following code words and elements:

Ruby: infiltration of the Democratic camp;

Emerald: use of a "chase plane" to eavesdrop on the Democratic candidate's aircraft and buses when his entourage used radio telephones;

Quartz: microwave interception of telephone traffic;

Sapphire: the use of prostitutes to compromise Democrats aboard an opulent houseboat fitted with video-tape recorders (the houseboat was to be moored near the site of the Democrats' National Convention);

Crystal: electronic surveillance;

Garnet: counterdemonstrations;

Turquoise: operations making use of the air-conditioning system at the Democrats' convention hall;

Topaz: photographing the Democrats' documents in the course of Crystal emplacements; and

Opal: four clandestine entries (or break-ins). The proposed targets, according to Liddy, were the Washington headquarters of Senator Edmund Muskie and Senator George McGovern, the Fontainebleau Hotel in Miami, and a fourth "target of opportunity" to be determined at a later date.

In addition to these aspects of the overall operation, Liddy had also provided for a special action group to carry out *Nacht und Nebel* (Night and Fog) missions involving the kidnapping, drugging and forcible deportation of antiwar leaders. This group, Liddy said to Mitchell, would be staffed by "professional killers who have accounted between them for twenty-two dead so far, including two hanged from a beam in a garage."[5]

The naïveté of this Maxwell Smart proposal—what with Liddy lapsing into Germanic references to *Einsatzgruppen* and using the hard G when addressing John Mitchell as *General*—is its most

---

[4]Ibid., p. 193.

[5]Ibid., pp. 197–98. Liddy attributes the remark about the twenty-two dead men to information offered by Hunt in the course of introducing Liddy to his Cuban associates.

striking feature. But before we look at the reactions of those who attended the January 27 meeting, a few points are worth considering.

First, Liddy was apparently quite confident that the plan would be approved. Even before the meeting with Mitchell had taken place, Bernard Barker had been dispatched to acquire architectural plans for the Miami Convention Center, in which the Democrats would select their presidential candidate (this was done in December 1971 or early January 1972).[6] Moreover, according to Liddy, he and Hunt traveled to Miami prior to the first meeting with Mitchell, there to interview goons and prostitutes for work at the Democratic convention.[7] These were all aspects of the yet to be presented (let alone approved) Gemstone plan—a circumstance that might suggest that Hunt and Liddy had jumped the gun. In an interview with the author, however, Liddy denied that, saying that his and Hunt's trip to Miami, and Barker's efforts to obtain the blueprints, were merely preparations taken in case Gemstone should be approved.

Second, the Gemstone plan is remarkable for what it omits as well as for what it contains. There is, for example, no reference to Alabama Governor George Wallace. While there are rumors to the effect that the Nixon and Wallace forces had reached an accommodation, with Wallace agreeing to run as a Democrat rather than as an Independent, the fact is that Wallace remained a constant, major worry to the Nixon forces.[8] The January polls indicated that about 13 percent of the electorate preferred Wallace to be President, leaving Nixon more or less dead even with the Democrats. The Wallace swing vote might therefore have seemed crucial, since so many in the Governor's camp preferred Nixon as their second choice.

With this in mind we may return to Liddy's initial presentation of the Gemstone plan. By the agreement of all who were present, the reaction was one of amazement bordering on shock. As Mitchell told the Senate: "I think it can be best described as a complete horror story that involved a mish-mash of code names and lines of authority, electronic surveillance, the ability to intercept aircraft communications, the call girl bit and all the rest of it. The matter was

[6] June 26, 1972, interview of Robert Swartburg by FBI special agent John R. Ackerly, obtained under the Freedom of Information Act. Swartburg was an employee of the architectural firm that designed the Miami Beach Convention Hall.
[7] Liddy, *Will*, pp. 191–92.
[8] Jeb Stuart Magruder, *An American Life* (New York: Atheneum, 1974), p. 188.

of such striking content and concept that it was just beyond the pale. As I recall, I told him to go burn the charts and that this was not what we were interested in. What we were interested in was a matter of information gathering and protection against demonstrators."[9]

Dean's recollection of Mitchell's reaction is more detailed. "He was amazed," Dean testified. "At one point I gave him a look of bewilderment and he winked. Knowing Mitchell, I did not think he would throw Liddy out of the office or tell him he was out of his mind. Rather, he did what I expected. When the presentation was completed, he took a few long puffs on his pipe and told Liddy that the plan he had developed was not quite what he had in mind and the cost was out of the question. He suggested to Liddy that he go back and revise his plan, keeping in mind that he was most interested in the demonstration problem. . . . [A]fter the meeting ended, as the charts were being taken off the easel and disassembled . . . , Mitchell indicated to me that Mr. Liddy's proposal was out of the question. . . . At that point, I thought the plan was dead, because I doubted if Mitchell would reconsider the matter."[10] Indeed, as Dean observes in his memoirs, Mitchell disdained direct confrontation, preferring to leave the hatchet work to his subordinates.[11] When, for example, Dean's assistant, Tom Charles Huston, sent an utterly insensitive memo using Dean's name to John Mitchell, it had been Mitchell's deputy, Richard Kleindienst, who had called from the Justice Department to read the riot act to the embarrassed Dean.[12]

Magruder's account conforms with John Dean's: in an understated but firm way, the Attorney General "indicated that this was

[9]Ervin committee *Hearings*, Book 4, p. 1610.
[10]Ibid., Book 3, p. 930.
[11]Dean, *Blind Ambition*, pp. 77–78.
[12]Huston was a twenty-nine-year-old libertarian who was reassigned by Haldeman to Dean's staff after he had alienated FBI Director J. Edgar Hoover. Huston's historical notoriety is a consequence of President Nixon's order in June 1970 that he draft a plan for redirecting and coordinating domestic intelligence-gathering activities. Huston responded by putting together a 43-page document that recommended (1) intensification of electronic surveillance and penetrations against individuals and groups "who pose major threats to national security"; (2) increased use of mail covers; (3) more surreptitious entries; (4) increased efforts to recruit informants on campus; (5) the deployment of undercover military intelligence operatives to work against certain groups in the United States; and (6) the creation of an interagency intelligence command responsible for internal security. This last group was to include representatives of the FBI, CIA, NSA, DIA and counterintelligence units from the Army, Navy and Air Force—reporting to the White House. Mussolini would have loved it. See Ervin committee *Hearings*, Book 4, pp. 1453–64, and Exhibits 35–41 of those same *Hearings*, Book 3, pp. 1319–37.

not an acceptable project," and sent Liddy back to the drawing
board.[13] With others, Magruder says that he was "appalled" by the
proposal, adding that he telephoned H. R. Haldeman's staff assistant, Gordon Strachan, to inform him of Liddy's effort and Mitchell's disapporval.[14] In an apparent effort to distance himself from
both Magruder and the Gemstone plan, Strachan vehemently denies
having received any such call.[15]

We may wonder, of course, why Mitchell did not simply defenes-
trate the *Dummkopf,* Liddy, at the January 27 meeting. Asked by the
Senate why he did not throw Liddy out of his office, Mitchell
replied, "In hindsight, I not only should have thrown him out of the
office, I should have thrown him out of the window."[16] That he did
not was due in large measure to the fact that the Nixon campaign
had a legitimate need for political intelligence concerning the
Democrats and antiwar demonstrations, and also a need for making
its own political apparatus secure. Liddy, Mitchell told the Senate,
was capable of producing a plan that would satisfy these objectives,
and so he was given a second chance. In the end, it seemed only a
question of soothing the spook's fevered brain. Nevertheless, it is
abundantly clear that Liddy should have been told, explicitly, that
the intelligence plan was *not* to include bugging, kidnapping, mugging, pandering, drugging, blackmail or any other criminal activity.
In fact, however, Liddy was never given any such advice.

The plot thickens with Magruder's account of the revised plan,
submitted to Mitchell on February 4. According to Magruder,
Liddy now hoped to deploy the hookers in Washington—a plan
that Magruder says he and the others opposed.[17] Once again, however, Magruder is contradicted. Liddy writes that more than a
month later, in March, prostitutes were retained as a component of
the Gemstone operation, and that, moreover, they were retained
with Magruder's enthusiastic approval. Liddy writes:

> Magruder approved the drastically revised plan. He had only one sug-
> gested change: that the prostitutes to be used at the Democratic conven-
> tion next summer be brought up to Washington from Miami and put
> to work immediately.

[13]Ervin committee *Hearings,* Book 2, p. 788.
[14]Ibid., pp. 2788–89.
[15]Ibid., Book 6, pp. 2440–41.
[16]Ibid., Book 4, p. 1610.
[17]Magruder, *American Life*, p. 180.

I told Jeb that bringing whores to Washington was like shipping cars to Detroit, with all the free stuff being given away on Capitol Hill. . . . Besides, the budget was bare bones; there wasn't a nickel left over for their transportation and payment for all those months until summer. Magruder replied that they could be paid through ["Bart"] Porter if necessary.[18] Again, I stressed that it just wasn't practical to bring hookers to Washington.

Magruder didn't want to let the subject go. If he could justify a trip to Miami, could I fix him up with our girls? Jesus, I thought, the wimp can't even get laid with a hooker by himself. I saw an opportunity to turn Magruder's lust to advantage. If GEMSTONE were approved, I told him, he'd be paying for them anyway and could take his pick. From the look on his face as I left the office, I had the feeling that if Magruder had anything to say about it, GEMSTONE would be approved.[19]

Liddy's revised plan was submitted to Mitchell on February 4 in the presence of its author, Magruder and John Dean (who arrived late for the meeting). The revisions in the plan consisted largely of eliminating its most expensive and outrageous components (the chase plane, microwave interceptions, kidnappings and rent-a-thug provisions), with the result that the $1 million budget was halved. Despite this reduction, Dean recalls that Mitchell was clearly unhappy with the presentation. Watching the Attorney General "wince" at Liddy's ideas, Dean finally intervened:[20] "Mr. Mitchell, I felt, was being put on the spot. The only polite way I thought I could end the discussions was to inject that these discussions could not go on in the Office of the Attorney General of the United States and that the meeting should terminate immediately."[21] Which is just what occurred: looking startled, Liddy and Magruder rose from their seats and wordlessly shuffled from the room.

In the hallway outside the Attorney General's office, Dean found himself standing beside Liddy, waiting for the elevator. "I told Liddy I would never again discuss this matter with him. I told him that if any such plan were approved, I did not want to know."[22] Dean had intended to express his complete disapproval of the plan —and, by extension, Mitchell's blunt disapproval as well. In fact, however, his advice was ambiguous: as Dean later came to realize,

---

[18]Herbert L. Porter was the CRP's scheduling director.
[19]Liddy, *Will*, p. 207.
[20]Dean, *Blind Ambition*, pp. 86–87.
[21]Ervin committee *Hearings*, Book 3, p. 930.
[22]Ibid.

Liddy apparently interpreted his message as an effort to protect Mitchell and to build "deniability" into the intelligence operation. In a sense, Dean's impression of urgency and his seeming concern with tradecraft encouraged Liddy in the mistaken belief that his plans were being seriously considered by the Attorney General.[23] In fact Mitchell was unaware that Dean had elaborated on the injunction that he had issued at the meeting. Mitchell knew only that the plan had been brought to him on two occasions, that on both occasions he had expressed dissatisfaction with it and, obviously, nothing had been approved. On the contrary, Liddy and Magruder had been all but ordered out of his office.

For Liddy and Magruder, it was the second humiliation in less than a week. Throughout both of their meetings with Mitchell the Attorney General appears to have played a mostly passive role— puffing on his pipe, listening to Liddy's ideas and, finally, rejecting them. Magruder, however, would have us believe (contrary to the testimony of everyone else) that Mitchell was more actively involved. According to Magruder, "[E]ither Mr. Mitchell or Mr. Dean . . . had information relating to Senator Muskie, [which information was said to be] . . . in Mr. Greenspun's office in Las Vegas. Mr. Liddy was asked to review the situation in Las Vegas to see if there would be potential for an entry into Mr. Greenspun's office."[24] Elsewhere, Magruder testifies that it was at this same meeting, on February 4, that the DNC was first discussed as a target, with Mitchell raising the subject. Magruder claims that Mitchell was upset that Larry O'Brien had become "a very effective spokesman against our position on the ITT case."[25]

Mitchell's rebuttal of Magruder's testimony is convincing, particularly when one takes into account the fact that Mitchell was responsible for administering euthanasia to two earlier intelligence plans: one submitted by Tom Charles Huston, which both Mitchell and J. Edgar Hoover opposed, and the one drafted by Jack Caulfield under the code name Operation Sandwedge.[26] More-

[23]Dean, *Blind Ambition*, pp. 86–87.

[24]Ervin committee *Hearings*, Book 2, p. 790.

[25]Ibid. ITT, then in antitrust litigation with the administration, had offered the GOP $400,-000 in cash and services if the Republicans would hold their national convention at the San Diego Sheraton Hotel, which ITT owned. This suggested a cozy relationship between the administration and ITT, and the promise of cash and services raised obvious questions about the eventual settlement of the litigation.

[26]The Sandwedge plan is published as an exhibit in the Ervin committee's *Final Report*, pp. 240–51. That same *Report* discusses the Huston plan, pp. 3–7.

over, with respect to Magruder's specific testimony, Mitchell pointed out that Magruder was in error about both the ITT case and the DNC. Mitchell said that he did not become concerned about O'Brien's interest in the ITT case until Jack Anderson began publishing a series of columns quoting a memorandum written by ITT lobbyist Dita Beard. "Mr. Anderson did not publish his column until the 29th of February," Mitchell pointed out, "which was more than three weeks *after* the February 4 meeting."[27] The Anderson column, therefore, could hardly have influenced what was planned at that meeting. Mitchell said that he "violently" disagreed with Magruder's testimony, and added that the "basically ceremonial" DNC was never of interest to him as an intelligence target.

Gordon Liddy's account of the matter confirms Mitchell's testimony. Liddy makes it clear that the DNC was not targeted until more than a month after the February 4 meeting, and then only upon Jeb Magruder's orders. As for Mitchell's supposed interest in Greenspun, Liddy writes (and others confirm) that it was the Mullen Company's Robert Bennett who first suggested (to Howard Hunt) that the publisher had explosive information about Nixon's rival. Hunt, in turn, relayed that tidbit to Liddy, who conveyed it to Magruder. Magruder then ordered Liddy to pursue the feasibility of a Las Vegas break-in. Contrary to what Magruder says, Liddy insists that the Greenspun matter did not come up until after February 4, and that it was never discussed with Mitchell in his, Liddy's, presence.[28]

In heaping the blame for Watergate on John Mitchell, Magruder is obviously protecting someone else. Just who that might be is an important question to which we will soon return. The point here, however, is that while Liddy remained in the dark as to the fate of his Gemstone plan (thanks to John Dean's ambiguous intervention at the February 4 meeting), and while Dean and Mitchell apparently thought the matter at an end or in indefinite abeyance, operations were in fact rushing forward. On February 17 Hunt and Liddy were dispatched to Los Angeles by Magruder, there to plot the Greenspun break-in with a Howard Hughes operative. A few days later

---

[27]Ervin committee *Hearings*, Book 4, pp. 1610–14. Quoting from Anderson's first column on the subject, "The memo . . . not only indicates that the anti-trust case had been fixed but that the fix was a pay-off for ITT's pledge of up to $400,000 for the upcoming Republican Convention in San Diego. . . ."

[28]Liddy's account is taken from *Will*, pp. 204–5, and from the author's interviews with him.

the Ruby I intelligence operation was consolidated under Liddy's aegis, and funds were authorized for recruiting Ruby II.[29] On March 1 Ruby II was in place in the headquarters of Senator Edmund Muskie, and began reporting. Two weeks later Magruder instructed Liddy to provide Hunt with an envelope containing $1,000 in cash, which Liddy did, not knowing that the money was to finance Hunt's trip to Denver—there to secretly interview hospitalized ITT lobbyist Dita Beard.

Despite all this activity, Magruder refused to tell Liddy that Mitchell had rejected the plan submitted on February 4. For more than a month, from early February until mid-March, Liddy badgered Magruder for some word and, with Hunt's help, persuaded Colson to urge Magruder to "get off the stick." Finally, as spring loomed around the corner, Magruder told Liddy that the project had been turned down as "too expensive." Once again, Liddy returned to the drawing boards and redrafted the proposal, reducing the budget to $250,000, a fourth of its initial total.

In relying upon Liddy to ascertain the truth about some matters that are disputed, one should take into account his contempt for Magruder and his admiration of Mitchell. Nevertheless, while Liddy has been called many things, "liar" is not one of them. However perverse his values may be, his account of the Watergate affair is widely regarded as one of the best and most candid of the memoirs that have been written on the subject.[30] And Liddy's description of Magruder's enthusiasm for Gemstone is far more credible than Magruder's claim that he disapproved of it. The fact that Magruder viewed Liddy's *third* plan in advance and then brought the matter up for approval at yet a third meeting with Mitchell is evidence enough of both Magruder's own inclinations and the near certainty that he was being pushed by someone higher up—presumably the person that Magruder attempted to protect throughout his testimony and in his memoir.

The third, and last, time that Gemstone was submitted for Mitch-

---

[29]Ruby I and Ruby II were Gemstone terms for intelligence operations against the Democrats' presidential candidates. Ruby I had been set in motion in late September 1971. Its principal operative was a private detective and Nixon loyalist named John Buckley, a.k.a. Fat Jack. Buckley planted a chauffeur in the Muskie campaign. When the chauffeur became a courier, Buckley was able to photograph various campaign documents. Ruby II was Thomas Gregory, a friend of Robert Bennett's nephew.
[30]Bob Woodward, "Gordon Liddy Spills His Guts," *Washington Post Book World*, May 18, 1980.

ell's consideration was on March 30 at Key Biscayne. Present, besides the vacationing Mitchell and the visiting Magruder, was Fred LaRue. This was not a meeting specifically organized for the purpose of discussing Liddy's intelligence plan. On the contrary, there were some thirty items submitted by Magruder having to do with the campaign, and each of them required Mitchell's decision. According to LaRue, he reviewed papers on each subject beforehand and then arranged the papers in order of priority, with the most important matters to be discussed first. He was concerned that with so many things to decide there would not be time to deal with them all at one session.

Among the papers to be discussed, LaRue recalled, was one that "outlined a plan of electronic surveillance." This he placed at the very bottom of the pile. As LaRue recalls, the meeting lasted several hours before this last matter was reached. "Mr. Magruder, as in the previous proposals, handed this paper to Mr. Mitchell. Mr. Mitchell read it, he asked me if I had read it and I told him I had. He asked me what I thought of it and I told him I did not think it was worth the risk." Mitchell then replied, "Well, this is not something that will have to be decided at this meeting."[31]

Mitchell's recollection of the meeting is much the same with respect to LaRue's description of only the briefest discussion of the intelligence plan. But, according to Mitchell, he was more forceful in his rejection of that plan than LaRue remembers. As Mitchell recalls, he said, "We don't need this. I am tired of hearing it. Out—let's not discuss it any further."[32] The discrepancy between LaRue's recollection and Mitchell's own is significant. Yet both men agree that the proposal was not approved, and one suspects that Mitchell's recollection is colored by the *wish* that he had been more forceful and had said what he recalls having said.

Magruder's recollection of the March 30 meeting, however, is entirely at odds with that of the other men. According to Magruder, Mitchell approved the $250,000 plan; there was extended discussion about "targets"; and in the end it was agreed that Liddy's first task should be to wiretap Larry O'Brien's telephone at the Watergate.

If Magruder is telling the truth, then obviously both Mitchell and

[31]Ervin committee *Hearings*, Book 6, pp. 2280–81.
[32]Ibid., Book 4, p. 1614.

LaRue are lying. And yet, if Magruder is telling the truth, we would expect him to have informed Liddy that the former Attorney General had approved the new plan and wanted him to bug O'Brien's phone.[33] In fact Magruder did tell Liddy that the budget had been approved. But it was not until a month had passed that Magruder approached Liddy with the instruction to bug O'Brien. This occurred at the "end of April," when O'Brien's bags had already been packed for Florida, and Liddy expressed the opinion that by then the target was not worth the effort. Still, he told Magruder, he would give it a try. As it happened, however, it would not be until the end of May that the break-in would be attempted—more than four months after the subject was first broached (according to Magruder), and fully two months after John Mitchell supposedly issued the order to carry out the bugging.

Would Magruder have waited a month before passing along an order of that magnitude from someone as important as John Mitchell? Hardly—not with Hunt and Liddy champing at the bit, with Colson calling to complain about delays, and with Strachan "tickling" him with queries about the status of the intelligence project. Would Mitchell, in any case, have silently tolerated a two-month hiatus in the implementation of an order to bug O'Brien? Of course not. Clearly, then, the order to bug O'Brien originated outside the CRP. Which is to say that Mitchell was a scapegoat for someone whom Magruder regarded as even more important. Who?

In his testimony before the Senate, John Dean recalled that, following Nixon's reelection, the President had said that Magruder could not return to the White House. Shortly thereafter, Dean testified, "Magruder had a conversation with Mr. [Paul] O'Brien [counsel to the CRP], in which he told O'Brien that he had received his final authorization for Liddy's activities from Gordon Strachan and that Strachan had reported that Haldeman had cleared the matter with the President. I reported this to Haldeman, who expressed concern over Magruder's statement. After I reported this information, the White House efforts to find a job for Magruder became intense."[34]

If Dean's testimony is accurate, Mitchell was made a scapegoat to protect the President and his chief of staff, whose knowledge of Liddy's operations was apparently more extensive than anyone

---

[33]Mitchell resigned as Attorney General on March 1, 1972, in order to become chairman of the CRP.

[34]Ervin committee *Hearings*, Book 3, p. 990.

wished to admit. This is not, of course, a complete surprise. Magruder was a protégé of Haldeman's, and it was logical that he would protect his patron. Moreover, the wish for a campaign intelligence capability had first arisen in Haldeman's office, and it was he who had approved the hiring of Donald Segretti to carry out dirty tricks against the Democrats.[35] Indeed, Magruder later testified that he had given Haldeman's deputy, Gordon Strachan, "complete information about the plans for bugging and burglary as they were developing."[36] As for Strachan himself, he would testify to having passed along instructions from Haldeman to Liddy. In early April 1972, for example, Liddy had been summoned to Strachan's office. There Strachan read a message from Haldeman, ordering him to switch his intelligence capabilities—whatever they were—from Senator Muskie to Senator McGovern.[37] Haldeman's responsibility for Liddy's activities seems well established, then, and the news that Nixon himself may have approved Liddy's operations—in what detail we do not know—is less than a shock. On the contrary, it is predictable inasmuch as the almost irrational interest in a politician such as the DNC's Larry O'Brien and Las Vegas's Hank Greenspun clearly reflected Nixon's own worries about his family's past and present ties to industrialist Howard Hughes. Such ties had helped him to lose a presidential election once before, and Nixon may well have feared new revelations.[38] Both O'Brien and Greenspun were deeply enmeshed in the reclusive billionaire's affairs, and no one could be certain how much either man knew about the President's own entanglements with Hughes.[39] There is no question, however, but that Nixon was concerned about the budding relationship between his brother, Donald, and Hughes aide John H. Meier.[40]

However deeply implicated Nixon and Haldeman may have been, it would be wrong to absolve Mitchell entirely of any respon-

[35]Ibid., Book 6, p. 2489.
[36]Ibid., Book 2, p. 858.
[37]Ibid., Book 6, p. 2476; see also Liddy, *Will*, pp. 215–16.
[38]Nixon's loss of the 1960 election is blamed in part upon revelations about a $205,000 loan made by the Hughes Tool Company to Donald Nixon. The loan was made in 1956, shortly after Nixon was elected to the vice presidency. Inadequately secured by Nixon family real estate, the loan was made public in the heat of the 1960 campaign, and created a scandal from which presidential candidate John F. Kennedy profited.
[39]O'Brien had recently held a "public relations" contract with the Hughes organization—which contract had been taken over by Robert R. Mullen Company in the wake of Robert Maheu's ouster as Howard Hughes's chief executive in Nevada. Greenspun was the recipient of memoranda between Hughes and Maheu.
[40]Meier became controversial for having spent millions of dollars buying worthless mining claims for Hughes. He later became a fugitive.

sibility for the Gemstone operation. Following the March 30 meeting in Key Biscayne, campaign finance chairman Maurice Stans asked Mitchell if Magruder had the authority to issue funds to Gordon Liddy. Mitchell replied that Magruder had *continuing* authority to do so, alluding to the fact that Magruder had been issuing funds to Liddy for months prior to Mitchell's arrival at the helm of the CRP. According to Mitchell, the inquiry seemed routine to him, and he did not inquire as to the amount of funds that Liddy wanted from Magruder (in fact it was $83,000).[41] While one is inclined to believe Mitchell, if only because Magruder's story is contradicted on so many points by Gordon Liddy, the one man whose silence Magruder wrongly counted on to remain golden, the former Attorney General's role in the Watergate affair seems most aptly comparable to that of a latter-day Pontius Pilate. As LaRue has testified, he procrastinated at the March 30 meeting, and, as Maurice Stans suggests, he turned a blind eye toward much of what was happening around him. In effect, Mitchell appears to have given Haldeman, Strachan and Magruder enough rope to hang themselves and, as it turned out, everyone else in the administration as well—including, not least of all, himself.

In a curious sidelight to the matter, "documentary proof" that Magruder lied was offered to the FBI, but for reasons that remain uncertain the information was declined by the bureau. According to Norman Karl McKenzie, who became a fellow inmate of Howard Hunt's at the federal penitentiary in Danbury, Connecticut, Hunt confided in him that he had a document or documents to prove that Magruder perjured himself throughout his Senate testimony. McKenzie offered to deliver this "proof" to the FBI in return for a pardon. In his interviews with the bureau, McKenzie claimed that the document(s) would exonerate Nixon with respect to the Watergate break-in itself while incriminating Magruder more deeply than before. The FBI declined McKenzie's offer despite the fact that it appeared to be fail-safe. That is, McKenzie said that he expected nothing unless all of the following conditions were met:

1. That he could produce the promised document(s).
2. The bureau proved able to authenticate the document(s).

---

[41]Erwin committee *Hearings*, Book 4, pp. 1616–20. According to Mitchell, Magruder had already expended upward of $3.5 million in his capacity as deputy director of the CRP.

3. The bureau agreed that the information had a material impact on the Watergate affair.

4. The document(s) constituted proof of Magruder's perjury.

Incredibly, the FBI refused even to examine the evidence that McKenzie was prepared to provide.[42]

While the FBI's indifference to McKenzie's information is a disappointment, the bureau can at least rely on the excuse that the information was offered at a time when the Watergate affair appeared to be all but over. Hunt had been sentenced to prison, and the prospect of "startling new developments" and rekindled controversy cannot have seemed to be in the national interest.

The CIA, however, had no such excuse when, in the spring of 1972, it suppressed the warnings of Eugenio Martinez.[43] In March, shortly before the disputed meeting between Mitchell and Magruder at Key Biscayne, Martinez met with his CIA case officer to raise the subject of his relationship to E. Howard Hunt. Just how much detail Martinez went into is unknown, but it was enough for the case officer to arrange an interview between Martinez and the CIA's chief of station in Miami, Jake Esterline. In that conversation, Martinez told Esterline that Hunt was employed by the White House and asked if Esterline was certain that he had been apprised of *all* CIA activities in the Miami area. Esterline, familiar with Hunt's reputation as a "black operative," was alarmed by the implications of the question, and immediately queried CIA headquarters as to Hunt's White House status.

More than six months had passed since the Fielding break-in, and so far as anyone knows, the Cubans had been operationally idle since then. Why Martinez should have suddenly felt the need for guidance is therefore a mystery. It may be, of course, that the Cubans engaged in activities of which we have yet to learn; it is also possible that Hunt somehow anticipated Magruder's imminent go-ahead on the Gemstone project, and communicated that information to the Cubans in Miami. But whatever the stimulus, Martinez was worried.

The reply to Esterline's inquiry was written by Cord Meyer,

[42]See FBI serial 139-4089-2400, obtained by the author through the Freedom of Information Act.

[43]My account of Martinez' warning, and the CIA's actions with respect to that warning, derives mostly from the Baker Report, published in the Ervin committee's *Final Report,* pp. 1145–51.

assistant deputy director of plans to Tom Karamessines, Hunt's former case officer. Meyer's message arrived in Miami on March 27 and, in the words of Senator Baker, it was "cryptic." In essence, Meyer told Esterline "not [to] . . . concern himself with the travels of Hunt in Miami, that Hunt was on domestic White House business of an unknown nature and that the Chief of Station should 'cool it.' The tone of the letter infuriated the Chief of Station and left him uneasy about the matter. . . . The Chief of Station requested that Martinez prepare in Spanish a report on the Hunt information."[44] Before Martinez sat down to write his report, however, he was instructed by his case officer that he should instead compile a "cover story," and that he should not put anything in the report "which might come back to haunt him." With these instructions in mind, Martinez wrote a vague account of the matter, an account that did not contain any of the alarming innuendos that he had made in earlier conversations. The report was then delivered to Jake Esterline on April 5, 1972, whereupon it was placed in a file and forgotten until after the Watergate arrests.

In effect, Esterline had been shut down from above *and* from below, by CIA headquarters *and* by his own subordinate, the case officer for Martinez. Whether this was a coincidence or a calculated effort to squelch Esterline's incipient investigation is uncertain because, as it happens, Martinez had *two* case officers during this same period. Following Martinez' conversation with Esterline in March, the Cuban's first case officer was suddenly replaced and sent abroad on an extended tour of duty. A second case officer, the portly Robert D. Ritchie (a.k.a. Buddha) was dispatched from Langley headquarters to take charge of Hunt's talkative agent. The exact date on which this changeover occurred cannot be ascertained. The CIA has resisted every Senate inquiry on the subject. It cannot be determined, then, whether the first or second case officer was responsible for muting Martinez' written report to Esterline. The question is anything but academic: if the report was bowdlerized at the direction of the second case officer, Robert Ritchie, then it would appear that someone in CIA headquarters was working overtime to protect Hunt's operations, and that Ritchie may have been dispatched to Miami for that purpose.[45]

---

[44]Ibid., pp. 1146–49.
[45]Ritchie subsequently became an employee of rogue CIA agent Edwin P. Wilson.

8.
Operation Sapphire

The first two weeks in April, beginning with Esterline's filing of the Martinez report and the April 7 disbursal of $83,000 to Gordon Liddy, were critical to the Watergate affair. On April 12, James McCord was given $65,000 out of that amount and told to purchase electronic eavesdropping equipment. That same day, the Office of Security issued orders to terminate the surveillance against Jack Anderson and dismantled the photographic observation nest across the street from the columnist's offices. It was three days later, on April 15, that William Haddad wrote to Anderson for the first time, informing him of plans to spy on the Democrats. Things were heating up.

In particular, they were heating up for a Washington, D.C., attorney named Phillip Mackin Bailley.[1] On April 6, the day before Liddy's first large appropriation was approved, Bailley was defending a client in the courthouse of the District of Columbia. Amid the proceedings, he received an urgent message that caused him to ask for an immediate adjournment. As he explained to the judge, the adjournment was necessary because he had just learned that the FBI was in the process of "raiding" his apartment and law offices. Astonished, the judge granted the adjournment, and Bailley departed posthaste to the offices of a friendly bail bondsman. There, he told me, he "hid out" in a back room, wondering what to do about the bureau's investigation of his private and business affairs.

The FBI probe centered on alleged violations of the Mann Act, a law prohibiting the transport of persons across state lines for

---

[1]My principal sources of information concerning the nature of Bailley's activities, and the identities of his playmates and victims, are court records, newspaper reports in the *Washington Post* and *Star*, and interviews with Bailley and John Rudy. It was Rudy who investigated the Bailley case for the U.S. Attorney's office.

immoral purposes.[2] One of the complainants in the case, an attractive University of Maryland coed, accused Bailley of seducing her with the help of wine and marijuana. Drugged, she had acquiesced to Bailley's taking pictures of her, photographs that were described as "pornographic." According to the Terrapin coed, Bailley then threatened to send the photographs to her parents and to school authorities if she did not submit to the attentions of his political cronies and business associates. So she did submit, on one occasion having sex with fifteen consecutive partners at a party hosted by Bailley in a suburban Maryland house. In her complaint, the young woman reported that one of her partners told her that he had paid Bailley $20 for her services.[3]

Bailley denies that. "We pulled a train on her," he says. "There wasn't any blackmail or money involved. It was just a party."

To understand the fear that coursed through Washington as a result of the ensuing grand jury investigation of Phil Bailley, it is necessary to know a bit more about Bailley, his life-style and his business. To begin with, he is a charmer, the essence of what some women think of as "cute." At 5 foot 6, he is an admitted "health nut," a jogger; he has curly black hair, twinkling blue eyes, a pug nose, and a face that instantly evokes the proverbial "map of Ireland." A compulsive raconteur on the subject of sex, he was named by his classmates in law school as the graduate "most likely to be disbarred," and the result of the 1972 FBI investigation would prove his classmates to have been clairvoyant. During his career as a lawyer, a career that lasted three years, he specialized in the defense of women charged with prostitution. Whether this was a business decision or a libidinous one is uncertain. Possibly it was both. The FBI decided at the end of its investigation that Bailley had at least four professional prostitutes working directly for him (as distinct from the numerous "amateurs" and part-timers who gathered at his side).[4] It was, in a way, an ideal situation: at once the women's pimp

[2]In June, Bailley would be charged in a 22-count indictment alleging violations of the Mann Act as well as interstate travel in aid of racketeering enterprises, extortion, procuring and pandering. Bailley would profess his innocence of all wrongdoing except fornication, while accepting a plea bargain in which he pleaded guilty to a charge of transporting a woman in the District of Columbia for the purpose of prostitution. See Winston Groom and Woody West, "Capitol Hill Call-Girl Ring," *Washington Star*, June 9, 1972, p. 1, and Lawrence Meyer, "Lawyer Pleads Guilty in Call Girl Case," *Washington Post*, September 30, 1972.
[3]Jim Mann, "Lawyer Indicted in Hill Call-Girl Ring," *Washington Post*, June 10, 1972, p. 1.
[4]Interview with former Assistant U.S. Attorney John Rudy. See also Lawrence Meyer, "Lawyer Pleads Guilty in Call Girl Case."

and their lawyer, his conversations with them were protected by attorney-client privilege.

To consider Bailley only in terms of prostitution, however, is a mistake. He was, in his own words, "the man who brought the good times back." He was young, on the make, and well connected in political circles. His friends and business associates included appointees and career employees of the Department of Health, Education and Welfare (HEW), the Law Enforcement Assistance Administration (LEAA), secretaries on Capitol Hill, a brigade of Young Dems, White House employees, Maryland pols and veterans of Senator Edward Kennedy's political campaigns. Indeed, Bailley liked to brag that he had been intimately involved with one of the young secretaries who had been at Chappaquiddick.

Among the business that he mixed with pleasure was a vest-pocket investment corporation that Bailley claims he founded in a Washington bar. According to Bailley, the firm was created as "an excuse to have parties"—meetings of the board of directors at which little business seems to have been transacted. All of the firm's officers, except one, were personal friends of Bailley's—young professionals who enjoyed a good time. The exception was a man who, Bailley says, happened to be in the same bar drinking with his friends when the firm was conceived and its articles of incorporation discussed. "Everyone thought [he] was someone else's friend," Bailley told me, "so we just included him [as an officer of the firm]." In fact the young man was an employee of the Defense Intelligence Agency (DIA).

According to Bailley, the man was present at a meeting of the "board of directors" that quickly became controversial. The cause of the controversy was a handful of pornographic photos that Bailley passed around the conference table while the minutes of the previous meeting were being read. The woman reading the minutes was a beautiful young attorney employed in the Office of the President. She enjoyed the parties that often followed the board meetings, and occasionally performed secretarial chores for the firm. The photos snickered at by the men around the table were of her, though she was unaware of that. When the pictures reached the DIA man, Bailley says, he reacted violently, protesting that the woman posing in flagrante delicto was an employee of the President in one of the most sensitive components of government. The photos were therefore a national security matter, and, as a DIA employee, he would

have to report the incident. It was this report, Bailley believes, that
led to the FBI investigation that was to ruin his career.

Whatever the cause of the investigation, alarm spread in the city
after the raid on Bailley's apartment. Among the evidence that the
bureau had seized were various "marital aids"—dildos, a bullwhip,
pornographic still photos and "home movies" of a related kind—as
well as a pair of address books with a great many names in them.
It was these address books that represented the FBI's most important lead, and many of those named in the books were soon subpoenaed to appear before a grand jury.

It was an explosive situation. Bailley's playmates were by no
means confined to single college students, typists and whores. On
the contrary, he was amorously and photographically involved with
the wife of at least one powerful senator, the wife of one of the most
important liberal thinkers in the United States, a White House
attorney with a penchant for being horsewhipped and an executive
secretary on Capitol Hill who was not only beautiful and politically
active but more than a little inclined toward voyeurism, sadomaso-
chism and zoophilia. In all, more than a hundred people were interviewed in connection with the Bailley case. As former Assistant
U.S. Attorney John Rudy recalls, "We had them coming up and
down the back elevator to my office so no one would see them. They
were beautiful girls and they were terrified of being connected [in
public] to Bailley's activities."

One of the key aspects of the relationship of the Bailley scandal
to the Watergate affair was Bailley's friendship with workers at the
DNC's headquarters and in particular, Bailley told me, his familiarity with the comings and goings of DNC worker R. Spencer Oliver.
It was because Bailley knew that Oliver was often traveling that the
latter, through no fault of his own, became a central figure and
victim in the Watergate scandal.

The received version of that scandal, the version propounded
over and over again in the courts, the Congress and the press, tells
us that it was Spencer Oliver's telephone that James McCord
bugged. As to why Oliver was allegedly singled out, the record is
anything but clear. Reporters have speculated that it had to do with
the fact that Oliver's father was an employee of the Robert R.
Mullen Company and a rival of Howard Hunt's.[5] But that was just

[5]The rivalry between the senior Oliver and Hunt was caused by the former's responsibility
for the lucrative Howard Hughes account at the Mullen Company and, also, by his having
made overtures to Robert Bennett about making young Oliver a partner in the firm. For

speculation, as, indeed, was Oliver's own theory: that he was singled out because of his frequent contact with Democratic state leaders. As for the burglars themselves, they are by turns mum and self-contradictory on the subject of Spencer Oliver and his telephone.

In reality, what made Oliver's DNC telephone uniquely sensitive was its relationship to a complex of prostitution activities located in the nearby Columbia Plaza Apartments. These are a group of luxury residential buildings that form a line-of-sight triangle with the Howard Johnson's motel and the Watergate office building, each of which is within a short walk from the others and each of which would play an important part in the bugging activities that would soon send McCord and his colleagues to jail. The prostitutes working at the Columbia Plaza were many. They included "a lush blonde" (this is Bailley's description) whom we may call Tess.[6] There were at least two madams, Lil Lori and Helen Henderson, who used the apartments at the Columbia Plaza and, farther away, the Woodner Hotel.[7] One of the apartments used for assignations was in the Columbia Plaza building at 2440 Virginia Avenue, directly behind the apartment in which Tess resided. Like Tess's rendezvous, the one rented by Lori faced the Watergate and, because it was in a taller building, was also in line of sight with the Howard Johnson's motel.

Besides their location at the Columbia Plaza Apartments, the prostitutes had at least two things in common. The first was the homogeneity of their clients. With few exceptions, they were professional men—lobbyists, lawyers, stockbrokers, physicians, congressional aides and real estate developers. They were among the movers and shakers of the capital, and included at least one U.S. senator, an astronaut, a Saudi prince, a clutch of U.S. and KCIA intelligence agents and a host of prominent Democrats.[8] The pre-

---

Hunt's feelings on the subject, see *Undercover*, p. 142. Apparently Hunt suspected that Oliver was a CIA agent—a suspicion that Oliver himself vehemently denies.

[6] The blonde that Bailley referred to was living and working under an alias. Tess is neither her real name nor the alias that she used.

[7] Lil Lori is still in business in Washington, the proprietor of the King's Kastle Health Salon ("Beautiful Attendants, Plush Decor"), in the Capitol Hill section of the city. She declined to be interviewed. As for Helen Henderson, she seems to have disappeared from the Washington scene.

[8] The identities of these clients derive from a trick book seized by Washington police in a raid on the Columbia Plaza. The trick book consists of names and referrals with coded notations having to do with the clients' sexual preferences and payments.

ponderance of Dems in the boudoirs of the Columbia Plaza was probably due to the proximity of the DNC's headquarters at the Watergate. According to a 1971 police intelligence report, a Washington pimp associated with Lori and Henderson had issued orders for their girls to "solicit in major hotels in the Washington area. The Watergate Hotel . . . was a prime source of business."[9]

The second thing that Lori, Henderson and Tess had in common was Lou Russell, a man whose life was devoted to booze, whores and anti-Communism (roughly in that order). His attorney, Bernard ("Bud") Fensterwald, sometimes hired him to perform investigative assignments. When the time came to pay Russell for this work, Fensterwald preferred to do so on a daily basis lest the private eye be tempted to blow a week's pay on a lost weekend. According to Russell's friends, his Q Street apartment was a kind of way station for depressed hookers, a safe place with someone who did not mind listening to sad stories. No one objected, then, when Russell chose to idle away his leisure time in the apartments at the Columbia Plaza. He was a friend to many of the girls, a sometime customer, a free-lance bouncer and a source of referrals. In addition, he was a formidable presence: his training as a specialist in making difficult apprehensions for the FBI and his years of hardening as a professional baseball player "in every league but the majors" made him a threat to unruly customers.

The relationship of Phil Bailley to Tess was more ambiguous than Russell's. In Bailley's mind, he and the call girl were having an affair. That conclusion was reasonable, since, after all, they were making love and she demanded no payment. But there was more to it than that. During the late winter of 1971–72, Tess asked a favor of Bailley, and he quickly granted it. She wanted him to use his connections at the DNC to facilitate her trade. The pols would make good customers, and the arrangements could be made in a most discreet way. That is, a prostitution out-call service could be set up inside the Democrats' headquarters. All that was needed was an office, a spare telephone that did not connect to the DNC's switchboard, and someone inside the DNC who would help with referrals.

Bailley soon found all three. As executive director of the Associa-

[9]"Intelligence information concerning call girl and prostitution house activities of Walter R. Riggin," by Morals Division plainclothesmen Michael W. Hartford and George E. Bradford, February 8, 1971, addressed to Lieutenant George F. Richards, Prostitution and Perversion Branch of the Washington Metropolitan Police Department.

tion of Democratic State Chairmen, Spencer Oliver was often on the road. At those times his office—whose elegant appointments matched the important sound of his title—was empty. With the help of a secretary at the DNC, a woman whom Bailley sometimes dated, the lawyer says that, unknown to Oliver, he was able to arrange for Oliver's personal business telephone to be used for arranging assignations between Tess and the Democrats.[10]

Bailley's friend would tell the prospective clients that soon after entering Oliver's vacant office the telephone would ring twice. They were not to answer it. Immediately afterward, the telephone would ring again, and this time they were to pick it up. Bailley's girlfriend would then show photos of Tess to the would-be johns, explaining that these were pictures of the woman on the other end of the line. When the john went into Oliver's office to await his call, Bailley's girlfriend would telephone Tess to say that a client was waiting. Tess would then place a call to Oliver's phone, ring twice, hang up and call again.

The advantages of the arrangement were obvious. At the least, it locked Tess into a lucrative trade while providing the visiting pols with a service that seemed entirely discreet. The risk of embarrassing police involvement was nil. There was no need for either the call girl or the client to loiter in the Watergate Bar, hoping to make contact. All negotiations were handled over the telephone, before the parties met, so the awkwardness of face-to-face haggling was eliminated. The client knew what the woman looked like, and as for the call girl herself, she could take comfort in the fact that her customers were, however indirectly, vouched for by no less than the Democratic National Committee. What the politicians did not realize, however, was that Lou Russell was recording their telephone conversations with some of the prostitutes at the Columbia Plaza, including, as we will see, those with Tess.

At about the time that Bailley had established Tess's liaison with the DNC, Russell purchased $3,000 in electronic eavesdropping equipment from a former partner of his, John Leon, the proprietor of Allied Investigators Inc.[11] That this equipment was purchased on

---

[10]Because the telephone in question was a personal appliance that did not belong to the DNC, it was not connected to the DNC's switchboard. As a result, it was widely regarded as the most private and secure telephone in the Democrats' headquarters. Because of this, DNC workers sometimes borrowed it to make calls that were uniquely sensitive.

[11]Interview of Charles F. Knight and Gordon Hess conducted on August 16, 1973, by the

behalf of McCord is likely: Russell was McCord's employee and had neither funds nor a bank account of his own. Leon himself was of the opinion that Russell had made the purchase for McCord, and so was Gordon Hess, a former Washington police officer in whom Russell confided.

That Russell was bugging the whores at the Columbia Plaza is unquestionable. Shortly after McCord's arrest, attorney Bud Fensterwald hired Russell to investigate certain non-Watergate-related events in which the Committee to Investigate Assassinations (CtIA) was interested. Accordingly, Russell had frequent occasion to converse with CtIA worker Bob Smith in the foundation's offices. As Smith told me, Russell regaled him with anecdotes about intimate conversations between prostitutes and the politicians at the DNC. "This was long before Alfred Baldwin came forward with his story about McCord's eavesdropping activities," Smith recalled. Bob Smith wasn't the only one to hear Russell's stories. The private eye also bragged to Fensterwald and told another investigator, former Treasury agent Kennard Smith, that he was tape-recording conversations between Columbia Plaza prostitutes and their clients. The prostitutes, Russell told Ken Smith, were cooperating in the venture.

Still, many questions about Russell's bugging activities remain unanswered. It is uncertain, for example, whether Russell listened to tape-recordings of conversations that another agent monitored, or whether he himself was responsible for monitoring the Columbia Plaza bugs.

Certainly Russell thought enough of the operation to go to unusual lengths to protect it. According to John Rudy, the lead prosecutor in the Bailley case, Russell went out of his way to affect the direction of his investigation. Rudy said that in the spring of 1972 the private eye urged him to investigate a bordello near Dupont Circle. There, Russell told the prosecutor, video cameras had been installed to document the sadomasochistic proclivities of certain Washingtonians, including a number of local judges and attorneys. Rudy had no choice but to check out that information. Verifying it, he established an investigative file, using the code name House Calls. Subsequently, evidence was obtained which suggested to

---

Ervin committee's minority counsel, Fred D. Thompson, and Don Sanders, staff assistant to Senator Howard Baker.

Rudy that some judges had been blackmailed, and that others had accepted sexual favors in return for acquittals or lenient sentencings. In retrospect, however, Rudy says that while Russell's information was accurate, it was apparent that Russell was trying to divert him from the Bailley case and from the Columbia Plaza. As we will see, that effort would prove unnecessary: the Justice Department would bring pressure upon Rudy to turn his attention "to more important things," and the judge who was to try the case, Nixon appointee Charles Richey, would all but order the litigants to settle the case in chambers.[12]

While many details about the Columbia Plaza operation remain uncertain, its purpose must be obvious. This cannot have been to collect "political intelligence"—not, at least, in the conventional sense of that term—because prostitutes and their clients do not often hold political discussions in bed. In bugging the Columbia Plaza's whores, eavesdroppers could expect to learn details of sexual liaisons between particular individuals, but not much else.

As to the destination of the product generated by the monitoring operation, we know that Russell's employer, James McCord, was secretly in league with Howard Hunt. Hunt, as we have seen, had established within the White House a clandestine means for reporting "gossip" on a regular basis to psychologists at the CIA. According to Senate investigators, this gossip was sexual in nature. Since it was McCord's friend and employee Lou Russell who was directly responsible for carrying out the eavesdropping operation with the prostitutes at the Columbia Plaza, it seems reasonable to infer that Tess's liaison with the DNC was contrived to generate that gossip. Details of her dalliances with the prominent might be used for blackmail, but, less crudely, they would also prove useful in construction of the psychological "machines" mentioned earlier.

The reader may recall that prostitutes were an original part of Gordon Liddy's Gemstone plan. The hookers were to be deployed on a houseboat across the avenue from the Fontainebleau Hotel in Miami Beach, where, presumably, they would have been patronized by Democrats attending their party's national convention. This aspect of Gemstone, code-named Sapphire, was scuttled, however, when Liddy revised the plan in an effort to meet a lower budget;

[12]It was Judge Richey, also, who presided over the critical civil litigation brought by the DNC against Nixon et al. in the aftermath of the Watergate arrests.

at Magruder's suggestion, prostitutes were to be used in Washington instead, when the time seemed ripe.[13] And yet, so far as Liddy and Magruder knew, this particular component was never activated. To the best of their knowledge, there were no prostitutes involved in the Watergate affair and no take from any operations of that kind.

According to fugitive ex-CIA officer Frank Terpil, CIA-directed sexual blackmailing operations were intensive in Washington at about the time of the Watergate scandal. One of those operations, Terpil claims, was run by his former partner, Ed Wilson. Wilson's base of operations for arranging trysts for the politically powerful was, Terpil says, Korean agent Tong Sun Park's George Town Club.[14] In a letter to the author, Terpil explained that "Historically, one of Wilson's Agency jobs was to subvert members of both houses [of Congress] by any means necessary. . . . Certain people could be easily coerced by living out their sexual fantasy in the flesh. . . . A remembrance of these occasions [was] permanently recorded via selected cameras, I'm sure for historical purposes only. The technicians in charge of filming . . . [were] TSD personnel.[15] The unwitting porno stars advanced in their political careers, some of [whom] may still be in office. You may now realize the total ineffectiveness of the 'Watchdog Committee' assigned to oversee clandestine operations."[16]

In considering Terpil's allegations, it must be emphasized that he

13Liddy, *Will*, pp. 203, 206.
14Revived from near bankruptcy by Tong Sun Park, the George Town Club is located in Suter's Tavern, a historic building in Washington's prestigious Georgetown section. The club's first president was Park's friend Robert Keith Gray, who was also a director of Ed Wilson's flagship firm, Consultants International, Inc. (In 1981 Gray would serve as co-chairman of the Presidential Inaugural Commission for Ronald Reagan.) A business associate of Wilson's, Park was the central figure in a 1978 investigation by the Senate Select Committee on Ethics. A belated investigation, the probe concerned Park's activities in Washington during the early 1970s. According to the testimony of a former director of the Korean Central Intelligence Agency (KCIA), the George Town Club was an intelligence front created to facilitate the "lobbying activities" of the Korean government and the KCIA, whose agent Park was. As such, the club was part of a network of "assets" (the Diplomat National Bank was another), used by the KCIA in efforts to manipulate members of Congress, the White House, U.S. intelligence agencies and the press. For further details, see the Senate's 1978 report entitled *Korean Influence Inquiry*.
15TSD: the Technical Services Division of the CIA.
16Terpil's letter was sent to me in the fall of 1981. At the time, Terpil was in hiding in Beirut, a fugitive from an array of federal charges having to do with the illicit transport of explosives aboard a commercial airliner, the training of terrorists and solicitation to murder. Terpil wrote to me because I had interviewed him in connection with a documentary film, *Confessions of a Dangerous Man*, which I had helped to produce for British television and the Public Broadcasting Service (PBS).

is their only source, and that federal prosecutors doubt his veracity. Even if the allegations are true, it may turn out that the activities of Wilson and Park were separate from each other and from those taking place at the Columbia Plaza. The only evidence that would connect Wilson and Park to the Columbia Plaza consists of the entries in Lil Lori's trick book, mentioning men named Ed Wilson and "Tungsten Park," and perhaps the circumstances surrounding the rental of Tess's apartment.

According to a prosecutor in the U.S. attorney's office in Washington, Tess's apartment was rented in the name of Bailley's former girlfriend, the White House attorney who was fired for posing in the nude. Bailley, however, says that Tess told him that the apartment had been rented on her behalf by a wealthy defense contractor, a sometime lobbyist on Capitol Hill who owned a huge farm and claimed to "hail" from Houston, Texas. Bailley cannot recall the man's name, but remembers that "he was a big guy, about six two. Tough-talking, rich. We used to kid him because he said he had this ranch, or farm, in Texas. But he was always in Washington, so you wondered why the place didn't fall to pieces. He must have been a gentleman farmer, though, because he knew a lot about it. Horses, cattle—like that."

The circumstances surrounding the rental of Tess's apartment are something of a mystery, then. From the standpoint of "tradecraft," the "gentleman farmer" had done a good job: any investigation of the apartment would yield the information that it had been rented, apparently as a convenience address, by an attorney in the Office of the President.[17] That information would either end such an investigation immediately or target it directly at 1600 Pennsylvania Avenue. In either case, the gentleman farmer would probably be untraceable.

One wonders if this was Ed Wilson. Like Tess's sugardaddy, Wilson was a big tough-talking defense contractor. He was also a lobbyist, albeit secretly on behalf of the CIA, and met often with Capitol Hill legislators to discuss a wide range of issues. Indeed, he was so successful at this that his friend and frequent weekend guest, Hubert Humphrey, urged in 1968 that Wilson be appointed Assistant Secretary of the Army. The laird of a 16,000-acre estate in

[17]Questioned about the apartment's rental, the attorney told me that she knew nothing about it, or about "Tess."

Centerville, Virginia, Wilson was a gentleman farmer and a million-aire twenty-four times over. His business affairs, moreover, often took him to Houston, Texas, the headquarters of Around World Shipping and Forwarding, Inc., one of his more important firms.

Wilson, of course, fits Bailley's description to a T. But beyond that one cannot go. Federal prosecutors feel certain that had Wilson been engaged in the kind of blackmailing operation that Terpil has described, Wilson himself would have confessed it in the hope of receiving a reduced sentence. However intriguing the circumstances, the possibility is real that where Wilson—and Park—are concerned, we are in the presence of nothing more than coincidence.

9.

Mr. Hoover's
Secret Files

While the Bailley case was simmering before a grand jury, Gordon
Liddy "introduced" James McCord to Howard Hunt. The introduction took place in April in the offices of the Mullen Company,
across the street from the CRP. According to Hunt, McCord and
Liddy "came to my office one afternoon after five o'clock. . . . Mr.
McCord and I had never seen each other. We only knew one or two
people in common. . . .[1] We did not play 'Whom do you know' very
long. Mr. McCord was rather taciturn. He wasn't a field man, he was
a home office type; we had very little to exchange in terms of war
stories, if I may put it that way. And Liddy said, in effect, 'McCord,
here, is going to handle all the electronics side of things. Now we
can go ahead, and the DNC will be the first target.' "[2]

According to Liddy, the DNC had been scheduled as one of the
later targets in a series of Gemstone operations calculated to wreck
the Democrats' election campaign. He was somewhat surprised,
therefore, when Jeb Magruder called him to his office at the end of
April and asked if he could get into the Watergate. Liddy was
confident that he could, but pointed out that an entry at such an
early date was premature: the DNC would not be a worthwhile
target unless and until it became the headquarters of the Democrats'
presidential candidate. But Magruder would not be forestalled. He
wanted DNC Chairman Larry O'Brien's office bugged—a waste of

[1]As we have seen, McCord and Hunt had many acquaintances in common, including such
close acquaintances as Richard Helms, Howard Osborn, Dr. Edward Gunn and, it appears,
Harry Ruiz-Williams.
[2]Nedzi report, p. 519. Cf. Hunt's *Undercover*, p. 210.

time and money, in Liddy's view, because O'Brien had already decamped for Florida and was spending most of his time there in preparation for the Democrats' convention. Nevertheless, Magruder said, he wanted O'Brien's office wired, his phones bugged, and any available documents photographed. He didn't care if it used up the only "optional entry" in the Gemstone plan; he wanted it done as soon as possible. It was important, he said.[3]

Why was it important? And why was it important so suddenly? Liddy was never told. A good soldier, he followed his orders unquestioningly, while privately surmising that the operation was motivated by political counterintelligence concerns. But that was just a guess.

Whatever the reason for Magruder's sudden interest in the DNC, McCord began to acquire electronic eavesdropping devices and related equipment that April. His sources were several, his needs extraordinary. Besides the transmitters (or bugs) themselves, he needed a sophisticated receiver, walkie-talkies, tape recorders and more—most of it legal, some of it not. The receiver came from the Bell & Howell Corporation. It was sold to McCord by its representative William McCuin, who was under the false impression that McCord was a Secret Service agent. This impression was understandable. McCuin had met McCord at a demonstration of equipment at the White House, a demonstration for the benefit of McCord's friend Alfred Wong. That demonstration took place in late November 1971, and it is uncertain how and why McCord came to be present. It is a fact, however, that McCord made quite an impression on the Bell & Howell representatives. An FBI interview with McCuin elicited the information that McCord behaved so obnoxiously, interjecting a constant stream of querulous questions, that McCuin lost his temper and upbraided him. Subsequently McCuin reconsidered the wisdom of offending a lucrative client (the Secret Service), and so wrote an apology to McCord. The practical effect of the incident, however, was to identify McCord in the minds of the Bell & Howell representatives as an important Secret Service official in the White House.[4]

The supplier of the actual bugging devices, however, was not Bell & Howell. It was a Chicago wireman named Michael Stevens, the

[3]Liddy, *Will*, pp. 219–20.
[4]FBI interview with William McCuin, July 5, 1972.

proprietor of Stevens Research Laboratories. According to Stevens and two of his associates, McCord visited him in early May to place an order for ten eavesdropping devices, including a room microphone and assorted telephone bugs. Not only was Stevens a supplier of sophisticated electronic equipment to the CIA and other U.S. intelligence agencies, but he was also a sometime contract agent of the CIA.[5] One of the men whom Stevens approached for assistance in putting together the eavesdropping devices was Robert F. Barcal, owner of Electronic Specialty Products (ESP). According to Barcal, he agreed to help on the condition that Stevens could demonstrate that he was authorized by a federal agency to make the equipment. Stevens then produced a letter from the CIA providing that authorization.[6] In the aftermath of the Watergate arrests, Stevens would contact the FBI, requesting "immunity" in return for his testimony. According to Stevens, McCord justified his purchase of bugging equipment by displaying CIA identification.[7] What made Stevens approach the FBI was the December 1972 plane crash that killed Dorothy Hunt. Stevens told the FBI that his life had been threatened anonymously, and that he believed Mrs. Hunt's death to have been a homicide. He claimed that the more than $10,000 in cash found among her personal effects was intended for him in return for his silence.[8] He was breaking that silence out of fear, and in the hope that the FBI could protect him against those who, as he believed, had murdered Mrs. Hunt.

The circumstances of Dorothy Hunt's death are not at issue here, though others have questioned the official finding that the crash was an accident.[9] The significance of Michael Stevens' story rests, in some measure, with the fact that it provides even more evidence of the CIA's complicity in the affairs of Hunt and McCord—complicity long after the alleged termination of agency assistance to the

[5]FBI serial 139-4089-2398 makes reference to an assignment that Stevens undertook for the CIA in Arizona during September 1970. Other FBI reports concerning Stevens are black with deletions justified on the grounds of "national security."
[6]Ibid., reflecting the FBI's May 24, 1973, interview with Robert F. Barcal.
[7]Ibid. According to a Jack Anderson column of May 8, 1973, these CIA credentials were in the name of "George Russell."
[8]Also found among Mrs. Hunt's belongings at the site of the crash were a $100 bill, with the notation "Good Luck FS" written on it, and a piece of paper with the words "Dr. Gary MORRIS—Hypnotist" (FBI serial 139-4089-153, December 15, 1972).
[9]Among those who advocated a conspiratorial interpretation of the crash was Sherman Skolnick, a free-lance investigator. See Carl Oglesby, *The Yankee and Cowboy War* (Mission, Kansas: Sheed Andrews and McMeel, Inc., 1977).

White House spooks in August 1971. Stevens' reason for approaching the FBI seems genuine: he sought protection, and had nothing else to gain. On the contrary, by coming forward he had everything to lose. On its surface, however, Stevens' assertion that Mrs. Hunt was flying to Chicago to pay for his silence seemed to make little sense. Why should anyone pay to ensure the silence of a man whose testimony, after all, would only implicate himself in a felony that, in effect, had been solved months before by the Watergate arrests? If anyone was to pay anyone else for his silence, one might have imagined that Stevens would be sending cashier's checks to McCord. But no. The significance of Stevens' information was that it directly implicated the CIA in the Watergate affair. According to Stevens, he agreed to supply eavesdropping equipment to McCord in the spring of 1972 because McCord claimed, and the agency apparently confirmed, that he was engaged on a mission for the CIA. It was this, Stevens believed, that Mrs. Hunt was paying to conceal.

For reasons that apparently had to do with "national security," Stevens was neither questioned by the Senate's Ervin committee nor prosecuted for his role as a supplier to McCord. Still, we are not quite done with him. FBI files contain an extraordinary report concerning the equipment that McCord ordered from Stevens.[10] According to the FBI, McCord spent $15,000 to $20,000 at Stevens Research Laboratories. Among the equipment he ordered were four telephone bugs (believed to be those seized in the June 17 arrests), eight high-fidelity tape recorders concealed in briefcases, and three eavesdropping devices with astonishing capabilities. That is, the last three devices, consisting of two room bugs and a telephone bug, were "capable of feeding into the nation's highly-classified satellite communications network."[11] McCord was arrested before the satellite bugs were completed.

A detailed description of this equipment will be provided shortly, but for the moment let us consider whether Stevens' story is to be credited, and if so, what use McCord could possibly have made of such equipment, because, obviously, the Committee to Re-elect the President did *not* have a satellite into which to feed. As to the first part of the problem, Stevens had no obvious motive to lie—on the

[10]FBI serial 139-4089-2159, May 16, 1973.
[11]Ibid. Chicago *Today* articles of May 14–16, 1973.

contrary, barring his panic at the death of Mrs. Hunt, he had every reason to remain silent. Moreover, those parts of Stevens' account that can be checked are true: McCord admits that Stevens was his supplier and that he had sophisticated equipment on order with Stevens at the time of the June 17 arrests.

Stevens' interviews with the FBI and other investigators were leaked to the Chicago press, whose reports were made part of the FBI's own file. In that file the following account is given: "Investigators said that [Stevens'] shop, which opened in 1971, was partly financed by a federal intelligence organization, probably the DIA [Defense Intelligence Agency]. The three bugs that could transmit to the communications satellites were never picked up by McCord, Stevens told investigators. Stevens destroyed them after the Watergate arrests. . . . Knowing the orbit of a satellite, a person using a simple compass could point the antenna of the bug toward the orbit. Because of the supersensitivity of the satellite, it could pick up the extremely low-powered signal. . . . The antenna is built into the case of the small device." The report then goes on to say that the satellite in question is "parked" in a synchronous orbit 22,500 miles above the earth. Once the satellite receives the signal, it is relayed to a ground receiving station, and retransmitted to the appropriate agency—e.g., to the NSA, DIA or CIA. "Stevens told investigators that the bugs were set to transmit on the frequency used by the CIA to track suspected double-agents in Viet Nam. Stevens reportedly said that McCord never mentioned the satellite network, but that, based on his [own] knowledge, Stevens was certain that it [the bugging device] was intended for feeding into the network. Investigators said that the special high-powered bugs even included a device capable of sending a special signal to 'unlock' the satellite. Without the signal, it is impossible to feed into the satellite. . . . Stevens told investigators that he was assisted by [unidentified] 'experts' in assembling the special bugging equipment. . . ."[12]

Of what use would this equipment have been to McCord? All of the bugging activities of which we have knowledge, whether only planned or actually realized, involved a nearby human monitor— that is to say, someone across the street who could intercept and listen to the bugged conversations. These conversations, moreover, were to have taken place in Washington and Miami, not in Albania

[12]Ibid.

or East Kurdistan. Why, then, would McCord have needed satellite facilities designed for the use of agents in places so remote that conventional communications would not have sufficed? Only one explanation suggests itself. The devices described by Stevens had a unique advantage in that they eliminated the need for a monitor to be on the scene. By transmitting the bugged conversations to a stationary satellite, the intercepts would have gone directly to the ultimate consumer—in this case, to the CIA, since it was to CIA frequencies that Stevens says McCord's apparatus was tuned.

It was at about the time of McCord's visit to Stevens in Chicago that the U.S. intelligence community, and the Nixon administration at large, experienced a profound change. On the night of May 1–2, 1972, FBI Director J. Edgar Hoover died in his sleep. Immediately, on the orders of Acting Attorney General Richard Kleindienst, Hoover's office was sealed, and the locks to its doors were changed. Even as this process was under way, and as the director's body was en route to the mortician's, Hoover's lifelong companion, Clyde Tolson, packed a suitcase and moved into the director's home.

Hoover's death represented an opportunity that the Nixon administration was determined to seize. For more than fifty years Hoover had presided over one of the largest investigative/intelligence agencies in the world. More than any other figure in American history, he was privy to the deepest secrets of the superpower and those who managed it. As journalist Anthony Lukas has written, the "files in his private office . . . detailed the private lives of Presidents, members of Congress, federal officials, and those who merely tried to oppose him and his policies. Many of the files . . . contained highly derogatory information on the sex lives, drinking habits, and other indiscretions of these people. . . . Hoover had enough dirt on most public figures to tar their reputations irredeemably if not put them in jail."[13] And he used those files, intimidating some of the most powerful men in the world, including, not least of all, President Richard Nixon.[14] Compared with the contents of

[13]Lukas, *Nightmare*, p. 35.
[14]Among the sources that refer to Hoover's threats to Richard Nixon, two may be cited here: *Inquiry into the Destruction of Former FBI Director J. Edgar Hoover's Files and FBI Recordkeeping, Hearings before the Government Information and Individual Rights Subcommittee of the House Committee on Government Operations*, 94th Cong., 1st sess., December 1, 1975, p. 11; and the October 22, 1971, memorandum from Gordon Liddy to Bud Krogh entitled "Subject: The Directorship of the FBI."

Hank Greenspun's Las Vegas safe, the chatter inside the DNC and the gossip of Clifton DeMotte, the FBI director's secret files were thought to be the end game of American politics.

Hoover's death was convenient for the Nixon administration in that it solved the problem of bringing the FBI to heel, while also presenting an opportunity of historic dimensions—that is, to take possession of the legendary files. It should come as no surprise, then, that Acting FBI Director Patrick Gray (appointed to the post within hours of Hoover's death) arrived at FBI headquarters on the afternoon of May 2 in quest of the files. The man he went to was John P. Mohr, assistant director of the FBI in charge of administration.

> MR. MOHR: Mr. Gray came up to see me, that is the afternoon that Mr. Hoover died, I believe. He wanted to know where the secret files were. I told him that there were no secret files that I knew of. . . . He left. The meeting, I would say, was fairly amiable. He called me the next morning before nine o'clock and said he wanted to see me. He came into my office and sat down and he was agitated. He wanted to know again where the secret files were. This time, I got a little agitated myself. I had told him there were none. . . . Judging from his conversation and his comments, not specifically what he said, I thought he was looking for secret files that would embarrass the Nixon administration. . . . We got to the point where I told him in no uncertain terms that there were no secret files. I will not cuss here, but I think I did cuss at him a little bit. I think the secretaries even heard me out there talking to him. . . . At that point he sat down in his chair and he said, "Look Mr. Mohr, I am a hard-headed Irishman and nobody pushes me around." I looked him right in the eye and said, "Look Mr. Gray, I am a hard-headed Dutchman and nobody pushes me around." With that, he left.[15]

There had been a shouting match, then, and the upshot of it was that the Nixon administration was frustrated in its efforts to secure what it regarded as its rightful legacy—the personal and political intelligence dossiers that Hoover was thought to have been compiling for nearly half a century.

What happened after Gray's conversation with Mohr is as uncertain as the fate of the files themselves. What is known is that on May 3 a contingent of ten Miami Cubans was brought to Washington on

---

[15] *Inquiry into The Destruction of Former FBI Director J. Edgar Hoover's Files and FBI Record-keeping*, pp. 88–89.

an emergency basis, and at considerable expense, on the orders of
G. Gordon Liddy and E. Howard Hunt. Liddy was, of course, an
ex-FBI man and (considered himself) the administration's resident
"expert" on the subject of J. Edgar Hoover and the FBI. Indeed, in
October 1971 Liddy had written a lengthy memorandum on the
subject, recommending that Hoover be replaced. The memo received considerable praise not merely from the Plumbers' Bud
Krogh but (Liddy tells us) from John Ehrlichman and the President
himself.[16] Given the administration's sense of urgency with respect
to Hoover's files, and the frustration it felt at being unable to acquire
the files legitimately, the sudden arrival of Barker's men in Washington suggests that they may have been brought to the capital to
accomplish by stealth what Patrick Gray could not accomplish
openly. At once a black operative for the White House and an
expert on Hoover, Liddy was a logical recourse—if only on a contingency basis—for an administration in search of the largest intelligence prize of all.

Whether or not Liddy and his men actually made an attempt to
acquire the files is uncertain. We will see what it was that the Cubans
claimed to have done in Washington, but first, some attention
should be given the physical location and identity of the files themselves.

The subject was of sufficient interest that it generated (once again,
thoroughly unsatisfactory) congressional hearings. In those hearings, Helen W. Gandy, Hoover's executive assistant and personal
secretary since 1918, testified at some length. She stated that John
Mohr had placed a literal interpretation on Kleindienst's order to
secure Hoover's office. That office consisted of one room, which
Mohr had indeed caused to be locked, but Hoover's suite had consisted of nine rooms, and eight of these had remained open. Since
Hoover kept many files in his suite but none in his office, Mohr's
literal compliance with Kleindienst's order frustrated the order's
actual intent: to preserve the director's most sensitive files intact,
exactly as they were at the time of his death.

It was under these circumstances that Gandy and an assistant
began to purge more than a hundred linear feet of files in the suite.
There were, Gandy testified, two kinds of files in the suite. One was
marked "Personal and Confidential," and the other "Official and

[16]Liddy, *Will*, pp. 172–80.

Confidential." The latter set of files was turned over to Assistant FBI Director Mark Felt and stored in a special vault at the bureau.

The so-called Personal file was purged in the following way. Gandy and her assistant began at opposite ends of the alphabet, with Gandy taking those files that began with the letter Z, and her assistant handling those files that began with the letter *A*. They then began to read the files with an eye toward destroying those that were truly "personal" (e.g., the registration papers for Hoover's pets), and toward preserving those that might be of "official" interest to the bureau. According to Helen Gandy, the purge was completed in a matter of weeks. Some of the Personal files were destroyed at FBI headquarters, but most of them were removed to the late director's home on the eve of Patrick Gray's confirmation as the bureau's new chief. There, Gandy said, the remainder of the files were destroyed —all one hundred five feet of them. Nowhere in all that yardage, she said, was there a single piece of paper that might have been considered sensitive or official.

To which Congressman Andrew McGuire remarked, "I find your testimony very difficult to believe, Miss Gandy."

"That," she sniffed, "is your privilege."

And, indeed, Gandy's testimony did seem to be in error. Given access to some of the FBI's files, congressional investigators found eight that had been processed by Gandy's assistant immediately after Hoover's death. These dossiers had been part of the Personal and Confidential files in Hoover's suite, but had been shifted by Gandy's assistant to the Official and Confidential files under the control of Mark Felt. The dossiers were entitled "Agreement between the FBI and Secret Service concerning Presidential Protection"; "Bentley, Elizabeth—Testimony"; "Black Bag Jobs"; "Black, Fred B. Jr."; "Black, Fred B. Jr. (#2)"; "Bombing at the U.S. Capitol"; "Bureau Recording Instruments"; and "Butts, E.R."[17] Obviously, none of these files could sensibly have been regarded as "personal." Fred Black, for example, is a Washington resident (of the Watergate Apartments, as it happens) who has long been of interest to the FBI's organized crime section. Elizabeth Bentley was an apostate Communist whose congressional testimony contributed greatly to the travails of Alger Hiss. And so on.

[17] *Inquiry into the Destruction of Former FBI Director J. Edgar Hoover's Files and FBI Recordkeeping*, Appendix, p. 173.

Congress questioned Gandy as to why such sensitive and patently official files should have been included among those that Hoover had marked "Personal and Confidential." The discovery of these eight files suggested that there may have been others equally sensitive and official that had been among those Personal files that Gandy had destroyed. Not so, she insisted: the eight files in question had been mistakenly included by Hoover among his Personal files—they were the only such mistakes among the entire one hundred five feet of paper (since destroyed).

Congress was skeptical of that answer, and one of the grounds for that skepticism was the fact that all eight files (with the exception of the first) began with the letter *B*. If mistakes had been made, they would presumably have been made at random, rather than in alphabetical sequence. Accordingly, a statistician was consulted as to the probability of such an error. His answer was that such an event had a probability of one in several million.

Because Gandy's congressional inquisitors found her testimony about the *nature* of the files to be unworthy of belief, they were skeptical also of her claim that she had destroyed the files. Ascertaining the truth about either matter, however, proved impossible. To begin with, the FBI's filing system was a nightmare that contained more than 6 million volumes of files and more than 58 million index cards relating to those files. These were grouped within 186 categories, but in addition to these volumes and indexes, there were Hoover's "Official and Confidential" files, his "Personal and Confidential" files and a "Do Not File" file, as well as files assigned to the FBI's field offices and to the offices of its assistant directors. Who, then, could say just where "the secret political files" were kept, or under what designation, let alone what eventually happened to them.[18] But that such files existed, contrary to the statements of Helen Gandy, was never doubted by the Congress or by the Nixon administration itself. Indeed, no less an authority than William Sullivan, formerly the number three man in the FBI, vouched for their existence, described the manner in which they were collected and used, and asserted that they simply "disappeared" following Hoover's death.[19]

In fact, as Gandy testified, Hoover's personal files were brought

[18]Information concerning the FBI filing "system" derives from the testimony and prepared statement of John J. McDermott, assistant director of the FBI (ibid., pp. 96ff.).
[19]Ibid., pp. 58–59.

to Hoover's residence, supposedly for final disposition. An FBI truck driver, Raymond Smith, recalls delivering more than twenty filing cabinets to the house shortly after the director's death. Congressional investigators, however, were never entirely convinced that this was the final destination of the files. More than one congressional investigator and Washington journalist was convinced that the secret files had been preserved, but where, and by whom, no one could say for certain.[20]

It is in the context of this conflicting testimony and the welter of lacunae that the Cubans' summons to Washington on May 3, 1972, must be considered. Led by Barker, the Miami team had come to the capital at the urgent request of Howard Hunt, who had telephoned Barker on the preceding night. The purpose of the trip was said to be twofold: to capture a Vietcong flag from antiwar demonstrators who were planning to rally at the Capitol and to prevent those same demonstrators from overturning Hoover's catafalque in that building. Should the demonstrators surge toward the embalmed FBI director, the Cubans were to encircle the catafalque and repel all attackers.

The assignment was, to be blunt, as ludicrous as it was expensive. It would take at least $3,000 from an already dwindling intelligence budget, and for what? Hoover's catafalque was under Marine and police guard, and ten Cubans were not going to make much differ-

---

[20]According to a former staff member of the House Intelligence Committee, the files were suspected by some to have been transported to the Blue Ridge (Rod & Gun) Club in the Shenandoah Valley. The club was an old and beautiful 27-room lodge on a hill overlooking the Potomac River near Harpers Ferry. The lodge was the weekend retreat of more than two dozen top FBI agents and CIA officers (including John Mohr and James Angleton). Weekends there were devoted to hunting, fishing and seven-card stud, and the tab was usually picked up by Joseph Tait, president of the U.S. Recording Co. (Tait was apparently reimbursed by the others for the $600 tabs.) U.S. Recording was itself a subject of congressional interest. Among other things, it was a "cut-out" for suppliers of secret surveillance equipment to the FBI. One of those suppliers, Martin Kaiser, discovered in 1972 that U.S. Recording was adding a 30 percent markup to the price of all equipment invoiced through its offices. This was, for the convenience of mere paperwork, a questionable practice, and three years later, when news of the markup was made public by Kaiser, an investigation was undertaken by the House Intelligence Committee. The committee quickly focused on the weekends spent by the counterintelligence establishment at the Blue Ridge Club—the question being whether Tait or the others benefited improperly from the cut-out arrangement with the FBI. To answer that question, committee staffers journeyed to Harpers Ferry to examine the books at the Blue Ridge Lodge. When they arrived, however, they found only a smoldering ruin and the standing remains of huge stone fireplaces. The Blue Ridge Club, they learned, had burned to the ground that very morning, shortly after dawn. According to a former staff member of the Intelligence Committee, it was suspected that Hoover's files had been among those destroyed in the blaze. (The origin of the fire has never been determined with certainty, though fire marshals believe that it was probably caused by an electrical failure.)

ence against tens of thousands of demonstrators, even on the unlikely assumption that the Cubans could get close enough to the
catafalque to protect its dead occupant. An impossible assignment,
it was peculiar also for the fact that it made no political sense
whatsoever. Hoover, for all his faults, was a national hero. For
antiwar demonstrators to have desecrated his remains on national
television would have amounted to a public relations coup for the
Nixon administration and for the right wing in general—it was
hardly something that Liddy et al. would have wished to prevent.

The second part of the supposed assignment was just as silly: to
capture a Vietcong flag from the antiwar demonstrators so that the
flag might be presented to the President.

On its face, then, the "assignment" seems to have been contrived
by Liddy and the others as an afterthought, following the arrests at
the Watergate, in order to explain the Cubans' presence in Washington at that time. Clearly, having recommended Hoover's re-
moval from office six months earlier, Liddy was not spending
thousands of dollars just to supplement the dead man's honor guard,
and neither was he spending money to provoke a fight for some
college student's flag.

As for the Cubans, their accounts vary. Depending upon who is
telling the story, Barker, Sturgis or Reinaldo Pico (or all three) got
into a fight with some demonstrators, whereupon they were either
escorted from the scene or arrested and taken to jail. Barker claimed
there was actually an arrest: Sturgis was supposedly taken to police
headquarters, but in the best tradition of a pulp thriller, "a man in
a gray suit" appeared and secured his release before he could be
booked. Hunt relates much the same, wholly unverifiable story, but
concludes his account with the observation that the Cubans' "stories
matched."[21] In fact they did not, not quite, but what is interesting
is Hunt's assertion that they did. Why should Hunt wish to empha-
size that everyone was telling the same tale unless Hunt knew, or
suspected, or feared, that the tale was false?

According to an article in the Harvard *Crimson*, the Cubans were
brought to Washington to burglarize Hoover's residence in an effort
to get at the secret files. Felipe De Diego told the *Crimson*'s reporter
that he himself had made a successful entry into the late director's

---

[21]Hunt, *Undercover*, p. 213. Barker's testimony about his assignment during the Hoover
funeral is published in the Ervin committee *Hearings*, Book 1, pp. 358, 365–66. For Hunt's
testimony, see Book 9, pp. 3711–12.

house, though he later denied making that statement when questioned by others.[22]

Knowing what we do of Liddy, his priorities and his men, the Cubans' visit to Washington in early May is more plausibly explained in terms of a plan to recover Hoover's files rather than to protect his catafalque.

While Hoover's death and speculation about his files filled the newspapers for days an important step toward the Watergate scandal was secretly taken by James McCord. That is, at about 6:15 P.M. on May 1, only a few hours before Hoover breathed his last, McCord telephoned Alfred C. Baldwin III with an offer of a job.

A wisecracking bachelor, Baldwin had fallen upon hard times. A law school graduate and ex-marine, he had repeatedly failed the Connecticut bar examination. A stint with the FBI in Tampa, Florida, had ended in resignation, and so, when McCord said there was a place for him with the Committee to Re-elect the President, Baldwin readily agreed to catch the next flight out of Hartford, Connecticut, for Washington, D.C.

That McCord chose Baldwin as a bodyguard for Martha Mitchell is puzzling. The former G-man lived more than three hundred miles from Washington, a circumstance that required his new employers to provide him with both housing and living expenses in addition to his salary. McCord says he selected Baldwin's name from a registry published by the Society of Former Special Agents of the FBI. A look at that registry for the year 1972 reveals the unsurprising fact that hundreds of such retirees lived in the Washington metropolitan area at that time. For McCord to have reached out to Connecticut, particularly when a bodyguard had to be on the job by the afternoon of the following day (when Martha Mitchell was scheduled to visit the Midwest), is more than a little strange. Indeed, one gets the impression that, for whatever reason, McCord was interested not so much in hiring a bodyguard per se as in hiring Baldwin in particular. This implies that Baldwin was somehow special and perhaps well known to McCord. McCord and Baldwin deny that, however, by insisting that their first contact with each other was by telephone on May 1.[23]

---

[22]Mark C. Frazier, "Ervin Committee, FBI Investigate Hoover Death," Harvard *Crimson*, November 10, 1973.
[23]An FBI interview with Robert L. Houston, McCord's deputy at the CRP, may shed some

Whatever the reason for McCord's choice, there was some urgency to it. Reached by telephone at 6:15 P.M., Baldwin was on an Allegheny Airlines flight to Washington two hours later. The flight, however, was subject to repeated delays caused by mechanical problems, with the result that he did not actually arrive in Washington until about 1:00 A.M. Baldwin says that he telephoned McCord from the airport, notifying him of his arrival, and learned that a reservation awaited him at the Roger Smith Hotel. Interestingly, a map found among Lou Russell's personal effects has a red circle inked around that hotel, with a dotted line running from it to the Columbia Plaza Apartments. That line is then scratched out, perhaps because Baldwin later changed hotels.

On the afternoon of May 2, within hours of his arrival in the capital, Baldwin entrained for Chicago with Martha Mitchell, who was on a speaking tour. In the course of that journey the Amtrak passenger train, then on its maiden trip to the Midwest, killed a pedestrian on the tracks. McCord's deputy, Bob Houston, told the FBI that "Baldwin could see the man's remains out of the train window, and he related a vivid description to Mrs. Mitchell. After this trip Baldwin was replaced by another security man. . . ."[24] Subsequently Martha described Baldwin as "the gauchest character I've ever met," criticizing him for being overly garrulous and wandering about in his bare feet.[25] By May 9 Baldwin was back from his tour and reassigned. McCord sent him home to Connecticut to get more clothes, and told him that his new assignment would involve surveillance of antiwar activities in Washington. On May 11 Baldwin returned to the capital, but not to the Roger Smith Hotel. McCord told him that he was to move to the Howard Johnson's motel, across the street from the Watergate complex. The reason for the change, McCord said, was to reduce expenses.

As we have seen, McCord could easily have eliminated all such expenses simply by hiring someone who lived in the Washington

---

light on the matter. According to Houston, "Baldwin had stopped in to see McCord during the first two weeks of April, 1972 (to the best of Houston's recollection), and this was the first time he (Houston) saw Baldwin." If Houston is correct about the date, then McCord and Baldwin (like McCord and Hunt) are concealing a prior acquaintance. It may be, of course, that Houston misspoke, in which case the matter remains a mystery. See the FBI's interview with Houston, conducted June 27, 1972, by special agents John E. Denton and Joseph C. Kelly.
[24]FBI interview with Robert Houston, June 27, 1972.
[25]In Baldwin's defense, it must be said that Mrs. Mitchell disliked every security guard assigned to her. A difficult and volatile person, however admired by the public, her situation was complicated by a serious problem with alcohol.

area. Rental records at the Howard Johnson's, moreover, show that Room 419 was rented on May 5, six days before Baldwin's shift from the Roger Smith Hotel. If economizing was the purpose, McCord did not accomplish it with much efficiency—or why would he have retained Baldwin's redundant room at the Roger Smith? The truth, of course, is that McCord knew of the plans to break into the Watergate offices of the DNC. The Hojo (as it is affectionately known) was to serve as the operation's "listening post"—that is, as the site from which the bugging devices would be monitored. As such, the Hojo was ideal, having a clear view of both the Watergate and the Columbia Plaza Apartments down the street. There was nothing unusual, then, about moving Baldwin to the Howard Johnson's except, of course, for the timing and for the fact that his room was rented in the name of McCord's own firm, McCord Associates.

This was an inexcusable blunder, and it deserves comment. In his undercover work for McCord Associates, Baldwin would be required to use a series of aliases.[26] The use of aliases was a standard precaution of tradecraft, a precaution taken in order to limit the damage in the event that any part of the operation was blown. Renting a room in the name of one's own firm while knowing that the room would be the headquarters of a felony in progress makes veteran intelligence agents suspicious of McCord's actual motives. The blunder, if that was what it was, was compounded even further by the fact that while resident at the Hojo, Baldwin received mail in his own name, entertained friends, and made long-distance calls to his mother and others on a regular basis. Each of those calls was a matter of record, and the FBI later found no difficulty at all in tracing them to Baldwin.

If Baldwin's blatancy at the Howard Johnson's was foolish, the foolishness was repeated elsewhere in the affair. For example, when the Cubans registered at the Watergate Hotel (on May 26), their assignment was to burglarize the DNC. Accordingly, they took the precaution of using aliases when registering at the hotel. This, however, was merely a gesture, a curtsy to tradecraft rather than an application of it, because reservations had been made for them in

---

[26]Baldwin's employment status is somewhat ambiguous. Hired by the CRP (with the routine approval of Fred LaRue), he was actually in the pay of McCord Associates. The same was true of Lou Russell: a sometime guard, "working for the CRP," he too was on the payroll of McCord Associates.

writing by the secretary of Ameritas, Inc., a Miami real estate firm with which Barker was closely associated.

Four days after Baldwin moved into the Howard Johnson's, Washington was shocked by the near assassination of Governor George Wallace. At a shopping mall in suburban Prince Georges County, Maryland, a "lone nut" named Arthur Bremer fired a fusillade of bullets at the right-wing Southern populist, crippling him for the rest of his life. An FBI investigation concluded that no conspiracy existed, and a diary apparently written by Bremer supported that conclusion. According to the diary, the assassination was designed "to prove Bremer's manhood" to the world.

10.
The May Break-ins

On Monday, May 22, while Governor Wallace lay recovering in the hospital, a contingent of anti-Castroites arrived in Washington from Miami. They were Bernard Barker, Eugenio Martinez, Felipe De Diego, Frank Sturgis, Virgilio Gonzalez and Reinaldo Pico. The first three had participated in the Fielding break-in nine months earlier and, with the others, had been present three weeks before at the Hoover rites. This time the Cubans were put up in the Manger Hamilton Hotel (which, like the Roger Smith, was circled in red on Lou Russell's Exxon map).

On previous occasions the Cubans had been brought to their operative destinations on or about the day that the operation was to have taken place. That they should have been brought to Washington four days in advance of the intended break-in over the long Memorial Day weekend is therefore somewhat disconcerting in view of Liddy's professed concern about the dwindling Gemstone finances. (What made the Cubans relatively expensive was not merely the cost of their room and board but the fact that each of them was to be recompensed for "lost income" while on assignment in Washington.) The possibility suggests itself, then, that the Cubans may have been given some other assignment to occupy themselves with prior to the weekend. If any other political break-ins occurred at this time, however, they seem never to have been reported.[1]

---

[1] See the *Congressional Record*, Vol. 120, No. 153, October 9, 1974: "The Unsolved Break-Ins," by Robert Fink, reprinted as Exhibit 1. Among these unsolved break-ins, which appear to have been politically motivated, were those at the New York residence of Victor Rioseco, economic counselor for the Chilean mission to the UN, on February 10, 1972; the residence of Humberto Diaz Casanueva, Chilean delegate to the UN in New York, on April 5, 1972; the New York apartment of Javier Urrutia, chief of the Chilean Development Corporation, on April 11, 1972; the home of television commentator Dan Rather on April 9, 1972; the Chilean

Meanwhile, Hunt and Liddy had a great many things on their minds. At the time, a plan existed to bug George McGovern's campaign offices with the assistance of Tom Gregory, who, some weeks before, had infiltrated the McGovern camp at Howard Hunt's request. That break-in would never get off the ground, but in the meantime Hunt and Liddy were concerned that McCord had yet to receive all of the equipment, including some small transceivers, that he had ordered. These were sophisticated walkie-talkies, identical with the kind used by the Washington Police Department's Intelligence Division (with which McCord had established liaison several months earlier).[2] Part of the delay was attributed to the fact that McCord was seeking FCC clearance for the transceivers' use—a formality that Liddy has since compared to "registering a gun you're going to use in a holdup."[3]

On Friday afternoon, May 26, four days after their arrival, the Cubans changed hotels, moving into the Watergate under the aegis of Ameritas, Inc. Earlier that week the reservations had been confirmed by the secretary of Ameritas, and Howard Hunt's wife, Dorothy, had consulted by telephone with the Watergate staff in helping them plan a menu for a small banquet to be held that evening in the Continental Room. The Watergate management was told that the reservation was for ten persons.

The location of the banquet room was key to the projected entry. The Watergate Hotel is adjacent to the Watergate office building, in which the DNC had its headquarters on the sixth floor.[4] Both the hotel and the office building are directly across the street from the Howard Johnson's motel in which Alfred Baldwin was ensconced. To reach the DNC, three routes were available.

The first would take a visitor through the front door of the office

---

embassy on April 13–14, 1972; the law offices of Fried, Frank, Harris, Shriver & Kampelman, a prominent Democratic firm, on April 15, 1972; and the Federal Reserve Board's Watergate offices on May 8, 1972.

[2] McCord's liaison with the WPD Intelligence Division was established with Officer Garey Bittenbender and Inspector Leo Herlihy. Ostensibly, the liaison was arranged in an effort to coordinate intelligence between the CRP and the police with particular attention to antiwar/ anti-Nixon demonstrations. In the course of his liaison with McCord, Bittenbender was provided by McCord with a demonstration of the electronics equipment in his CRP offices; the demonstration caused Inspector Herlihy to caution Bittenbender not to become involved in any surveillance activities with McCord.

[3] Liddy, *Will*, p. 227.

[4] There are in fact two Watergate office buildings. The only one that concerns us, however, is the building on Virginia Avenue that housed the headquarters of the Democratic National Committee.

building, past the GSS security desk, and then by elevator to the sixth floor. This was the conventional way to go to the DNC, but its disadvantages were manifest: it would require the burglars to sign in and out with the GSS guard prior to each entry and exit—hardly an ideal circumstance.

The second way to reach the DNC was through an underground garage, which served both the hotel and the office building. Near the entrance to the garage, at a point only a few feet below street level, was a locked door leading into the basement of the office building. By means of that door a visitor (or burglar) could gain access to a stairwell leading to the floors above, including the floor on which the DNC was located.

Yet a third route, and the one first selected by Hunt, required the use of the Continental Room. This was a large room in the basement of the Watergate office building, seven floors below the DNC. Not equipped with a kitchen—there was only a bar—the room was serviced by the hotel. Waiters had to carry the diners' meals across a driveway that passed between the office building and the hotel. The front door to the Continental Room gave access to a small courtyard; a second door—the one in which the burglars were most interested—opened onto a corridor that led to both the underground garage and a stairwell going up to the DNC.

In choosing the third route, Hunt's plan was comparatively simple. A banquet for "Ameritas executives" would be held in the Continental Room. When the deliberately prolonged dinner meeting was finally ended, the table cleared and the check paid, the bogus executives would remain in the room to watch an industrial film that Hunt had rented for the occasion. The purpose of the film was twofold: to give the board meeting an air of authenticity and to extend the banquet until such time as the last person left the DNC. News of that departure was to come from Room 419 of the Howard Johnson's, where McCord and Alfred Baldwin (equipped with walkie-talkies) were supposed to have the DNC under visual surveillance. Once the word arrived that the DNC was empty, the entry team would proceed down the corridor to the door leading into the underground garage. There they would admit McCord, walk to the nearby stairwell, and climb to the sixth floor. Virgilio Gonzalez was then to pick the lock to the DNC. Once inside, McCord was to deploy his bugging devices while Barker and Martinez photographed the most sensitive documents they could find.

That, at least, was how the plan was supposed to work. In reality, it was to turn out very differently.

Hotel records show that reservations were made for ten people. The guests were to arrive at 8:00 P.M. that Friday night, and for half an hour cocktails would be catered from a buffet-bar set up in the Continental Room. Dinner would be served at 8:30 P.M., beginning with shrimp cocktail and including filet mignon, baked potato (with sour cream), a bouquetière of fresh vegetables, tossed green salad, frozen parfait cake and Cutty Sark Scotch. The charge was to be $14.95 per person, plus taxes and tip, but in the end, after Hunt had selected the wine and cigars had been passed around, the bill amounted to $236 and change.

According to Franco Rovere, the waiter who served the party, only eight men attended the banquet.[5] Of these eight, Rovere said, only two were Americans, "the others being of mixed origin."[6] Various accounts make it apparent that the gringos were Hunt and Liddy (Rovere having lumped in the swarthy Sturgis with the Cubans in attendance). There seems, then, to have been some small snafu in the banquet's planning because two reservations were wasted. The likelihood is that those who made the reservations simply counted heads and found the number of co-conspirators to be ten, forgetting, or not realizing, that it was essential to the burglary plan that McCord and Baldwin stay away from the banquet so that they could surveil the DNC from their Hojo motel room and sound the all-clear when the Democrats' headquarters was empty.

But even that part of the plan concerning the surveillance presented a problem, though it seems never to have been remarked upon by anyone. That is to say, only a small part of the DNC could be observed from the Howard Johnson's because of the layout of the DNC's headquarters. It consisted of a large rectangular space, compartmented into 53 offices, and of these, 31 offices formed the rectangle's four sides, enclosing the remaining 22 rooms.[7] From their location in the Hojo, Baldwin and McCord would have had a partial view of (at most) those 14 rooms that faced Virginia Avenue. The

---

[5] Despite this, the group was billed for ten dinners, since that number had been guaranteed by those renting the Continental Room.

[6] FBI serial 139-4089-734, pp. 94–96 (interview of Franco Rovere conducted by special agent Harvey W. James, dictated June 27, 1972).

[7] A floor plan of the DNC is reproduced as Exhibit 13 in Book 1, p. 102, of the Ervin committee *Hearings*.

remainder of the headquarters would have been wholly obscured, with 39 rooms invisible from view. Indeed, the problem is compounded even further when one considers that Baldwin's room was two floors lower than the DNC, and that the headquarters itself was recessed into the office building, making the view even poorer (as, in fact, does a large terrace separating the offices from the building's façade).

But to return to the banquet. According to an FBI interview of Franco Rovere, "the main topic of conversation was night clubs in the Miami area and women. The women were prostitutes that hung out in these clubs. ROVERE cannot recall any names of either clubs or women."[8] As to what happened next, there is massive confusion, the sort of confusion that occurs when people have reason to lie but have not had time to get their stories straight.

According to Howard Hunt, the group dispersed at about 10:00 P.M., with Hunt and Gonzalez remaining behind in the Continental Room. The intention was for the two men to hide in the closet of the darkened room. Armed with a walkie-talkie, they were to stay in contact with McCord, and when word came from the Hojo that the DNC was empty, they were to enter the corridor and walk to the stairwell. Gonzalez would continue up to the DNC's sixth-floor offices and set to work on the locks. Meanwhile, Hunt was to linger in the stairwell, taping open the locks to doors that led into the underground garage. When that was done, Hunt was to return to the "command post" in the Watergate Hotel, while McCord and the remaining Cubans were to link up and enter the stairwell by means of the doors that Hunt had taped open. They were then to proceed to the sixth floor, where, if all went according to plan, Gonzalez would have picked the lock to the DNC.

Hunt tells us, however, that a complication arose which eventually defeated this plan. The complication was said to be an alarm in the corridor leading from the Continental Room to the stairwell in the office building. According to Hunt, he had previously discussed the alarm with McCord, and it was understood between them that the "electronics expert"—McCord—would find some way to defeat it. It was now after 10:00 P.M., however, and nothing seemed to have been done about it. Worried, Hunt telephoned (or radioed) to McCord to ask him what he intended to do. Hunt felt that McCord

[8]FBI serial 139-4089-734.

was phlegmatic about the problem. Hunt says McCord told him that the alarm would not be armed until eleven o'clock, by which time the DNC should be empty and the break-in under way. If someone decided to work late that night inside the DNC and stayed there until after the alarm was armed, the entry would just have to be aborted. Hunt comments that this reply irritated him, but there was nothing that he could do about it.[9]

McCord's account is much the same as Hunt's. He says that because the DNC continued to be occupied after 11:00 P.M., when the alarm was activated, the operation could not go forward.[10] There is, however, a rather massive stumbling block to the credibility of both accounts. Before we confront this particular issue, though, a general point should be made. So many elements of the Watergate story have been repeated so often that they are taken on faith by the public, which has the impression that every aspect of the affair was thoroughly investigated. That impression is entirely mistaken: virtually no investigation was made of the attempted break-ins over the Memorial Day weekend. Neither was the June 17 break-in much investigated because, after all, the burglars were caught red-handed. In any case, the intent of most investigators was to identify those who were *ultimately* responsible for the burglaries, which, in and of themselves, held little interest for anyone. So it was that demonstrably false accounts of these events became an accepted part of history.

Those who have read Liddy's autobiography will recall that his account of the attempted break-in on the evening of the banquet conforms with the accounts of Hunt and McCord. They forget, however, that Liddy's version is almost entirely hearsay: although he attended the banquet, he did not learn of the problematic alarm until afterward, when Hunt and McCord informed him of it. As for the version recounted by Anthony Lukas in *Nightmare*—an excellent book, though it amounts to the received version of the Watergate affair—it depends almost entirely upon Hunt's rendition of the events that night. Lukas repeats that rendition simply because he has no reason to doubt the word of Hunt and McCord on a subject that

[9]Hunt, *Undercover*, p. 223. If, as Hunt claims, McCord said that the DNC had been empty after 10:00 P.M. on the preceding nights, then McCord was lying or badly mistaken. Logbooks maintained by General Security Services Inc. (GSS) make clear the fact that the DNC was routinely occupied until after midnight.
[10]McCord, *Piece of Tape*, p. 24.

appears to be of merely academic or historical interest. No one was prosecuted for the break-in attempts over the Memorial Day weekend, after all, and the U.S. attorney's office preferred to ignore FBI reports that flatly contradicted the story put forth by Hunt and McCord.[11] For Lukas, then, as with so many of Watergate's historians, the banquet break-in is recounted in the spirit of comic relief and for the purpose of lending a (mistaken) sense of completeness to their accounts.

The problem with the story told by Hunt and McCord is not merely that the Howard Johnson's was inadequate to the surveillance of the DNC, but that—astonishingly—*there was no alarm* in the corridor or on the door of the Continental Room. Nor was there any object that could have been mistaken for an alarm. Bob Fink, who helped to research this book, remembers walking through the building with Royce Lea, Watergate's maintenance supervisor.

"Lea's been with the building since the concrete was poured," Fink said. "He's a guy who takes pride in knowing every electrical outlet, every light socket in the entire complex. He showed me how the door was unencumbered by an alarm, and categorically stated that if there ever was an alarm on the door, he'd have known when it was installed and when it was removed. In fact, he'd have a work order on file in his office but, of course, there isn't one because there wasn't any alarm.

"It's funny," Fink said. "We crawled through the building, tracing the supposed movements of the burglars, and it was obvious that the break-ins couldn't have happened the way McCord and the others said. They'd have had to walk through concrete walls, and go through doors where there were no doors. But despite all the investigations, and the millions of words that were written, as far as Lea knew, no one—not the police, the prosecutors or the reporters—had actually walked through the place the way we did."

[11]In fairness, it should be said that the U.S. attorney's office was by no means alone in overlooking important evidence. The press, the Senate, and the special prosecutor's office reacted in the same way to information that threatened to refute or complicate their view of the affair. The most egregious example of such neglected information—the planting of evidence in the DNC to support McCord's tale of the bugging—will be examined in later pages. Here, however, it should be pointed out that the FBI deserves a portion of the blame for the falsification of the Watergate story because, while the bureau's investigative effort was at least adequate, its analytical performance was nothing less than abysmal. Moreover, even when the bureau's analytical efforts rose to the level of competency, it remained submissive in the face of the prosecutors' efforts to tell a particular story—whether or not that story happened to be true.

So Liddy was misled. Hunt and McCord blamed the ruination of the mission on a nonexistent alarm that was supposedly set to go off at 11:00 P.M. Disgruntled by the information, Liddy never checked to see if what he had been told was true. He simply assumed that his accomplices were telling him the truth.

According to Hunt and McCord, the DNC remained occupied (how could they be sure?) until after 11:00 P.M. This meant that the door to the corridor outside the Continental Room could not be opened without setting off the imaginary alarm. Compounding the difficulties even further, according to Hunt, was the alleged fact— we have no way of knowing if it was true—that a GSS guard had locked the only other exit from the Continental Room, the front door leading into the courtyard of the Watergate complex. This lock (like so many others that later confronted them) defied Gonzalez' efforts to pick it—assuming it was locked, as Hunt reported —with the result that Hunt and Gonzalez were compelled to remain in the Continental Room until 6:00 A.M. (when the nonexistent alarm was allegedly scheduled to be deactivated). It was dawn, therefore, when Hunt and Gonzalez returned to their hotel rooms. Hunt says that he woke Liddy and told his partner to inform McCord that they would try a different means of entry that same night.[12] The banquet routine was too problematic to repeat.

According to Franco Rovere (and, as we will see, his information is corroborated elsewhere), "When dinner had been served, [he] lowered the screen [for the industrial film], then left the room. . . . [He later] checked to see if he could render further service after serving dinner. He was not needed, so he left work around 12:30 A.M. He learned later [that] this party had remained until approximately 2:00 A.M."[13] This information is confirmed by none other than Frank Wills, the GSS guard who came on duty at midnight, and who, on June 17, would notify the police of a burglary in progress at the Watergate. According to the GSS security log maintained by Wills, he made his rounds through the office building between 1:00 and 2:00 A.M. As he noted in the book:

> CONTINEAL ROAM OPEN
> HAVING MEETING CONT
> ROOM CLOSE AT 2:10 A.M.

[12]Hunt, *Undercover*, p. 224.
[13]FBI serial 139-4089-734.

McCord and Hunt, however, would have us (and Liddy) believe that the banquet had come to an end shortly after 10:00 P.M. An hour later, they claim, Hunt and Gonzalez were effectively trapped inside the Continental Room, with no way to leave before 6:00 A.M. As we have seen, they were not trapped. There was no alarm in the corridor, nor anything that could be mistaken for an alarm, and had they wanted to, they might have done cartwheels down that corridor at whatever hour they wished. The question might be raised, of course, as to whether Hunt was under a false impression about the supposed alarm: might not McCord have deceived Hunt by telling him that an alarm existed when in fact none did? No. Hunt is quite specific about the alarm, stating on more than one occasion that he noticed it and worried about it. Discussing an earlier reconnaissance, for example, he writes that "[O]ne afternoon we entered the Continental Room, which was vacant, and noted that the door between the Continental Room and the corridor was equipped with a magnetic alarm system. McCord said he was familiar with the system and would be able to defeat it when the time came."[14] Later, "I checked the door leading to the corridor and again noticed the burglar alarm. So far McCord had said nothing about his plans to defeat the system. . . ."[15] That Hunt's story depends, therefore, on his having repeatedly hallucinated something that did not exist makes it obvious that he is party to a lie, rather than that he is merely mistaken.

Moreover, even if the canard about the alarm is set aside, Hunt's account of the banquet remains suspect. As he would have it, after the diners had dispersed, leaving Gonzalez and him alone in the Continental Room, "About ten thirty a building guard opened the door and said we would have to leave. We agreed to do so, but when he left, we turned out the lights . . . and concealed ourselves in a closet."[16] This is impossible because, as GSS security logbooks reflect, there was no "building guard" on duty between 6:00 P.M. and midnight on the evening of May 26. Frank Wills was the building guard that night, and he did not arrive at work until shortly after midnight on the morning of May 27 (Saturday). The waiter, Franco Rovere, was on duty during the time of the purported visit from the building guard. But Rovere did not leave until 12:30 A.M., and there is no way that he would have permitted his guests to be *ejected* from

[14]Hunt, *Undercover*, p. 220.
[15]Ibid., p. 223.
[16]Ibid., pp. 223–24.

the Continental Room by a rent-a-cop: after all, the Ameritas group had rented the room for the ostensible purpose of holding a "board of directors meeting." They had Scotch and setups to occupy them after Rovere left. Nor would any GSS guard have acted so presumptuously; at most, their job was to note in the security log which rooms were open or occupied and at what time—which, as we have seen, is exactly what Frank Wills did, reporting that a meeting was in progress in the Continental Room as late as 2:00 A.M.

Clearly, a hoax is in the works. For whatever reason, Hunt and Gonzalez have connived with McCord—and perhaps with others— to lie about their activities and whereabouts in the early-morning hours of Saturday, May 27. Why? The intention seems to have been to provide Hunt and Gonzalez with a phony alibi for the hours after 11:00 P.M. To what end? We can't be certain. But *someone* was meeting in the "Contineal Room" after midnight—while Liddy was being escorted on what turned out to be a fool's errand.

While Hunt and Gonzalez were supposedly locked inside the Continental Room, McCord, Liddy and Baldwin conducted a reconnaissance of McGovern headquarters (with an eye toward breaking in). This was between 1:00 and 4:00 A.M. that Saturday. Of this reconnaissance (whose purpose was frustrated by a derelict's presence on the front steps of McGovern headquarters), Baldwin says that he and McCord drove into downtown Washington and, by prearrangement, met with Liddy there. The car in which Liddy was riding, Baldwin remembers, held four others: three men in the backseat, whose faces were obscure, and a driver.[17] Thus, it would seem that five of those who had attended the banquet that night were present for the McGovern reconnaissance, which leaves Hunt, Gonzalez and one other elsewhere. Just where, and doing what, is unknown. Obviously, they were not at McGovern headquarters, and neither were they locked inside the Continental Room. Their whereabouts and doings are therefore a matter of speculation, but it seems significant that it was Gonzalez, the locksmith, who remained with Hunt in the banquet room, a short walk down the corridor to the stairwell that led to the DNC.

Late that Saturday night, May 27, the would-be burglars rendezvoused for a second attempt. There were seven of them, including

---

[17]In an interview with the *Los Angeles Times*, Baldwin identifies Howard Hunt as the driver of the other car, but corrects himself immediately, saying that he couldn't be certain who the driver was.

McCord, and they were all wearing business suits. At 12:30 A.M.—
which made it Sunday morning, May 28—the seven presented
themselves at the security desk in the Watergate office building.
There each of them signed an alias (e.g., "John Smith") in the GSS
visitors' log, indicating their destination was the Federal Reserve
Board (FRB) on the eighth floor.

Briefcases in hand, they must have been holding their breath as
they waited for clearance. They were a small task force of mostly
Hispanics abroad on a holiday weekend, signing in after midnight
for one of the most sensitive destinations in the capital. One can only
wonder why Frank Wills, who seems to have been the guard on
duty at the time, did not choose to question these late arrivals.[18]
Even granting that Wills is a less than clever man, the chutzpah of
McCord and the Cubans is mind-boggling. Having reconnoitered
the DNC on repeated occasions, and having made it a point to chat
with the guards, McCord ought to have known that the FRB had
been burglarized earlier that month and security had been tightened
as a consequence. Moreover, as McCord knew, the FRB guard was
due to make his rounds at about the time of their entry. If the guard
had glanced at the visitors' log for that evening, which was a standard procedure, he would have known immediately that seven men
had entered the FRB after midnight—a circumstance that he would
have been obliged to investigate. Finding no one in the Federal
Reserve's offices, he would have realized that the men were elsewhere in the building, and that they had entered under a pretext.
The consequences would have been swift, with McCord and the
others almost certain to be apprehended in possession of alias identification, cameras, bugging equipment, surgical gloves and more.[19]

Eugenio Martinez recollects the operation with a sense of utter
bafflement:

> [A]ll seven of us in McCord's army walked up to the Watergate complex
> at midnight. McCord rang the bell, and a policeman came and let us in.
> We all signed the book, and McCord told the man we were going to
> the Federal Reserve office on the eighth floor. It all seemed funny to me.

[18]That it was Wills who was on duty that night seems likely, given his schedule, but there
can be no certainty about it. The GSS security log, located in the National Archives, has had
two pages torn from it. Those pages covered the last two nights of the Memorial Day
weekend.

[19]Unlike the GSS guards, those protecting the FRB were responsible for several buildings,
only two of which were located in the Watergate complex. Watergate was but one of several
stops that the FRB guards made in the course of their evening tour.

Eight men going to work at midnight.[20] Imagine, we sat there talking to the police. Then we went up to the eighth floor, walked down to the sixth—and do you believe it, we couldn't open that door, and we had to cancel the operation.

I don't believe it has ever been told before, but all the time while we were working on the door, McCord would be going to the eighth floor. It is still a mystery to me what he was doing there. At 2:00 A.M. I went up to tell him about our problems, and there I saw him talking to two guards. What happened? I thought. Have we been caught? No, he knew the guards. So I did not ask questions, but I thought maybe McCord was working there. It was the only thing that made sense. He was the one who led us to the place and it would not have made sense for us to have rooms at the Watergate and go on this operation if there was not someone there on the inside. Anyway, I [re]joined the group, and pretty soon we picked up our briefcases and walked out the front door."[21]

McCord had in fact worked at the Watergate in the sense that earlier in the year, he had performed what we are told were counter-measures sweeps in John Mitchell's apartment.[22] It is conceivable that he may have met some of the Watergate guards in the course of that task, but that hardly resolves the issue raised by Martinez. For one thing, he would have avoided the FRB guards, who visited the eighth floor after midnight, and, in any case, had he known the guards, he would hardly have used an alias ("E.J. Warren") when signing in.

The reader may recall that Hunt and Liddy had agreed that this second entry was to be made by means of the garage-level door. McCord's method is therefore even less comprehensible because it went against orders. Interestingly, Howard Hunt's memoir, in describing this second entry, is entirely mistaken: according to Hunt, McCord taped open the locks at the garage level and admitted four of the Cubans, who then proceeded up to the DNC.[23] It is an open

[20]Note that Martinez mentions eight men taking part in the mission: McCord himself and the seven men in his "army." So far as we know, however, there were only six men from Miami who were involved. The visitors' log, with its scribbled alias entries, is somewhat unclear and does little to resolve the matter.

[21]Martinez, "Mission Impossible," p. 55.

[22]It was Martha Mitchell's belief that McCord was actually engaged in bugging her husband, since the sweeps were made redundant by the FBI's weekly search for eavesdropping devices in the apartment. See Winzola McLendon, *Martha* (New York: Random House, 1979), pp. 204–7, and the FBI's interview of Martha Mitchell on April 3, 1973 (conducted by special agents Angelo Lano and Vincent Alvino), FBI serial 139-4089-2393, p. 222.

[23]Hunt, *Undercover*, p. 225. The four "Cubans" that Hunt mentions are Barker, Sturgis, Martinez and Gonzalez.

question as to whether Hunt deliberately falsified his version of these events or whether his memory failed him. It is true (and frustrating) that memoirs do not constitute sworn testimony, but they must nevertheless be relied on where Watergate is concerned. This is because federal investigators and the press consistently ignored operational details of the break-in, declining to question the perpetrators at any length about the burglaries themselves. The few questions that were asked about the break-ins tended to be ill informed or pro forma, or both—with the result that false, evasive and contradictory testimony constitutes the official record to date. To establish what actually happened in the course of the break-ins, one must consider the testimony in light of the memoirs, and the memoirs in light of the physical evidence (e.g., the visitors' log alone makes clear that Hunt's account of the second entry attempt is entirely false).

In any case, despite the brazen means of entry, the second attempt to penetrate the DNC was also a failure. According to McCord and the others, "Villo" Gonzalez proved unable to pick the lock to the DNC door, saying that he required special tools. Confronted with this news, Liddy (who had awaited the entry's results in the comfort of his hotel room) expressed his disappointment, and then concern. In emphasizing his futile struggle with the lock, Gonzalez caused Liddy to fear that he had mangled it, with the result that the Democrats might notice the attempted entry and notify the police.

Liddy questioned Gonzalez to ascertain just how badly the lock was damaged, but lacking confidence in the accuracy of the Cuban's report, he decided to see for himself. So it was that Liddy, in a reprise of the earlier opéra bouffe, signed into the GSS visitors' log at 2:55 A.M. Accompanied by at least two other men, he listed the Federal Reserve Board as their destination. As he later recalled, the DNC's lock was damaged, but not in a way that anyone seemed likely to notice. Relieved, he and his men returned to the lobby, scrawled aliases in the visitors' log and went back to their hotel rooms. Against Hunt's wishes, Liddy told Gonzalez to fly immediately to Miami to obtain the right tools for the job. When he returned to Washington later that same day, they would try once again. The idea of admitting failure to a wimp such as Magruder was more than Liddy could stand.[24]

[24]Liddy, *Will*, p. 232.

So a third attempt was mounted at about 11:00 P.M. that Sunday night (May 28). Gonzalez had flown round-trip to Miami, picked up the tools he needed, and returned. This time they were to use the third entry method: taping open the locks to the doors leading from the underground garage to the basement stairwell. If this failed, they would presumably have resorted to using Gurkhas. But it did not fail. Hunt says McCord had earlier taped open the locks to the doors, and shortly after 11:00 P.M. he and the four Cubans finally succeeded in their surreptitious entry. An hour later, however, Barker, using his walkie-talkie, radioed back to the command post to say that the team was getting out. Hunt recalls that the news of this "premature departure" came as a surprise and a disappointment to both himself and Liddy. They had expected that Barker and his men would remain inside the DNC, photographing documents, throughout the night. The photography mission had been even more important, in fact, than McCord's placement of eavesdropping devices. Hunt tells us in his memoirs that when Barker returned to the command post the Cuban explained that he and Martinez had photographed some of the correspondence on Larry O'Brien's desk. Before they could break into the filing cabinets as instructed, however, McCord had ordered them to leave. Altogether, the entry team had exposed fewer than two cassettes of film—about fifty frames.[25] In terms of Howard Hunt's expectations, that yield was minimal at best: when arrested in the DNC some three weeks later, Barker would have thirty-nine rolls of film in his possession—enough for more than fourteen hundred exposures.[26] Curiously, though, Hunt's version of these events is at odds with Gordon Liddy's. Liddy claims that both he and Hunt were "delighted" by the way the operation had gone.[27]

[25]Hunt, *Undercover*, pp. 227–28.
[26]Government Exhibit GX 22, criminal case 1827-72, U.S. District Court for District of Columbia. According to Liddy (*Will*, p. 233), each film cassette contained thirty-six exposures. While Hunt says in *Undercover* (pp. 227–28) that he had expected nearly a hundred frames of film to be exposed, it is clear from his disappointment and the context—not to mention Barker's subsequent arrest while in possession of so many film cassettes—that Hunt had actually hoped for many more pictures to have been taken. Barker and his cohorts were to use an assembly-line method in photographing documents at the DNC. This meant that two people were to select documents while a third person turned each page for the photographer. In this way Hunt's men might have been expected to expose perhaps five frames a minute (or about eight rolls of film each hour).
[27]Liddy, *Will*, p. 233.

By any standard, the break-ins over the Memorial Day weekend are perplexing in the extreme. What we have been told (by Hunt, Liddy and McCord) of the first attempt, on Friday night, is demonstrably false, and as for the second break-in attempt, the modus operandi can only be described as foolhardy—and even bizarre. Physical evidence (i.e., a critical portion of the GSS logs) that might shed light on the various break-ins has been destroyed. The number of persons involved in each of the efforts fluctuates in the telling, as do the identities of those participating. The burglars were fraternizing openly with the security guards assigned to protect the target, and insofar as the mission's goal can be stated, either eighty frames or eighty *rolls* of film were to constitute the take. The result of the operation was, according to Hunt, disappointment, while, according to Liddy, the reaction was one of "delight." Clearly, something else was going on.

Just what that might have been is suggested in the testimony of Alfred Baldwin, testimony that shows—conclusively, to my mind—that a second "track" or "secret agenda" was in the works.

Interrogated by the FBI, and subsequently by the press and the Congress, Baldwin insisted that his first transcription of an intercepted telephone conversation occurred in Room 419 of the Howard Johnson's motel on Friday, May 26—two days *before* the first successful entry is said to have taken place. In an interview with H. William Shure, assistant minority counsel for the Senate's Ervin committee, Baldwin discussed the circumstances of that interception in considerable detail. I quote from Shure's report of his interview with Baldwin:

> On May 23, Baldwin said, he returned to Connecticut and came back to Washington on Friday afternoon, the 26th. He had gone to Connecticut to get his own car at the instruction of McCord. He arrived back from Connecticut at approximately 1 P.M. and returned to his room, where he found McCord with all of the bugging equipment set up in the room. McCord very casually told Baldwin that after he had unpacked and showered and gotten organized, he, McCord, would explain to Baldwin what he [Baldwin] would be doing. Baldwin indicates that McCord was already attempting to listen to phone calls over the bugging devices and Baldwin was therefore convinced that a break-in of the Democratic headquarters had to have taken place prior to the 26th [of May]. That

afternoon McCord in fact showed Baldwin the equipment and McCord himself attempted to pick up conversations and did. . . .[28]

In an earlier interview with the FBI, Baldwin told the same story, adding further details. "McCord was fiddling with . . . a Communication Electronics, Inc., . . . Receiving System. . . . During McCord's tuning of this instrument at 118.9 megacycles, a conversation was picked up to which Baldwin listened. The conversation was in regard to a man talking with a woman and discussing their marital problem."[29] The same story, emphasizing the same date and the fact that the first telephone conversation was intercepted from Room 419 of the Howard Johnson's, was provided by Baldwin to the *Los Angeles Times*.[30]

The implications of Baldwin's account are profound, and it is therefore worth emphasizing that his recollection of the matter has never varied in any significant detail. He recalls the circumstances perfectly, having just returned from Connecticut to find his motel room transformed into a miniature electronics studio. He recalls the nature of the conversation on which he came to eavesdrop, and is emphatic in his assertion that the event occurred in the afternoon of the twenty-sixth in Room 419. This last detail is important because on Monday morning, May 29, hours after the third and finally successful break-in, Baldwin shifted to a room on a higher floor of the Hojo in hopes of improving reception. Clearly, then, if the first interception occurred on a weekend afternoon prior to that move, the DNC had to have been bugged earlier than McCord and the others would have us believe.

In fact, however, all Baldwin knew was what McCord told him and whatever he might have surmised from the conversations of those on the line. He could not say from personal knowledge which telephone, in the DNC or elsewhere, had been bugged. Obviously, then, since the DNC was not broken into until May 29, and since Baldwin is emphatic about having monitored a telephone conversation on May 26, he must have been listening to the transmissions of a bug on a telephone in some location other than the DNC. On

---

[28]H. William Shure report of interview with Alfred Baldwin, March 30, 1973, pp. 5–6.
[29]FBI "Summary of Investigative Reports in the case: James Walter McCord, Jr., and Others; Burglary of Democratic National Committee Headquarters, June 17, 1972; I.O.C.," prepared April 23, 1973, p. 106–7.
[30]District Court copy of *Los Angeles Times* interview of Baldwin, sealed January 17, 1973, pp. 44–45. The interview was unsealed October 3, 1980, at the request of this writer and his researcher, Robert Fink.

whom, then, was Baldwin eavesdropping? We cannot be sure, but one possibility that immediately suggests itself is that Baldwin was monitoring a telephone that McCord's employee Lou Russell had bugged earlier in the spring. That is to say, a telephone in the Columbia Plaza Apartments, in line of sight with the Howard Johnson's, two blocks from the Watergate, and intimately bound up with the telephone in Spencer Oliver's DNC office.

But it is not only Baldwin's recollection of the May 26 interception that makes his reminiscence so fascinating. In his interview with the *Los Angeles Times*—the first insider's account to be made public—Baldwin recalled that on the evening of May 26 McCord suddenly appeared at the window of Spencer Oliver's office in the DNC. This would have been at about the time that McCord's colleagues were sitting down to their famous banquet in the Continental Room. As Baldwin told the *Times*, McCord "turned on a light in [Oliver's] office, came over to the window, pulled the drapery and shut the light off. . . . I saw McCord. I can specifically say I saw McCord. His features are distinguishable, and he came right over to the window and pulled the drapery. He had the light on."[31]

This was on Friday night, and yet the burglary team would not gain entrance to the DNC until two more days had passed. We may well wonder what McCord was up to inside the DNC that night and who, besides Baldwin, knew that he was there. We may wonder, also, how he was able to gain entrance when, some twenty-four hours later, the burglary team would be stymied by the locksmith's inability to pick the lock to the DNC's front door.[32] Whatever the

---

[31] Ibid.

[32] The possibility suggests itself that McCord had somehow obtained a key. Lou Russell, for instance, might have obtained one while working for General Security Services Inc. For that matter, McCord was almost certainly a veteran of the CIA's "DAMES and DACES" curriculum, which teaches "defenses" against mechanical entry and electronic eavesdropping. If so, he would have known how to pick the DNC's lock, or how to cut a key to fit it. And, in fact, someone appears to have attempted exactly that. Viz.: at 8:00 A.M. on the Monday following the third and ultimately successful attempt at entering the DNC, GSS guard Leroy Brown notified the police that there had been an attempted break-in over the Memorial Day weekend. In their report of the incident (Complaint 27-735, dated May 29), the police noted that an attempt had been made to unscrew the DNC's lock from its front door, and that this effort had damaged the lock. Mistakenly, the police concluded that entry had not been gained to the DNC—never realizing that a successful break-in had been carried out after the lock had been damaged. In his report of the incident, Leroy Brown noted in his security logbook that the building maintenance man had discovered a key that morning in the cigarette receptacle beside the front door to the DNC. GSS Investigator Thomas McGillicuddy subsequently told the FBI (on June 20, 1972) that this key fit the lock to the DNC—i.e., it could be inserted into the lock—but that it could not turn the lock's tumblers. The key, then,

answer to those questions, however, McCord's apparent ability to enter and leave the DNC at will made a mockery of the burglars' subsequent attempts to pick the DNC's lock. Taken together with McCord's sabotage of the "banquet break-in" (citing an imaginary alarm), and Baldwin's interception of a telephone conversation (before the DNC had been bugged), the apparition of McCord in Oliver's office two days before a break-in succeeded can only be explained in terms of McCord's duplicity and his commitment to a secret agenda.

Further evidence that such an agenda existed is manifest in FBI reports concerning the fate of the film that Bernard Barker had exposed inside the DNC. According to Barker and Martinez, some forty or fifty pictures had been taken—all of them of documents on Larry O'Brien's desk. Howard Hunt adds that McCord "had been given the films . . . to develop. After a few days, Liddy asked him . . . where the developed prints were. McCord apparently reported to Liddy [that] the photographer he knew was not in the vicinity, he was on vacation or something, and Mr. McCord could not get the films developed. Therefore, Mr. Liddy asked Mr. McCord to turn the films over to me. . . . At about the time Mr. McCord turned the films over to me, I was going down to Miami. . . . I had called Barker to ask him if he had or knew what we call a 'person of confidence' to print the film. He said certainly. He met me at the airport within a day or so, I delivered the film cassettes to him . . . [and] within an hour or so . . . he came back to me and said the films were all set . . ."[33]

Barker's "person of confidence" turned out to be Michael Richardson, the proprietor of Rich's Photos in Miami. As Richardson later told the FBI, he developed and printed two cassettes of film for Barker on June 10, 1972 (about two weeks after the break-in over Memorial Day weekend). The printing was done on a "rush" basis, and it was immediately clear to Richardson that some sort of "cloak-and-dagger" activity was involved. The photos showed surgically gloved hands holding down political documents against the background of "a shag-type rug."[34] There were thirty-eight photos in all. "There was a mention of a Kennedy name," Richardson subsequently testified, "and Hubert Humphrey's name was mentioned

appears to have been an imperfect copy, perhaps one made from a wax impression, of the key to the DNC's front door.
[33]Nedzi report, pp. 520–21.
[34]FBI "Summary of Investigative Reports," April 23, 1973, p. 22.

and there was more or less a file on this woman who headed up Humphrey's campaign—but nothing derogatory or anything. It just told about the woman."[35] In addition, Richardson recalled, there were some interoffice memos and shorthand notes—all in all, rather innocuous stuff made interesting only by the gloved hands. But what concerned the FBI most about Richardson's information was the fact that the documents in question were held against the background of a shag rug with a long nap. Because there was no such rug in the DNC's offices. Neither was there a rug of that kind in the Watergate Hotel rooms rented by the burglars.[36] Obviously, then, the documents depicted in Richardson's prints—containing information that was later described as "worthless" by Jeb Magruder—were not the same ones that Barker had photographed inside the DNC.

A switch must have taken place during the time that McCord was in possession of the film cassettes that Barker had exposed. It should not come as a surprise, therefore, to learn that Alfred Baldwin's room in the Hojo contained a "shag-type" rug similar to the one described by Richardson.[37] What appears to have happened, then, is that McCord somehow obtained his own (utterly innocuous) set of DNC documents. Taking them to the room that he had rented at the Howard Johnson's, he—or an accomplice—donned a pair of surgical gloves and exposed two cassettes of film.[38] These cassettes were subsequently given to Howard Hunt, who in turn delivered them to Barker for Richardson to develop; for all that Barker knew, these were the same cassettes that he had exposed a few days earlier.

A double cross had taken place, and the effect of it was that Jeb Magruder and his bosses at the White House were deprived by McCord of campaign intelligence obtained in the course of the first break-in. As for the film that Barker had exposed, its fate remains unknown. It may have been destroyed. Then again, it may have been among the contents of the packages that Hunt was sending to CIA headquarters at Langley.

---

[35]FBI "Summary of Watergate Trial Testimony," serial 139-4089-2144. (Richardson's testimony was given on January 26, 1973.)

[36]FBI special agents Harvey W. James and John E. Denton conducted the search for the missing rug on June 23, 1972, the day after Richardson contacted the FBI with his information. See, for example, FBI serial 139-166-247.

[37]FBI serial 139-4089-156. Paul Chapman, manager of the Howard Johnson's in 1972, and janitorial personnel there confirm that Baldwin's room was carpeted with a shag rug.

[38]McCord did not necessarily require an accomplice to effect the switch, but having one would certainly have made the photography easier to accomplish.

II

IT COMES DOWN

11.
The Surveillance and the Reports

On Monday afternoon or evening, May 29, Alfred Baldwin packed his bags, borrowed a luggage cart and moved upstairs into Room 723 at the Hojo, there to begin the monitoring routine that was to end abruptly some three weeks later. According to the FBI, which reported and then forgot Baldwin's interception of a telephone conversation on May 26, "Baldwin began monitoring the receiving system through an earphone on May 29–30, 1972, during the period 8:00 A.M. to 6:00 P.M., daily, on McCord's instruction. McCord also told him if he was in the room after hours he should continue to monitor. Baldwin was instructed to keep daily logs of the conversations overheard, setting forth the date, time and conversational activities. McCord would pick up the logs prepared by Baldwin on a daily basis, either at night or the following morning. McCord would type up summaries of the monitoring logs in memorandum form, with each memorandum beginning with 'a reliable source.' "[1]

According to Baldwin, in his interview with the *Los Angeles Times* and elsewhere, he was able to provide McCord with "almost verbatim" accounts of the overheard telephone conversations. "Sometimes," he said, "the logs would be only a page or two long, but on a busy day they might run to six pages." On other days (e.g., Friday, June 16) no conversations were overheard, though Baldwin remained at the ready. On still other occasions the surveillance was suspended while Baldwin was in Connecticut to visit friends and relatives.

[1]FBI "Summary of Investigative Reports," pp. 107–8.

Surely this was one of the sloppiest telephone surveillances ever undertaken. And yet each of the men directly involved in the surveillance—Baldwin, McCord and Liddy—was a former special agent of the FBI, well trained in the methods of electronic eavesdropping. Despite this expertise, only one person (Baldwin) was assigned to monitor the receiver through which the telephone calls could be overheard. Necessarily this meant that gaps would occur in the surveillance, if only because Baldwin was taking weekends off and handling other assignments for McCord. Moreover, even on those days when Baldwin was supposed to be monitoring, he cannot have been very effective. If he left the room for any reason, the receiver remained untended. And Baldwin must have left the room on many occasions if his paltry receipts for room service are any indication. According to those receipts, Baldwin ordered only the following during the period May 29 through June 17: two cheeseburgers, $4.04 (May 30); two grilled cheese sandwiches, $2.20 (June 2); room service, $2.65 (June 8); and room service, $2.10 (June 15). Obviously, despite his ten-hour workdays, Baldwin almost never ate in his hotel room. Nevertheless, Baldwin claims to have monitored an estimated two hundred telephone calls during the thirteen days or so that he was actually engaged in eavesdropping.[2] This works out to about three calls every two hours, hardly what one would expect in a presidential year at the headquarters of the Democratic National Committee.

It was an odd surveillance on any number of grounds, and it would have resembled nothing so much as a Chinese firedrill had the supposed bug on O'Brien's telephone actually worked. Because, of course, Baldwin would then have been expected to monitor two bugs simultaneously. What makes it all even more peculiar is Baldwin and McCord's claim that no tape recorders were used, despite the fact that two tape recorders were present in Room 723 throughout the operation. Electronic eavesdroppers and countermeasures technicians alike agree that it is virtually unheard of not to employ tape recorders in the course of an electronic surveillance. The advantages of tape-recording are overwhelming. To begin with, the recorders are usually (and easily) voice-actuated, so that constant attention to an unengaged telephone line is unnecessary; the ma-

[2]The May 29–June 17 period covers twenty days. Of these, seven days were a total loss, with either no telephone activity or Baldwin unavailable to overhear it.

chines will record what is said *when* it is said. Secondly, the purpose
of an electronic surveillance is to produce raw intelligence or evidence of something. Baldwin's scribbled accounts were useless as
evidence of anything, and as raw intelligence they were equally
flawed. Gordon Liddy makes the point in *Will.*

Liddy asked McCord why he didn't use one of the tape recorders
that he had in his room. McCord replied that the receiver and the
tape recorders were incompatible. Liddy retorted that McCord
could either buy compatible equipment or, if he didn't want to be
bothered, he could just tape the telephone conversations with a
microphone. For some reason, McCord demurred. He told Liddy
that the system they were using was working well, and that, moreover, it enabled McCord to "edit out the junk," thus saving Liddy's
time. Liddy replied acidly that he would prefer to do the editing
himself, and that he expected McCord to rectify the situation.[3]

When I questioned Liddy about McCord's method, he was even
blunter: "It was the most ridiculous fucking electronic surveillance
operation I've ever seen. With all the equipment he had, the money
he spent . . . goddamn it, he could probably have gotten what he
needed at the Radio Shack. I don't know why he disobeyed my
orders—they were simple enough. The last thing I wanted was him
and that goofball, Baldwin, deciding what was important and what
wasn't."

As it is, only Baldwin knows what Baldwin heard; and only
McCord can say with certainty who was actually bugged and, therefore, to which telephone(s) Baldwin was listening. Having deliberately failed to provide his agent with a functioning tape recorder,
McCord could easily have invented some (or all) of the conversations that he summarized for Gordon Liddy—and perhaps, in a few
cases, that is what happened.

McCord's summaries were the basis of the Gemstone File. Because that file was burned to ashes by Jeb Magruder shortly after the
Watergate arrests, its dimensions can only be inferred from the
procedure that was used to compile it. To recapitulate, that procedure was as follows:

Baldwin wrote his "almost verbatim" accounts on a yellow legal
pad (later he would use an electric typewriter and onionskin paper).
On any given day he would produce up to six pages of material,

[3]Liddy, *Will,* p. 235.

which he would then give to McCord. It was McCord's intention, at first, to summarize this material for Liddy, but the latter objected, insisting that he must see the raw data. Accordingly, when Liddy received Baldwin's reports from McCord, he would edit them himself, reading aloud to his secretary, Sally Harmony. Using a special letterhead, one with the code word GEMSTONE on top, Harmony would commit Liddy's summations to paper. According to her, she typed eight of these memos for her boss.[4]

Of what, then, did the Gemstone File consist? Certainly it consisted of the eight memos that Harmony had typed—perhaps ten pages—and the thirty-eight photos that Richardson had developed. As for Baldwin's raw product, he cannot have been monitoring for more than thirteen days. Based upon his own estimate of his productivity—two to six pages per day—he seems to have turned out about fifty pages. Whether these pages were included in the Gemstone File is uncertain, however, because Liddy is known to have regarded Baldwin's typing as execrable. Believing that John Mitchell himself would study the file, and that Baldwin's product would reflect poorly on the professionalism of his operation, Liddy may have omitted the raw reports when submitting the take to Magruder.[5] But even if we assume that Liddy included Baldwin's "transcripts" in his submissions to Magruder, the Gemstone File cannot have amounted to more than sixty pages at most. Add Richardson's photographs to this, and one has a file that is rather less than an inch thick.

It is surprising, therefore, to read Magruder's version of the file's destruction after the Watergate arrests. According to him, the file "was about four or five inches thick, about half photographs and half transcripts of telephone conversations."[6] If this was so, then it would appear that the Gemstone File ran to a length of about four hundred pages, with perhaps another hundred photographs thrown in—an impossibility.

The monitoring operation had not gone well in its first few days. There was no work product, according to Liddy, because McCord allegedly had trouble tuning his receiver to the narrow frequency that the transmitters were supposed to have used. Sometime around

[4]Ervin committee *Hearings*, Book II, pp. 458–89.
[5]Liddy, *Will*, p. 235.
[6]Magruder, *American Life*, p. 226.

June 1, however, McCord reported to Liddy that he had isolated one of the bugs and that some conversations had been monitored. Less happily, McCord said that the bug in Larry O'Brien's office seemed not to be working. This was a particular disappointment to Liddy because he was under the mistaken impression that the device in question was an ultrasophisticated room bug for which McCord claimed to have paid $30,000, about an eighth of the entire Gemstone budget.[7]

According to Liddy, the first logs prepared by Baldwin and McCord were handed to him by the latter on or about June 1, 1972. The logs were sloppily typed, Liddy writes, and it was clear that they were based on telephone conversations rather than on anything picked up by a room bug. None of the people quoted appeared to be Larry O'Brien. For these reasons, then, Liddy decided not to send the logs to John Mitchell. He would wait, instead, until McCord was able to make the room bug work in O'Brien's office, at which point the take could be expected to improve. As it happened, however, Liddy's expectation that the take would improve was optimistic. Day after day, the take remained the same, and none of it quoted the DNC's chairman. On Monday, June 5, Liddy could wait no longer. He summarized the logs aloud for Sally Harmony to transcribe and, on June 8, delivered them in a sealed envelope to Jeb Magruder for him to forward to John Mitchell. At this point, Liddy had still not received the photographs that Barker had taken inside the DNC and that Hunt was apparently having developed in Miami.[8]

Jeb Magruder's account of this first delivery of Gemstone material

[7] A room bug (as distinct from a telephone bug) is capable of picking up and transmitting conversations taking place in the room in which it has been secreted. Together, a room bug and a telephone bug would complement each other, providing the monitors with complete coverage of the office that is under surveillance.

With respect to McCord's receipts and expenditures of Gemstone funds, a more general point is worth making. Questioned by the Senate (see Book 1, p. 448, of the Ervin committee *Hearings*) about the financing of the Gemstone operation, McCord claimed to have received $76,000. Asked to account for his expenditures from this amount, McCord provided figures that, literally, do not add up. According to him, some $38,050 was spent on electronics equipment, of which $17,750 represented "miscellaneous purchases" or monies spent in "unidentified stores." Another $12,000 was written off as "overhead," while $18,800 in receipts were retained by McCord for "legal fees." In other words, less than a third of the funds given to McCord could be accounted for in terms of purchases of electronics equipment. The Senate did not question McCord's arithmetic, even when his expenditures—incorrectly listed as $76,000—actually added up to $78,650 ($2,650 more than he claimed to have received).

[8] Liddy, *Will*, pp. 235–36. These are the "correspondence photographs" developed by Michael Richardson on June 10.

generally reflects Liddy's own, though Magruder is mistaken in his belief that the June 8 delivery included the so-called correspondence photographs taken inside the DNC. Magruder writes that Liddy's first delivery occurred in early June, and that the take was found to be "worthless." Most of the material concerned the private lives of workers at the DNC, and none of it was of any political interest. It was for that reason, Magruder tells us, that he decided not to forward the material to John Mitchell but to wait, instead, until something more substantial came in.[9]

Magruder's unhappiness with the first intercepts, and his decision to withhold their contents from Mitchell temporarily, did not come as a surprise to Liddy. He had argued from the very beginning that the DNC was a useless target. If anything, the Gemstone File made his argument seem prescient.

Which makes Jeb Magruder's testimony before the Ervin committee all the more confusing. According to Magruder, "I brought the [Gemstone] materials in to Mr. Mitchell in my 8:30 morning meeting I had each morning with him. . . . He, as I recall, reviewed the documents, indicated, as I did, that there was really no substance to these documents, and at that time, as I recall, it was at that time he called Mr. Liddy up to his office and Mr. Mitchell indicated his dissatisfaction with the results of his work." Asked by Chief Counsel Sam Dash if Mitchell gave any specific orders with respect to improving upon the information being gathered, Magruder said no. "He [Mitchell] did not ask for anything more. He simply indicated that this was not satisfactory and it was worthless and not worth the money that he [Liddy] had been paid for it. . . . There was no information relating to any of the subjects [which Mitchell allegedly] hoped to receive, and Mr. Liddy indicated there was a problem with one wiretap and . . . he would correct these matters and, hopefully, get the information that was requested."[10]

Mitchell denies all this, saying that he and Magruder were never alone at any of the morning meetings, that he was never shown the Gemstone File, and that he never discussed its contents with Gordon Liddy.[11] Liddy concurs, suggesting that Magruder has confused Mitchell with H. R. Haldeman's staff assistant. According to Liddy, it was Gordon Strachan—not John Mitchell—who sum-

[9]Magruder, *American Life*, p. 209; the Ervin committee, *Hearings*, Book 2, pp. 796–98.
[10]Ervin committee *Hearings*, Book 2, p. 797.
[11]Ibid., Book 4, pp. 1619–20.

moned him to the White House to say that the contents of the first batch of telephone intercepts were useless. Liddy says he believed that Strachan was speaking on Haldeman's behalf, and so informed him that one of the bugs had malfunctioned and that the break-in team intended to reenter the DNC to correct the problem.[12]

Elsewhere, Liddy tells us about his last contact with John Mitchell, a contact that took place on June 15, roughly thirty hours before the fateful break-in. While the meeting was not intended to serve as a forum for the discussion of intelligence matters, Liddy hoped for the opportunity to say a private word to Mitchell about plans for reentering the DNC, correcting the broken bug, and photographing more documents. Doing so, however, was not going to be easy, since others would be present at the meeting, and among them would be some who lacked a need to know about the operation. In the event, Liddy carried a thick envelope with him. In it were an accumulation of Gemstone transcripts. Taking a seat near the distracted Mitchell, who was reading and puffing on a pipe, Liddy says that he placed the envelope discreetly on a corner of the desk beside them. Telling Mitchell that the envelope was for him, and that "the problem we have" would be solved that weekend, Liddy says that Mitchell only nodded, "making no move to pick up the envelope. Indeed, the entire time I was in his office he never touched it."[13]

And, in fact, Liddy was not in Mitchell's office for very long. In an effort to ingratiate himself with the CRP's chieftain, Liddy says that he began to tell Mitchell of his prankish plans for embarrassing McGovern in Miami. Mitchell's reaction was to order Liddy to cease and desist, with the result that Liddy scampered away to tell Bernard Barker to call off his dogs. The meeting, then, had not even begun before Liddy was forced to leave. Once again, Mitchell had put the kibosh on the spook's fatuous schemes.

Liddy's account is interesting not merely because it contradicts Magruder's, but also because its narrator assumes that Mitchell understood his reference to "the problem." Since there were others present at the meeting, Liddy felt constrained to speak only in the vaguest way about the difficulties with the O'Brien bug, hoping that Mitchell would get his drift. There is no evidence that Mitchell did —perhaps because he did not want to.

[12]Liddy, *Will*, pp. 239–40.
[13]Ibid.

The meeting took place on Thursday evening, June 15, after normal working hours; on the following morning Mitchell, Magruder and other administration officials enplaned for San Clemente, California. While it would have been physically possible for Mitchell to have read the transcripts late that same night, he says that he did not. And, in fact, for him to have done so would have entailed a sense of urgency on Mitchell's part vis-à-vis Liddy's operation, a sense of urgency to be found nowhere else.

Mitchell says that he knows nothing about any envelope from Liddy. As he told the Senate in support of his testimony with reference to a meticulously kept appointments book, he had only one encounter with G. Gordon Liddy after their meeting on February 4, 1972. This encounter occurred in Mitchell's office on June 15 —obviously the same meeting to which Liddy makes reference. Mitchell says that he does not recall Liddy's remark about "a problem," nor does he recall that Liddy left anything on his desk. This is not to say that neither event occurred, Mitchell points out, but that if they did occur, he took no notice. According to Mitchell, his June 15 conversation with Liddy was brief. At the suggestion of DeVan Shumway, the CRP's public information officer (who was present at the June 15 meeting and who confirms Mitchell's account), they discussed a letter that Liddy had written to the *Washington Post* and that required Mitchell's approval before it could be sent. Mitchell gave his approval, and that was that.[14]

There was, according to Mitchell, no early-morning meeting at which Magruder claims he, Mitchell, upbraided Liddy for the unsatisfactory contents of the Gemstone File. That story, Mitchell insists, is "a palpable, damnable lie."[15] As he points out, a conversation of that kind simply would not have taken place. The morning meetings were crowded ones, as his office calendar reflects; on no occasion was Mitchell alone with Magruder and/or Liddy, and he would certainly not have discussed such sensitive matters (had he been aware of them) in the presence of others. Finally, and once again Mitchell is supported by his office calendar, Liddy did not attend any of the morning meetings. To believe Magruder, then, one must also believe that everyone else is lying, and that, moreover, the office calendar has been "cooked."

[14]Ervin committee *Hearings,* Book 4, p. 1620.
[15]Ibid., p. 1619.

12.
"Why?
Who Wants to Know?"

In an appearance before the Senate's Ervin committee, Jeb Magruder was asked about the June 16–17 break-in.

"Where were you when this occurred?" Chief Counsel Sam Dash inquired.

"I was in Los Angeles, California," Magruder replied.

"Were you aware," Dash continued, "that this break-in was to take place?"

"No," Magruder said.[1]

That testimony was false; given in the mistaken belief that Gordon Liddy would never come forward with his own account of events, Magruder's testimony accomplished two ends. First, it appeared to absolve him of any responsibility for the final break-in, and, second, it obviated any questions that might have been asked of Magruder concerning the reasons for the break-in. Obviously, if the break-in took Magruder by surprise, he could not testify as to the motives that lay behind it.

But, the question of motive was eventually put to him by his own accomplices, who, unlike the Senate committee, were skeptical of Magruder's veracity and all-American image. According to John Dean, the question arose during a 1974 prison conversation between himself and Charles Colson:

"Chuck, why do you figure Liddy bugged the DNC instead of the Democratic candidates? It doesn't make much sense. I sat in Mitchell's

[1] Ervin committee *Hearings*, Book 2, pp. 797–98.

office when Liddy gave us his show, and he only mentioned Larry O'Brien in passing as a target. I confess that Magruder once told me you were pushing for information on O'Brien because of the ITT case, and I—"

"Magruder's full of shit," Chuck interrupted. "That bastard tests my Christian patience to the breaking point. I have to say special prayers to temper my feelings about that asshole. I'd like to hear him say that to my face."

"Why don't we ask Jeb to come over?" I suggested. "And I'll ask him why the hell Liddy went after O'Brien. What do you think?"

"I think it's a capital idea," Chuck replied. . . .

I went down to Jeb's room. . . .

"Jeb, [Dean asked] we've been trying to put some pieces together about why we're here," I began, "and one of the questions we can't answer is why Larry O'Brien was targeted. I guess you and Mitchell agreed to that in Florida. But why O'Brien?"

Jeb froze. His pallid face flushed crimson. He tried to find words, but only stuttered. The question had more than caught him off guard. It had overwhelmed him. "Why do you want to know?" he asked haltingly.

"Just curiosity," Chuck said.

"Well, it just seemed like a good idea," Jeb said evasively.

"Well then, why was Spencer Oliver's phone bugged?" Chuck pressed. . . .

Jeb looked at me. Then at Colson. "Why? Who wants to know?" he asked as his confusion turned to suspicion and headed toward anger. "I don't think we ought to talk about that stuff," he said sharply. Jeb turned on his heel and walked out, leaving Chuck and me staring at each other in dismay.

Chuck broke our silence. "You know, I think I know why Jeb's so damn depressed. I think he's still holding back what he knows."

"You think maybe Mitchell didn't approve O'Brien as a target?"

"No. Well, I'm not sure. . . . But it looks suspicious to me. It's incredible. Millions of dollars have been spent investigating Watergate. A President has been forced out of office. Dozens of lives have been ruined. We're sitting in the can. And still nobody can explain why they bugged the place to begin with."[2]

Years later Gordon Liddy shed some light on the question. In his memoir he describes two meetings with Magruder that led directly to the last break-in. The first meeting took place on June 9, less than twenty-four hours after Liddy had delivered the first installment of the Gemstone File.

[2]Dean, *Blind Ambition*, pp. 388–91.

At that meeting, Liddy writes, Magruder complained that the contents of the Gemstone logs had proved to be a waste of time and money, and asked if the "defective bug"³ could be fixed or relocated. Liddy said that it could be, but that doing so would entail an unbudgeted entry into the DNC. Still, if Magruder and his principals wanted it done, Liddy would see to it. Magruder promised to give him a decision on the matter the following Monday.⁴

Which he did. Liddy and Magruder met in the latter's office. To Liddy's annoyance, they were discussing the number and placement of filing cabinets in the DNC when suddenly Magruder exclaimed, "Here's what I want to know."

> He swung his left arm back behind him and brought it forward forcefully as he said, "I want to know what O'Brien's got right here!" At the word *here* he slapped the lower left part of his desk with his left palm, hard. "Take all the men, all the cameras you need. *That's* what I want to know!"
>
> There was a world of significance in Magruder's gesture. When he said "here!" and slapped that particular portion of his desk, he was referring to the place he kept his derogatory information on the Democrats. Whenever in the past he had called me in to attempt to verify some rumor about, for example, Jack Anderson, it was from there that he withdrew whatever he already had on the matter. *The purpose of the second Watergate break-in was to find out what O'Brien had of a derogatory nature about* us, *not for us to get something on him or the Democrats.* [Emphasis in the original.]
>
> Magruder didn't tell me what he either expected, or was afraid, we'd find in O'Brien's files. He instructed that we go in there with all the film, men, and cameras necessary to photograph everything in his desk and in those files. . . .⁵

From Liddy's description of the event ("Take all the men, all the cameras you need!"), it is clear that Magruder has been galvanized into action. His sense of urgency is palpable, and Liddy acts upon the order immediately. Whereas more than a month had passed

³The "defective bug" to which Magruder referred was the bug that McCord had supposedly placed in O'Brien's office. Liddy had passed along McCord's explanation for the absence of "take" from O'Brien, saying that no transmissions had been received from the putative bug either because it was defective in manufacture or architecturally "shielded." As mentioned earlier, Liddy was under the impression that the bug was an ultrasophisticated room microphone.
⁴Liddy, *Will*, pp. 236–37.
⁵Ibid., p. 237.

before Liddy attempted to carry out Magruder's initial order in April to burglarize the DNC, this time only four days would separate the command from the response. Clearly, something had happened between the afternoon of June 9 and the morning meeting on June 12.

What that seems to have been was the publication of a newspaper article in the *Washington Star* on Friday afternoon, June 9. The article, headlined "Capitol Hill Call-Girl Ring," hit very close to home. According to that article:

> The FBI here has uncovered a high-priced call girl ring allegedly headed by a Washington attorney and staffed by secretaries and office workers from Capitol Hill and involving at least one White House secretary, sources said today.
>
> A 22-count indictment returned today by a special federal grand jury names Phillip M. Bailley, 30, as head of the operation.
>
> Sources close to the investigation said that among the clients of the call girl operation were a number of local attorneys holding high positions in the Washington legal community and one lawyer at the White House.
>
> The clients were not named in the indictment, but sources at the U.S. Attorney's Office said some of them will be called to testify at the trial.
>
> The indictment, handed down this morning before U.S. District Court Chief Judge John J. Sirica, alleges that Bailley violated the Mann Act, a federal law which prohibits the transportation of women across state lines for the purpose of prostitution or immoral acts. He is also charged with interstate travel in aid of racketeering enterprises, extortion, procuring and pandering.
>
> The indictment says that Bailley "compelled, induced and enticed the girls to engage in prostitution."[6]

According to prosecutor John Rudy, White House reaction to the *Star* article was swift. Within an hour of its publication, John Dean called Rudy to say that "They were very concerned about White House personnel being involved, about potential embarrassment during an election year." Rudy further recalled: "He told me he was the President's counsel, and that he wanted me to come over to the White House. He wanted me to bring 'all' the evidence but, mostly, what I brought were Bailley's address books. Dean said he

[6]Winston Groom and Woody West, "Capitol Hill Call-Girl Ring," *Washington Star*, June 9, 1972, p. 1.

wanted to check the names of the people involved, to see if any of them worked for the President." Within minutes of speaking with Dean, Rudy was en route to the White House in a chauffeured black Mercury sedan. Sitting in Dean's office, Rudy discussed the case with Dean while the latter's secretary took the address books from the room to copy. This done, Dean studied the copies page by page, circling names with a Parker pen.

The involvement of some White House employees was indisputable. Among the evidence that Rudy took to the White House were sexually explicit photos of a female attorney who, with upwards of two thousand other federal employees, worked in the Executive Office of the President. (This was the same attorney whose name appears to have been used—without her knowledge—to rent Tess's apartment at the Columbia Plaza.) Dean recommended that she be fired immediately, and she was. But there were many other names in the books, and not all of them were Republicans. On the contrary, according to Bailley, the books contained the names of DNC secretaries and pols, past and present girlfriends of his, prostitutes at the Columbia Plaza and elsewhere, clients, colleagues, and not a few johns. While it would serve no purpose to identify those who Bailley says were in those books, it should be emphasized that they included the secretaries and wives of some of Washington's most important people—Republicans and Democrats. Not all were involved in the seamier side of Bailley's life, but more than a few were, which raised the specters of blackmail and scandal at the height of the presidential campaign.

All the circumstantial evidence suggests that concerns about the Bailley case led to the June 16 break-in. This evidence has to do with timing, and with the chain of command between the White House and the CRP. As we have seen, it was John Dean who recruited Liddy for the CRP intelligence operation, offering him a seven-figure budget, and it was Dean who expressed such interest in the Bailley address books. Like Magruder, Dean reported to H. R. Haldeman, who, perhaps more than anyone else at the White House, had been pushing for clandestine political intelligence operations. Haldeman was kept fully apprised of Donald Segretti's dirty-tricks campaign against the Democrats.[7] Moreover, according to Dean, Haldeman had dispatched Gordon Strachan to urge Ma-

[7]Hersh, *Price of Power*, p. 590.

gruder to "get this [intelligence operation] going . . . : the President wants it done and there's to be no more arguing about it."[8] In view of Haldeman's demonstrated interest in such matters, it would be surprising if Dean had failed to discuss Phil Bailley and the *Star* article with him—or with his agents, Strachan and Magruder. In terms of prurient political intelligence, the scandal was a potential embarrassment to *both* parties.

Whether a connection was made between the Bailley scandal and the contents of the Gemstone File is unknown. It is undeniable, however, that it was on June 9, when the Bailley story broke and Dean summoned Rudy to the White House, that Magruder declared that a second foray into the DNC might be required. It was on the very next working day (Monday, June 12) that Magruder met with Liddy again, and this time he insisted on a second break-in, saying that he expected to obtain information of a scandalous kind—in a word, "dirt."

Principal AUSA Earl Silbert was also convinced that the DNC was a repository of scandal. "Hunt was trying to blackmail Spencer [Oliver],"[9] Silbert later insisted. That belief was based upon what the prosecutors had been told about the contents of telephone calls that Baldwin had monitored, and the information that the younger Oliver was having marital problems. The intercepted telephone conversations, Silbert said, were "extremely personal, intimate, and potentially embarrassing."[10] According to an assistant of Silbert's, who interviewed Baldwin on several occasions, the conversations were "primarily sexual. What you had were the secretaries at the DNC talking to their boyfriends, arranging dates. Apparently, they were pretty explicit about what they were going to do on a given night." In reality, the attribution of those conversations to DNC secretaries and their boyfriends is mistaken, as the reader may have already surmised from the fact that Baldwin recalls having intercepted a conversation on May 26, prior to the alleged installation of any bug inside the DNC.[11] Baldwin's naïve belief that he was listening to a horde of sexually aroused typists is based upon what he was

---

[8]Lukas, *Nightmare,* p. 187.
[9]*Nomination of Earl J. Silbert to be United States Attorney, Hearings before the Senate Committee on the Judiciary,* 93d Cong., 2d sess., Part 1, April–May 1974, p. 52.
[10]Ibid., p. 65.
[11]The installation of bugging devices at the DNC is alleged by McCord to have taken place on the night of May 28–29.

told by McCord: that he was monitoring phone calls originating from a bug inside the Democrats' headquarters. In fact, as we will see, what Baldwin was actually listening to was a bug, or bugs, inside the Columbia Plaza (and perhaps elsewhere as well).

The sexual character of the Gemstone File, and the attendant threat of blackmail, would not be revealed in court (for reasons discussed in a later chapter). Outside the courts, however, the whiff of blackmail was pervasive. *New York Times* reporter Anthony Lukas wondered about it even while writing what is widely regarded as the definitive account of the Watergate scandal. According to Lukas, "Several secretaries used Oliver's phone because they thought it was the most private one in the office. They would say: 'We can talk; I'm on Spencer Oliver's phone.' Some of the conversations, Baldwin recalls, were 'explicitly intimate.' . . . Ehrlichman, after debriefing Magruder (in the wake of the arrests), reported, 'What they were getting was mostly this fellow Oliver phoning his girl friends all over the country lining up assignations.' So spicy were some of the conversations on the phone that they have given rise to unconfirmed reports that the telephone was being used for some sort of callgirl service catering to congressmen and other prominent Washingtonians."[12]

---

[12]Lukas, *Nightmare*, p. 201. Just as everyone was mistaken about the identities of the "secretaries," Ehrlichman was mistaken about Oliver: it was his telephone that was used, but he was not the caller.

13.

The Last Break-in

Magruder's order to hit the DNC a second time was transmitted by Liddy to Hunt and McCord on the same day that it was issued. That afternoon, June 12, McCord instructed Baldwin to visit the DNC's headquarters, using a pretext. Though the visit has never been controversial, it should have been.

According to Baldwin, his trip to the DNC was a casing visit: McCord wanted him to pinpoint the location of Larry O'Brien's office. To accomplish that, he took advantage of the fact that Spencer Oliver was out of town. Pretending to be the nephew of former DNC Chairman John Bailey, Baldwin says that he told DNC receptionist Clota Yesbek that he had stopped by to see his old school chum Spencer Oliver. Feigning disappointment at the news that Oliver was in Texas, Baldwin was introduced to Oliver's secretary, Ida ("Maxie") Wells (later secretary to presidential candidate Jimmy Carter). She gave him a guided tour of the DNC and, at Baldwin's request, provided him with O'Brien's private telephone number in Miami.

Questioned later by the FBI, Maxie Wells remembered Baldwin's visit only vaguely, but generally confirmed the account that he had given of it. The only discrepancies that emerged in connection with that account had to do with the alias that Baldwin used and Clota Yesbek's memory of the visit. With respect to the alias, Baldwin himself was somewhat mixed up: he told the *Los Angeles Times* that he used the name Bill Johnson, whereas he later informed the Senate that Bill Bailey was his nom de guerre.[1] Wells was herself unable to recall her visitor's name, while Yesbek's recollection of the visit

[1] *Los Angeles Times* interview with Baldwin, p. 99 of the transcript; see also March 30, 1973, interview of Baldwin by Senator Lowell Weicker and attorney William Shure.

was entirely at odds with the account that Baldwin had given and Wells had confirmed. According to Yesbek, Baldwin paid *several* visits to the DNC and, on each occasion, asked to see Maxie Wells, not Spencer Oliver. Yesbek was under the impression—an impression that Wells and Baldwin both deny—that the two were dating. Finally, Yesbek thought that Baldwin had used his real name during these visits.[2]

Resolving these differences is probably impossible. The explanation, however, may be that Yesbek confused Baldwin and his "Bill Bailey" alias with Phil Bailley, who was, indeed, a frequent visitor to the DNC and who, moreover, resembled Alfred Baldwin. Asked in a telephone interview whether she had ever dated Phil Bailley, Maxie Wells said that she did not recall, but would not rule out the possibility that she had. "We were certainly not close friends. I had a lot of passing acquaintances up there [at the DNC]. . . . The name sort of rings a bell."

What is most peculiar about Baldwin's visit, however, is not the discrepant accounts of the witnesses. Rather, it is the motive that Baldwin and McCord gave for the excursion, because, of course, McCord knew exactly where Larry O'Brien's office was located. According to McCord, he had bugged that same office some two weeks earlier, and on that occasion Bernard Barker was said to have photographed documents on O'Brien's desk. While those documents were considered uninteresting, and while the alleged bug did not transmit, the location of the office itself was never in doubt. What, then, was the real purpose of Baldwin's mission?

The answer has to do with Baldwin's requesting to see Spencer Oliver, knowing that he was out of town. In claiming that he was a personal friend of Oliver's and the nephew of an important Democrat, he ensured that he would be turned over to Oliver's secretary, Maxie Wells. At the very least, then, he would have an opportunity to see her office, and her desk. And that Maxie Wells's desk was a target of the Watergate break-in is beyond a doubt. As we will see, in the course of making the arrests inside the DNC, Washington police would wrest a key from Eugenio Martinez. The FBI later determined that that key opened the drawers to Maxie Wells's desk.[3] Baldwin, then, seems to have been sent to the DNC to locate

[2]Executive session interview of Yesbek before the Ervin committee: "Memorandum, Subject: Clo Yesbek Interview Digest," dated July 19, 1974 (noted in the unpublished version of the Baker Report, Section IV).

[3]The relevant FBI reports with respect to Wells's key are serialized 139-166-356, -358, and -359;

that particular desk—to identify it from among the scores of other desks on the sixth floor.

Having said that, there are many questions about Baldwin's tour and Wells's key that remain unanswered. While the key was perhaps the only piece of prima facie evidence that spoke directly to questions concerning what the burglars were after, almost no attention was paid to it by those responsible for investigating the affair. The existence of the key raised the specter of an "inside person" at the DNC (for how else could the burglars have gotten it?) and, what's more, hinted at a secret agenda to which neither Magruder nor Liddy was privy. Neither man mentions the key in either his testimony or his memoirs, and when asked about it by this reporter, Liddy protested—sincerely, I believe—that he knew nothing about it.

On Friday morning, June 16, Judge Charles Richey ordered that Phillip Mackin Bailley be committed to fascist poet Ezra Pound's alma mater, St. Elizabeths Hospital, to determine whether or not the attorney was sane. The commitment was resisted by Bailley's lawyer, and by Bailley himself. That he had been practicing before that same court some two months earlier militated strongly against the possibility that he was insane. He had pleaded not guilty to the charges against him, and however lurid the evidence might be, there was nothing to suggest that he was mad—kinky and corrupt, yes, but not "certifiable." For different reasons the prosecution was equally unenthusiastic about the prospect of commitment. To John Rudy and others handling the case, the investigation of Bailley had been intensive, and the evidence showed that he had committed criminal acts. Rudy wanted a conviction, therefore, and the resort to St. Elizabeths threatened its likelihood because it raised the possibility of an insanity defense. Despite the objections of both the defense and the prosecution, however, Bailley was told to pack his toothbrush.[4]

---

these are interviews, conducted June 27, 1972, with Wells and DNC secretary Barbara Kennedy. According to Wells, there were only two examples of the key in existence: one in her possession, which she wore around her neck, and one in Kennedy's possession. (Both keys, in addition to the one taken from Martinez, were accounted for by the FBI.)

[4]Following an observation period in the mental institution, Bailley was allowed to plead guilty to one of the twenty-six counts filed against him (in return for which the remaining twenty-five counts were dropped). In the fall, he was sent to the federal penitentiary in Danbury, Connecticut, where, ironically, he came to serve on the Inmates' Committee with Howard Hughes's biographer, Clifford Irving, and Watergate burglars E. Howard Hunt and G. Gordon Liddy. See Jim Mann, "Mann Act Suspect Due Mental Test," *Washington Post*, June

Even as Bailley listened to the judge's order that he undergo a
mental examination at St. E's, the Cubans arrived at National Airport, where, in yet another coincidence, they were hailed by Jack
Anderson. As the columnist recalls:

Outside the terminal, as I headed for the entrance closest to where my
Cleveland flight was already loading, I spotted a familiar face [Frank
Sturgis] bobbing hopefully above the incoming bustle, a face at home in
the world's depots of eternal expectations. . . .

"Frankie!" I hollered, waving him down. He turned and a look of
unease crossed his eyes, resembling an errant husband who at the point
of rendezvous bumps into a well-meaning neighbor. But he came over,
shook hands warmly, and we chatted for a moment in the banalities of
airport encounters.

"What brings you to Washington?" I asked.

"Private business," he said. But he could not resist an exaggerated
smile, a telegraph that he was off on one of his peculiar missions. He
introduced me to a companion; the other two confederates hung back.
We parted jovially, talking of getting together soon. Then Frank and
his group disappeared in the direction of the taxicabs. They would
momentarily depart for the Watergate Hotel, where they had two rooms
reserved under aliases.

On the plane, in the enforced idleness of waiting for our turn in the
take-off pattern, a loose chord jangled in my head, agitating to be
plugged in. One of the Cubans who had hung back, his face turned
away, I knew him from somewhere. Yes. Sturgis had introduced me to
him in Miami years before. Barker was his name. Bernard Barker.
"Macho," Sturgis had called him. . . .

I wondered what the four Cubans were doing in Washington. Something murky, I thought, probably for the CIA. As soon as I got back
from Cleveland, I planned to check back with Sturgis. There might be
a story in it.[5]

16, 1972; and Lawrence Meyer, "Lawyer Pleads Guilty in Call Girl Case," *Washington Post*,
September 30, 1972.
[5] Jack Anderson (with George Clifford), *The Anderson Papers* (New York: Ballantine, 1974),
pp. 35–37. The encounter, and Anderson's explanation, have raised any number of eyebrows.
Questioned by the Senate about the meeting, the columnist proved unable to document the
trip to Cleveland. His calendar did not reflect it, he could not recall to whom his speech had
been given, and there seemed to be no mention in the Cleveland newspapers of the famous
man's public visit. It was natural, then, that the "chance encounter" should cause some to
charge that Anderson was engaged in his own cover-up. Those charges became even more
heated when it was learned that, months earlier, Anderson had been apprised by William
Haddad and A. J. Woolston-Smith of plans to bug the DNC—information with which the
columnist seems to have done very little. In fact, however, Anderson's presence in the
Cleveland area that night can be documented. He was a featured speaker at the annual dinner

While the country's foremost investigative reporter was en route to Cleveland the Cubans were ensconced under aliases at the Watergate Hotel and the stage was set for Richard Nixon's final crisis.

The evening of June 16, 1972, was a Friday night like any other in the Washington summer. The temperature was uncomfortably high, the light polluted by rush-hour traffic, the air heavy and stagnant with humidity. Cars rolled along Virginia Avenue toward Rock Creek Park and Georgetown, passing the Columbia Plaza, the Howard Johnson's motel and the Watergate office building. A few blocks away the orchestra began tuning up in the Kennedy Center for a performance of Leonard Bernstein's *Mass*. (The composer himself would conduct that night.)

At about 6:00 P.M., Lou Russell climbed into his car, a battered Plymouth, and drove southeast toward his daughter's house in Benedict, Maryland. The trip would take a bit more than an hour. Meanwhile, as Howard Hunt and Gordon Liddy dined with their families in suburban Maryland, James McCord finished his week's work in the offices of the CRP. According to those who worked with McCord, he left the CRP shortly after 6:15 P.M. They assumed that he was going home. In fact he drove to the Howard Johnson's, parked his car, and went up to Room 723. It was 6:30 when he arrived. Alfred Baldwin was waiting.[6]

The two men sat down amid the electronics equipment, including a smoke detector that McCord planned to wire as a room microphone, supposedly for installation in Larry O'Brien's office. As it happened, however, McCord had forgotten to bring the batteries that the device required. This, at least, is what he told Baldwin, who was dispatched to buy the batteries and some "speaker wire." As it turned out, Baldwin had a difficult time finding what was needed,

meeting of Sigma Delta Chi (SDX), a fraternity of professional journalists. That the speech was not covered by the Cleveland press was due to an editorial decision that it was not newsworthy. The speech *was* mentioned, however, in the Willoughby (Ohio) *News-Herald* edition of June 19, 1972, in which a photograph of Anderson appears, showing him in rapt conversation with that newspaper's editor. That no one, including Anderson, was able to uncover this documentation was apparently due to the *Herald*'s late publication of the photo. The airport encounter with the burglars, therefore, seems to have been precisely what Anderson said it was: a remarkable coincidence, and nothing more.

[6]The chronology of events for June 16–17 is established primarily by consensus obtained in interviews (by the author and the FBI) with the staffs of the Howard Johnson's and Watergate restaurants, the statements and testimony of those involved in the break-in, and reference to physical evidence, such as GSS security logbooks.

and ended up, ironically, at the Spy Shop in downtown Washington, the same enterprise whose proprietor, a few months earlier, had offered to "de-bug" the DNC. McCord, then, was alone in Baldwin's hotel room at 6:45 P.M. and for some time afterward.

Russell reached Benedict at about 7:00 P.M. There were almost two hours of light left when he tried the small gate to the front yard of his daughter's house and, finding it locked, climbed over it. Calling out to her, he received no response and so went next door to ask the neighbors where she might be. They did not know, but assumed that she had gone to the store for groceries and would return before long. Would Russell like to wait at their house? No, he said, he would visit a friend, the coroner, Dr. George Weems, whose office was near, and return in an hour. Russell repeated that he'd be back in a little while; he intended to spend the night in Benedict, he said, adding that it was good to be out of Washington on the weekend. Having impressed his supposed intentions upon the neighbors, he got back into his Plymouth, waved good-bye, and drove straight to the Howard Johnson's motel near the Watergate.

At 8:00 P.M. James McCord was seated in the Howard Johnson's ground-floor restaurant and, clearly, he was waiting for someone—though who that might have been is anyone's guess. Lou Russell was on his way, and so were Frank Sturgis and Eugenio Martinez. Coincidentally, however, the first person to join McCord on the scene was an acquaintance named Peyton George, a former FBI agent.[7] George and his son were on their way to a waterfront concert and, with time to spare, had stopped for an ice-cream cone at the Hojo. Seeing McCord, George had chatted briefly with him, and then left. Questioned about the encounter by the FBI, George could not recall if McCord had been alone or with company.[8]

It was just as George left that the Howard Johnson's restaurant became a kind of crossroads for real and theatrical espionage agents. At 8:15 P.M. Sturgis and Martinez entered the restaurant, supposedly to have dinner, but in fact to meet McCord. In one of those bizarre coincidences that afflicted the Watergate affair, Sturgis literally

[7]What made this a coincidence was the fact that, six weeks earlier, McCord had offered George a job as chief of security for Martha Mitchell. George's salary demand of $30,000 had been high, but Fred LaRue had given his approval. George, however, would not take the post unless he was also guaranteed a position with the law firm of Mitchell, Mudge, Rose & Alexander—a condition that apparently was not met.
[8]FBI serial 139-4089-744, p. 95 (interview of Peyton George conducted by special agent Howard Slack on June 29, 1972).

bumped into his idol, film actor Burt Lancaster.

"I saw him," Sturgis told me, "and, you know, he's about my favorite movie actor. My wife says I look a little like him. So I went up and shook his hand. Told him I was Frank Fiorini—I didn't wanna use Sturgis—and that I thought he was terrific. He said he was in town to make a movie and, later, when I got out of jail, I went to see it. Burt Lancaster in *Scorpio*. It's funny—the movie's about this CIA guy who's betrayed by the agency. Sorta like what happened to us, y'know? I mean, it doesn't take a genius to figure out that Watergate was a CIA setup. We were just pawns. Anyway, I met Burt Lancaster."

According to Sturgis, he and Martinez had dinner in the Howard Johnson's. They ate alone, he claims, and saw no one whom they knew (except the film star). In fact, however, Sturgis is mistaken. He and Martinez dined with Gonzalez and McCord at 8:30 P.M. in the Watergate Hotel—this according to the hostess who seated them, the waiter who served them, and the dining-room captain.[9] (According to the waiter, they had lobster tails.) Why the burglars should wish to conceal this fact is uncertain.

It was at about this same time, though, that Lou Russell arrived at the Howard Johnson's. In an interview with the FBI, he said that he dined in the Hojo restaurant that night from 8:30 until 10:30 P.M.[10] He did not see McCord, he said, and his presence there on that historic evening was only coincidental. He was there, he said, on what amounted to "a trip down memory lane." He had once dated a girl, he told skeptical G-men, who was in the habit of having her hair done in the Watergate complex across the street. On those occasions, he claimed, he would have lunch with her at the Howard Johnson's. That evening, he said, he had suffered a sudden attack of nostalgia for the girl, and so had gone to the Hojo, there to dine by himself and to reminisce about the good times that they had had.

This was, purely and simply, a cock-and-bull story. To say that his previous "girlfriend" had had her hair done at the Watergate was something of an understatement. She was a weekend prostitute at the Columbia Plaza who picked up johns in the Watergate bar, and her coiffure was by no means the only reason for her presence there.

[9]Ibid. (interviews conducted on June 26, 1972, with Theresa Acuna, Kgah Win, and Chris Tesimbidis).
[10]Ibid., pp. 26–27 (interview conducted by special agents Rodney C. Kicklighter and James M. Hopper on July 3, 1972, one of several FBI interviews with Russell).

The FBI agents who interviewed Russell were certain that he was lying about his reasons for being at the Howard Johnson's that night, but they were ill-equipped to disprove his story. He had not told them that he had driven all the way from Benedict to relieve his nostalgia.

Indeed, Russell told different stories to different people about his whereabouts that evening and why he was in one place or another. To some he said that he was at the Hojo's from 8:30 to 10:30 for sentimental reasons. He then went, depending upon who was listening, either to his own apartment or to his daughter's house in Benedict. To others he claimed that he had gone to the Howard Johnson's *after* 10:30 P.M., having spent the earlier part of the evening at the Kennedy Center listening to Bernstein conduct his *Mass*. Still others were told that he had spent the whole evening in Benedict.

James McCord's version of the matter contradicts all of Russell's accounts. McCord testified that Russell "was not there the night of the break-in at the Howard Johnson Motel or anywhere in the vicinity. He told me that the night before, which would have been the night of June . . . 15—the Thursday night [prior to the break-in] —that he had gone to the Howard Johnson Motel restaurant to have dinner and that he had gone there with a woman companion who —they on a regular basis ate at the Howard Johnson restaurant as a custom over some years; that she normally went to the Watergate hairdresser, one of them, for her hairdo, and they would go over to the Howard Johnson restaurant and have dinner."[11]

Obviously, McCord's testimony is mistaken. Not only did Russell admit to the FBI that he dined at the Hojo that Friday night, but McCord should have known that Russell had *not* dined there the night before. On that evening, Thursday, June 15, the two of them had had dinner *together* at a downtown Washington restaurant, either the Black Rose or Blackie's House of Beef.[12]

Establishing Russell's whereabouts on the evening of June 16–17 is an important matter that is made difficult by his efforts, and McCord's, to conceal that same information. Russell's motives for concealing his whereabouts are themselves complicated, but they certainly include his wish to keep secret any role that he played in the break-in. That role is something of which McCord himself has

[11]Ervin committee *Hearings*, p. 218.
[12]FBI serial 139-4089-744, pp. 26–27.

been understandably protective. When, for example, I sought to interview him on the subject of Lou Russell, his attorney, Rufus King, said that McCord refused to discuss Russell under any circumstances, and that, moreover, he would not discuss Watergate with any writer who so much as expressed an interest in Lou Russell. In addition, King said, he had received two telegrams from McCord after passing on my request for an interview, and these telegrams instructed him to threaten suit against me, and to say that both Alfred Baldwin and "the Pennington family" would also bring suit should I choose to write about Russell. King confided that he was baffled by his client's attitude, but was obliged to pass the messages along. No, he said in response to a question, he himself did not know who Lee Pennington or Lou Russell was, nor did he know why McCord would link the one to the other.

As we have seen, Russell performed a number of tasks for McCord, patrolling the offices of the CRP at night, infiltrating the Jack Anderson apparat by day, and eavesdropping on the Columbia Plaza in between. (Perhaps, unlike Baldwin, Russell had voice-actuated tape recorders to help him in his work.) But this was not all that Russell did for McCord. On at least one occasion he appears to have handled part of the Gemstone File itself. This occurred in early June, when McCord went to Miami for three days. In his absence, Baldwin was instructed to deliver his eavesdropping logs to a night guard at the CRP. Baldwin told the FBI that he did so —though neither Liddy nor Magruder seems ever to have received this particular batch of conversations—but added that he could not remember the guard's name. He did, however, recall that the guard in question was a man in his fifties, and that he seemed to have two first names. According to Robert Houston, McCord's subordinate at the CRP, there were only two night guards at the CRP who could be described as men in their fifties. They were Walter Braydon, a retired CIA officer, and Louis Russell.[13]

At 8:30 P.M. on the evening of the break-in, Lou Russell was ordering dinner at the Howard Johnson's restaurant as McCord and three of the Miami men were ordering lobster tails at the Watergate. Alfred Baldwin had gone to Georgetown in a fruitless search for

[13]On several occasions, the Ervin committee questioned McCord about the unusual delivery of eavesdropping transcripts to the night guard at the CRP. McCord, however, refused to identify the guard, insisting that he had nothing to do with Watergate. In line with its tender treatment of McCord throughout the investigation, the committee accepted that refusal and probed no further.

speaker wire and batteries while Hunt and Liddy were en route from home to their room in the Watergate Hotel. It was expected that the DNC would be vacant by 9:00 P.M. (the time of Hunt's arrival at the hotel), and that the break-in would occur at approximately 10:00 P.M.

It was shortly after 9:00 P.M. that McCord left the Watergate, saying that he was going to the Howard Johnson's. In fact he went first to his office at the CRP. In an interview with the FBI, CRP security officer Millicent ("Penny") Gleason recalled that "Sometime between 9:30 and 10 P.M., Mr. McCord came in the office and jokingly remarked that he had dropped by to make sure they had plenty of work. McCord's appearance was unusual in that his shirt sleeves were rolled up and he was not well dressed. He was usually dressed very well. McCord stated that he had come to pick up his raincoat. Upon leaving, he said words to the effect, 'Penny, I want to thank you for what you've done for our office.' Her impression was that McCord's remark seemed more like a 'goodbye' than a 'thank you.' "[14]

It was at about 10:00 P.M. that McCord returned to the Howard Johnson's. If he and Russell told the truth, they did not see each other, despite Russell's vantage point in the coffee shop. Taking the elevator to Room 723, McCord found the room empty. Minutes later, however, Baldwin arrived to say that he had found the batteries McCord had wanted, but that he had not been able to locate any speaker wire. McCord took the batteries and, sitting on the bed, instructed Baldwin in the proper method of wiring them together in series, using a soldering gun. Baldwin nodded his understanding, and McCord took leave yet again, telling Baldwin that he knew of an all-night Lafayette radio store where he might be able to buy the needed speaker wire. When the door closed behind McCord, Baldwin sat down to solder the batteries together and, within a minute or two, melted them.

It was about 10:15 P.M. as McCord went down the elevator to the Howard Johnson's ground floor. Minutes earlier Gordon Liddy had reached a decision: since the DNC was still occupied, the break-in would be delayed until after the GSS guard made his midnight inspection. Clearly, that information had been communicated to McCord because, otherwise, with the break-in set to go at 10:00 P.M.,

[14]FBI interview with Gleason conducted July 1, 1972, by FBI special agents Charles W. Harvey and Paul P. Magallanes.

McCord would not have sallied forth into the night when he did. The likelihood is that McCord had spoken to Liddy by telephone from his room in the Hojo, informing the latter that lights continued to burn inside the DNC, and Liddy, weighing the information, had made his decision. And just as likely, McCord had passed that information along to Lou Russell, because Russell also chose that moment to depart the Howard Johnson's restaurant. Climbing into his battered Plymouth, his nostalgic and prolonged cafeteria meal at an end, Russell drove yet again to his daughter's house in Benedict, Maryland, hoping that this time she would be at home.

At 10:50 P.M. (according to GSS security logs), James McCord signed in at the Watergate office building. Taking the elevator to the eighth floor, where the Federal Reserve Board had offices, McCord proceeded to neutralize a series of locks on doors leading from the building's stairwell to corridors and reception areas on the eighth and other floors. Since the circumstances and method used in neutralizing the locks would prove critical to the Watergate arrests, the matter is worth examining in some detail.

To begin with, the burglars could not prudently use the building's elevator (though, in fact, they had done so in May when signing in at the Federal Reserve Board). This meant that they had to use the stairwell that connected all the floors in the building, from the basement to the roof. Access to the stairwell could be obtained through the underground garage, the doors to which would also need to be kept open in some way.

To accomplish this, McCord carried with him a roll of ordinary tape. As police and GSS records later showed, McCord wedged open the locking mechanisms on certain doors, stuffing the latches with bits of balled-up paper. He then placed strips of tape vertically along the edge of each door, covering the latches and making certain that each lock was held in a permanently open position. To a casual passerby there would be nothing odd about the doors: they appeared to be closed and securely locked. Only by pulling at the doorknobs, or by examining the edges of the doors, would it become obvious that the locks were secretly disengaged. All in all, McCord spent ten minutes taping open the stairwell doors to the eighth floor, the sixth floor, the B-2 and B-3 levels, and the doors leading to the underground garage.

Years afterward, Liddy attempted to explain away certain suspicions that had arisen with respect to the taping procedure:

... McCord agreed to tape [the doors] open. It was an old maintenance man's trick.... Experienced guards are used to finding doors taped open no matter how often the maintenance people are admonished. It is done across the lock bolt and around the edge of the doors, rather than along the inside edge of the door, for a very good reason; with the commonly carried electrician's tape, that's the only way it will work. Tape placed edgewise hasn't enough purchase to restrain the strongly spring-loaded bolt of commercial building doors. Even if it did work we wanted it to look like a maintenance man's routine, and they don't do it that way (i.e., they don't place the tape vertically over the lock along the edge of the door). Why should they? They're not trying to burglarize the place and have nothing to fear from discovery. Burglars don't tape the locks. They wedge a matchstick in between the bolt and the bolt opening, then snap it off flush. I would not have approved that method; if discovered by a guard, it's a dead giveaway; he knows immediately he has a burglary on his hands.[15]

The impression given by Liddy in this passage is that he and McCord discussed the taping procedure to be used, and to this day he believes that the tape was placed horizontally across the doors—that is, in the way that maintenance men do it. This is clever of Liddy inasmuch as it is his intention to rebut those Watergate skeptics who insist that the procedure used in taping the locks amounted to sabotage—that it was a deliberate effort to alert the guards. In fact, however, Liddy is mistaken, and his argument has no strength because his knowledge of the actual break-in (and taping procedure) is only a compendium of hearsay and reports in the press —themselves compiled without any critical understanding of the facts involved. McCord did *not* place the tape in the blatant manner that Liddy supposedly recommended. On the contrary, McCord placed the tape vertically along the edges of the doors, so that when the doors were closed the locks were kept open in such a way as to be invisible to casual passersby.[16] It is a small point, perhaps, but it

---

[15]Liddy, *Will*, p. 232.

[16]Establishing this was by no means an easy matter, despite the fact that the senior arresting officer at the scene, Sergeant Paul Leeper, testified clearly and concisely to this effect before the Ervin committee (*Hearings*, Book 1, pp. 95–114). He said that on the B-2 level and the sixth and eighth floors tape had been placed vertically along the edges of various doors, keeping the locks open in such a way that the tape could not be seen when the doors were shut. The press, however, publicized photographic "reconstructions" that mistakenly showed the tape placed horizontally around the edges of the doors in such a way that the tape would be visible even when the doors were shut. One might imagine that the police would have taken photographs at the scene of the crime, and that these photos would show conclusively just

illustrates the bias of Liddy and others who have gone out of their way to twist the facts to make them conform to their own theories about the affair. One wonders if Liddy, on the basis of his own argument, would now take the position that McCord sabotaged the break-in by placing the tape in such a manner as to be, in Liddy's words, "a dead giveaway."

By his own reckoning, McCord completed taping the doors in the Watergate office building at 11:00 P.M. This accomplished, he went to the so-called command post (the room rented by Hunt and Liddy) in the Watergate Hotel. There he told Hunt and Liddy that the doors had been taken care of, and then returned to the "listening post" (the room he shared with Baldwin in the Howard Johnson's). Going to the room's balcony, McCord glanced at the DNC's offices across the street. There was a light on, and a volunteer continued to work inside. (This was a young man named Bruce Givner, and he was not so much working as taking advantage of the DNC's WATS line to telephone friends around the country.) Accordingly, McCord notified Liddy that the target remained occupied.

It was now 11:30 P.M., fully an hour and a half after the break-in had been scheduled to occur. The revised plan called for an entry after the building guard's midnight inspection, and so, with half an hour to go, Hunt and Liddy crossed the street to the Howard Johnson's for a late-night snack. Some forty-five miles away, Lou Russell pulled up in front of his daughter's house and went inside; he told his daughter and son-in-law that he had been at Dr. Weems's office throughout the evening.

At 11:51, a black security guard named Frank Wills arrived at the

---

how the tape had been placed. In fact there is one such photograph in existence (it shows the taped door to the sixth-floor offices of the DNC). In that photo the tape has been placed in the vertical manner that Liddy disparages (and Leeper describes). This photo, however, is useless as evidence: a police "reconstruction," the photo was not taken until June 26, nine days after the arrests. That no other photographs were taken is due to the fact that within fifteen minutes of the Watergate arrests there was no tape on any of the doors in the Watergate office building. This rather startling fact was elicited from GSS supervisor Captain Bobby Jackson by Senate investigator Donald Sanders. In an October 8, 1973, memorandum on his interview with Jackson, Sanders reports that Jackson arrived at the Watergate office building at 2:30 A.M. After conferring with the police and the GSS guard on duty, Jackson checked every stairwell door in the building and found tape on none of them. Asked about this recently, arresting officer Carl Shoffler expressed surprise, and then vaguely recalled having removed the tapes as they were discovered. At the author's suggestion that this seemed an unusual procedure, Shoffler surmised that it was done to prevent any burglars from exiting into the stairwell or out of the building. The problem with this explanation is that removing the tapes would not have prevented either; on the contrary, it would only have stopped someone from breaking in rather than out.

Watergate office building to work the midnight to 8:00 A.M. shift. An unassuming man, he had no way of knowing that his actions (and inactions) during the next two hours would change the course of his life and, perhaps, that of the nation.[17] Standing in the lobby, Wills greeted a second guard, Fletcher Pittman, who was on his way home, and learned that a third guard, LeRoy Brown, had left work early, saying that he felt unwell. Brown was to have been on duty with Wills that night; in signing out, he had inaccurately indicated his time of departure as 1:30 A.M. (possibly so that his employers, General Security Services Inc., would not dock his pay). Immediately upon coming on duty, Wills began to make his rounds in accordance with a standing order of the private security firm that required the relieving watch at midnight to check the basement-level doors for evidence of tampering. At the witching hour, then, Wills discovered McCord's handiwork. As the guard wrote in his security log, "B-2 level stuff with paper. Both doors. Also, one Door on B-3 level was open, the other was stuff with paper and the Door annex outside of office building was open."

This sort of thing had happened before, what with maintenance men going in and out of the building. Often the GSS guards did not bother to report such incidents, preferring simply to free the locks and get on with their rounds. Whether because McCord's taping method was (as Liddy suggests) "a dead giveaway," or because of Wills's own insecurities, the guard decided not to take any chances. Stripping the tape from the B-2 locks, Wills returned to his desk in the lobby of the office building. There he noted his discovery in the log and, uncertain what to do, attempted to telephone his "roving superior," Captain Bobby Jackson. It was impossible to reach Jack-

---

[17]Receiving credit for the Watergate arrests, Wills would become an instant celebrity—a folk hero en route to becoming a public embarrassment. He was an undereducated young man whose race and class had been victimized by the Nixon administration's policy of "benign neglect," and there was poetic justice in whatever contribution he made to that administration's downfall. For a while Wills served as an inarticulate but honored guest on the liberal banquet circuit, accepting plaques and small honoraria before settling into a troubled obscurity. His entirely unrealistic dreams of establishing the Frank Wills Detective Agency seem pathetic in retrospect, and one can only wonder at author Alex Haley's intention to write Wills's biography. Unable to find work in the years after the Watergate arrests, Wills recently told me that he spends much of his time "reading the Bible backwards" (so as to learn secret truths) and studying the legends of Atlantis. Arrested for shoplifting in 1979, Wills was apprehended a second time in 1982. On that occasion, he was sentenced to one year in jail in Georgia for attempting to steal a pair of tennis shoes. A *New York Times* editorial of February 18, 1983, compared Will's sentence with those received by Nixon's men and remarked that "it is probably correct to say that Frank Wills, the first Watergate hero, has become the final Watergate convict."

son immediately, however, since he was making his rounds at a building in Takoma Park, Maryland, twenty minutes away by car. Wills therefore left a message with the GSS answering service, saying that there was a problem at the Watergate office building and asking that Jackson be contacted by beeper for instructions. The answering service signaled Captain Jackson, but as it happened, he did not have the necessary change to make a telephone call from a public booth and was unable to contact the answering service (or Wills) until he could get to his next inspection site, the Carnegie Institution of Washington, where he could use an office phone.

His uncertainty increasing, Wills sought advice from Jackson's own supervisor at GSS, Sergeant Major Ira O'Neal. O'Neal remembers that the call awakened him in bed "a few minutes after midnight." Wills explained to O'Neal what he had found, and O'Neal instructed him to check the doors on other floors in the office building to see if they had been taped open as well. If they had not been taped open, O'Neal said, the incident was probably unimportant. But if other doors had tape across their locks, there might well be a burglary in progress. Wills was to find out and report back to O'Neal in about fifteen minutes to let him know the results of this second tour.

Before Wills could begin checking the other doors, however, DNC volunteer Bruce Givner came bounding down the stairwell into the lobby. According to Givner, he had been the last person in the DNC that night, and at 12:05 A.M. he had shut off the lights before leaving. ("I always wear a watch," Givner told me, "and I always shut off the lights when I go out. I guess you could say I'm pretty compulsive about that sort of thing.")

It was at about this same time that Hunt and Liddy finished their snack at the Howard Johnson's restaurant and, crossing Virginia Avenue, returned to the Watergate Hotel. Hunt recalls the surprise he felt at sharing the elevator with French film actor Alain Delon, Burt Lancaster's co-star in *Scorpio*. (Delon played a contract assassin for the CIA.) The actor chatted amiably with the real-life spies as the elevator ascended, and then stood aside to let Hunt and Liddy exit at their floor.

Meanwhile, in the lobby of the adjacent office building, Wills insisted that "the white boy" Bruce Givner sign out on the visitors' log, but Givner playfully refused, saying that it was unnecessary to sign out because he had not in fact signed in. Becoming friendly, the two men turned to the subject of food, and each said that he was hungry. Then, like Russell, Hunt, Liddy, Sturgis, Gonzalez, McCord, Burt Lancaster and Peyton George, they went together to the Hojo for something to eat. In the end, Givner did not sign out on the visitors' log. According to both Givner and Wills, it was about 12:15 A.M. when Wills turned off the lights in the lobby of the office building and, accompanied by Givner, crossed Virginia Avenue. In doing so, Wills had failed to follow his superior's orders to immediately check the building's other doors, and then to report whether any other locks had been jammed with paper and taped open. Had Wills done as Sergeant Major O'Neal had instructed, he would have found locks taped open on both the eighth and sixth floors. This information would have led O'Neal, as a matter of standard procedure, to notify the police. The police would then have responded to the scene of a crime *that had yet to be committed.* And had the police done so, Baldwin and McCord, watching from the balcony of the Howard Johnson's, would presumably have notified Hunt and the others that the operation had been blown and must be called off, in which case the Watergate scandal might not have occurred. It is ironic, then, that it was Frank Wills's *neglect* of his duties, and not his diligence or perspicacity, that ultimately led to the Watergate arrests.

Between midnight and 12:15 A.M. Lou Russell told his daughter that he must return from Benedict to Washington to do "some work for McCord" that night. Asked whether he had placed or received a telephone call that may have prompted his late-night return to the capital, Russell's daughter says that she is unable to recall if he had. Depending upon the time that Russell actually left for the city, he arrived at the Howard Johnson's as early as 12:45 or as late as 1:00 A.M.[18]

The ideal time for the break-in was, of course, in the absence of Frank Wills. So far as McCord and Baldwin knew at the time, the basement doors to the office building remained open, the lights were out in the lobby, the DNC was finally vacant, the security guard had abandoned the building, and there had been no unusual activity accompanying Wills's arrival at work half an hour earlier. Despite the propitiousness of the situation, however, the go signal was not

---

[18]In ordinary daytime traffic, the trip from Washington to Benedict takes an hour. In the absence of traffic, such as one would expect to find after midnight, the trip requires less time —about forty-five minutes.

forthcoming. This was because McCord, for reasons known only to himself, falsely informed Hunt and Liddy by walkie-talkie that lights continued to burn inside the DNC (Givner had shut them off) and that a man could be seen still working there (Givner was the last worker, and he had left). No mention was made of the fact that the guard had left the building, which even the most casual surveillance would have revealed, since Wills had shut out the lights in the lobby upon leaving for the Hojo.

Why McCord should have lied to his co-conspirators, thus delaying the break-in, is uncertain.[19] The most that one can say about it is that he was waiting for something to happen before he would permit the entry to take place. What that "something" may have been is a matter of speculation, but the timing of events suggests that he was awaiting the arrival of Lou Russell, who at that point was motoring back to the Howard Johnson's.

Whatever we may think of Wills for having left the Watergate unguarded after finding tape on the basement doors, he at least had the prudence to order his food from the take-out counter rather than sit down to a meal in the restaurant itself. While he waited for the order to be prepared he stood beside the seated Givner and made small talk. When his order was made up, Wills returned to his post in the Watergate lobby. He could not have been absent for more than twenty minutes.

Back on duty, Wills received a call from his roving supervisor, Bobby Jackson, for whom Wills had earlier left a message and who was now at the Carnegie Institution. Jackson logged his conversation with Wills as having taken place at 12:30 A.M. He gave Wills the same advice that Ira O'Neal had offered earlier: Immediately check the other doors in the building and report back within fifteen minutes. For some reason, Wills again delayed carrying out the order;

[19]Once again Liddy offers a nonconspiratorial explanation of seemingly mysterious events, and I suspect that I may be the cause of it. While *Will* was in preparation, Liddy and I had perhaps a dozen lengthy telephone conversations on the subject of Watergate. In those conversations I pointed out to him a number of peculiarities about the affair (e.g., questions surrounding the taping procedure that was used). The delay described above was one such "peculiarity." In his autobiography Liddy goes out of his way to say that this delay was deliberate—that is, the break-in was postponed in order to see if Givner would return to the DNC. In fact, however, this seemingly plausible explanation begs the underlying question because it does not take into account the fact that McCord *deceived* Hunt and Liddy about the DNC's occupancy and lighting conditions. As we will see, the break-in took place *immediately after* McCord's report (at about 12:45 A.M.) that the DNC was finally empty. Liddy, then, did *not* delay the entry (contrary to what his autobiography suggests).

nearly an hour would pass before he would examine another door. (To make the same point twice, had Wills carried out this second order when told to do so by Jackson, the police would have been notified and the break-in would probably not have occurred—no arrests, hence no Watergate affair.)

At about the same time that Wills returned to the Watergate, Alfred Baldwin paid a visit to that hub of espionage and glamour, the Hojo coffee shop. There he waited while two hot fudge sundaes were prepared, and then returned with them to Room 723 at about 12:45 A.M.—which is to say, at more or less the time that Lou Russell arrived from Benedict. Meanwhile Frank Wills sat at his security desk across the street, paying close attention to a cheeseburger, french fries and a shake.

Whether Baldwin crossed paths in the restaurant with Wills, Givner or Russell is unknown. In subsequent interviews, Baldwin told the FBI and the press that upon returning to the listening post, he found McCord on the telephone saying that someone continued to work inside the DNC. Here, however, Baldwin's accounts are at variance with one another. To the FBI he reported that McCord received a telephone call, said "I'll be there," and left the Hojo for the Watergate. In his interview with the *Los Angeles Times*, however, Baldwin gave a more dramatic account. In that interview, Baldwin said that he stepped out onto the balcony while McCord was still on the telephone complaining that the DNC remained occupied. Baldwin told the reporters that looking across the street, he saw a man get up and turn off the light inside the DNC. Returning inside, Baldwin reported this information to McCord, who, in turn, relayed it over the phone to Hunt, saying that the operation was a go.[20] It was about 12:50 A.M.

That Baldwin embellished his account to the *Los Angeles Times* may or may not be of significance. In either case, the account cannot be true because, as we have seen, Bruce Givner was the last worker inside the DNC—having left those offices, and turned off the lights, at 12:05 A.M. That neither Givner nor Wills has any reason to lie about the time is apparent. So, too, there does not seem to be any possibility that they are mistaken: both the timing and the sequence of events that night are established beyond any doubt by reference

[20]See FBI serial 139-4089-745, p. 21, special agent Angelo Lano's account of his interview with Baldwin, dated July 11, 1972, and pp. 119–21 of Baldwin's interview with *Los Angeles Times* reporters Jack Nelson and Ronald Ostrow.

to the telephone calls between Wills, the answering service and Wills's supervisors at GSS. How, then, are we to explain Baldwin's erroneous account to the *Los Angeles Times?* Was he simply mistaken about what he saw? Perhaps, but probably not. If we wish to give Baldwin the benefit of every doubt, we may surmise any number of remotely plausible reasons to explain his story in terms of innocent human error. In the end, however, each of these reasons collapses of its own weight.[21] Baldwin's account to the press, therefore, is more than incorrect. It is suspect. The question is: Did he lie in order to facilitate McCord's contrived delays (while awaiting Russell's arrival from Benedict), or did Baldwin merely embellish his story so as to make a better one? We cannot be sure.

Whatever the stimulus, it was at about ten minutes of one in the morning when McCord hung up on Hunt and turned to Baldwin, saying that he was on his way "over there." Hefting his kit bag containing the ruined smoke alarm and other equipment, McCord provided Baldwin with a walkie-talkie and instructed him to keep watch for any unusual activity. Baldwin agreed, flicking on the television set, and inquired as to what McCord intended to do about his melting hot fudge sundae. McCord said that Baldwin could have it and, with that, left the room. Eating the sundae, Baldwin sat back on the bed and began watching a 1958 horror film entitled *Attack of the Puppet People.*[22]

It is here that James McCord lies for the second time (the first lie being his insistence that the DNC was occupied when, unquestionably, it was not). He says that he went across Virginia Avenue and descended into the underground garage to make certain that the doors to the office building remained open. He claims that upon ascertaining this he then proceeded to the command post, where he informed Hunt, Liddy and the Cubans that everything was well. As

[21]For example: perhaps someone was working late that night on a different floor, and Baldwin momentarily confused that floor with the sixth. This would legitimately explain his report to McCord that the DNC was finally empty. And, indeed, we may even find some evidence for this: i.e., in his interview with the *Los Angeles Times* (p. 122 of the court transcript), Baldwin mistakenly refers to the Democrats' headquarters as being located on the seventh floor. In the context of Baldwin's remarks, however, it is clear that while he has confused the number of the floor housing the Democrats, he knows very well what that floor actually looked like. It was distinct from every other in the Watergate office building because it had a large terrace. Baldwin, then, could not have *visually* mistaken the sixth floor for the seventh, and so this explanation will not stand up.

[22]"A newly hired secretary to a doll manufacturer correctly suspects that her boss turns human beings into robots. John Agar, June Kenny."—*Washington Star* television guide, June 17, 1972.

we know, this was by no means the truth: Wills had cleared the tape
and other debris from the doors an hour earlier.

The purpose of McCord's second lie, which subsequently bewildered the police and every other investigator and journalist, was a
simple one. In brief, it was to explain his delay in arriving at the
command post after leaving the Howard Johnson's. Ordinarily it
should have taken him no more than five or ten minutes to go from
one hotel room to the other, but in this case roughly fifteen minutes
elapsed between the time that McCord left the Howard Johnson's
and the time (1:05 A.M.) that he arrived at the Watergate command
post. Usually a short delay of this kind would not have called for
an explanation, but Hunt, Liddy and the Cubans were impatient to
proceed. Indeed, the break-in was already three hours behind schedule, which worried all who were involved, so that McCord was
chided for the time he had taken in crossing the street. McCord
therefore offered the false explanation that he had gone to check the
taping on the locks.

What McCord had to conceal was, obviously, his actual whereabouts during the five to ten minutes that accounted for his delayed
arrival at Hunt's hotel room. Clearly, he could not have gone far in
that short time. The possibility suggests itself that he met briefly
with Lou Russell for a last-minute consultation outside the Watergate—in its garage, perhaps, or in the restaurant of the Howard
Johnson's. To explain that delay without reference to his secret
accomplice, McCord falsely told Hunt, Liddy and the Cubans that
he had been checking on the office building's B-2 entrance.[23]

[23]The discrepancies in McCord's account of the June 16–17 break-in have been noted by
others, including Anthony Lukas, in Nightmare. Lukas et al., however, were unaware of the
GSS security logs establishing the actual time of Wills's first discovery concerning the locks,
and were unaware, also, of Wills's telephone calls to his GSS supervisors, Jackson and O'Neal.
Accordingly, McCord's discrepancies were shrugged off as "perplexing" or, ironically,
blamed on the supposed confusion of GSS guard Frank Wills. Understandably, many journalists based their accounts of the break-in and arrests in large part on Frank Wills's statement
to the police. That statement, however, is false, not because Wills lied, but because the
interviewing officer, Carl Shoffler, later changed Wills's statement to conform with what
amounted to the received version of the affair. Shoffler says he did this because Wills's account
of the "timing" of events "just didn't make sense"—which, indeed, it did not if one was to
believe Alfred Baldwin and James McCord's version of the affair. Because the authorities seem
to have been unaware of the information available from Jackson and O'Neal, Shoffler apparently tried to make sense of the break-in by changing the times supplied by Wills. In doing
so, he simply crossed out what Wills said in his statement and inserted different times, creating
the impression that certain events (e.g., Wills's first discovery of tape on the B-2 door)
occurred an hour later than they actually did. It should be emphasized that in making these
changes Schoffler did not intend to deceive anyone. On the contrary, his intention was to
clarify what was otherwise obscure. In effect, he "fixed something that wasn't broke."

It was at about 1:10 A.M. that the entry team arrived in the underground garage at the B-2 level of the Watergate office building, whereupon they found the door locked, the tape missing and their entry barred. Questioned about this by his astonished Cuban cohorts, McCord said that the tape must have been removed in the past ten minutes, since, after all, he had only just reported that everything was in order. The five-man break-in team went into a huddle with McCord as the leader, and it was decided that McCord, Barker and Martinez would consult with Hunt and Liddy about what should be done. Virgilio Gonzalez was to remain in the underground garage and, while waiting there, to pick the B-2 lock in case the decision was made to proceed with the operation. Sturgis was to be a bodyguard for Gonzalez; while the latter picked the lock, the former was to stand in a nearby telephone booth and talk animatedly to a dial tone. So Barker, Martinez and McCord (according to all but McCord) returned together to the command post in the adjacent Watergate Hotel. There they informed Hunt and Liddy of the tape's discovery. Hunt says that he urged Liddy to scratch the operation.[24] Liddy agrees, adding that McCord took the opposite position, suggesting that the tape had been removed by a maintenance man in the routine performance of his chores.[25] In the end, Liddy decided to go ahead with the break-in because McCord was willing to do so, and McCord was more at risk than he and Hunt.

Here, however, McCord's own story has diverged entirely from the accounts of everyone else—that is, from the accounts of Barker, Martinez, Hunt, Liddy and even Baldwin. According to McCord, he did not return to the Watergate command post (at 1:15) after finding the tape missing from the B-2 door. Instead, he says that Sturgis and Gonzalez were dispatched to pick the B-2 lock while Barker and Martinez went to confer with Hunt and Liddy. As for himself, McCord says that he returned to the Howard Johnson's, rejoining Alfred Baldwin. Before long, McCord tells us, Liddy telephoned to say that the operation was to proceed. That decision, in other words, had been reached without any input from McCord himself.[26]

Alfred Baldwin disagrees. According to him, McCord did *not* return to the listening post after leaving it (for the last time) at about 12:50 A.M. Barker, Martinez, Hunt and Liddy all agree that McCord

[24]Hunt, *Undercover*, pp. 240–41.
[25]Liddy, *Will*, p. 244.
[26]McCord, *Piece of Tape*, pp. 29–30. See also the Ervin committee *Hearings*, Book 1, pp. 239–40.

returned instead to the Watergate Hotel room that served as the command post.[27]

However disputed McCord's whereabouts at this time, the question of whether to proceed was moot. Sturgis and Gonzalez had already picked the B-2 locks, retaping them in the "dead giveaway" manner, with the tape running over the lock and vertically along the edge of the door. That accomplished, they had then taken it upon themselves to climb the six floors to the DNC, where they set to work on a recalcitrant lock. Meanwhile, Barker and Martinez had left the command post and arrived at the underground garage. Finding the locks taped open, they entered at the B-2 level and joined their companions on the sixth floor. There Sturgis and Gonzalez labored mightily to gain entry to the DNC. When the lock defied all efforts at picking it, the men proceeded to remove the door from its hinges.

As for McCord, he had disappeared. According to Martinez, "McCord did not come in [to the office building] with us. He said he had to go someplace. We never knew where he was going [when we left the command post]."[28] So far as the Miami men were concerned, their operations leader had simply vanished after the discussion with Hunt and Liddy about the tape's discovery. They had no way of knowing when, or even if, he would join them inside the DNC.

Once again McCord has seen fit to lie about his whereabouts at a crucial moment in the Watergate break-in. And once again he cannot actually have been far away, and the only explanation that appears to make sense is that he was informing Lou Russell of recent developments, namely, the problem created by the tape's discovery and the decision to carry on in spite of it.

At this point it may be useful to clarify the timing of events. As we have seen, the entry team first learned of Frank Wills's discovery at about 1:10 A.M., when, to their shock, they found themselves locked out of the Watergate office building. They conferred about this among themselves, McCord delegated various responsibilities,

[27]Subsequently, Martinez would put yet another twist on the story. Writing in a national magazine, he would suggest that the decision to proceed with the break-in (following the discovery of the tape) was reached by Hunt, Liddy and McCord after they had allegedly consulted by telephone with an unidentified fourth party. See Martinez, "Mission Impossible," p. 56.

[28]Ibid.

and then they split up. Since the men were concerned about their conspicuousness and worried about the discovery of the tape, their conference in the garage was short. If we allow a few minutes more for McCord, Barker and Martinez to return to the command post, the argument between McCord and Hunt must have begun shortly after 1:20 A.M. Since this argument required that McCord report the tape's discovery, make his recommendations, and listen to Hunt's rebuttal, this second discussion may well have consumed ten minutes. It was about 1:30 A.M., therefore, when McCord, Barker and Martinez left Hunt's hotel room. McCord then went off on his own, apparently to confer with Russell, while Martinez and Barker returned to the garage and entered the stairwell to the office building through doors that their colleagues had just retaped. The time was just after 1:30 A.M.

According to Martinez, he and Barker had been standing in the stairwell outside the DNC for five minutes prior to McCord's rejoining them on the scene. Having entered the building at 1:30 and having taken about five minutes to scale the eight landings to the sixth floor, Barker and Martinez cannot have reunited with McCord until about 1:40 A.M. Wherever McCord had been, his absence had been brief—a few minutes, no more.

But during this absence Frank Wills had finally gotten around to satisfying the orders of his superiors that had been issued more than an hour before. Going to the basement, he found the new tape that Sturgis and Gonzalez had placed on the locks a few minutes earlier. This time, Wills did not remove the tape but returned instead to the lobby to confer with Walter Hellams, the Federal Reserve Board guard who had just arrived to inspect the FRB's premises. Wills was uncertain as to whether he should notify the police. Hellams insisted that he should, saying that a burglary was obviously under way even as they stood there. But Wills still hesitated, deciding instead to check with his predecessor, GSS guard Fletcher Pittman, and his superior, Captain Bobby Jackson.

According to Pittman, Wills called him at 1:30 A.M. and asked if he had found any locks taped open during his watch. Pittman said that he had not.[29] Wills then telephoned Jackson to tell him of his most recent discovery: the B-2 level door had been *re*taped. According to Jackson, he received this call about "an hour to an hour and

[29]Statement of Fletcher Pittman to Officer Carl Shoffler, June 27, 1972.

fifteen minutes" after his previous conversation with Wills—which is to say that Jackson and Wills spoke together for the second time between 1:30 and 1:45 A.M. It was during this same time, with Hellams, Jackson and Wills debating whether to call the police, that McCord entered the building through the taped-open doors in the basement. And that is one more ironic aspect of the affair: had Frank Wills removed the materials holding open the locks, as he did on the occasion of his first discovery, McCord would have been locked out of the office building, as also, depending upon the exact time of the second discovery, Barker and Martinez might have been. Had this occurred, the subsequent arrests would have netted no more than a locksmith and a soldier of fortune from Miami, neither of whom had any obvious ties to the CIA, Howard Hunt, Gordon Liddy or the director of security at the Committee to Re-elect the President. There would have been a crime, in other words, but no scandal.

When McCord entered the stairwell and climbed to the DNC's offices, he found Sturgis banging on the hinges of the rear door, making a racket that resounded in the stairwells and terrified Martinez. Gonzales had been unable to pick the lock, apparently because it was rusted and jammed, so Sturgis had taken it upon himself to remove the door in its entirety. Standing in the stairwell beside McCord, the worried Martinez inquired if McCord had remembered to remove the tapes on the way up so that they should not be discovered yet again. McCord falsely assured Martinez that he had done so.

It was at 1:47 A.M. that Frank Wills finally acquiesced to Hellam's arguments and made his historic telephone call to the Washington Police Department, saying that a burglary seemed to be taking place in the Watergate office building.[30] Across the street, in Room 723 of the Howard Johnson's, *Attack of the Puppet People* was moving toward its climax.

At 1:52 A.M., according to the police dispatcher, a unit was requested to respond to the Watergate office building. Officer Carl Shoffler, breaking with the tradition that the senior officer in a squad car is responsible for replying to the dispatcher, grabbed the microphone in the unmarked squad car. "We got it," he said, and with that, three plainclothesmen were on their way. Not that they had far to go. When the dispatcher's call came, Shoffler and his col-

---

[30]It would be interesting to know just what Wills said to the police in his telephone call, but, unfortunately, the recorded call was erased (as a matter of routine procedure) sometime after the arrests.

leagues were parked a block and a half from the Watergate.

In the lobby of the office building, Wills attempted to explain his discoveries while the plainclothesmen listened patiently. Shoffler (who had hair down to his shoulders and was very much in need of a shave) could not understand just what it was that the guard was saying. So Wills led the cops down to the B-2 level of the building and showed them the taped doors leading out to the underground garage. By this time the three police officers and Wills had been joined by Walter Hellams, and a brief conversation ensued about the burglary that had taken place some weeks before in the Federal Reserve Board offices on the eighth floor.

With this information in mind, the police went up one of the stairwells to the Fed. Their progress must have been noisy because it alarmed Martinez. Turning to McCord for an explanation, Martinez was told not to worry; McCord said that the cause of the disturbance was only the GSS guard making his two o'clock rounds. As a precaution, however, McCord told Barker to turn off his walkie-talkie, saying that its static might attract unwanted attention. Barker complied, in effect cutting off the entry team's communication with its leaders, Hunt and Liddy, and its lookout, Alfred Baldwin—this at the very moment when advice and warning were most needed.

By then the police had arrived on the eighth floor, where they found that the door leading to the stairwell had been taped in the same manner as the doors on B-2. To their frustration, however, Hellams and the police were unable to inspect any of the offices on that floor; Hellams simply could not get his keys to work. So it was that the police descended to the seventh floor and, finding no tape there, went down to the sixth.

Here it may be useful to estimate the time. According to McCord, testifying in a civil suit, an estimated thirty to forty-five minutes were consumed in removing the DNC's rear door from its hinges. Now, since McCord did not arrive at the door to the DNC until 1:40 A.M., it follows that the entry to the DNC did not actually occur until sometime between 2:10 and 2:25 A.M. Or to put it another way, the police were inside the building—interviewing Wills and Hellams, examining the taped doors and searching for the burglars—for at least fifteen minutes before the crime itself was committed (that is, before the DNC was entered).[31]

In the meantime, Alfred Baldwin had not been of much use,

---

[31]Shoffler et al. were dispatched to the Watergate at 1:52 A.M. and made the arrests at 2:30 A.M.

engrossed as he seems to have been in the puppet people's plans to conquer the planet. He did not report the arrival of the plainclothesmen until after the film had ended, and after the search for the burglars had begun. As Hunt put it: "Here we have a darkened building, let us say, at around 2 o'clock in the morning. Abruptly, lights begin going on on the eighth floor, men must be able to be seen running through the eighth floor. Those lights go out, there is a repetition on the seventh floor, and on the sixth floor the same procedure begins. At this point, a rather casual inquiry comes over the walkie-talkie from Mr. Baldwin to the effect, are any of your men wearing hippy clothes? The answer which Mr. Liddy gave him was, no, they are all in business suits."[32]

According to Liddy, Baldwin next said, "They're on the sixth floor now. Four or five guys. One's got on a cowboy hat. One's got on a sweat shirt. It looks like . . . guns! They've got guns. It's trouble!"[33]

Indeed, it was. Inside the Watergate, Shoffler and his colleagues discovered McCord and his colleagues hidden behind a desk in the secretarial cubicle adjacent to Larry O'Brien's office. Ordering the men to put their hands in the air and to "assume the position" against the wall, the officers were surprised by what they had found. They described the men under arrest as "Mafia types" because of their swarthy complexion, business suits and surgical gloves. In McCord's kit bag they found three small transmitters and the wired-up "smoke detector," which, to the police, appeared to be a bomb. When Martinez surreptitiously reached inside his jacket, Shoffler slammed him in the back and ordered him not to move. Used to dealing with the capital's lumpen, the cops were made nervous by the apparent sophistication of the suspects; they might have started shooting at any moment, and according to Shoffler, when Martinez yanked something from under his jacket, they very nearly did. Instead, Shoffler smacked the Cuban a second time, and wrestled him against the wall to prevent him from disposing of what the FBI later determined was a key to Maxie Wells's desk. Martinez was desperate that it should not be found.[34] It was, quite literally, the key to the break-in.

[32]Ervin committee *Hearings*, Book 9, p. 3737.
[33]Liddy, *Will*, p. 245.
[34]When this reporter asked Martinez about the incident in 1984, the former CIA agent denied knowledge of it. The key's existence, however, is demonstrated by police photographs and FBI reports. It was taped to the cover of a small notebook that Martinez carried with him on the break-in.

Meanwhile, Baldwin had gone out onto the balcony and was continuing to supply Hunt and Liddy with reports by walkie-talkie. He told them that he could see "our people" standing in the DNC with their hands in the air—an unhappy circumstance, Baldwin realized, and one that caused him to opine that the newly arrived gunmen in plainclothes might be the police. And, indeed, that wild surmise was soon corroborated.

Shortly after the arrests, squad cars began pulling up in front of the office building with lights flashing and radios crackling. Frank Wills, standing in the lobby next to what was later described as "an unidentified white male," admitted the uniformed police into the building and directed them to the sixth floor. Then Wills reopened the locked lobby doors so that the unknown man could leave. That done, he then began fielding questions from those policemen who had remained in the lobby. One of the questions that Wills was asked was, "Who was that?"

"Who?"

"The guy you just let out."

Wills replied that he didn't know. Immediately the police rushed out into the street in search of what the FBI later decided was "the sixth man" on the entry team.[35] By then, however, the man had vanished.

Hunt and Liddy could see the activity in the street from their room in the Watergate Hotel and, judging by what they did next, were in a panic. According to Liddy, Hunt exclaimed, "We gotta get out fast. I just remembered. Macho's [Barker's] got this room key."[36] Indeed he did, and one can only wonder *why* Hunt had permitted him to take it with him on the break-in, since the Cubans had been instructed to leave the keys to their own room with Hunt and Liddy. In the event, what Hunt and Liddy did next (or, more accurately, what they failed to do) sealed their fate. That is, they neglected to sanitize either their own room or the room in which the Cubans were to stay, with the result that police and FBI agents soon uncovered a trove of evidence establishing the real identities of the men under arrest and their connection to E. Howard Hunt and the White House.

Rushing out of the hotel, Hunt gave Liddy a ride to the latter's Jeep, parked down the street, and then circled back to the Howard

[35]The five men under arrest were McCord, Martinez, Gonzalez, Sturgis and Barker, all of whom were using aliases at the time.
[36]Liddy, *Will*, p. 245.

Johnson's motel. Going upstairs, he found Baldwin watching McCord and the others being led out of the office building and into a paddy wagon. Hunt recalls:

> He encouraged me to lie down on my belly on the balcony and join him in watching what was going on across the street. I thought this was a very unrealistic reaction to what was going on, and I said to him, "For God's sake, get out of here."
>
> And he said, "Well, I have got all of this stuff to load."
>
> I had still never seen any of the electronic equipment in the apartment. I said, "Load [McCord's] van and get out of town."
>
> He said, "Where shall I go?"
>
> I said, "I don't care where you go, but go far and go fast."
>
> He said, "Shall I take the van to Mr. McCord's home?"
>
> I said that would be the last place to take it. I said, "Anyplace but that."
>
> I opened the door, left, and never saw him again until I saw him on television.[37]

Baldwin's recollection is diametrically opposite from Hunt's. According to Baldwin, Hunt specifically instructed him to take the van, which contained the receiver, walkie-talkies and other incriminating equipment, to McCord's home in Rockville. Which, Baldwin says, is what he did, awakening Mrs. McCord and prevailing on her for a ride back into the city. By 5:00 A.M., Baldwin was in his own car, racing toward his mother's house in Connecticut.

"The Watergate affair" had finally begun.

[37] Nedzi report, pp. 523–24.

14.
An Operational
Overview

Since McCord and his men had been caught in the act, the burglary did not seem to warrant much investigation in its own right. The identity of the target, coupled with the eavesdropping devices and photographic equipment that had been seized, made it apparent that political skulduggery was afoot. The task that remained for investigators, therefore, was to establish what other crimes had been committed and on whose orders. And quite naturally, the Nixon White House was the chief suspect.

So the break-in went almost unexamined. Bud Fensterwald,[1] who came to represent McCord before the Senate's Ervin committee, complained to this writer that "Sam Dash [chief counsel and staff director of the committee] never [publicly] asked McCord why they'd singled out Spencer Oliver, or what they hoped to get from Larry O'Brien." While there were some (Carl Oglesby on the left, Miles Copeland on the right) who suspected that the break-in had been sabotaged, they were unable to prove it, and the suggestion

[1]Fensterwald was one of two attorneys who represented McCord during the Watergate inquiry. (The other was Gerald Alch.) Regarded by some as a bit of a mystery figure in his own right, Fensterwald is an independently wealthy graduate of Harvard Law School and Cambridge University. He worked for the State Department in the early 1950s, and in the 1960s was chief counsel and staff director of subcommittees of the Senate Judiciary Committee under Senator Edward V. Long. The founder of the Committee to Investigate Assassinations (CtIA), he has a consuming interest in uncovering the truth behind the assassination of President John F. Kennedy. Well-connected in intelligence circles, Fensterwald was a friend of the Plumbers' CIA liaison, the (probably) late John Paisley. His clients have included Marianne Paisley, bug-designer Martin Kaiser, James Earl Ray (Dr. Martin Luther King's assassin), the arms-dealer Mitch WerBell and a contingent of Task Force 157 agents (who successfully sued the government for retirement benefits).

itself was considered almost subversive. Because, of course, if the break-in had been sabotaged, then Nixon and the CRP were, in some sense of the word, victims in the affair, however culpable they may have been in other areas. Similarly, to suggest that the CIA played a secret role in these events would also have seemed to exculpate the Nixon White House. For the affair to be seen in black-and-white terms that everyone could understand, there was room for only one victim and one villain. Accordingly, it was politically expedient for both the press and the prosecutors to gloss over or ignore any contradictions that arose. The case was to be treated as a moral fable: an open-and-shut case of political espionage carried out by the bad guys in the White House against the good guys in the Democratic party. In this, ironically, the White House itself became a collaborator, acquiescing to the image of the burglars as "bunglers" while characterizing the break-in as "a third-rate burglary" unworthy of serious investigation. By taking this view, and by destroying so much evidence, the administration was hoist by its own petard; in its reflexive pursuit of the cover-up, the White House discouraged scrutiny of the burglars' own motives, and buried evidence that was at least mitigating.

In considering the break-in, it is immediately obvious that McCord had a secret agenda. Why else would he have lied to his own accomplices? But what is not so obvious is whether that agenda had sabotage as its objective. The evidence that it did includes the method that McCord used to tape open the locks, the number and locations of the doors that he taped open, and the lies that he told throughout the evening. With respect to the method that McCord used, Gordon Liddy has described it as "a dead giveaway" because it is, to coin a phrase, "openly clandestine." In the mistaken belief that McCord used a more blatant method than this, Liddy congratulates him on his subtlety—the idea being that locks so obviously taped open would have seemed innocent to the building's guards. In the end, however, it doesn't matter which method McCord actually used; one can make the same argument, for or against a theory of sabotage, using either method.

What is more substantive, though, is McCord's peculiar resort to taping open so many locks when only those on the B-2 level and sixth floor needed to be kept open. Indeed, McCord placed tapes on as many as eight doors, including the stairwell door to the eighth floor. Why? The eighth floor was occupied by the Federal Reserve

Board, and it was not—so far as we know—a target of the break-in; neither did it provide a means of escape from the building if the burglary was interrupted. And yet, putting the tape on that door cannot have been a casual act: McCord knew that the Federal Reserve Board was patrolled twice nightly by its own guards, in addition to the routine inspections carried out by the GSS men. As we know, those same offices had been burglarized only a month before, and so the guards were perhaps even more alert than usual. It was quite likely, then, that if the GSS guards did not find the tape in the basement, the Fed's men would find it on the eighth floor. In either case an alarm would go up.

As for McCord's lies to his accomplices, there were many. He lied about the occupancy of the DNC between 12:05 and 12:45 A.M. He lied again (about inspecting the tape on the garage-level door) at 1:00 A.M. and, subsequently, prevaricated further when trying to conceal his brief disappearance following the emergency meeting with Hunt and Liddy at 1:15 A.M. (there to decide whether or not to proceed). Finally, he lied to Martinez, saying that he had removed the telltale tapes from each of the doors on his way back into the Watergate office building. In sum, McCord's behavior on the night of the break-in was defined by a pattern of deception. Moreover, in considering that pattern, it becomes clear that every element in it —every lie—can be explained in terms of Lou Russell's whereabouts and suspected assignment. Indeed, while this explanation is circumstantial, one would be hard put to find another that takes into account all of the known facts. It seems obvious, therefore, that McCord lied about the occupancy of the DNC in order to give Russell time to return to Washington from Benedict. Similarly, he lied about the tape being on the door at 1:00 A.M., apparently to conceal a brief meeting between himself and the newly returned Russell. Fifteen minutes later, at 1:15 A.M., he lied yet again, and probably for the same reason: to hide a second conference with Russell (this one to report that although the guard had found the tape on the B-2 level door, the operation was proceeding nonetheless). Finally, McCord's calamitous deceit of Martinez can only be explained as an effort to allay the Cuban's fears while, at the same time, leaving Russell a means of entry into the building. Had McCord actually removed the tapes, as he told Martinez that he had, Russell would not have had a safe way in.

But what was Russell's role? Clearly, not to help the Cubans—else

McCord would not have lied to conceal the detective's presence. Was he there to provide protective surveillance? No, that was Alfred Baldwin's job. The only role left to Russell, then, seems to be that of a saboteur. Why McCord should have wanted to sabotage the break-in, and who else may have been privy to that intention, are matters that will be considered shortly. For now, however, it is enough to say that McCord was the pivot man in a conspiracy within a conspiracy; and though he might leave clues throughout the Watergate office building, hoping that the FRB or GSS guards would find them, there was no certainty that they would or, if they did, that they would notify the police. On the contrary, in fact, the same building had been repeatedly and incompetently burglarized during the past few months, and no one had been apprehended— this despite the fact that on at least one occasion the burglars had actually signed the security logbook prior to committing their felony. McCord, therefore, could not be blamed if, wishing for the break-in to be discovered, he had taken the precaution of assigning Lou Russell to the task of creating a disturbance at a strategic moment or otherwise making certain that the GSS security staff called the police to report a break-in. How Russell was to accomplish this is unknown. It may be relevant, however, that only three months before, Russell had been an investigator for GSS and, as such, was at least technically a superior of Frank Wills and the other guards.[2] He was familiar with GSS methods and personnel, and may have retained his GSS identification after leaving the firm. It is even possible that one or more of the GSS guards were bribed, but suffered a failure of nerve at the last moment.[3]

What seems most important, however, was that the police should not be called until the proper moment. Because, of course, McCord

[2]There is some uncertainty as to the exact dates of Russell's employment at GSS. According to F. Kelly Chamberlain, executive vice-president of GSS, Russell started work at the firm on December 4, 1971, and was discharged on February 1, 1972. Senate sources claim that Russell worked for GSS until March 24 of that year, leaving the firm voluntarily to work for McCord.
[3]A newspaper report in which Gonzalez is alleged to have boasted that GSS guards had been bribed to permit more than forty illicit entries into the DNC generated only skepticism at the FBI. See Jeremiah O'Leary and Patrick Collins, "Were Guards Bribed?," *Sunday Star and Washington Daily News*, October 1, 1972, p. A-1; the FBI interview with GSS exec Kelly Chamberlain (conducted October 4, 1972, by special agent Michael J. King), and FBI interviews with Martin Dardis, chief investigator for the Dade County (Florida) State's Attorney's office, and employees of Rich's Photo shop. According to Chamberlain, polygraph tests were administered by Fausto E. Molinet to five GSS guards. The results showed that none of those tested had been "paid off." Among those tested were Frank Wills and Fletcher Pittman. (See FBI serial 139–66, p. 56.)

did not intend that he himself should be arrested. Once inside the DNC, he needed only fifteen minutes or so to install the eavesdropping devices and then, with his work finished, he could leave. But the Cubans were equipped with three dozen rolls of film and would therefore remain on the scene, photographing documents, for some time after McCord's departure. This would appear to be the reason for McCord's repeated conferences with Russell: to make certain that his warning was timely but not premature. Despite this precaution, Russell's assignment was mooted by FRB guard Walter Hellams, who insisted that Wills notify the police that a burglary was in progress. Because the door to the DNC was so unexpectedly recalcitrant, McCord and the others had yet to enter the Democrats' headquarters when the cops were called. In the end, Russell's work had been co-opted—catastrophically. All that was left to him was to make good his own escape as the unidentified "sixth man."

Again, this explanation of the behavior of Russell and McCord is based on circumstantial evidence, and in the absence of a signed confession from either man, proof is wanting. No one, however, has suggested an alternative explanation that plausibly takes into account the strange behavior of both men: the extraordinary number of doors that McCord taped open; the lies that he told to explain his disappearances; the deception of Martinez; Russell's repeated trips to Benedict and his long cafeteria meal at the Howard Johnson's; and the coincidence in timing between Russell's movements and various turning points in the break-in operation. There also remains the otherwise unexplained presence of the "sixth man."

Who, then, were McCord's accomplices, and what was the motive? Just as certainly as Russell was a partner in the scheme, Gordon Liddy was not: Hunt and McCord had been deceiving him for months. As for the Cubans, they were clearly McCord's fall guys. While it is true that there are discrepancies in the Cubans' accounts of the evening, and while they made their share of mistakes that night, the most critical error attributed to them was not their own but Howard Hunt's. It was he who insisted that they register at the Watergate Hotel, rather than at a hotel farther from the scene of the crime. It was he, also, who went to the trouble of collecting their ID's before the burglary. The purpose of this precaution was defeated, however, when Hunt placed the ID's in a briefcase, left the briefcase in their hotel room, and then told the Cubans to keep the keys to their room while embarking on the break-in. Why? Martinez can hardly believe that it happened: "I don't know why. Even today, I don't know."[4] The effect of this decision, however, has never been in doubt: because the burglars had the room keys in their possession when arrested, the police knew immediately where they were staying and were able to obtain search warrants the same day. As a result, evidence linking Hunt (and the White House) to McCord and the Cubans was obtained on the very day that the arrests were made. There is no reason, however, to believe that Hunt knew that the Cubans' hotel room contained address books with his own telephone number in them, or that his personal check could be found among Barker's belongings. Indeed, rather than conspiring with McCord to bring about the Cubans' arrest, Hunt seems to have argued that the operation should be canceled (this upon learning that the GSS guard had removed the tape from the B-2 level door). Either Hunt did not have a "need to know" about the plans for sabotaging the break-in, or he got cold feet at the last moment.

As for Alfred Baldwin, the evidence of his complicity in McCord's secret scheme is ambiguous. His report of a light winking out inside the DNC at 12:45 A.M. may have been an outright lie, told to shore up McCord, or it may have been no more than a raconteur's imagined detail. One may be inclined, in view of Baldwin's veracity on so many other issues, to give him the benefit of the doubt. But Howard Hunt would disagree: to him, Baldwin was a double agent.[5] And, indeed, some of the events surrounding Baldwin are suspicious. The curious parallels between his movements and those of Lou Russell on the night of June 16, his pretext visit to Oliver's secretary on June 12, his laconic performance as a lookout, his "unnatural" reaction to those arrests, and his decision to take the incriminating van to McCord's home—all of this weighs heavily against Baldwin's pose as an innocent in the midst of scoundrels.[6]

---

[4]Martinez, "Mission Impossible," p. 56.

[5]Asked by Senator Edward J. Gurney if he thought that the arrests were the result of a double agent's sabotage, Hunt replied affirmatively: "The series of events that night . . . have suggested to me . . . that we might have been . . . trapped by information having been provided beforehand to local law enforcement authorities by a member of our unit." Asked which member this might have been, Hunt answered: "[T]he most likely suspect would be Mr. Alfred Baldwin." See the Ervin committee *Hearings*, Book 9, pp. 3736–38.

[6]The decision to take the van, which was packed with electronic eavesdropping paraphernalia, is seen as suspicious because Hunt and McCord feared that the FBI would obtain a search warrant for McCord's premises. In the event, the bureau failed to do so, which gave McCord an opportunity to ridicule the bureau in an article written for the *Armed Forces Journal* ("What the FBI Almost Found," August 1973). An eccentric article at best, its purpose was obviously to make the FBI appear incompetent in order to cast doubt on the bureau's findings

If we compare the characters directly involved in the last Watergate break-in to the layers of an onion, we will find that the outermost skin corresponds to Frank Wills and the police—who knew only that a burglary had been committed, and that it was obviously politically motivated.[7]

Beneath that layer are Jeb Magruder and Gordon Liddy, who knew that the break-in was the last in a series and, moreover, part of a much larger operation that had White House sanction.

Yet another layer closer to the core of the mystery were Eugenio Martinez and, perhaps, one or more of the other Cubans; as the key in his possession proved, Martinez knew that the break-in was secretly targeted at the desk belonging to Maxie Wells. Depending on how Martinez obtained that key, Magruder (and Strachan and Haldeman) may or may not have been privy to that same information.

Even nearer to the heart of the enigma was Howard Hunt. Hunt knew that his work for the White House was but a cover for CIA activities and that, as a part of those activities, the fruit of operations such as the Fielding break-in were being diverted from the White House to the agency.

While Alfred Baldwin's role in the affair is finally ambiguous, those of Hunt and McCord are not. They knew that the break-in was to be compromised—but why?

The answer should not be surmised from the effect that the sabotage had on the Nixon presidency. McCord could not have predicted that the arrests would cause a scandal of such dimensions that the Nixon administration would collapse. Indeed, all that could have been foreseen at the time was that the sabotage would lead to the temporary embarrassment of the administration, and, just as certainly, that it would put an end to any further assaults on the DNC.

Clearly, it was this second goal that McCord pursued—not because he wished to protect the DNC per se, but because he was concerned that Magruder's operations would jeopardize the DNC's relationship to the Columbia Plaza. His actions in the past—the

with respect to the "September bug" (see Chapter 17). A point-by-point in-house rebuttal of McCord's article was written by the FBI on August 3, 1973 (see FBI serial 139-4089-2544). In tearing apart McCord's article, the rebuttal notes that McCord's newfound "desire to 'tell all' . . . contrasts singularly to McCord's refusal to be interviewed when we contacted him on 6/21/72 at the District of Columbia jail."

[7]The suggestion that the police may have been party to a setup is explored (and rejected) in Appendix II, "If I Was a Jury, I'd Convict Me."

business at the Continental Room with the imaginary alarm, the
substitution of the shag-rug photos for those that Barker had taken
in the DNC, and the refusal to use a tape recorder while monitoring
—had one common denominator: they preserved the Democrats'
secrets for the CIA's exclusive consumption.[8] Still, sabotage was a
painful and dangerous course of action—even if McCord himself
escaped unscathed. It would have been far simpler for McCord to
have demurred, telling Liddy that he would have nothing to do with
the operation. But McCord was replaceable. Had he balked at the
assignment, another wireman would have been found to carry it out.

The question of what was so important about the DNC bewilders
Haldeman, Mitchell, Colson and others; so far as they knew, the
DNC held no secrets worth stealing. But Haldeman and the others
were never informed of the fact that when arrested, Martinez had
a key to Maxie Wells's desk.

As we know, the DNC contained an explosive secret: its relationship to prostitutes at the Columbia Plaza Apartments. And what
McCord was determined to preserve was the monopoly that his
secret principals held on that relationship. Neither he nor the
agency wanted the Columbia Plaza operation exposed, and neither
were they willing to share everything with the Nixon administration.

That the surveillance of the Columbia Plaza and the DNC was
an intelligence operation mounted by the CIA is demonstrated by
a long chain of evidence. That chain includes McCord's secret relationship to Hunt, the clandestine relationship of both men to the
Office of Security, the Office of Security's operational use of prostitutes in the past, the CIA's continued assistance to Hunt long after
the August 17 "cutoff," the circumstances of Hunt's "retirement,"
his reports to the agency while working at the White House, the
precedent or parallel established in the Furbershaw operation—and
more to be related subsequently. The conclusion is inescapable that
McCord sabotaged the June 16 break-in to protect an ongoing CIA
operation. In doing so, he cannot have acted spontaneously; sabotaging the break-in was a desperate action. Those who know McCord
are of the unanimous opinion that he is a man who acts upon orders,
a patriot who, as his friend James Angleton has put it, "never did

---

[8]In subsequent pages we will see that McCord's cleverest act of sabotage was the illusion that
he created with respect to the supposed bugging of the DNC. This, too, shielded the DNC
from Nixon's spies.

anything unless he was wrapped in a flag." It seems relevant, then, that in the week prior to the break-in, McCord chose to visit CIA headquarters in Langley. Both Bill McMahon and Clare Petty, McCord's former colleagues on the security and counterintelligence staffs, separately recall seeing him at headquarters a few days prior to his arrest. McMahon remembers greeting McCord and asking him about his destination. "He just smiled," McMahon told me, "and wouldn't answer."

It is possible, of course, that McCord was visiting the agency on some innocuous mission—a pension problem, perhaps, or a retirement ceremony for a fellow officer. If so, then the timing of his visit —his only known visit to headquarters since the day he retired— would be an exquisite coincidence. But knowing what we do, it is likely that McCord was personally conveying the bad news that Magruder had insisted upon yet another sally against the DNC. What should be done about it? McCord had already done his best to foil the previous break-ins, and Magruder would tolerate only so many pratfalls. To quit, however, would be fruitless, to go forward foolhardy, and to go back impossible. Sabotage was the only way out.

15.
Summer Fires

Taken to police headquarters, the arrested men had little to say. Mugged and fingerprinted, they were booked under the aliases "Frank Carter" (Barker), "Raoul Godoy" (Gonzalez), "Gene Valdez" (Martinez), "Frank Fiorini" (Sturgis) and "Edward Martin" (McCord). The evidence against them was overwhelming. When arrested, they were in possession of lock-picking devices, surgical gloves, $2,400 in sequentially numbered new $100 bills, assorted blank keys and screwdrivers, thirty-nine rolls of film, two Minolta cameras, a light stand for document photography, the (yet to be identified) key to Maxie Wells's desk, false identification, three miniature electronic transmitters (bugs), the ARI smoke detector converted into a room bug and, most imprudent of all, a pop-up telephone desk directory—the metal kind—that belonged to Martinez and contained a listing for *Howard Hunt—W. House.*

Within an hour of the arrests news of the incident began to travel. Alfred Baldwin arrived at McCord's house at about 3:30 A.M. and explained to Mrs. McCord about her husband's plight even as he abandoned the incriminating van in her driveway. At about the same time, Police Chief Jerry Wilson was awakened by a call from headquarters, and notified of the arrests. By 4:00 A.M. the *Washington Post* had also been told of the incident. According to Carl Shoffler, "We couldn't get anything out of them—the 'suspects,' I mean. They wouldn't tell us who they were, what they were doing, where they were from—zero. So, I figured, what the hell, I'll put some pressure on them, get the papers interested, see what happens, y'know? So I . . . uhhh . . . dimed the *Post* and more or less told them what we had—five mystery men."

Whether or not CIA Director Richard Helms was also informed of the arrests at a very early hour is uncertain. Helms says that he was not, but he has lied before, and evidence bearing on the matter is disputed.[1] According to Helms, he learned of the arrests from news reports, but did not learn of the arrested men's identities until about 10:00 P.M. Saturday night (some nineteen hours after the arrests). It was then, Helms testified, that Howard Osborn telephoned him from the Office of Security to say that McCord was in jail and that Howard Hunt was somehow involved in the affair.[2]

There are persistent reports, however, that Helms may have been told about the break-in even earlier—indeed, before any of the arrested men were properly or publicly identified. If true, these reports would suggest that the CIA had prior knowledge of the break-in. Unfortunately, the accounts are flawed. We may dismiss, for example, a story by journalist Andrew St. George saying that Helms was notified of the arrests by the CIA watch officer in Langley at 7:00 A.M. that Saturday. When questioned by the Senate Armed Services Committee about his quotation of an alleged conversation between Helms and the watch officer, St. George proved unable to verify his account in any way.[3]

A more credible report on the subject of what Helms knew and when he knew it comes from an acquaintance of his, columnist Carl Rowan. The former U.S. Ambassador to Finland and onetime chief of the U.S. Information Agency, Rowan has written that he and Helms bumped into each other at a film screening a few days after the arrests. They discussed the incident, and Helms remarked that "Cynthia [Helms's wife] and I had been up late [Friday night] and had just fallen asleep when they telephoned to tell me that these fellows had been arrested in the Watergate."[4] To Rowan, the implication was clear: Helms had learned of the arrests in the early-morning hours of June 17—which is to say, within an hour or two

---

[1] On November 4, 1977, Helms was sentenced to two years in jail (suspended) and fined $2,000 after pleading nolo contendere to two misdemeanor counts charging him with having failed to testify "fully, completely, and accurately" before the Senate in 1973. Helms's plea was part of a bargain arranged by his attorney, Edward Bennett Williams. The testimony in question concerned the CIA's role in destabilizing the administration of Chilean President Salvador Allende. Had Helms not agreed to the plea bargain, the Justice Department was prepared to indict him on at least eight counts of perjury.

[2] Ervin committee *Hearings*, Book 8, p. 3237.

[3] Andrew St. George, "The Cold War Comes Home," *Harper's*, November 1973, and the Ervin committee's *Final Report*, p. 1120. St. George is a controversial journalist in certain respects, having admitted to helping fake documentary film sequences for CBS. (See *Network News Documentary Practices—CBS "Project Nassau," House Committee on Interstate and Foreign Commerce*, 91st Cong., 1st and 2d sess., July–November 1969, February–April 1970.)

[4] Carl Rowan's column, *Washington Star-News*, May 11, 1973.

of the break-in itself, and long before any of the arrested men had been identified by the police.

To be fair to Helms, Rowan's report is anything but conclusive. It may well be that the report was, as the former CIA director insists, the result of a misunderstanding. After all, had Helms been notified of McCord's arrest before McCord himself had been identified, would Helms then have made the remark that Rowan attributed to him? Of course not—unless Helms was unaware of the fact that the arrested men were using aliases. In which case, he might have.

If anyone telephoned Helms that Saturday morning to report the arrests, however, it was probably not a lowly watch officer at CIA headquarters. On the contrary, if any such call was made—and there is only Rowan's report to suggest that one was—the most likely person to have dimed the director was Helms's friend E. Howard Hunt. It was to Helms, after all, that Hunt was secretly reporting "gossip items," and the Watergate arrests were certainly one of the biggest gossip items to which Hunt was personally privy. Hunt, moreover, had ample opportunity to place a call to Helms.

After leaving Baldwin at the Howard Johnson's, Hunt had gone to his office in the old Executive Office Building. There he placed some materials in his safe and removed $10,000 in cash to be used for bail and as a legal retainer. He then telephoned Douglas Caddy to ask that Caddy represent the men who were under arrest. While not usually a practitioner of criminal law, Caddy could be trusted so far as Hunt was concerned: he had recently served as the Washington representative of the General Foods corporation, working out of an office at the Mullen Company. As such, he had been standing at an important intersection between the public and private sectors: it was General Foods' account with the Mullen Company that provided cover to CIA officers abroad.[5] Whether Caddy knew of this, or was himself a CIA "asset," is unknown. The Senate seems never to have questioned him about his work for Mullen or General Foods.[6]

In the event, it was to Caddy that Hunt turned for help, promis-

[5]Ten years earlier the Mullen Company had established an office in Stockholm, Sweden, which was staffed by two CIA officers, James Everett and Jack Kindschi. Under cover of the public relations firm, Everett and Kindschi pretended to be working on the General Foods account. In fact they were engaged in debriefing Soviet and Chinese defectors. (See Lukas, Nightmare, p. 38.)

[6]With respect to a bizarre allegation that Officer Carl Shoffler is said to have made about Caddy, see Appendix II.

ing to meet him within the hour. That done, he crossed Pennsylvania Avenue to the building that housed the Mullen Company. In his office there, Hunt telephoned Clara Barker and, breaking the news of her husband's arrest, instructed her to contact Caddy and formally retain him. That Hunt's visit to the Mullen Company's offices entailed some risk, or was at least something that he wished to conceal, is clear from the fact that he used an alias when signing the security log. Why, then, did he bother to go there after leaving his offices in the EOB? Did he think that because the Mullen Company was a CIA cover, its telephones were more secure than those in his office across the street? And did he have someone more important to call than either Douglas Caddy or Bernard Barker's wife? Only two people can say for certain—Hunt and Helms—and neither is renowned for his candor.

Evidence of Hunt's own involvement in the break-in or, at least, of his involvement with the men under arrest was obtained by the police exactly twelve hours after the arrests. At 2:30 P.M. that same Saturday, police and FBI agents arrived at the Watergate Hotel, armed with search warrants to examine Rooms 214 and 314. Officer Shoffler was by then in his seventeenth hour of overtime when he entered the rooms rented to the burglars. There the police found more surgical gloves, electronic equipment, $3,200 in sequentially numbered $100 bills, an address book belonging to Bernard Barker that contained the initials "H.H.—W.H" and Hunt's telephone number at the White House. The identity of "H.H." was ascertained immediately and without reference to either telephone company or White House records because among Barker's belongings was a check for $6.36 made out by E. Howard Hunt to the Lakewood Country Club in Rockville, Maryland. Before long, that information would be leaked to the *Washington Post*, and a reporter named Bob Woodward would begin placing telephone calls to Hunt at the White House, the Mullen Company and at home.

Meanwhile FBI agents Dennis W. Fiene and Allen B. Gilbert conducted "a physical check" of the DNC's headquarters "in an effort to locate hidden electronic surveillance equipment. Results of the check were negative. . . ."[7] According to Fiene, four offices were checked initially, including the DNC's conference room and Larry

[7] FBI serial 139-166-60A, written by special agent Dennis W. Fiene, June 19, 1972, describing the events of June 17.

O'Brien's office. "Nothing unusual or out of order was detected," Fiene reported. The check was made because no one could be certain just how long the suspects had spent inside the DNC prior to their arrests. Four eavesdropping devices had been recovered from them at gunpoint, but the possibility existed that other bugs had been installed earlier—hence the need to check the DNC's offices. Later that same Saturday, Earl Connor, chief of security for the Chesapeake and Potomac Telephone Company, and his assistant conducted a security check on *all* telephones and communications equipment in the DNC. Again, no bugging devices were found, which led the police, FBI and telephone company agents to conclude that the arrested men had not had time to install eavesdropping equipment prior to their arrests. The place was clean. Clearly, then, there had been a conspiracy to eavesdrop, but no eavesdropping had actually taken place. Or so, at least, it seemed.

Even as the FBI and telephone company technicians arrived at this conclusion, McCord and his accomplices were being led to their arraignment. Earlier that morning, at about 10:00 A.M., McCord's cover had been blown through a chance encounter at the police station. Garey Bittenbender, the police officer who served as McCord's liaison between the CRP and the police Intelligence Division, had recognized him and informed his superiors. Bittenbender and McCord were friends, but their relationship would quickly deteriorate when Bittenbender would be quoted in the Senate as having said that McCord told him, on the day of the arrests, that the Watergate break-in was "a CIA operation"—an allegation that McCord would vehemently deny.[8]

Whether McCord was misquoted by Bittenbender or whether the police officer simply jumped to a conclusion is uncertain, but it is easy to see how Bittenbender might have been under the impression that McCord was working on behalf of the CIA. His agency background was manifest: photographs of Richard Helms and McCord hung on the CRP's walls; the Miami men were straight out of Central Casting; and the operation itself was of the sort that one associates with the CIA. Bittenbender, moreover, seems to have been mesmerized by McCord's professional manner, his shadowy background and the displays of equipment that McCord had assembled at the CRP. It is easy, then, to imagine Bittenbender arriving

[8]Nedzi report, pp. 442–43.

at a conclusion that, in his mind at least, must have seemed exculpatory: that McCord's presence at the Watergate was CIA-connected —which is to say, patriotically motivated.

Washington Post reporter Bob Woodward subsequently recalled:

> [At the arraignment that afternoon] The Judge asked [McCord] his occupation.
>
> "Security consultant," he replied.
>
> The Judge asked where.
>
> McCord, in a soft drawl, said that he had recently retired from government service. [Bob] Woodward moved to the front row and leaned forward.
>
> "Where in government?" asked the Judge.
>
> "CIA," McCord whispered.
>
> The Judge flinched slightly.
>
> Holy shit, Woodward said half aloud, the CIA.[9]

Within CIA headquarters much the same reaction ("Holy shit!") seems to have occurred. Given the ambiguities surrounding the precise time that Helms was told of McCord's arrest, it cannot be said just when the agency first acted upon the news. It is known, however, that on the afternoon of June 17 Secret Service agent Michael Mastrovito made inquiries about McCord to the CIA, and was told that the agency was concerned about McCord's "stability" prior to his retirement.[10] On Sunday, June 18, the CIA's chief of station in Miami sent to headquarters a cable concerning Martinez, which detailed his maritime activities but deliberately omitted Martinez' earlier reports about Howard Hunt. On Monday Helms and other officials at the agency met to discuss the implications of the break-in, the arrest of McCord and Martinez, and the apparent involvement of E. Howard Hunt. Counterintelligence Chief James Angleton expressed the fear that the press might blame the affair on the agency, and all present at the meeting were determined to prevent this from happening. Photographs of Hunt, including those depicting him under aliases and in disguise, were ordered up and

[9]Bob Woodward and Carl Bernstein, *All the President's Men* (New York: Simon & Schuster, 1974) p. 18.

[10]"Agency documents indicate that Mastrovito agreed to downplay McCord's Agency employment . . . , and that Mastrovito was advised by the CIA that the Agency was concerned with McCord's emotional stability prior to his retirement."—Baker Report, appendix to the Ervin committee's *Final Report*, p. 1157. The report cites "CIA cable traffic shortly after the Watergate break-in" with respect to the question of McCord's "emotional stability."

passed around; Angleton, while well acquainted with McCord, was relieved to find that "I'd never seen [Hunt] before in my life." What was not discussed at the meeting, however, were Hunt's secret reports to Helms and the Medical Services Staff and the materials that McCord had transmitted to the Office of Security. Of these matters Helms said nothing. Angleton and the others did not have "a need to know."

That same Monday the CIA's chief of station in Miami was rebuked for failing to keep in better touch with his agents (i.e., with Martinez) even as the CIA was misinforming the FBI that with the exception of McCord none of the arrested men was known to them. Angered by the rebuke, the Miami station chief sent to headquarters a copy of the report that Martinez had been asked to write some months before. The station chief had done his best to warn headquarters in March about Hunt's activities, and for his trouble he'd been ordered to keep quiet, and then reprimanded. He later told the Senate that he was "confounded" by the fact that the agency did not order him to terminate Martinez' contract upon learning of the Cuban's involvement with Hunt and Hunt's partisan political activities. Queried about this, Cord Meyer, the assistant deputy director of plans, replied that his cable, ordering the station chief to "cool it" some months before, had been predicated on the fact that the station chief had wanted to check on Hunt's activities domestically. That allegation was denied, however, by the chief of station and, indeed, there is nothing in the CIA's own correspondence to suggest that any such intention ever existed.[11]

Even as the heat came down on the Miami station chief, it came down also on Martinez' case officers. The reader will recall that there had been two. The first case officer had been closer to Martinez, and he had been replaced by Robert Ritchie in March following the chief of station's inquiry to headquarters concerning Martinez and E. Howard Hunt. The second case officer was Robert Ritchie. On or about June 19 Ritchie was ordered to return immediately to Langley headquarters from Miami. His orders were that he was not to come by commercial airline but to drive his own car along the Interstate. He was not to stop, except to eat and purchase gas; and on those occasions when he did either, he was to telephone

[11]Ervin committee's *Final Report*, pp. 1148–49. See also Cord Meyer, *Facing Reality* (New York: Harper & Row, 1980), pp. 149–51.

CIA headquarters to report upon his exact whereabouts.[12] Clearly, then, the agency was determined to debrief Ritchie as soon as possible, but it did not want him to leave a paper trail on his way to Washington (hence the order that he drive rather than fly). As for Martinez' original case officer, testimony is conflicting. According to Ritchie, the first case officer was still in Miami on June 19. According to the CIA, however, the case officer had left the United States at the end of May to go on "an African safari." While abroad he was reassigned to Indochina and, despite Senate requests, was never made available for questioning.

The agency's reaction to the Watergate arrests was schizophrenic. Some CIA officers were clearly determined to get to the bottom of the matter, while others seem to have gone out of their way to prevent just that from happening. Helms concealed critical information (e.g., Hunt's secret reports) from his colleagues, even while taking the public position of calling for a full investigation. The FBI was lied to by the CIA, and witnesses who might well have shed light on the affair (e.g., the first case officer) were effectively sequestered so that their testimony could not be taken.

As for the Nixon administration itself, its reaction to the Watergate arrests was more predictable. Top officials at the White House conspired to obstruct justice by destroying evidence, suborning witnesses, exercising improper influence on federal investigators, buying the silence of the men in jail, and cynically invoking national security in fruitless attempts to conceal what they believed were their own misdeeds. In later months these efforts would become synonymous with "the Watergate scandal," and the burglary would diminish in importance to the role of a mere catalyst. That said, there is no need in these pages to replicate what has already been exhaustively documented in Congress, the courts and countless books on the subject of the cover-up. Neither does it seem necessary to bludgeon the obvious by repeating the condemnations that it has deservedly received. It is enough to say that attempts to bury the scandal began, as Jeb Magruder has testified, on the very day of the arrests: "I do not think there was ever any discussion that there

---

[12]Information concerning Ritchie's trip was obtained from nonpublic sources familiar with Ritchie's testimony before a federal grand jury investigating Ed Wilson's alleged role in corrupting public officials. Ritchie testified before that grand jury as a former employee of Wilson's. Ritchie is alleged to have resigned from the CIA after refusing to undergo a polygraph examination on these and other subjects.

would not be a cover-up."[13] Or, as John Mitchell put it: "What'd they expect us to do—advertise it?"

On Sunday, June 18, McCord's deputy security chief, Robert Houston, arrived at the CRP to remove certain files belonging to his boss. Houston was a recently retired military policeman, having served twenty-eight years in the U.S. Army, and had been hired by McCord in January on the basis of a referral from the Department of Defense.[14] Just what it was that Houston removed from McCord's files is unknown, but there is reason to suspect that these items included tape-recorded conversations and onionskin copies of Baldwin's reports (the raw material of the Gemstone File). What makes this seem likely is a set of facts that includes the timing of an unusual security precaution taken by McCord at the CRP, a bonfire that occurred at McCord's home shortly afterward, and the disappearance of those same onionskin logs.

In interviews with McCord's security staff, FBI agents learned that on June 17 Mrs. McCord telephoned the CRP to say that her husband's "personal pictures and plaques" should be removed from the walls of his office. (This included the curiously inscribed photograph of McCord receiving an award from CIA Director Richard Helms.)[15]

From these same CRP staffers the FBI learned that on or about June 1, two weeks before the Watergate arrests, McCord changed the combination lock on one of the filing cabinets in his office. Previously, that cabinet had been accessible to nearly everyone in the CRP's security section. With the change in combination, however, McCord and Houston became the only ones to have access to this particular filing cabinet. Was it merely a coincidence that this cabinet became restricted at precisely the moment when Alfred Baldwin commenced his monitoring operation at the Howard Johnson's?

As FBI reports show, Houston arrived at the CRP's offices at about 7:00 A.M. on Sunday, June 18. According to two of his coworkers, he "proceeded to remove all of McCord's writings . . . , accomplish[ing] this without any direction, as if the procedure were

[13]See Magruder's testimony before the Ervin committee on June 14, 1973.
[14]FBI interview with Robert Houston, July 3, 1972, conducted by special agents Michael J. King and John W. Minderman, FBI serial 139-166, p. 130.
[15]FBI interviews with Millicent ("Penny") Gleason and Stephen T. Anderson as reported by special agents Harvey W. James and Charles W. Harvey, FBI serial 139-166, pp. 110–20.

part of a prearranged plan."[16] Questioned by McCord's assistant, Penny Gleason, Houston reportedly announced that the papers were to be burned. At first Houston denied this account when questioned by the FBI. Houston "stated he stayed at the office until about 3 P.M., when he went home. He was asked if he took anything from the office that day, at which time he replied 'no.' . . . Houston was again asked if he had removed any items from the office on June 18, 1972, at which time he advised that he did remove some cassette-type tapes, a tape recorder and some personnel files, which he was working on at home. He further stated he also took an electronic sweeper, which was used to detect 'bugs.' He stated that all of the aforementioned items he returned to the office since June 18th, and that the tapes were blank when he removed them and they still are. . . . Houston stated that he did not want to be contacted again by the FBI concerning this matter, at which point he requested the interview to be terminated."[17] Houston's changing story, his insistence on having an attorney present during his interview with the FBI, his contradiction of other witnesses' statements and his abrupt termination of the interview generated no small concern within the bureau. Why would Houston have bothered to remove cassette recordings if, as he claimed, the cassettes were empty (and still were)? A suspicion arose that the tapes or files had been destroyed by Houston or removed to another location. Penny Gleason informed the FBI that—contrary to what Houston said—all of the tapes had certainly not been blank (if, indeed, any of them were). She said that she recognized one of the cassettes that Houston removed as a recording that McCord had brought back with him from a trip to Miami; its contents, she said, included information from "a sensitive source" concerning antiwar demonstrators and plans for security arrangements at the Miami convention site.[18] Finally, in connection with Houston's account, the FBI was told by another source that Houston's son, an officer with the Army Security Agency, had bragged that his father "spent several hours" on

---

[16]Ibid., p. 119.

[17]Ibid., p. 130.

[18]Ibid., p. 119. With respect to this "sensitive source," it may be relevant that, according to CIA case officer Robert Ritchie, Martinez' reporting requirements included information pertaining to possible demonstrations at the Miami conventions. (See executive session testimony before the Ervin committee, February 4, 1974, pp. 25–26, 41–42.) Ritchie's testimony in this regard contradicted earlier CIA testimony on the same subject. The matter has never been resolved.

the evening of June 18 "destroying files."[19]

As we will see, at least some of McCord's files and other materials were in fact destroyed shortly after the Watergate arrests. But even before this occurred, a conflagration took place in the home of Jeb Magruder—on the evening of June 19, following Magruder's return from California. As Magruder tells it:

> Gail [his wife] and the children were asleep. I went to the kitchen and drank a glass of milk, then I walked into the living room to burn the Gemstone papers in our fireplace.
>
> The file was about four or five inches thick, about half photographs and half transcripts of telephone conversations. I couldn't just toss the whole thing in; I had to get the fire going and feed the papers in, a few at a time. I sat cross-legged on the floor in front of the fireplace, glancing at the Gemstone papers before I tossed them into the fire, chuckling at . . . the graphic details of the social lives of some of the Democratic staff people.[20] The photographs, I discovered, blazed brightly, the way Christmas trees and certain kinds of paper do; for a moment the fire seemed to leap out at me. A sudden thought crossed my mind: what if a passing policeman saw the blaze through the window and came to investigate?[21]

Magruder was hardly alone in the destruction of evidence. Liddy made intensive use of the shredder at CRP headquarters within a few hours of the arrests. Whatever Liddy missed that might have been of interest was apparently destroyed a day or two later in what has been described as a "general housecleaning" at the CRP. Elsewhere, other search-and-destroy missions were undertaken. At the White House, for example, John Dean recalls that Gordon Strachan was instructed by H. R. Haldeman "to go through all of Mr. Haldeman's files over the weekend and remove and destroy damaging materials. He told me that this material included such matters as memorandums from the reelection committee, documents relating to wiretap information from the DNC" and more, including a Political Matters Memorandum that made reference to the CRP's intelligence plans.[22] Meanwhile, Charles Colson fruitlessly tried to eliminate all references to E. Howard

[19]FBI serial 139-4089-2187 (interview with Sergeant Douglas E. Kramer, May 18, 1973).
[20]In the complete text, Magruder makes reference to a specific conversation, monitored by Baldwin, that took place between CRP and DNC officials.
[21]Magruder, American Life, pp. 226–28.
[22]Ervin committee Hearings, Book 3, p. 934.

Hunt from White House telephone directories, while Hunt himself laid a summer fire at Witches' Island, his home in Potomac, Maryland, burning an array of materials that he considered sensitive or incriminating. Just what these materials may have been is unknown, but they could not have included what John Dean later referred to as the "political dynamite" in Hunt's White House safe. This latter trove included the CIA's psychological profiles of Daniel Ellsberg; interviews with Clifton DeMotte and others on the subject of Chappaquiddick; real and bogus State Department cables concerning former President Kennedy and his putative role in the assassination of Vietnamese President Ngo Dinh Diem in November 1963; a pop-up address book; classified sections of the Pentagon Papers; a .25-caliber handgun; and two black clothbound journal notebooks (Hermès), which Hunt had acquired years earlier in Paris. Dean had opened Hunt's safe in the presence of Secret Service agents, and so, when John Ehrlichman suggested that he should "deep-six" the materials on his way home across the Potomac, Dean declined. Instead, it was decided that the least sensitive documents should be given to the FBI, while reserving the more sensitive materials for FBI Director L. Patrick Gray himself. In that way Dean and Ehrlichman could have their cake and eat it too; if questioned at a later date, they could truthfully testify that they had turned over everything from Hunt's safe to the FBI. In fact, however, it was suggested to Gray that the documents reserved for him were of "national security interest," had nothing to do with the Watergate affair, and should be destroyed. Which is what happened—though not immediately. Gray waited six months, the files languishing in his shirt drawer, before burning the documents shortly after Christmas. Even then, not everything in Hunt's safe had been destroyed. Unknown to Gray or anyone else, John Dean had chosen to withhold the most sensitive materials of all: the black Hermès notebooks that Hunt had used as an operational diary during his CIA years. These reportedly contained the names of CIA agents and officers, their telephone numbers, code words and operational details that collectively amounted to a diary of E. Howard Hunt's clandestine career.[23] It was the fate of these journals, more than anything else in the safe, that seems to have turned Hunt's knees to water. But, according to John Dean, he need not have worried: the journals

[23]Lukas, *Nightmare*, pp. 226–27.

were shredded in January 1973, a few weeks after L. Patrick Gray's
fire in Vermont and Dorothy Hunt's death in a Chicago plane
crash. As to why both Gray and Dean should separately have
waited more than six months to destroy the evidence in their possession, the matter can only be one of conjecture.

But we have gotten ahead of the story.

On June 21, two days after the Gemstone File was reduced to
ashes in Jeb Magruder's fireplace, other evidence was discovered by
the FBI, only to disappear shortly afterward, and yet another fire
was set in yet another home.

The evidence that was to disappear consisted of a notebook that
seems to have been very much like Hunt's own. The notebook was
one of two that belonged to Eugenio Martinez, and it was found in
his car at the Miami airport on June 21. The circumstances of its
discovery are appropriately mysterious. Two days earlier, on June
19, the CIA claims to have learned from an informant or agent that
Martinez' car could be found at the airport. Inexplicably, the agency
waited forty-eight hours before notifying the bureau of the automo-
bile's whereabouts—a circumstance about which Senator Howard
Baker repeatedly queried the CIA, only to be stonewalled.[24] However belatedly, the FBI arrived at the airport with a search warrant.
Inside the car, they found (among other things) a knife; various
business cards; copies of *The Doctor's Quick Weight-Loss Diet*, *The
Brand-Name Calorie Counter*, *Basic Developing, Printing, and Enlarg-
ing*; a parking stub, which showed that the car had been left at the
airport four days earlier, on June 17; a Marquette Page-A-Day calendar notebook; and a second "notebook containing various names
and numbers," as well as "Spanish writing."[25] The parking stub is
of interest because it proves that Martinez' car was brought to the
airport after his arrest and, necessarily, by someone else—perhaps
the CIA operative whose tip to the agency led to the bureau's
delayed notification. In any case, the CIA and its agents had sole
access to the vehicle for four days before notifying the FBI of its

[24]The subject is discussed on page 1149 of the Baker Report (appendix to the Ervin committee's *Final Report*): "Despite conflicting evidence from the FBI and the CIA, it is known that
the Agency received information on June 19, 1972, from an operative that Martinez' vehicle
was at the Miami airport and contained compromising documents. Our staff has yet to receive
a satisfactory explanation regarding the aforementioned time lag and an accounting of
Agency actions during the interim." Senator Baker notes that "The testimony we received
[in executive sessions] from the agents revealed discrepancies as to the manner in which the
FBI was notified, and raised questions about just what the FBI found."
[25]FBI serials 139-4089-1205, June 22 and June 26, 1972.

whereabouts. As for the two notebooks that the FBI reportedly found, only one has survived: the Marquette calendar containing a single, apparently irrelevant name and telephone number—a notation so small, in fact, that it cannot even be used for purposes of handwriting comparison. In other words, it might have been written by Martinez or by anyone else. As for the notebook with the "Spanish writing" that contained "various" names and numbers, it is thought to have been the operational diary that Martinez was required to keep as a contract agent to the CIA.[26] Like Hunt's own, it has disappeared without a trace.

To the evidentiary devastation already listed—ranging from the disappearance of Martinez' notebook to Magruder's destruction of the Gemstone File, as well as the pillaging of McCord's office files and Hunt's safe and the shredding activities of Gordon Liddy and the "housecleaning" at the CRP—must be added yet another instance of destruction.

This was the conflagration in James McCord's home on the afternoon of June 21 or 22 (a Wednesday or Thursday). Among those present at the fire was a former top-ranking official of the FBI, the seventy-six-year-old Lee R. Pennington, Jr. At the time, Pennington was director of the Washington office of the ultraconservative American Security Council (ASC). He was also, and had been for more than fifteen years, a contract agent of the CIA's Security Research Staff. In that capacity, he reported (at various times) to three people: SRS chief Paul Gaynor, and two case officers.[27] Pennington's contract with the CIA was oral rather than written; he filed no written reports of his own (or so we are told); he was paid by means of "sterile checks"; and his affiliation with the agency was unknown to anyone outside the Security Research Staff—including the CIA's own director.[28]

[26]The question naturally arises: If the CIA was concealing evidence, why did it not "sanitize" Martinez' car prior to informing the FBI of its whereabouts? To which one would have to answer with another question: What is the evidence that the CIA did *not* sanitize the car? The only object in the car that seems to have been of more than passing interest was the notebook with "Spanish writing," names and numbers, which, as we have seen, quickly disappeared.

[27]Pennington's two case officers were Louis W. Vasaly and a woman who cannot be identified in these pages without violating the law. The woman, however, is of particular interest because it was she who analyzed Howard Hunt's "David St. John" novels to assess the likely reaction of the KGB to those works.

[28]Information concerning the so-called Pennington incident is based on testimony provided to the Nedzi committee by Lee Pennington and CIA officers Paul Gaynor, Howard Osborn, Stephen L. Kuhn, Edward F. Sayle, Louis W. Vasaly and two unidentified security officers (see the Nedzi report, testimony of February 25–26, 1974, pp. 940–1039).

Pennington was a close friend of McCord's, having been recruited by the younger man in the early 1950s while serving as director of the American Legion's National Americanism Commission. In that capacity he helped McCord to identify those members of the CIA who, for one reason or another, might be regarded as politically suspect. He was able to do this because one of his principal duties with the Legion was to compile and maintain a watch list of Americans who had attended the wrong rallies, signed the wrong petitions, or joined the wrong political party. Pennington's secretary, Donald Sweany, himself a veteran of the House Committee on Un-American Activities, had married McCord's secretary, Lucille. It was something of a reunion, then, when Pennington "just happened" to drop by McCord's house a few days after the break-in. There Pennington says that he found the Sweanys and Mrs. McCord standing before the fireplace, destroying every shred of paper that was to be found in McCord's office—books, magazines, files, photographs, everything. (Apparently, because the fire had been lighted in some haste and perhaps the flue had not been opened beforehand, the house was engulfed in smoke, and later would require repainting; the walls were blackened with soot, and the furniture was smoke-damaged as well.) Eager to be of help, Pennington sat down before the fire and began tossing folders into the flames. Asked later about the contents of these folders, Pennington could not be of much help: as he said, it was not as if a selection process had taken place—if it was paper, it got burned.

This, at least, is what Pennington claims occurred and, lest anyone jump to the conclusion that they were destroying evidence, Mrs. McCord has stated that this summer fire was set at her husband's direction. According to Mrs. McCord, she had received a telephone call from Houston, Texas, on June 19, two days after the arrests, in which a bomb threat had been made. In a telephone conversation with her jailed husband, Mrs. McCord informed him of the threat. He, in turn, recalled that his office at home was filled with papers of every kind. Should a bomb go off in the house, these papers might catch fire, and so Mr. McCord told Mrs. McCord to burn every piece of paper in his study. In effect, it was a preemptive strike, and, surely, some important personal papers must have gone up in flames. However odd this must seem, so also must Mrs. McCord's information that the alleged telephone threat came from

Houston, Texas. How could she have known that? Was the threat made *collect?*[29]

What is most astonishing about this conflagration, however, is not the fatuous explanation put forward to justify it but the Ervin committee's failure to question McCord about the matter. Clearly, there was every reason to suspect that the committee's principal witness had ordered the destruction of potentially valuable evidence, and yet, because the committee found McCord's testimony so convenient to its own biases, Senator Ervin and his colleagues were loath to ask questions of McCord that might impugn his credibility as a witness or complicate the morality play that the committee had chosen to put on.

The Pennington incident (as it became known) came to light (or, more accurately, to twilight) indirectly through the thoroughness of the FBI's investigation and directly through the integrity of two unidentified CIA employees in the Office of Security. On August 18, 1972, FBI agent Donald L. Parham inquired of the CIA as to the identity of a "Mr. Pennington," who was believed to have been a past supervisor of McCord's at the CIA. The inquiry came as a result of the bureau's having learned that someone named Pennington—a man much older than McCord—had driven the indicted burglar to his Rockville home following the latter's release on bail. The bureau made the twin assumptions that Pennington was a former CIA colleague of McCord's and, in view of his years, a probable past supervisor.

The inquiry generated considerable concern within the Office of Security. Pennington was regarded as a "very, very sensitive source" whose value would be diminished if the CIA were to "give him up" to the FBI. Why the agency took this attitude is unclear: Pennington, after all, had at one time been the number three man in the FBI, a protégé of J. Edgar Hoover's who was so completely trusted that he had had the responsibility of preparing Hoover's personal income tax returns. In other words, he was the Bureau's long before he became the CIA's. Moreover, if we are to credit the testimony of General Paul Gaynor, head of the Security Research Staff, Pennington appears to have done nothing for the

---

[29]By comparison, this writer and his wife have also suffered bomb threats. Unlike the McCords, however, our reaction was not to reduce our records to a *tabula rasa*, but rather to notify the FBI in the hope that they would handle the matter. (They did, and quite competently.)

agency but clip newspapers and, on one occasion, to purchase a copy of the publicly available *Congressional Directory*. According to his operational file, he had not been given a single assignment for the CIA since 1969, though he met regularly with his case officer and General Gaynor, and continued to be paid by sterile check. It is strange, therefore, in light of this testimony as to Pennington's supposed unimportance, that the CIA's response to the FBI's inquiry was to give the bureau the name of a different Pennington—not Lee R., Jr., but Cecil H. The latter was a retired employee of the Office of Security. He had nothing whatsoever to do with the Watergate affair and had not, of course, driven McCord anywhere at any time. Grilled by the FBI for reasons that he could not comprehend, his alibi was quickly verified, with the result that the Pennington lead turned into a dead end for the bureau, just as the CIA had intended.

There is no question that the bureau was deliberately misled, and for the following reasons. On June 22, immediately after the fire at McCord's home, Pennington contacted his CIA case officer, Louis W. Vasaly (an employee of the Security Research Staff). Pennington told Vasaly what had occurred, and Vasaly passed the information to his boss, General Gaynor. Gaynor was amused by the detail about the house needing to be repainted as a result of the fire and, in casual conversation with a subordinate named Edward F. Sayle, related the anecdote with a chuckle. A conscientious man, Sayle took the information to Security Officer number one, who, three days before, had been appointed as one of the agency's "focal point" officers on the burgeoning Watergate affair. According to Security Officer number one, Sayle provided him with a limited account of the story, saying that he had received it from General Gaynor and that the general had mentioned that Howard Osborn was aware of the incident. Because the story was hearsay, and because the director of security supposedly knew all of the details, Security Officer number one did nothing with the information at the time, filing it only in the back of his mind. When, two months later, on August 18, the FBI inquired about a Pennington who was an associate of McCord's, Security Officer number one recalled his conversation and went back to Sayle.

"He [Sayle] told me at that time . . . that Mr. Lee Pennington had entered Mr. McCord's office at home, destroying any indication of connections between the Agency and Mr. McCord," Security

Officer number one recalled.[30] Disturbed by this and uncertain what to do, he went to the man in charge of Personnel Security. Telling him of the FBI's request, and of Lee Pennington's actions in June, Security Officer number one suggested that the FBI be given the name of the man whom it was clearly seeking. The head of Personnel Security dissented, saying that Pennington was too sensitive and the decision had been made to sacrifice Cecil Pennington instead.[31]

Security Officer number one was upset by his superior's decision to send the FBI on a fool's errand, so he took the matter to Stephen L. Kuhn, deputy director of the Office of Security. After recounting his story, Security Officer number one was told by Kuhn to "Get a memo in the record. Get the thing down, just what happened."[32] In Washington this is impolitely described as "covering one's ass," and on August 25, 1972, the memo was filed.

The matter might have ended there, with the FBI effectively short-circuited and the Pennington incident buried, were it not for an action taken by Richard Helms some five months later in January 1973. This was Helms's decision to have all records pertaining to the CIA's "mind-control" and drug experiments destroyed and, also, to erase all tapes and burn all transcripts of conversations secretly recorded on what has been described as the CIA's "central recording system." This system was a constellation of room and telephone bugs in the office of the director of Central Intelligence and in the French Room (a conference room separating the offices of the director and deputy director of the CIA). More than four thousand pages of recorded conversations were destroyed, obliterating the behind-the-scenes record of Helms's six and a half years as DCI. An equally enormous historical loss, and one that may have had even greater relevance to the Watergate affair, however, was the destruction of all known materials pertaining to the agency's oldest and most nightmarish program: "mind-control." Because of the outgoing Helms's decision to destroy these records, we can only speculate as to whether that program impinged on the Watergate affair. What makes it appear that it may have is the use of prostitutes in both the

[30]Nedzi report, p. 973.
[31]Senator Howard Baker has suggested that Pennington's extreme sensitivity may have been due to the possibility that he was an illegal "domestic agent" of the CIA. If so, then Pennington would certainly have undertaken assignments far more sensitive than clipping newspapers —and, unquestionably, he did.
[32]Nedzi report, p. 975.

mind-control and Watergate operations,[33] as well as Hunt's secret reports to CIA psychologists charged with creating psychological models, or "machines," for predicting and affecting the behavior of targeted individuals. Helms, of course, denies that anything so interesting was at stake.

According to Helms, he was only "tidying up" while preparing to assume his new post as U.S. ambassador to Iran. The tapes and transcripts had been no more than a personal aid, a diary of sorts, and there was no need for them to be retained. In fact, however, Helms's decision was taken in defiance of a January 18, 1973, letter from Senator Mike Mansfield to a host of government agencies, including the CIA. The Mansfield letter ordered that all materials having to do with the Watergate affair be preserved, pending the Senate's scheduled hearings on the subject. When news of Helms's housecleaning became known, the reaction was both predictable and understandable. It was suggested that Helms was guilty of destroying evidence, and of obstructing justice: it was inconceivable that there had not been a single reference to Watergate in the thousands of pages that had been destroyed. But that could not be proved. The tapes were gone, and Helms insisted that none of them had anything to do with the Watergate affair. He had not, therefore, violated Senator Mansfield's order—or so, at least, he claimed, and no one could dispute him. As Helms summed it up: "[W]hen I heard about tapes and destruction of Watergate-related tapes, the thing that immediately struck me was: who knows what was on those tapes except me or my secretary . . . ? [W]ho in the public can make an allegation that there were any tapes that were Watergate-related?"

To which Representative Lucien Nedzi replied, "The problem is, if the shoe was put on the other foot, how can you prove they weren't Watergate-related?"[34]

Helms's "housecleaning" is relevant to the CIA's deception of the FBI in that Helms's action was inadvertently responsible for a congressional inquiry that ultimately forced the Pennington issue to surface. In August 1973, a year after Security Officer number one had written his memorandum and put it in the file on the Pennington incident, CIA Director William Colby (Helms's successor) ordered

[33]See Marks, *Search for the Manchurian Candidate.*
[34]Nedzi report, p. 1041.

that a package of representative Watergate materials be prepared for him. The package was to contain any materials that were to date unknown to the new director. Security Officer number one was responsible for preparing the package, and he was explicitly told, apparently by CIA officer Stephen Kuhn, to exclude the Pennington material from the file. Security Officer number one expressed his "concern" about this order, but complied with it.

Subsequently, on January 21, 1974, a year after Helms had ordered that the agency's central taping records be destroyed, the CIA inspector general's office announced that it was about to review the Office of Security's voluminous Watergate file. Security Officer number one informed Kuhn of that fact, and Kuhn paid a visit to the director of the Office of Security, Howard Osborn. Minutes later, Kuhn returned to say, " 'Remove the [Pennington] materials from the [Watergate] files and maintain them separately.' From the words [that Kuhn] used, [Security Officer number one] took Mr. Kuhn to be passing along instructions which he himself had just received. [The security officer] left [Kuhn's] office immediately, remarking . . . 'We'll see about that.' "[35]

Clearly, Lee Pennington was of profound concern to the top officials of the CIA's Office of Security. His identity, and his participation in the bonfire at McCord's home, had been concealed not merely from the FBI but from the new CIA director, William Colby, and from the CIA inspector general himself.

After his brief and unhappy conversation with Stephen Kuhn, Security Officer number one went to his colleague Security Officer number two. The men discussed the recent order, and both agreed that they would resign rather than comply with it. Number one remarked that "the Agency doesn't need its own L. Patrick Gray" (a reference to Gray's destruction of the materials from Howard Hunt's safe). To make certain that the attempted cover-up of the Pennington incident would not succeed, the two security officers copied all of the Pennington materials, including the August 1972 memo that number one had written, and placed them in sealed envelopes marked for the director's "Eyes Only." Expecting to be fired, they then placed these envelopes in their personal safes.

A month later, on February 20, 1974, "a review was being made of a draft Memorandum concerning Agency tapes and tape tran-

[35]Ibid., p. 979.

scripts, prepared by the [CIA's] Office of Legislative Counsel, which contained a statement that the Agency had provided *all* relevant data relating to the Watergate matter."[36] Both security officers were asked to sign the memo, but felt that they could not. Ever cautious, they telephoned the Office of Legislative Counsel and asked, in effect, "Do you really mean it? *All* relevant data?" They were told that indeed the memo meant what it said, whereupon the security officers surfaced the Pennington incident—nearly two years after it had occurred.

The Pennington matter is significant for several reasons. To begin with, an informational memorandum prepared over the signature of Howard Osborn specifically states that Pennington helped to destroy McCord's files in order to eradicate any evidence of a connection between McCord and the CIA. What is most meaningful about this is the fact that McCord's past connection to the CIA was already a matter of public record—indeed, the front page of the public record—at the time that Pennington fed the flames in McCord's home. The inference, then, is obvious and unavoidable: since McCord's past connection to the CIA was well known at the time, the only purpose to be served by destroying McCord's files in June 1972 was to eliminate evidence of an *ongoing* clandestine relationship between the CIA and the recently jailed spook.

The cover-up of the Pennington incident is important, also, for what it suggests, either in its own right or in conjunction with other evidence. Internal CIA documents make reference to the fact that Pennington repeatedly briefed his case officer on McCord's situation vis-à-vis Watergate, and that Pennington provided the Security Research Staff with investigative reports about Jack Anderson that McCord had prepared on the basis of Lou Russell's information. It appears, then, that Lee R. Pennington was McCord's cut-out to the Security Research Staff. So, too, as evidenced by the deliberate concealment of the Pennington incident from the CIA's own director and inspector general, it is clear that a secret agenda was at work within the CIA—a "second track" or "runaway operation" to which only a select few (e.g., General Gaynor) were privy.

---

[36]"Memorandum for: Director of Central Intelligence; Subject: Watergate Incident," February 22, 1974, from Howard Osborn. The memo's first sentence is "This memorandum is for *information* only."

16.
Signposts Ignored

While the June 19–21 period was an evidentiary disaster in many respects, certain successes were achieved. The most important of these was the establishment of a connection between the arrested men, E. Howard Hunt and G. Gordon Liddy, and the identification of Alfred L. Baldwin, Jr., as the occupant of Room 723 in the Howard Johnson's motel. One would like to congratulate the FBI on these successes, but the fact of the matter is that little investigation was required to produce the evidence in any of these matters. Hunt and Liddy were, as we have seen, both listed in Barker's and Martinez' telephone directories. As for Baldwin, he had made free use of the telephone in his hotel room, calling home with the frequency befitting a dutiful son. Routinely, the FBI obtained the telephone toll slips for his room, and quickly identified Baldwin as its previous occupant. Agents were sent to interview him, but on the advice of his attorney, John Cassidento, he had nothing to say. It would be a week before he would decide to tell all.

At the time, Lou Russell was living in the rooming house on Q Street. With his boss under arrest, he soon became a suspect in the case. Questioned by the FBI, Russell needed an alibi for the night of June 16–17, and he did not have one. Because his daughter had not been at home on the occasion of his first visit, his comings and goings in Benedict that night seemed somehow desperate and therefore suspicious. A shaky alibi was worse than none at all; accordingly, he told the bureau that he had eaten dinner at the Howard Johnson's that evening and then returned alone to his rooming house. No, he lied, no one had seen him that night; the bureau would simply have to take him at his word. When the FBI agents suggested that his word was of little value, and intimated that he had been directly involved in the Watergate break-in, Russell reacted angrily and told them to shove off.

It was at about this time that Russell received a telephone call from a prominent man—Carmine Bellino, an "investigative accountant," whose life had been spent in close association with the Kennedy family.[1] He had known Lou Russell when the latter had been chief investigator for the House Committee on Un-American Activities, and he was telephoning Russell at the suggestion of a mutual friend, John Leon.[2]

Leon later said that Bellino had wanted to learn everything he could about the attack on the DNC. Knowing of Russell's employment by McCord and suspecting his involvement in the break-in, Leon urged Bellino to contact the private detective. At the time, Bellino was the de facto point man of the congressional investigation then impending. Under the authority of Senator Edward Kennedy, the then chairman of the Senate's Administrative Practices Committee, Bellino was laying the groundwork for the day when he would be appointed chief investigator for the Senate Select Committee on Presidential Campaign Activities (the Ervin committee).

We do not know what Bellino said to Russell or what Russell said to Bellino. Soon after the call, however, a Good Samaritan came to Russell, offering sanctuary. The Samaritan was William Birely, Bellino's close friend and longtime stockbroker. Asked if there was any connection between his friendship with Bellino and his subsequent generosity to Russell, Birely insists that there was not. Similarly, Birely says, his friendship with Lee Pennington was also a coincidence: both he and Pennington had long served together as executive officers in various patriotic societies based in Washington.[3]

It was "out of the goodness of my heart," Birely recalls, that he offered to rescue Russell from his squalid quarters in the capital. Russell accepted the offer, and was soon resident in an apartment

---

[1] A former FBI agent, Bellino had served Attorney General Robert F. Kennedy well in the latter's campaign against corrupt Teamster President Jimmy Hoffa. According to two Justice Department officials who were questioned by the Senate's Church committee in its probe of CIA abuses and assassination attempts, Bellino handled President John F. Kennedy's personal matters. It was to Bellino, for instance, that complications such as Judith Exner (the President's sometime mistress) were referred.

[2] In fact, Bellino is said to have contacted Leon and Russell on June 18, twenty-four hours after the arrests. (This, according to an investigative memorandum prepared by Washington attorney Jerris Leonard, a prominent supporter of Richard Nixon. Leonard's memorandum is dated July 19, 1974, and is based on interviews with John Leon and others.)

[3] Birely and Pennington had worked together on the *Cross of Languedoc*, the official publication of the Huguenot Society of Washington. Birely adds that he and Pennington were also active members of the Sons of the American Revolution.

on the top floor of the Twin Towers complex in Silver Spring, Maryland, just across the District line. Provided with "walking-around money" and a better car than he had been driving until then, Russell found that his situation had improved dramatically.

"I pitied him," Birely told me. "There was nothing more to it than that. Lou had just picked himself up. He'd stopped drinking. He had great hopes for his work with McCord and then, all of a sudden, he was out of a job. The Watergate business just devastated him."

In fact Russell was not "out of a job." Despite McCord's arrest, and the apparent dissolution of McCord Associates, Inc., Russell remained in the employ of the Watergate burglar, albeit under different auspices. On June 9 McCord had rented office space at the Arlington Towers complex in Rosslyn on the Virginia side of the Potomac.[4] There McCord established a new firm, Security International, Inc., headed by a former CIA officer named William Shea (whose wife, Theresa, had previously worked as McCord's secretary). The new firm was to achieve remarkable success; whereas McCord Associates had won only two clients (the CRP and the RNC) after two years of trying, Security International signed twenty-five to thirty (never identified) new clients in its first nine months of existence.[5] Moreover, even while the Arlington Towers were unusually secure, so also was the suite of offices that McCord had rented for his new firm.[6] The doors of that firm were kept locked around the clock (even while its employees worked inside), and no outsiders were permitted to enter. Salesmen and others who called in person were told that all business had to be transacted over the telephone. It was while living at the Twin Towers in Silver Spring as a guest of William Birely's that Russell continued to work

---

[4]FBI serial 139-4089-681, interview of Patricia Marshall conducted by special agent Arnold Parham, July 10, 1972.

[5]Testimony of James McCord in executive session before the Ervin committee on March 28, 1973.

[6]Security in the Arlington Towers complex was tight because the complex was the domestic staging ground for CIA/military/State Department pacification programs directed against the Vietcong infrastructure under the auspices of the Civilian Operations and Rural Developments Support (CORDS) program. Among those "pacification" operations was the notorious Phoenix program, which, by official estimates, left 20,587 alleged Vietcong cadres dead. That McCord chose to locate his new offices in what might be described as "a nest of spooks" cannot have been an accident. As the former chief of Physical Security for the CIA, McCord had been at least nominally responsible for every CIA installation in the United States. The Arlington Towers' relationship to the CIA and CORDS was almost certainly well known to him.

for McCord under the auspices of Security International. According to Russell's daughter, Jean Hooper, "Mr. McCord was a pallbearer at my dad's funeral [in July 1973]. And when it was over, Mr. McCord came to me with my dad's last paycheck. I think it was for $285—something like that."

Which raises the question: Why did—*how could*—McCord keep Russell on the payroll for more than a year after the Watergate arrests and, indeed, even after the detective was incapacitated by a heart attack (in April 1973)? If we are to believe the impression given at the time, McCord was in desperate financial straits. Raising bail was said to be a serious problem, his family was allegedly hard put to make ends meet and so forth. And yet, despite these difficulties, McCord was able to pay Russell a good salary and, what is more, to reject a $105,000 publishing advance for what appear to have been artistic reasons.[7]

As we will see, it was not only for McCord that Lou Russell was working that summer, and neither was he living alone at the Twin Towers. Unknown to Birely, whose office was next door to the apartment he had provided for Russell, the detective was living with "Tess," the Columbia Plaza prostitute whom the U.S. attorney's office sought to question. Tess's friend Phil Bailley recalls talking by telephone to the blonde during the time that he himself was awaiting trial and a short stay in the bin. According to Bailley, Tess said her roommate was a strange man, much older than herself, who was living in a "penthouse" at the Twin Towers. She added that he had been an FBI agent years before, that he was a private detective now, and was writing a book about his experiences.[8] She said he had a drinking problem, spoke often about his work for HUAC, hunting Communists, and was somehow involved in "the Watergate business." It seems most unlikely that there could be more than one person fitting that description, which Russell did to a T. But what seems to clinch the matter is an idiosyncrasy that Bailley recalls Tess

---

[7]This was the amount of the contract offered to McCord and ghost-writer Eric Norden by Holt, Rinehart & Winston. (The authors were to receive 45 percent of the advance upon signing.) Additionally, Warner Brothers was negotiating for the movie rights to the book.
[8]Russell's book was not found among his papers after his death. Those closest to him—Birely, Russell's daughter and a second prostitute (with whom Russell seems to have been in love) —each claim that one of the others either has the book or destroyed it. Complicating the issue even further is the disputed existence of a second book that Russell is said to have been writing. The first concerned his experiences in the FBI, the second his experiences with McCord.

describing: she said that her friend distrusted banks and preferred to keep his money in cash, which he secreted in a roll of aluminum foil. So, too, did Lou Russell.

Russell performed a number of services for Birely while resident at the Twin Towers. On at least two occasions, for example, he fronted (there is no other word) for the stockbroker in highly profitable transactions involving bank shares—transactions that were later questioned by the Senate. According to Russell's daughter, moreover, her father began to travel quite a bit, going most often to Rhode Island and Connecticut. The purpose of those trips was never disclosed to her, but she recalls that her father told her they were taken in Birely's behalf. Birely denied this, as he denied any suggestion of improprieties concerning the questioned stock transactions. As for the Columbia Plaza Apartments and, in particular, Lil Lori's operation, he at first denied ever having been there. Told of entries in Lori's trick book, he then recalled having known her, but insisted that he "took no pleasure there." It is not my intention to embarrass Mr. Birely. As a friend of Lou Russell's who was interested in the detective's welfare and personal circumstances, the stockbroker could hardly have avoided incidental contact with Lil Lori and the girls. The prostitutes were, after all, Russell's solace in life and, more or less, his constant companions. That Birely should also have been well acquainted with Lee Pennington may give us pause, but by itself it proves nothing. In the same way, Birely's generosity, and the timing of it so soon after Russell's conversation with Bellino, would seem to be cause for wonder, but perhaps such a reaction would be mere cynicism. And as for Tess, her presence in Russell's apartment in the Twin Towers apparently had nothing to do with Birely; he claims not to have known that she was there. Still, the connections between these people and events are so suggestive that it is hard to understand why the Ervin committee failed to inquire about them. Apparently, Bellino, heading the committee's investigative task force, did not feel that these were useful leads to pursue.

One lead that was pursued, however, was Alfred Baldwin.

While at first refusing to answer the FBI's questions, Baldwin made repeated attempts to contact McCord by telephone, only to find that his phones had been disconnected. Becoming increasingly worried, he wrote to McCord, explaining that he had yet to be paid for his work, did not know if he was still employed, and was in a quandary as to what he should do about the FBI. The letter mailed, he then called the Committee to Re-elect the President and repeated his plight to Fred LaRue. A day later, CRP attorney Paul O'Brien came to New Haven to discuss the matter with him.

Like that of so many other lawyers in the affair, O'Brien's past included connections to the CIA.[9] And the position he took with Baldwin did much to break open the Watergate scandal. To Cassidento it was obvious that O'Brien and the CRP had no intention of helping his client. O'Brien's questions centered almost entirely on the issue of whether or not it could be proved that Baldwin had an official relationship to the Nixon reelection committee. If it could be proved that he did, that was a potential embarrassment; if not, well . . . To Baldwin, however, his employment by McCord Associates, Inc., rather than by the CRP itself, was a mere technicality, and he told O'Brien as much. The GOP attorney's response was to shrug, whereupon the interview was ended, and O'Brien returned to the capital. Baldwin felt that he was being abandoned by the big shots.

When McCord finally telephoned his former employee, on June 24, the tenor of the conversation was more sympathetic, but the content was much the same. McCord urged Baldwin to remain silent, except to say that he was employed by McCord Associates. Baldwin replied that his position was difficult, and suggested that he might have to seek a deal with the authorities. McCord replied that he understood, and that whatever Baldwin did, he would "understand."

[9]O'Brien was employed by the CIA until 1952 (see the *Final Report* of the Ervin committee, p. 1165), and is thought to have assisted the agency in later years. Robert McCandless, co-counsel for John Dean, was until 1973 a partner in Burwell, Hansen & McCandless (later, Burwell, Hansen & Manley). One of that firm's clients (and one, moreover, with which it shared office space) was Southern Capital & Management Corporation, the CIA proprietary responsible for managing the agency's investment portfolio. McCandless says that he was unaware of the CIA's involvement with his law firm. James Bierbower, counsel for another key witness against Nixon, Jeb Magruder, had served as vice-president of Southern Air Transport, one of the CIA's largest airline proprietaries. (With respect to McCandless and Bierbower, see John Marks, *The CIA's Corporate Shell Game* [Washington, D.C.: Center for National Security Studies, Reprint 103].) James St. Clair, who succeeded J. Fred Buzhardt, Jr., as Nixon's attorney, was a member of Hale & Dorr, the prestigious Boston law firm that *Newsweek* suggests is part of the CIA's Old Boy network. (It was from Hale & Dorr's offices that a number of important CIA proprietaries were established. See *Newsweek*, May 19, 1975, pp. 25–28.) As we have seen, David Young's counsel, Anthony Lapham, became general counsel to the CIA in the aftermath of Watergate. As for Edward Bennett Williams, his relationship to the agency goes back to the early 1950s, when he and CIA agent Robert A. Maheu worked together.

Two weeks later, on July 5, the U.S. attorney's office in Washington made a formal promise not to prosecute Baldwin in return for his complete cooperation. Five days afterward Baldwin sat down to a marathon session with two FBI agents, giving them a blow-by-blow description of his adventures.

News of Baldwin's confession, however, did not reach the public until September 6, two months after his interview with the FBI. It was then that Democrats Joseph Califano and Larry O'Brien staged a press conference. Referring only to an unidentified "informant" (Baldwin), the Democrats for the first time made public details about the June 16–17 break-in, the alleged bugging of Oliver and O'Brien in May, the delivery of eavesdropping logs to the CRP, and the abortive efforts to bug McGovern's own headquarters.

It was a sensational story, and the question naturally arises as to how the Democrats learned of Baldwin's confession. The answer is that Baldwin himself told them, albeit supposedly without knowing to whom he was blabbing. In late July, more than two weeks after his client's interview with the FBI, Cassidento telephoned Edward Bennett Williams, saying that he had a client who has "a lot to say about the Watergate . . . and wants to get it out."[10] Williams then notified his partner, Joseph Califano, who was representing the DNC in its civil suit against the Watergate burglars. Califano and Cassidento subsequently discussed the matter, and an attorney was dispatched from Califano's firm to Cassidento's offices in New Haven, Connecticut. There, in early August, a bizarre interview took place. While Baldwin sat in one room Califano's representative sat in another, each out of sight and hearing of the other. A question would be put to Cassidento, who would relay it to Baldwin. Baldwin would reply, and Cassidento would return with the answer to Califano's man. This procedure would be followed until Baldwin had exhausted his information—and two lawyers.

Subsequently Baldwin was questioned by the Ervin committee concerning his transaction with the Democrats' attorneys. He "vehemently denied" ever collaborating with the Democratic National Committee or its counsel, and said that he had never provided them with information concerning Watergate.[11] This was, of course, untrue, though Baldwin seems not to have known it. His

[10]Executive session testimony of Joseph Califano before the Ervin committee, October 3, 1973, p. 10.
[11]Executive session testimony of Alfred Baldwin before the Ervin committee, November 1, 1973, pp. 155–57, 167–71.

attorney had apparently made a private deal with the Democrats and had not informed his client of the identity of his interrogators. Why he took such precautions is a subject of dispute. According to Cassidento (later *Judge* Cassidento), he was protecting his client, though it is difficult to understand how the interview and resulting publicity could possibly have been in Baldwin's interest, especially in view of the fact that he had been promised immunity a month earlier. According to the Baker Report, "Joseph Califano [explained] . . . that there was no quid pro quo asked for or given Cassidento in return for his providing access to Baldwin. He did seem to recall a discussion concerning a judgeship for Cassidento, and thinks Cassidento may have wanted a good word put in for him with John Bailey [Connecticut State Democratic chairman]. Cassidento recalls some reference to Califano about putting in a good word with Bailey, and states that he knew Williams and Califano would be close to Larry O'Brien and in a position to help him . . . to run for Connecticut Attorney General."[12]

We may thank Cassidento's political ambitions, then, for Baldwin's speedy arrival on the scene of the unfolding Watergate story. But what is most significant about what Baldwin had to say is that in fact his tale threatened to unravel the evolving version of the affair as it was appearing in the daily newspapers. As we will see in the next chapter, the story that he told contradicted some of the FBI's most important findings to date, and pointed investigators toward the very heart of the affair—a signpost that no one wanted to follow.

[12]Ervin committee memoranda, dated January 17, 1974, and January 24, 1974, entitled "Interview with Califano Attorneys and Interviews of Cassidento and Mirto."

17.
The September Bug

What made Baldwin's story incompatible with the evidence already gathered was his dramatic assertion that he had monitored Spencer Oliver's telephone, that a bug had also been placed on Larry O'Brien's phone (but had failed to work), and that he had compiled eavesdropping logs of the conversations that he had overheard. Until Baldwin came forward with his story, little significance had attached to the fact that both the FBI and the Chesapeake & Potomac Telephone Company had searched the DNC and failed to find a single bug. Here, however, was the jolly Alfred Baldwin with his spectacular tale of eavesdropping transcripts delivered to the CRP, the reconnaissance of McGovern headquarters and so forth. If he was telling the truth—and there was never any doubt about that in view of his stay at the Hojo and his employment by McCord— where were the bugs that he had monitored? What had happened?

The principal prosecuting attorney in the case, Earl Silbert, was under tremendous pressure from the Democrats, the White House and the public to secure a conviction, and he recoiled at the complication that had arisen. If Oliver's telephone had indeed been monitored, and if a second bug had been installed on Larry O'Brien's line, only two possibilities existed to explain the FBI's failure to find any device: either the FBI and the telephone company's technicians erred in their searches or the purpose of the June 16–17 break-in was to *de-*bug the DNC's phones. (The latter possibility would explain the fact that four bugging devices were recovered from the burglars at the time of the arrest.)

This second possibility was at once farfetched and alarming, from a prosecutorial point of view. A smart defense attorney, eager to introduce an element of doubt in the case, might argue that his clients were in the process of rectifying a felony (by de-bugging the

DNC rather than bugging it) at the time of their arrest. It was, in others words, a juridical mess, and Silbert had no practical alternative to concluding that the FBI had "goofed."

Silbert was hardly alone in his unhappiness at these developments. The FBI was also plagued by the insinuation that its agents had overlooked important evidence. As the bureau's internal documents make clear, there had been no fewer than three physical searches for bugs in the DNC's headquarters: on June 17, June 29–30 and July 5. The telephones of both Spencer Oliver and Larry O'Brien had been taken apart and examined, and no bugs had been found. As an investigative agency, there was nothing more that the FBI could do. It reported to Silbert its interrogation of Alfred Baldwin and its findings, or lack of findings, within the DNC itself. How the conflicting evidence was to be reconciled was not the bureau's problem; it was Silbert's. And it was a big one.

It was then that the fortuitous occurred: exactly a week after Califano's press conference, in which Baldwin's account of the bugging was made public, a bug was found on Spencer Oliver's personal telephone in the DNC. The discovery occurred in the following way, and as FBI documents make clear, the bureau smelled a rat.

On September 12, Spencer Oliver's new secretary, Marie Elise Haldane, called the Chesapeake & Potomac Telephone Company to report a malfunction on the telephones in Oliver's office.[1] According to Haldane, "the telephone bell would ring, and no extension light . . . would come on to indicate on which extension the call was being received. After several rings of the bell, a light would appear to designate the extension. However, after answering the phone, the phone bell would continue to ring and make conversation impossible."[2]

A C&P telephone repairman was sent to the DNC to check the phones, but was unable to duplicate the problem. The phones seemed to work perfectly.[3] It was then that Haldane asked him to check the phones for bugging devices. The repairman declined, suggesting that Haldane was "paranoid," and saying that he would

[1]Maxie Wells resigned as Oliver's secretary one to two months after the Watergate arrests. (Her reasons for quitting, she said, were personal.) By coincidence, however, Wells happened to be visiting with her replacement, Marie Haldane, when the September bug was found.
[2]FBI teletype of September 15, 1972, 139-4136-3.
[3]FBI report of interview with Richard Walter Blackman, P.B.X. repairman for C&P Telephone Company, September 22, 1972.

not recognize a bugging device if he saw one. He suggested that she call the telephone company's security office, and that afternoon she did.

On the following morning, September 13, the telephones were checked for bugging devices by two employees of the C&P security office. Haldane was present during the inspection and, according to the repairmen, expressed surprise when no devices seemed to have been found. In fact a device *had* been located, but company policy forbade the repairmen to mention this to the customer before notifying their supervisor and then the FBI.[4] The chief of the telephone company's security office, Earl A. Connor, arrived on the scene at the DNC shortly after noon on September 13. He inspected the telephones and told Haldane that he had further checks to make. FBI reports say that the following conversation then took place:

Secretary: Did you find anything?
Connor: No.
Secretary: You didn't find anything at all?
Connor: No, we're still checking.

According to the same FBI report, "Mr. CONNOR advised that at the time the above conversation took place he felt that the secretary was expecting him to say he had found something in the telephone."[5]

In fact Connor had confirmed the existence of the eavesdropping device on Oliver's telephone and, following company policy, notified the FBI. The bureau's agents then came to the DNC and removed the device for their inspection.

While the bug was being examined at the FBI Laboratory, Haldane was questioned by bureau agents. According to their report: "The interviewing Agents advised [the Democrats' attorney] Mr. [Alan] GALBRAITH of the fact that HALDANE considered this interview and investigation by the FBI to be a 'laughing matter,' inasmuch as she constantly smiled and laughed during the interview. HALDANE was repeatedly advised by the interviewing Agents that this was no laughing matter and that it was a serious allegation being made against someone. She replied that her smiles or

⁴FBI report of September 13, 1972, interview of Earl A. Connor, dictated September 18, 1972, filed in WFO 139-170.
⁵Ibid., p. 2.

laughing had nothing to do with the interviews."[6]

Haldane's inappropriate reaction to the FBI's questions bothered the bureau, as, indeed, did the device itself. A quarter of an inch thick, it measured one by one and a half inches, and appeared homemade. It was anything but a sophisticated bug—on the contrary, it was something of a dinosaur, the sort of eavesdropping device that might have been used in the early 1950s. Its parts were so commonly available as to be untraceable, and their manufacturer had probably spent no more than ten or fifteen dollars to put it together. What's more, the device was inoperable: while it might broadcast as far as five hundred feet under perfect conditions (e.g., on a clear day in a log cabin on a mountaintop), it would not function effectively within a steel-and-concrete building, and, in fact, it would not function at all with the defective transistor that it had.[7]

Considering the device, and the circumstances under which it was found, the bureau was skeptical. As the bureau noted in one of its teletypes, "Possibility exists that malfunction described by secretary [Marie Haldane] had never occurred."[8] This speculation was echoed by the experts to whom photos of the device were shown. They confirmed the growing suspicion of many FBI officials that the device had been "salted," or planted in order that it would be found. As one expert, Jack Cardover, of Carl Cardover & Company, told the FBI, "It was [Cardover's] opinion that the individual who built this device knew it would be detected or had planned that it be detected. . . ."[9] The same view was held by another expert, Lewis Lunine, of Amerex Electronics, who told the FBI that he "cannot believe anyone serious about intercepting conversations would use such an outdated piece of equipment." The consensus of the experts whom the FBI questioned was that the device recovered from Oliver's phone was a "throwaway"—a device installed to be found.[10]

The initial reaction of Earl Silbert to the discovery of a bug on

[6]FBI report of interview of Marie Elise Haldane, conducted September 13, 1972, transcribed September 18, 1972, and made part of FBI file WFO 139-170.

[7]See FBI teletype of October 13, 1972 (139-4136-71).

[8]FBI teletype of September 30, 1972, from the Washington Field Office, recorded as 139-4136-99.

[9]FBI interview of Jack Cardover, transcribed October 31, 1972, from an interview of October 25, 1972, FBI file NY 139-314.

[10]FBI interview of Lewis Lunine, dictated December 21, 1972, from notes taken December 18, 1972. See FBI file NY 139-314.

Spencer Oliver's telephone was, predictably, one of delight. His enthusiasm, however, deflated as the FBI's analysis turned to the conclusion that the bug had been installed after the bureau's searches of the DNC in June and July.

In the opinion of the bureau, the September 13 bug should not be "captioned" under the same heading as the Watergate break-in. It was a new case with no known connection to the men under arrest. In sum, the bureau took the position that McCord et al. had been arrested in the Watergate while attempting to install eavesdropping devices. The arrests had taken place before those devices could be installed. Baldwin's statement indicated that monitoring had taken place prior to the arrests, which, in the opinion of the FBI, meant that some other, unidentified site had been bugged. As for the September 13 device, it had probably been installed following the Democrats' press conference about Baldwin on September 6. The principal suspects in relation to the September 13 bugging were, in the FBI's opinion, the Democrats themselves.

To Earl Silbert this was nonsense: the bureau had simply "fucked up." So it was that in late September a sometimes blistering (and to date unpublished) correspondence took place between the prosecution's lead attorney and the FBI's highest echelon. In a letter written to the Justice Department's Henry Petersen on September 28, 1972, Silbert inveighed against the FBI's September 26 report on the discovery of a bug in Spencer Oliver's telephone.

"The report contains virtually no useful information concerning who put that wiretapping device there," Silbert wrote. "As you will see, it is entitled Unknown Subjects and the case is assigned to an agent other than the one assigned to the Watergate; the Bureau is thus assuming that the Watergate defendants are not involved. ... Obviously, we do not want to be put in the position of challenging such testimony of the FBI, particularly its lab, while at the same time relying so heavily on the FBI in general, and the lab in particular, for other important aspects of our proof."

Bristling at Silbert's letter, the FBI Laboratory summarized each of the prosecutor's objections, and replied to them all in devastating detail in an internal FBI memorandum of October 2, 1972:

1. SILBERT: The device recovered [on September 13] operated at 120 MHz. Baldwin was receiving at 118.9 MHz, well within the range of the device. The three devices in the possession of those arrested operated at . . . 110,

[110, and] . . . 114 MHz, not at all as clearly within the range of the receiver at 118.9, . . . particularly the two operating at 110.

LABORATORY COMMENT: The frequency on which the recovered device originally may have operated, if at all, cannot be accurately determined since it was inoperative at time of recovery. It was made operable by replacing a defective transistor, after which the unit operated on 120 MHz. While this is the closest [frequency to the one cited by Baldwin] of the four mentioned devices, this fact is not conclusive because (a) there is no evidence to our knowledge that limits the original device tuned in by Baldwin to one of the four recovered . . . (b) the original operating frequency . . . cannot be determined; and (c) after repair, the operating frequency is not on the frequency reportedly received.

To which one is tempted to add that in any case the September 13 bug was defective and not functioning. How, then, did Baldwin monitor it (if he did monitor it), and how could the secretary have noticed an "anomaly" on the line if the supposed source of that anomaly was itself "inoperative"?

2. SILBERT: To assume that one of the three devices recovered upon arrest was the one used on Oliver's telephone assumes that the defendants removed it. I see no reason to assume that. A more, or at least equally, logical assumption is that they were going to put more taps on, not take those they had in out. Clearly, they were going to put the bugging device in. . . . [Secondly,] While the Oliver tap was not [a tap on Larry] O'Brien, . . . [McCord et al.] apparently had considered it to be producing useful information. There was, accordingly, no reason to remove it while putting in other taps.

LABORATORY COMMENT: Reason appears speculative. We do not know the basis [for] . . . the assumption, "Clearly, they were going to put the bugging device in." Laboratory tests of the batteries associated with the bugging device showed that some were partially run down. This would not be the normally expected condition for a new installation of batteries. However, more in point, the absence of a device in Oliver's phone at the time of the security check does not necessarily carry with it the assumption that one of the devices found in possession of defendants was the one heard by Baldwin.

What is perhaps most interesting about this particular exchange is Silbert's assertion that "the Oliver tap was not [a tap on] O'Brien." Indeed, it was not, though we are told that an eavesdropping device was in fact placed on O'Brien's telephone—a device whose transmissions could not be received because of the architectural "shielding" in the vicinity of O'Brien's office. FBI memoranda concerning the initial search at the DNC on June 17 specifically list O'Brien's telephone as one of those examined on that date. And yet no bug was found at that time, which duplicated and compounded the problems associated with Spencer Oliver's phone.

> 3. SILBERT: The location of the tap in the [Oliver] telephone is totally consistent with Baldwin's explanation of how the telephone calls were intercepted—only three specific extensions, one at a time.
>
> LABORATORY COMMENT: Questionable reason. Summary Bureau report dated 9/20/72 made available to Laboratory states on page 12 that Baldwin in his monitoring discovered that he could overhear telephone conversations on *four* extensions of one phone at the office of Oliver. General Investigative Division advises that Baldwin's interviews tend to indicate he believed he was monitoring conversations of secretaries and others from telephones which were extensions of Oliver's phone. The instant device, as installed at time of recovery, would not permit this type of operation.

To put the FBI lab's reply more succinctly: the bug discovered on September 13 was not merely defective, nonfunctioning and quite possibly on the wrong frequency, but also incapable, because of its very design, of carrying out the functions that Baldwin claimed for the bug he monitored.

> 4. SILBERT: I cannot imagine anyone planting a device in the Democratic headquarters after Watergate, particularly on Oliver's telephone. It is too ludicrous.

In reply, the FBI suggests two possible motives, but before quoting the laboratory, I would suggest yet another: that the September 13 bug was installed in the DNC with the intention that it would be discovered and thereby confirm the prosecutors' belief that it was Spencer Oliver who was bugged (rather than, for example, the Columbia Plaza Apartments). This evidence, in other words, was planted.

> LABORATORY COMMENT: [Silbert's reasoning is] speculative. . . . At least two other possibilities suggest themselves on the basis of reported information:

(a) Bureau Summary report dated 9/20/72 shows on page 11 that some intercepted conversations dealt with marital problems. Marital problems are a well-recognized basis for attempted wiretapping.

(b) Democrats or sympathizers, feeling they had [an] unusually good issue in the "burglary" and wiretapping incident, could have decided to make a more recent "installation" and call attention to it in order to keep the pot boiling. Baldwin had previously disclosed approximate frequency and fact [that] Oliver's office [was] cognizant of at least part of this information. Moreover, O'Brien has recently publicly alleged his office was bugged. In this regard it is of possible significance that *the device found on Oliver's phone on 9/13/72 was completely unlike the devices found in possession of defendants at time of arrest.* [Emphasis added.]

To this, the FBI Laboratory added a footnote, suggesting that the discovery of the September 13 bug was contrived by means of a "false trouble report. In this regard WFO [Washington Field Office] wire [of] 9/30/72 advises telephone repairman attempted to observe malfunctions reported by secretary *with negative results.* WFO suggests possibility reported malfunction had never occurred."

In sum, the FBI took the following into consideration and arrived at the previously unpublished opinion that false evidence had been planted at the DNC in order to bolster Baldwin's story:

· The September 13 bug was "completely unlike" McCord's own;

· it was set to a frequency different from that which McCord intended to use;

· it had not been uncovered in previous searches at the DNC, despite its large size and crude placement;

· and despite the fact that it was not functioning, it was reported to have caused a disturbance on the line—a disturbance that the FBI could neither detect nor duplicate.

Again, in its reply to Silbert's fourth point, the FBI refers to O'Brien's *allegation* that his telephone was bugged. The word "alleged" was carefully chosen because, despite several efforts to locate a bug on O'Brien's phone, none had been found. How Silbert planned to cope with this issue is a complete mystery, and one wonders, also, what O'Brien himself made of the fact that no bug was discovered.[11]

---

[11]According to James McCord, a bug was recovered from O'Brien's telephone in April 1973, eleven months after the supposed date of its installation (in May 1972). McCord claims that he led the prosecutors to the bug. This writer has attempted to verify McCord's claim, but has so far been unable to find any evidence substantiating it. Even if true, however, the

5. SILBERT: I think the FBI missed it because the location of Oliver's office in the Democratic headquarters is such that it is almost the last place one would expect a tape to be placed—nowhere near O'Brien's office or anywhere else of importance.

LABORATORY COMMENT: Totally erroneous reason. Laboratory's search was not keyed to relative location. Indeed, Laboratory technical personnel, in addition to knowing of attempted penetration by arrested defendants, also considered possibility [that] Democrat[ic] sympathizers might make additional installations to exacerbate the situation, and therefore *all rooms and all phones were considered highly suspect and were thoroughly searched.* [Emphasis added.]

SUMMARY: While we recognize the appeal, from a prosecution standpoint, of the situation postulated by AUSA Silbert, no facts known to us at present support the presence of a listening device on Oliver's telephone at the time of the security check[s] [June 17, June 29–30, and July 5]. There is no evidence to our knowledge that the device heard by Baldwin was heard by anyone after the arrest of the defendants. On the contrary, a check of the telephones by competent and experienced technical personnel, looking specifically for this type of device, showed no such device to be present at the time of the search. In this regard, Supervisor W. G. Stevens, who was in personal charge of and took part in the search, has previously stated that the device was large enough to be readily seen by physical search, and that, based on the search conducted, he is positive that the device was not on the phone at the time of the search. Further, in this regard, it is noted that the physical security of the Democratic National Committee space was such as to make subsequent access for the purpose of installing devices relatively easy. WFO wire to the Bureau dated 9/15/72 on page 6 states [that the DNC] maintained no limitation to access to offices after normal duty hours until about midnight, when premises [were] secured.

The FBI Laboratory's reply to Silbert's comment is clearly devastating, and seems even more so when one examines the sheaf of FBI reports and memoranda on which the lab's reply is based. I will quote from only one of these reports:

Washington Field Office letter of 6/19/72, . . . advises that Earl Connor, Chief of Security, Chesapeake and Potomac Telephone Company . . ., and his assistant, who originally installed the telephone equipment at the Democratic National Committee Headquarters, conducted a secu-

---

recovery of the bug at such a late date would not prove much: it, too, might have been installed long after the original arrests, just as the September 13 bug was.

rity survey of the telephone and communication equipment of the DNCH. At the conclusion of their survey, Connor reported to [FBI special agent] Fiene that nothing unusual or out of order was detected. [The check was made June 17–18, 1972, hours after the FBI had carried out its own search.]

In order to obtain further detail as to the extent of Connor's check . . . , personnel of the Radio Engineering Section met with . . . Connor. Connor advised that the objective of his survey was to physically examine all telephone instruments and telephone equipment on the sixth floor space of the DNCH for wiretap devices. This survey was made . . . [and Connor] was positive that all available phones were checked. A room by room tour of the sixth floor space of the DNCH was made with Connor to refresh his memory of all offices and the checks made in them. He identified only one room, that occupied by the Press Secretary, as having been unavailable and therefore as not having been included in the survey. This room . . . has no telephone service in common with Oliver's office.

Both Connor and the installer advised that the check included taking the phones physically apart and visually inspecting them for foreign items. None were found. . . . The telephone company installer, who assisted Connor in the survey and who is quite familiar with telephone service in the DNCH, agreed with Connor regarding the details of the survey made by them, and each also recalled Oliver's room as one of those included in the survey. (The Laboratory also found Oliver's phone to be free of wiretapping devices on 6/29–30/72.)[12]

Other FBI reports, written at the time that the searches were made, corroborate the fact that every telephone in the DNC, as well as every telephone line, was examined, physically and electronically, and that nothing was found to be amiss.[13] Finally, there is the fact that at one time or another all of the telephones in the DNC were replaced, dismantled and examined by the Western Electric Company's Arlington office, and no listening devices were ever found.[14]

Which is to say that Larry O'Brien was never bugged at the DNC, and that Spencer Oliver was bugged only in the aftermath of the arrests—after Baldwin's account of the monitoring operation

[12]FBI memorandum, from W. W. Bradley to Mr. Conrad, April 12, 1973.
[13]Among the FBI reports and memoranda referred to are those of Dennis W. Fiene to AC, WFO (June 19, 1972); C. Bolz to Mr. Bates (September 29, 1972), Daniel M. Armstrong III to L. Patrick Gray III (October 4, 1972); and various FBI Laboratory reports. All of these, and others, were obtained under the Freedom of Information Act from the FBI.
[14]See FBI serial 139-4089-2393 and, in particular, the statements of C&P Telephone Company installer Jimmy Hilton.

had been made public. The question then becomes: Who planted the September bug and why?

Clearly, the September bug was installed in order to be discovered, and this was done so as to substantiate Alfred Baldwin's story that he had been monitoring an eavesdropping device on Spencer Oliver's telephone. In the absence of such a device, the authorities would necessarily investigate the proposition that Baldwin was in fact monitoring a transmitter that had been installed elsewhere—in a telephone that, for whatever reason, communicated regularly with people using the phone in Oliver's office. Considering the personal nature of the telephone calls that Baldwin remembered overhearing, such an investigation might have led to Lou Russell and the Columbia Plaza.

As for the September bug itself, it appears to have belonged at one time to a private detective named William Pierce.[15] In the summer of 1971 Pierce was introduced by an employee, Jim Sherwood, to Nick Beltrante. A former detective with the Washington police department, Beltrante was a brawny private eye who, Pierce said, was to work for him as vice-president of a newly planned private security firm. Before a formal agreement could be signed, however, Beltrante and Sherwood decamped to form their own firm, Investigations, Inc., leaving Pierce in the lurch. That was in September 1971, and, according to Pierce, Beltrante did not leave empty-handed. The detective was suspected by Pierce of having taken two of his clients, the Pepsi-Cola Company and the Federal National Mortgage Association ("Fannie Mae"), as well as certain electronics equipment, including a telephone bug that Pierce claimed was similar to, or identical with, the one found on Spencer Oliver's phone a year later.[16]

In a peculiar interview with the author, secured only after leaving messages on his answering machine for two years, the private eye repeatedly contradicted himself. He declined to say whether the

[15]A decade after Watergate, Pierce would make headlines in the case against former CIA agent Ed Wilson. Pierce's statements to federal prosecutors seemed to implicate Wilson in both the assassination of former Chilean ambassador Orlando Letelier and alleged payoffs to Senator Strom Thurmond. While Pierce had indeed been employed by Wilson, federal investigators were unable to substantiate either charge. A spokesman for Senator Thurmond declared that Pierce's accusation was "categorically false."

[16]Memo to Fred Thompson (minority counsel to the Ervin committee) from Richard L. Schultz (assistant minority counsel), October 19, 1973, "Subject: Wayne Barber, William Pierce—Nicholas Beltrante."

September bug was in fact the one missing from Pierce's offices, but claimed that he was responsible for the bug's discovery on Oliver's phone. He said that he had noticed certain malfunctions on the telephone and instructed the secretary to report these anomalies to the FBI, which she did, with the result that the bug was found. Confronted with Pierce's suggestion that it was he who bugged the DNC, or that he had someone do it for him, Beltrante turned the question aside, seemingly refusing an invitation for a denial. He preferred to ramble on about "the conspiracy" that led to his early retirement from the police department years before, a retirement that came about amid allegations of instability. According to Beltrante, it was he who cracked the notorious "Mayflower Hotel bugging," a 1962 incident that led to the indictment (and rapid retirement) of the Runyonesque Joe Shimon, the then chief of detectives for the Washington police department—and Beltrante's boss. Beltrante recalled: "After I went to Congress [with allegations about Shimon and the Mayflower incident], I started gettin' served with papers for the shittiest little infractions. I was always defending myself in front of the Trial Board, day after day. I had a lot of commendations, [but] they were always carping. After a while, it was driving me crazy, and I couldn't take it anymore, so I told them, the next time somebody gives me papers, I'm gonna blow his head off. The next day, they made me take a medical examination, and they decided I was depressive, and I had to retire. Fucker said it was 'not service-connected.' Forty percent disability was all. But now I had some appeals, and it's up to a hundred percent disability. With back pay. Service-connected."

It was impossible, then, to get Beltrante to answer the question as to whether or not he had in fact bugged the DNC in September 1972. Whenever the question came up, he would chuckle or change the subject—once, he winked and made a gesture to the effect that the room we were in was bugged. What I was able to establish, however, was that Beltrante began working for the Democrats on September 7, 1972, one day after the dramatic press conference on the mysterious GOP informant (Alfred Baldwin) and his eavesdropping activities. Beltrante was a contract employee of the McGovern for President Committee and was responsible for security matters, including physical and electronic searches. According to Beltrante, Lou Russell was not an employee of his but a co-worker at McGovern headquarters. The private eye did not recall Russell's title (if

Russell had one), saying only that he knew that Russell had formerly worked for McCord. (In fact, as we have seen, Beltrante was in error: Russell was still on McCord's payroll at the time of his labors for McGovern.) "I didn't trust him," Beltrante said, "because of the McCord business[!]. He said he wanted to cooperate with me . . . so we could be 'mutually helpful.' That's the way he put it: 'mutually helpful.' So he was around a lot. He helped me with the [telephone countermeasures] sweeps [at McGovern headquarters and the DNC]."

Why would Beltrante, hired to secure the Democrats' communications equipment, "work with" a man whose boss had just been arrested for bugging those same telephones? Beltrante shrugged and flexed his muscles: "It just worked out that way," he said. Then who was it that hired Russell to work for McGovern headquarters? "I don't know. I'm not sure anyone did," Beltrante replied. "We just worked together."[17]

To summarize: the FBI found that the September device was installed *subsequent* to the Watergate arrests, and technicians for the C&P Telephone Company concurred in this. Following field tests, bureau agents concluded that the discovery of the device was a contrived event: the reported "malfunctions" could not be reproduced, the device was inoperative and therefore could not have interfered with the telephone. According to William Pierce, the September bug appeared to be one that Nick Beltrante had allegedly taken from his offices the year before. Finally, there is the sequence of events involving Lou Russell, his covert work for McCord, his presence at the Watergate break-in, his admitted bugging of the Columbia Plaza, and his mysterious labors within the Democrats' security apparatus so soon after he had worked for the Republicans'. While a flat assertion of fact cannot be made, since none of those involved were ever questioned under oath about these matters, the conclusion suggests itself that with or without Beltrante's knowledge or complicity, Russell bugged Oliver's telephone in September in an effort to shore up Baldwin's story, and, thereby, to prevent

[17]There does not seem to be any written record of Russell's employment by—or, in any case, *at*—the McGovern headquarters or the DNC. This is somewhat surprising, not merely in its own right but for the fact that it replicates the circumstances surrounding Russell's earlier employment—or alleged employment—at the CRP. A "night guard" at the CRP, he does not appear on any of the employee lists but was, instead, paid by McCord. Oddly, McCord does not seem ever to have been reimbursed by the CRP for Russell's services.

investigators from pursuing the "loose ends" implied by the absence
of a bug on Oliver's phone. That Baldwin needed "shoring up" is
clear. According to prosecutor Don Campbell, "Baldwin was nothing like his image in the press. I mean, he wasn't the hot-shot ex-FBI
agent that he pretended to be. I remember, Seymour [Glanzer] had
to question him one day. The idea was that Seymour would pretend
to be the defense attorney and, in effect, would cross-examine Baldwin in a hostile way. The guy—Baldwin—just came apart. He was
totally unnerved, screwed up his story, and made a complete ass of
himself. It worried us. We didn't know what would happen when
he got on the stand."

Employed by McCord and working with Beltrante, Russell had
access to both the DNC and any equipment (such as Pierce's bug)
that Beltrante may have had. Which is to say that he had both the
means and the opportunity to bug Oliver's phone in September.
That he also had the motive to do so is clear: not only was he a
co-conspirator of McCord's, but he was also responsible for bugging
the Columbia Plaza. If the prosecutors, in seeking to tie up loose
ends, had learned of the connection between the bordellos at that
address and the telephone in Oliver's office, Russell would have had
all the trouble in the world. So it was that just as evidence was
destroyed at the beginning of the summer, evidence was manufac-
tured at summer's end.

Lou Russell was anything but alone, however, in his wish to
eliminate loose ends. The principal prosecutor in the case, Earl
Silbert, was similarly inclined. As the sarcastic and querulous
memoranda exchanged between Silbert's office and the FBI make
clear, Silbert could not accept the FBI's conclusion about the September bug. The implications were too great, the complications too
many and too profound. It is not surprising, therefore, that Silbert
chose to dispute the evidence offered by the bureau, whereby the
FBI became a kind of scapegoat (albeit a secret one, inasmuch as the
issues dividing the bureau and the U.S. attorney's office were never
made public).

In a telephone interview with the author, the lead attorney in the
Watergate case defended his actions: "There wasn't any choice,
really. What the bureau had to say bothered us, of course, but—we
had Baldwin! There was no question that he was monitoring someone, and the problem we had was, if not Spencer Oliver, then *who*?"

The pressure that Silbert felt at the time came not merely from the FBI but from many other sources as well. The White House, of course, was interested in a quiet and speedy trial in which all of the defendants would plead guilty and shuffle off to Danbury. The Democrats, on the other hand, were convinced that the break-in was part of a complex political conspiracy whose ultimate origins were in the White House. They wished to see that conspiracy exposed in the most dramatic way possible, and feared that Silbert would yield to White House pressures for a narrow investigation. Like Silbert, however, the Democrats were angered by the FBI's belated discovery of a bug, and they were appalled by the bureau's conclusion that it had been put in place after the break-in. To the Democrats that conclusion conveyed the unwelcome suggestion that they may themselves have been responsible for the bugging—that, in other words, the Democrats had concocted a political hoax, manufacturing evidence in order to embarrass the Nixon White House. The bureau was criticized, therefore, not only by Silbert, who charged incompetence, but by the Democrats, who suggested that the FBI had dragged its feet in response to political pressure from the White House.

Each of them—the White House, the Democrats, the FBI and the U.S. attorney's office—was at the others' throats. And *all* of them were wrong about what had actually happened, and why.

The Democrats' hostility toward Silbert had another source as well. Because none of those arrested had so far proved willing either to implicate a superior or to explain their motivations in any substantive way, the federal prosecutor was hard put to establish a motive for the crime. The ringleader among those arrested, however, appeared to be Howard Hunt (to whom the Cubans were loyal), and Baldwin's statement clearly identified Spencer Oliver's telephone as the operation's target. Silbert quickly established that Oliver's father was an executive at the Robert R. Mullen Company, where Hunt also worked. To Silbert, this was more than a coincidence: Hunt and the senior Oliver were business rivals for control of the firm, and what is more, the White House consultant had successfully blocked Oliver's efforts to bring his son into the business. These facts, coupled with Baldwin's statements concerning the intimate nature of the conversations that he had overheard, suggested a motive to Silbert, which was that Hunt mounted the Watergate break-in for the purpose of blackmailing Spencer Oliver. To prove it he intended to question Baldwin on the stand about the substance of the telephone calls that he had overheard. Did they concern politics or sex and, if both, in what proportion? Who, moreover, had been overheard in these conversations, and what, if any, relation did the parties bear to Oliver?

Learning of Silbert's strategy, the Democrats were aghast. Political underdogs in the presidential election, McGovern's supporters saw the Watergate break-in as a useful issue for the purpose of dramatizing what they regarded as the cruel immorality of the Nixon administration—an immorality that was not confined to the war in Indochina but prevailed in the nation's capital as well. It was a point that might have swayed voters, but critical to it was the presumption that the Watergate break-in was somehow *political* and directed from above—that is, from responsible officials in the administration. To suggest, as Silbert intended to do, that the break-in was a parochial exercise in *business* espionage or blackmail—for which Hunt was ultimately responsible—was anathema to the Democrats. In effect, such an approach co-opted or neutralized the "political" issue, and carried with it the suggestion that some Democratic officials must be involved in hanky-panky of their own (else, how could they be blackmailed?).

It was to combat this thesis, then, that American Civil Liberties Union attorney Charles Morgan stood up in district court to make vehement and categorical objections to any testimony whatsoever concerning the nature of the conversations that Baldwin had overheard. Saying that he represented the Association of Democratic State Chairmen and their employees, Spencer Oliver and Ida ("Maxie") Wells, Morgan insisted that the court would itself be in violation of the law if it permitted testimony as to the contents of the monitored conversations or the identities of those who had been overheard. Silbert and Donald Campbell, an assistant prosecutor in the case, told me that they were "flabbergasted" by Morgan's sudden appearance in the matter, and by the "violence" of his objections.

In a report on the case that Morgan wrote to the special prosecutor, he explained his entry into the matter:[18]

---

[18]"A Report to the Special Prosecutor on Certain Aspects of the Watergate Affair, June 18, 1973," published in *Hearings before the Senate Committee on the Judiciary* (concerning Earl J. Silbert's nomination to be United States Attorney), 93d Cong., 2d sess., Part 1, April–May 1974, pp. 5–56.

Immediately after being told that Mr. Silbert intended to [establish] the contents of the illegally intercepted conversations, Mr. Oliver conferred with [top executives of the Association of Democratic State Chairmen]. They, of course, knew that the direct questioning of Baldwin as to the contents of the conversations he had overheard would open him to more specific defense cross-examination. And they knew that even though Mr. Silbert told Mr. Oliver he intended to ask him only about the general nature of the conversations, e.g., were they personal? were they political?, the opening of an area would subject him to more specific cross-examination.

They desired to prevent Mr. Silbert from doing to them that which not even the wiretappers had done—illegally disclose their private personal and political conversations to the world. They were not only at the mercy of the President's prosecutor and the attorneys defending the President's criminal supporters, they were also at the mercy of the "memory" of Baldwin, and he was subject to prosecution control. And if the public speech of the campaign was the music of politics, private gossip was its poetry.[19]

Continuing in what became an increasingly personal attack, Morgan accused Silbert of trying "to focus public attention on those on trial rather than higher-ups. . . ."[20] He cited a luncheon conversation with Silbert in which the prosecutor said, "Hunt was trying to blackmail Spencer, and I'm going to prove it."[21] Accusing Silbert of manufacturing a false motive in furtherance of a whitewash, Morgan charged that "Mr. Silbert's blackmail motive had been woven from whole cloth":[22]

[Silbert] intended to present a non-political and fictitious motive for the crime. . . . It then seemed certain that Mr. Silbert would prove the motive of the Cuban-Americans to be misguided anti-Castroism and the acquisition of money. To others, perhaps, he would attribute a misguided Republican loyalty. But to Mr. Hunt, or to Messrs. Hunt and Liddy, he would attribute an overriding and personal criminal—as opposed to political—motive. And their motive was to be personal blackmail and big money.

Thus, Mr. Silbert could argue to the jury and to the Court, and through them, to the public, that the higher-ups were not only not parties to the criminal conspiracy—they, too, were victims of it. For

[19]Ibid., p. 39.
[20]Ibid.
[21]Ibid., pp. 42, 53.
[22]Ibid., p. 42.

Hunt . . . , Mr. Silbert would argue, had converted CRP's money and
its legitimate political function to Hunt's personal use. . . . [A]nd by that
fraudulent conversion Hunt, or Hunt and Liddy, had injured the CRP
and its officials at least as badly—if not worse than—they'd injured the
Democrats. . . .

And we were convinced that once the contents were introduced into
evidence, the jury, the judge—and, through them, the press and the
public—might be so diverted to the contents of the conversations—
personal conversations about the personal and political lives of members
of the Democratic Party—that they would accept Mr. Silbert's presentation of the false motive, and would place ultimate responsibility for the
Watergate conspiracy on Mr. Hunt or Messrs. Hunt and Liddy.[23]

Morgan's complaints against Silbert, in which he characterized
the prosecutor's closing argument as "fiction unworthy of an
E. Howard Hunt novel," all but accused him of corruption.[24] Repeatedly Morgan harped on Silbert's suggestion that blackmail was
the motive, and criticized him for allegedly seeking to evade the
intent of the statute prohibiting testimony about the nature of intercepted telephone conversations. As "evidence" of Silbert's supposed
culpability in this regard, Morgan denounced prosecutorial questions that seemed to stress the intimate nature of the monitored
conversations (one is tempted to recall Magruder's remark, "What
we were getting was this guy Oliver lining up assignations. . . .").[25]
Neither did Morgan approve of Silbert's emphasis on the private
calls that were made on Oliver's telephone line, nor did it seem
relevant to the ACLU lawyer that McCord had instructed Baldwin
to monitor "all conversations of a personal nature, whether political
or otherwise. . . ." Finally, Morgan lambasted the FBI for conducting what amounted to an investigation of Oliver's personal life,
suggesting that the bureau was in cahoots with the supposedly
politically motivated prosecutor.

Of course, the opposite was more nearly the case. Far from being
in cahoots with each other, Silbert and the FBI were not even
investigating the same crime.

[23] Ibid., pp. 42–43.
[24] Ibid., p. 53.
[25] Lukas, *Nightmare*, p. 201.

18.
Robert Bennett, the Press and the CIA

In looking back at the confusion surrounding the Watergate break-in, and at the investigation that followed, it is surprising that any consensus about the affair—even the mistaken consensus that prevails—should ever have emerged. The destruction of evidence was broad and deep, with several of the burglars, CRP and White House officials, CIA officers and agents, and the director of the FBI all participating. The resulting gaps were, in many cases, ignored or downplayed by investigators who did not wish to impugn the testimony of felons who were about to become important witnesses—Magruder, Dean and McCord, for example, each of whom had burned, buried or deep-sixed materials of clear importance to the case, and then gotten "religion." Contributing further to the false certainties that emerged was the willingness of so many to ignore information of an inconvenient kind: the key to Maxie Wells's desk, the FBI's findings with respect to bugs inside the DNC, and Alfred Baldwin's account of the "intimate" telephone conversations that he had heard. Still other evidence (i.e., the September bug) was obviously fabricated in an effort—successful, as it turned out—to conceal flaws that would otherwise have been fatal to the official version of the affair.

Of all the media that helped to develop and popularize this version, none was of greater importance to the story than Watergate's "hometown newspaper," the *Washington Post*. In 1972 the *Post* was less influential, at least on the national scene, than it is today. It was considered a good newspaper, with any number of talented editors and reporters, but it lacked the depth, breadth and sophistication of the *New York Times*. On the other hand, the *Post* was uniquely well equipped to cover and influence this particular story. It was the newspaper that the scandal's principals read each morning at the breakfast table, and, as such, it contributed directly to shaping the debate within both the capital and the Capitol. Judge John Sirica read it on his way to court each day, with the result that its questions often became *his* questions. The *Post*, moreover, was a newspaper whose senior editors and reporters belonged to that part of the Washington establishment which is immune to changes of political administration: the President and his Cabinet might, if they were lucky, hold sway in Washington for as long as eight years, but a talented editor could preside at the *Post* for decades. Well connected in a general sense, the newspaper was particularly well placed vis-à-vis the Democratic Party; its attorney, Edward Bennett Williams, was not just any lawyer but the *Democrats'* lawyer. A mainstay of the Washington establishment, Williams had a long-standing relationship with the *Post* and powerful friends throughout the federal bureaucracy:[1] CIA Director Richard Helms,[2] for example, and Judge John Sirica. Indeed, Sirica could be described as a lifelong friend. Decades earlier, Sirica had been a "Fifth Street lawyer," hanging about the local courthouse in hopes of landing a client. Despairing, the future judge at the Watergate trial had been about to give up the practice of law when Williams rescued him, recommending Sirica as his own replacement at the prestigious law firm, Hogan & Hartson, that Williams' father-in-law had founded. Years later, Williams would become godfather to Sirica's son, and Sirica would tell Williams' biographer, Bob Pack, that "I owe my career to Ed Williams." In light of the way in which Sirica handled the trial, that debt has long since been repaid. As the *Washingtonian*, a liberal magazine, described Sirica's conduct of the trial: he "badgered, accused and castigated witness, prosecutors and defense lawyers. He read transcripts of confidential bench conferences to the

---

[1]Following the 1963 suicide of Philip Graham, Katharine Graham's husband, a controversy arose over the publisher's will. Williams saved the situation for Graham's widow, testifying that her husband had not been of sound mind when, by the terms of his will, he had left the bulk of his estate to his sometime mistress (a *Newsweek* reporter). This was an embarrassing admission for Williams to make, since it had been his own law firm that had drawn up the will whose validity he came to dispute.

[2]In the aftermath of the Watergate affair, the appointed President, Gerald Ford, offered Williams the job of CIA director. Williams turned down the position, accepting instead an appointment to the President's Foreign Intelligence Advisory Board (PFIAB). The initial offer is especially interesting, since Nixon and Haldeman, angered by Williams' role in the affair, had sworn to "get" Williams.

jury. He used the threat of lengthy sentences to force defendants into abandoning their constitutional rights. He turned the trial into an inquisition, and justice into a charade."[3]

To all of the advantages enjoyed by the *Post* should be added the aggressiveness and enterprise of the newspaper's young reporters Carl Bernstein and Bob Woodward, who were assigned to the scandal from its very beginning. Their approach to the story was to conduct a "vertical investigation"—that is, to learn what other crimes and dirty tricks had been committed and who within the administration was responsible. As a corollary, the *Post* focused also upon the administration's predictable (and often criminal) attempts to bury the affair.

To some the tenacity of the *Post*'s coverage smacked almost of malice. Day after day, the newspaper gave front-page headlines to Watergate articles whose importance seemed dubious. Conservative writers charged that a double standard was in use, insisting that the *Post* would not have accorded such attention to Watergate had the affair occurred under a liberal administration. However likely that may be, it is a fact that the newspaper's coverage would be rewarded with a Pulitzer Prize. Still, few would argue that the *Post* regarded Nixon dispassionately. On the contrary, the newspaper seemed to view the President as a mere suspect, and a sleazy one at that: duplicitous, authoritarian and vengeful. While there were well-meaning and talented people in his administration, they were fewer than statistical probability would seem to have allowed. And though the war in Indochina was not of his creation, Nixon waged it with unusual cruelty and enthusiasm, even as he used American police to punish American demonstrators. To the *Post*, opposed to both the content and the style of the administration, Watergate was a convenient symptom of a much deeper malaise. Extirpating that malaise, therefore, assumed the urgency and proportions of a patriotic crusade.

The *Post*'s determination to pursue the Watergate affair, while other news media were still inclined to shrug, delighted the Democrats, but it can only have alarmed the CIA. There were simply too many connections between the agency and the events in question. An unfettered investigation would be as likely to uncover the CIA's deep involvement in the affair as it would be to assign responsibility

[3] Harvey Katz, "Some Call It Justice Part II," *Washingtonian*, September 1973.

for it to Richard Nixon. Indeed, it was to prevent that from happening that James McCord wrote secretly to General Paul Gaynor at the CIA, urging him to "flood the newspapers with leaks or anonymous letters" discrediting those who would tie Watergate to "the company."[4] McCord's warning was probably unnecessary, however. Months earlier, the *Post*'s lead reporter on the story, Bob Woodward, had become the beneficiary of a uniquely well-informed source. This was Robert Bennett, Howard Hunt's boss at the Mullen Company. On July 10, less than a month after the Watergate arrests, Bennett met with his CIA case officer, Martin Lukoskie, in a downtown Washington cafeteria.[5] At that meeting, memorialized by Lukoskie in a handwritten memorandum of such sensitivity that he hand-carried it to CIA Director Helms, Bennett bragged that he had dissuaded reporters from the *Post* and *Star* from pursuing a "Seven Days in May scenario" implicating the CIA in a Watergate conspiracy.[6] Moreover, Lukoskie wrote, "Mr. Bennett related that he has now established a 'back door entry' to the Edward Bennett Williams law firm which is representing the Democratic Party. . . . Mr. Bennett is prepared to go this route to kill off any revelation by Ed Williams of Agency association with the Mullen firm."[7]

Bennett, then, was attempting to manipulate the press. That he was successful in the attempt—at least so far as he and the CIA were concerned—is established in a second memorandum, this one written almost a year later by Lukoskie's boss, Eric Eisenstadt: "Mr. Bennett said . . . that he has been feeding stories to Bob Woodward of the Washington Post with the understanding that there be no attribution to . . . Bennett. Woodward is suitably grateful for the fine stories and by-lines which he gets and protects Bennett (and the Mullen Company)."[8] Elsewhere in that same memo, Eisenstadt reports that Bennett spent hours persuading a *Newsweek* reporter that the Mullen Company "was not involved with the Watergate Affair."[9] In addition, the memo implies that Bennett helped to

---

[4]Ervin committee *Hearings*, Book 9, pp. 3441–46, and Nedzi report, p. 201. In all, McCord sent five secret letters to the CIA between December 1972 and January 1973.

[5]Lukoskie's memo, written July 10, 1972, is appended to this book. In it, Lukoskie says that his meeting with Bennett took place in the "Hot Shop Cafeteria." He was, of course, referring to the Hot Shop*pes* Cafeteria chain. The slip may well have been a pun, however, since a "hot shop" is CIA slang for any Washington office in which highly classified data are routinely handled or discussed.

[6]Nedzi report, p. 1071.

[7]Ibid., pp. 1071–72.

[8]March 1, 1973, memorandum of Eric Eisenstadt, published in the Nedzi report, pp. 1073–76.

[9]Ibid., p. 1074.

convince reporters for the *Washington Star*, the *Washington Post* and the *Los Angeles Times* that the CIA had not "instigated the Watergate affair" as the reporters seemed to suspect. As an example of Bennett's "achievements," Eisenstadt cited Bennett's inspiration of a *Newsweek* article entitled "Whispers about Colson" and a *Washington Post* story about Hunt's investigation of Senator Edward Kennedy.[10]

We do not know what Eisenstadt meant when he wrote that Woodward was "suitably grateful" for Bennett's help, or what the CIA official had in mind when he indicated that the reporter was "protecting" Bennett and the Mullen Company. The implication of the memo is that Woodward agreed to ignore Watergate leads that tended to incriminate the CIA in return for information that Bennett, himself a CIA agent, spoon-fed him. But is that conclusion fair? After all, it is possible that Bennett, in conversation with his CIA case officer, may have exaggerated his influence with the newspaper so as to enhance his own stature in the agency's eyes. Perhaps Bennett took credit for elisions in the *Post*'s reports with which he had little or nothing to do. Neither Woodward nor the *Post*, after all, required cajoling to pursue the theory that the Nixon White House was solely responsible for the Watergate break-in and every other dirty trick. Still, the newspaper's willingness to turn a blind eye toward the CIA's involvement is disturbing. Although leaks about the Mullen Company's relationship to the CIA had been published elsewhere in Washington only a few weeks after the Watergate arrests, nearly two years passed before the *Post* itself reported on the subject.[11] By then, of course, the information could have little or no impact on the scandal: the President's resignation was only a month away. Ten years later, in 1984, I asked Bob Woodward if he had agreed with Bennett to suppress the Mullen Company's links to Langley. Woodward said that he had not. He added that, on the contrary, "I think we were about the first to report it." Told that he was incorrect, Woodward became stubborn. "Are you sure?" he asked. "Have you read every story? *Every story?*" In fact Woodward is mistaken. However, one cannot be

---

[10]Ibid.

[11]The Mullen Company's ties to the CIA were a subject of speculation from the affair's inception. This was because of Hunt's employment at the firm, news of the Mullen Company's involvement with Radio Free Cuba after the Bay of Pigs invasion, and grand jury leaks of Douglas Caddy's testimony. (Caddy told the grand jury that, while working at the Mullen Company's offices, he had "intimations" that the firm provided cover to the CIA. See Dana Bullen, "Hunt's Wife Ridicules Link to Raid," *Washington Star*, July 6, 1972.)

certain that one has read every article that the *Post* published about Watergate. Between 1972 and 1975 the newspaper carried more than three thousand articles, cartoons and columns about Watergate—a million words or more.[12] Complicating the issue further is the fact that the Mullen Company is unlisted in the *Post*'s own *Index,* and the newspaper's library says that it has lost its file containing its cuttings about the firm. Nevertheless, it is a fact that the Mullen Company is described in *All the President's Men,* published in February 1974, as nothing more than "a Washington public relations firm."[13] Moreover, in his testimony before the Nedzi committee on July 2, 1974, Robert Bennett said, "I have told Woodward everything I know about the Watergate case, except the Mullen Company's tie to the CIA. I never mentioned that to him. It has never appeared in any *Washington Post* story."[14]

In fact the Mullen Company's ties to the CIA had been reported in the *Post* in a March 23, 1974, Jack Anderson column (anticipating the findings of Senator Baker's investigation). The first *Post* reporter to explicitly identify the Mullen Company as a CIA cover, however, was neither Woodward nor Bernstein but the late Laurence Stern. In a July 2, 1974, article about Senator Baker's dissent to the Ervin committee's *Final Report,* Stern acknowledged the Mullen Company's CIA involvement, and made reference to the memoranda written by the CIA's Martin Lukoskie and Eric Eisenstadt.[15] Nowhere in Stern's brief article, however, is Woodward mentioned, and neither he nor the *Post*'s executive editor, Benjamin Bradlee, was asked to comment about the CIA's suggestion that its agent had manipulated the *Post*'s reportage and planted stories in the press. Obviously, the *Post* was frightened of the subject.

Even so, Bennett must have been a valuable source. Aside from his connections to the intelligence agency, he was the employer of both Howard Hunt and Spencer Oliver, Sr. He had lobbied the White House on behalf of Hunt's consultancy there, and working with Liddy, he had helped to establish a battery of dummy commit-

[12]Bell & Howell's newspaper *Index to the Washington Post,* 1972–75, Volume 4.
[13]Carl Bernstein and Bob Woodward, *All the President's Men* (New York: Simon & Schuster, 1974), p. 24.
[14]Nedzi report, p. 1099.
[15]Laurence Stern, "Baker to Say CIA Helped Hunt Get Job," *Washington Post,* July 2, 1974, p. 1.

tees as conduits for the milk producers' contributions to Nixon's campaign funds.[16] He had helped to arrange Hunt's recruitment of Tom Gregory to spy on both the Muskie and McGovern campaigns, and, in fact, Bennett could take credit for Gregory's almost preternaturally timely, *formal* resignation as a spy. As Bennett told congressional investigators, Gregory had developed "moral uneasiness" over his role as the Ruby II facet of the Gemstone plan.[17] On Wednesday, June 14, therefore, Bennett met with the lad and counseled him with the words: "Tommy, . . . you have to draw the moral line and not step beyond it."

Turning to his fellow Mormon, Gregory replied, "Brother Bennett, I have gone way beyond that. I have long since crossed that line."

"Under the circumstances," Bennett told him, "I think you ought to get out." Accordingly, Bennett had Gregory write a letter to Hunt, announcing his resignation as a spook. The letter, Bennett told Congress, was given to him and placed on Hunt's desk at the Mullen Company on the night before the fateful break-in.[18]

It was Bennett, also, who had first suggested that Las Vegas publisher Hank Greenspun had information that could "blow [Senator Edmund] Muskie out of the water."[19] It was Bennett, too, who had arranged Hunt's visit in disguise to the hospitalized ITT lobbyist, Dita Beard, and he who had put Hunt together with Clifton DeMotte to discuss Chappaquiddick. When Howard Hughes's "autobiographers," Clifford Irving and Richard Suskind, were rumored to be writing a second book about Hughes, Bennett went to Hunt to ask about the feasibility and cost of examining the writers' trash.[20] Not finally, Bennett was the main point of contact between Hunt

---

[16]Ervin committee *Hearings*, Book 16, p. 7461, and Book 17, pp. 7545, 7604. See also the committee's *Final Report*, pp. 641, 689, and Lukas, *Nightmare*, p. 125.

[17]Nedzi report, pp. 1088–89.

[18]Ibid.

[19]Whether Bennett told Hunt that the damaging information was contained in Greenspun's *safe* is disputed. Bennett claims that he did not. Gordon Liddy claims that he did (*Will*, pp. 204–5). And while Howard Hunt has publicly testified (Ervin committee *Hearings*, Book 20, p. 9359) that it was a Hughes security agent who first mentioned the existence of a Greenspun safe, Senator Howard Baker cites Hunt's testimony in executive session to support his assertion that Bennett told Hunt that the Muskie data was in Greenspun's safe (*Final Report*, pp. 11222–23). The Senate's muddle is in no way clarified by the accounts of journalists. J. Anthony Lukas agrees with Liddy and Senator Baker (see "The Bennett Mystery," *New York Times*, January 29, 1976), while Howard Hughes's biographers Donald L. Barlett and James B. Steele echo Hunt's public testimony on the matter (see *Empire: The Life, Legend and Madness of Howard Hughes* [New York: Norton, 1979], pp. 501–2).

[20]Ervin committee *Hearings*, Book 20, p. 9404.

and Liddy in the wake of the Watergate arrests; as the Lukoskie memo makes clear, he continued to share confidences with Hunt and others who were privy to the operation's secret details (Bennett, for example, knew when others did not that the DNC had been broken into during May). All in all, Bennett's record is astonishing for someone who figures only peripherally in the *Post*'s reports and the Senate's investigation.

Indeed, Bennett's credentials as a Watergate source were so profoundly relevant that many reporters still consider him to be a leading candidate for Woodward's most important source, "Deep Throat." In fact, however, Bennett cannot have been Throat. A strict Mormon, he neither smoked nor drank (as we are told Throat did), and he was not an employee of the executive branch (as Woodward says Throat was). Bennett's task, moreover, was to steer Woodward and the *Post* away from leads implicating the CIA in the scandal, whereas Deep Throat had no compunction about suggesting that the CIA was involved in the affair.[21] Finally, and most unusually, we have Woodward's word that Bennett is not Deep Throat. While the reporter's usual practice is to avoid comment when others claim to have identified his supersource, Woodward feels different about Bennett. In my interview with him, Woodward issued a "preemptive denial" that Bennett and Throat were one— obviously, the *Post* reporter is concerned that the public should not come to believe that his best and most secret source was a CIA agent.

Lou Russell was another CIA-connected subject that the *Post* did not find newsworthy. Woodward knew of Russell's employment by McCord, his sudden good fortune in the wake of the Watergate arrest, and allegations that he had been at the Howard Johnson's restaurant on the evening of the break-in. That Russell had also worked for General Security Services, Inc., was well known in Washington, but the *Post* apparently regarded this as a mere coincidence. When Bob Fink, who helped Woodward and Bernstein with research on *All the President's Men*,[22] suggested in the summer of 1973 that Russell might be important, Woodward ignored the suggestion, saying that he had "checked into Russell and there was nothing to the story." In fact, Woodward had met with Russell and his patron, William Birely, on at least two occasions, though he

---

[21]See Woodward and Bernstein's *All the President's Men*, pp. 73 and 317–18.
[22]Fink does not recall whether his suggestion was made just before or after Russell's death that summer.

never reported on those meetings. Asked about them by this writer, Woodward recalled that he had "had a few drinks with Russell," and decided that the private eye had not not been near the Watergate on the evening of June 16–17. "He was just an old drunk, as nearly as I could see," Woodward said.

That the *Post* was soft in its coverage of Robert Bennett and the Mullen Company, blew the Russell story completely, and failed to follow up leads pertaining to the CIA is apparent. It is as wrong, however, to overemphasize the *Post*'s failures as it is to overemphasize its achievements. While it is true that the *New York Times* found Robert Bennett and the Mullen Company rather more newsworthy than the *Post*,[23] and while the *Washington Star* pursued the Lou Russell angle far more aggressively than "Woodstein" did, no newspaper or network covered the affair as a whole better or more completely than the *Post*. And while it is true that the *Post* was negligent in pursuing leads implicating the CIA in the scandal, so was virtually every other newspaper in the United States. Part of the blame for this, ironically, belongs to the Nixon administration. This is because the President's men, at a very early date, had attempted to use the CIA as a smokescreen in their efforts to thwart a full FBI investigation. It was suggested that such an investigation would compromise CIA operations and agents, and, in fact, the President himself had tried unsuccessfully to enlist Richard Helms's cooperation in laying down the smoke. By making that attempt, the administration poisoned all subsequent efforts to understand the CIA's involvement in the affair. No matter what evidence was found, it could be—and often was—deprecated as a diversion designed to provide the President with an undeserved escape hatch.

So it was that the *Post* ignored stories that deserved to be published. For example, it was obviously newsworthy that the Democrats had been warned months in advance of the opposition's plans to bug them. Learning of Senator Baker's investigation of the matter, the *Post* nevertheless decided not to print the story. Conservative press critic Reed Irvine, founder of Accuracy In Media (AIM), was infuriated. "I asked them why they wouldn't print the story, and all they'd say was 'It isn't proven.' I don't know what kind of proof they wanted." One suspects that the *Post* and Irvine were

[23]Two important articles that the *Times* published in connection with Bennett and the Mullen Company were Sydney M. Schanberg's "Employee of C.I.A. 'Cover' Quit Two Years Ago," July 6, 1974, and J. Anthony Lukas' "The Bennett Mystery," January 29, 1976.

talking at cross purposes. While no one has been able to prove that the Democrats set a trap for the burglars, Woolston-Smith's warning to Jack Anderson and Larry O'Brien was well established—and newsworthy. In the end Reed Irvine had to resort to publishing the story in a full-page *paid advertisement* in the *Post*. The *Post*'s critics, therefore, are not without ammunition when they contend that the newspaper's Watergate coverage was biased.

Though other newspapers failed to cover the Woolston-Smith story, one holds the *Post* to a higher standard because it had a unique responsibility: it was, in effect, the newspaper of record with respect to the Watergate scandal. It is especially disappointing, therefore, to find that years after Nixon's departure from the White House the *Post* shows little or no enthusiasm for correcting the record. Thus, when Gordon Liddy's autobiography, *Will,* was published in the spring of 1980, the *Post* consigned it to its book review section without reporting the book's contents on the news pages of the paper. This despite reviewer Bob Woodward's evaluation that the book contained "important new information." As Woodward wrote in the *Post*, "Liddy is meticulous. His story reads true, and balanced against the other evidence and testimony of the many Watergate investigations, it is credible. A hundred little facts and inferences convince me that he has been as honest as he could be." That said, Woodward then went on to list some of the book's most important revelations, including Liddy's report that the Gemstone charts had been prepared by the CIA. "For me," Woodward wrote, "this suggests more than anything available to date that top CIA officials must have known in advance about Liddy's illegal operations."[24] The implications of that conclusion, in terms of perjured testimony and of the CIA's involvement in the affair, are profound. But they would not be discussed any further in the paper.

Of those who believed that the CIA had a hand in the affair, Charles Colson was one of the few who attempted to prove it. The CIA's reaction to that effort was both predictable and unlawful: its agents, including Robert Bennett, tried to smear Colson by means of anonymous leaks to the press. Like Nixon, then, Colson was hoist by his own petard, having himself set out earlier to smear Daniel Ellsberg in the same manner—an effort that ultimately landed Col-

[24]Bob Woodward, "Gordon Liddy Spills His Guts," *Washington Post Book World*, May 18, 1980.

son in prison. Today Colson is more certain than ever, as he told me, of the CIA's culpability in the affair.

"I had access," he said, "to something that very few people had access to. In fact, it occasionally gives me a chill when I think about it, because several of the people who have seen the document that I know of are either very suspect, or dead. I don't know many people who are alive that have seen the whole CIA file. I saw the whole file. I had it in my possession."[25] Asked how he had obtained the classified file, Colson told me:

I was invited over to the White House in March of 1974, by Fred Buzhardt [then attorney for the President]. And Buzhardt said, "I've got something that you ought to take a look at."

I went over on a Saturday morning, walked into Fred's office, which was John Dean's old office, and he said, "Take a look at this." He handed me two folders—sort of gray-colored folders that were unmarked, with a binder on the end. A kind of standard-looking file. Two of them, to be exact: one kind of thick, a couple of inches, and one about half an inch.

While we were talking Fred said, "I may have to go over to the West Wing and spend a little time there. Would you like to go through these?"

I said, "You're going to leave me here with these?"

And he said, "I don't care what you do."

I said, "There's a Xerox machine down the hall."

He said, "Don't tell me your problems."

And then he left, and I went down and xeroxed the entire file. I think it had every CIA document, internal CIA document, relating to Watergate. Anyway, I wasn't indicted at that point. So I had the entire file, and my lawyer, David Shapiro, and I went through them with a fine-tooth comb. There were some really startling things. . . . I took my full set of copies and went to my home and buried them in the attic under ceiling insulation, because I figured I didn't want them stolen and I didn't want to leave them in the law office.

I had already been subpoenaed for everything I had from the White House, so these were safe—they weren't subpoenaed. I figured I would keep them for the authoritative records of what happened and . . . No, that's not true. I kept them because there was much in there that would have helped me in my trial. There was something in there that in a

[25]That Colson saw a file containing classified CIA documents pertaining to the Watergate affair is certain. But he is mistaken, when he claims that it was "the whole CIA file." The agency's Watergate file fills several filing cabinets, whereas Colson saw only two folders.

normal trial would have resulted in the case being dismissed, because the prosecution against me was tainted.

This was the fact that the CIA had gone and disseminated information to the press, deliberately trying to bag me as the bad guy of Watergate. And it was right in one of the memos that first Helms and then [CIA Director James] Schlesinger had approved it.[26] And so it was a piece of gold. Because, in a normal case, you would go and say that the government tried this man, me, in the press—the same thing I ended up pleading guilty to in the Ellsberg case.

In the end, however, Colson did not use the memo, or any other part of the CIA file, in his defense. Worn down by the scandal, and abandoned by his friends, he pleaded guilty in an effort to put the affair behind him. "And that same day, the day I pled guilty, I received a subpoena from the Watergate Special Prosecution Force asking for the CIA file. Shapiro and I, and probably Buzhardt, are the only people who knew that the file existed in my possession, so I found it sort of scary when the subpoena came. Anyway, I went home, pulled the insulation back, got the files out, and delivered it to the Watergate Special Prosecutor [Leon Jaworski]. Of course, they already had it, anyway. The file I had was a copy of Buzhardt's, and the White House had already sent the original over to Jaworski. We'd asked Jaworski to include it in his investigation, but he never did. Frankly, I don't know how they knew I had a copy—it baffles me. Baffles me? Hell, it frightens me." Colson paused, and shook his head. "I got such venom from Jaworski. He'd go out of his way with everyone he met, saying, 'That guy, Colson—he's a faker. He couldn't be converted. He's a liar. I never trusted him.' And why? I mean, why did Jaworski hate me? All I did was plead guilty, and that was it."

While Colson no longer had the CIA file in his possession, he did have verbatim notes quoting from parts of that file, including various CIA internal memoranda.[27]

You have to wonder why Bennett was never charged with obstruction of justice: he had all this information before the prosecutors. Instead, his lawyers were paid for by the CIA—a fact—and when he went to Silbert in December to give a deposition, there was a private agreement about

---

[26]Neither Helms nor Schlesinger would agree to be interviewed for this book.
[27]Colson was not the only person, besides Buzhardt and Jaworski, to see the file in question. Some members of the Ervin committee were also privy to some of its contents, and this writer has been able to verify independently the accuracy of Colson's notes.

what questions would be asked so that the CIA wouldn't come up in testimony.

Then there's [the] memo of March 1, 1973, which, to me, was the most critical document of all. It was from the chief of the Central Cover Staff, Eric W. Eisenstadt, to the deputy director for plans. In it, there were specific references to various articles published by Woodward, which had been fed to Woodward by Bennett. And the articles were attached. It was comical, actually. I opened the file, the first time, and here was a story from the *Washington Post* (February 10, 1973): "Hunt Tried to Recruit Agents to Probe Senator Kennedy's Life." And here was Eisenstadt, taking credit for the article, along with the "Whispers About Colson" story from the March fifth edition of *Newsweek*. It was all very self-congratulatory, about "what a good job the CIA is doing," and how Schlesinger had commended them "for diverting attention away from the agency."

And, in fact, Eisenstadt's memorandum is egregious. In it, the CIA official reports Bennett's claim that, if the CIA could "handle" Hunt, Bennett could "handle" the Ervin committee—noting that Bennett had prevailed upon a friend to intervene privately with Senator Ervin in an effort to divert the committee's scrutiny from the agency.

Colson chuckled ruefully as he recalled Bennett's work behind the scenes, and then continued reading from his notes on the CIA file. Those notes alluded to the Mullen Company's work for Radio Free Cuba in the 1960s, to the Mullen Company's subsidiary, Interprogress, and to the firm's ties to the Cuban Freedom Committee ("Whatever that is," Colson remarked). The notes described "negotiations" that the CIA had with the Mullen Company concerning the circumstances of Howard Hunt's hiring and the salary he was to be paid. They referred to the fact that Hunt reported to the CIA on each of his White House contacts (dating back to 1970), and to the agency's apprehensions over *Time* reporter Sandy Smith's access to the FBI's highest echelons. The notes reflected the CIA's efforts to find a lock-picker for Hunt to use in an eavesdropping operation that involved "monitoring phones" in Las Vegas, and they cited Hunt's reliance on a CIA proprietary (Anderson Security Consultants) for undescribed services. By no means finally, the notes referred to Lee Pennington, and to an operation involving the smuggling of gold bullion to Southeast Asia.

That the CIA attempted to manipulate the press, and was to some extent successful in doing so, is established by the agency's own memoranda. And what those memos make equally clear is that it was not merely the Mullen Company, or the Mullen Company per se, that the agency wished to protect, but rather an entire array of operations that in one way or another were connected to Watergate.

Colson's view of the affair is admittedly apocalyptic. According to his notes, the agency was concerned about "CIA defections in April [of 1972], and [about its] peculiar relationship with the Mullen Company." He cites the Lukoskie memorandum invoking the *Seven Days in May* metaphor that Pentagon investigator Donald Stewart also used (in his case, to dramatize the Moorer-Radford affair). As Colson told Richard Bast, a private detective who he hoped would investigate the CIA's role in the affair, Watergate was "a coup d'état in the making."[28]

That conclusion is a histrionic one: Nixon would be driven from office, but not by the military or the CIA. Nevertheless, in the climate of that time, one can understand how Colson and others might hold that opinion. Paranoia was a palpable factor in American politics, and the rhetoric on every side became increasingly extreme as the stakes mounted. It was not just Colson, Donald Stewart and others of a conservative bent who saw the country threatened by unconstitutional plots and "sinister forces." The same kinds of fears were shared by liberals. Among the staff of the Ervin committee, as well as in the Special Prosecutor's offices, nervous jokes about tanks being sighted on their way up Constitution Avenue became commonplace. That those jokes were not entirely playful is suggested by Secretary of Defense (later CIA Director) James Schlesinger's action in July 1974, countermanding *in advance* any "unwarranted military directives" that President Nixon might issue. As much as anyone else, Schlesinger realized that electoral politics in the United States was dependent, to some extent at least, on the goodwill of the serving administration and its adversaries: the mechanisms for a de facto dictatorship had been developed long ago in the form of contingency plans to cope with emergency circumstances. John Dean, for example, had written a series of memoranda outlining the conditions under which Nixon, like Franklin D. Roosevelt, might serve more than two terms in office. As we have seen, James McCord was also concerned with unconstitutional contingencies, having com-

[28]Bast turned down the job, saying that he would not be able to accomplish much without subpoena power.

manded a detachment of the Wartime Information Security Program (WISP), which was responsible for imposing censorship, travel restrictions and "preventive detention" during periods of national emergency.

In hindsight these fears must seem overblown. But the truth is that they were felt at the very heart of the administration, as President Nixon's chief of staff, General Alexander Haig, made clear in a 1979 interview. Asked what he felt was his "main accomplishment" while in the Nixon White House, Haig replied: "[W]ith respect to Watergate and its consequences, clearly one of the most dangerous periods in American history, change occurred within the provisions of our Constitution and established rule of law. *This was not a foregone conclusion* during those difficult days [emphasis added]."

"You mean that you persuaded President Nixon to resign," the interviewer asked, "and thus spared the United States the agony of impeachment?"

"I'll stick to what I told you," Haig said.[29]

Indeed. Haig's meaning is anything but obscure, and the interviewer's question almost deliberately missed the point, because, of course, impeachment would have been within the framework of the law. What Haig meant is that there was a possibility that unconstitutional means might have been used to keep Nixon in power.

As it turned out, of course, these fears were unjustified; the President resigned so as not to be impeached. Though Charles Colson, and others, suspected that this was the final goal of a CIA plot, it certainly was not. The agency's concern throughout the Watergate affair had been to protect its own operations, including its activities at the Mullen Company and the Columbia Plaza. While it was not an accident that the Nixon administration took a fall, it had only itself to blame for falling so heavily and so far.

According to Charles Colson's notes, the CIA's concerns were at least partly of a counterintelligence kind. Reading from his notes on the CIA file, Colson said that reporter Daniel Schorr had told him that "[P]rior to Dan Rather's first report about the CIA's destruction of files and tapes, [then CIA Director William] Colby admitted to Rather that there were tapes (which his predecessor, Richard Helms, had ordered destroyed). But the information was very sensitive, and Colby urged Rather not to use it. Rather went with his

[29]*Newsweek*, July 16, 1979, p. 54.

report [anyway], disregarding Colby's call. Shortly thereafter, Colby issued a public denial of the very things he had admitted to Rather. . . ."

The Ervin committee's minority counsel, Fred Thompson, "was advised by Colby that Colby's concern was directly related to disclosures of very high-level CIA defections which had occurred in the spring of 1972—and, also, with KGB infiltration of the CIA, which Colby . . . suggested is connected to the Bennett/Hunt disclosures."

We do not know of any CIA defections, whether in place or to Moscow, that occurred that spring. Neither is it clear how the KGB's supposed infiltration of the CIA impinged on the relationship between Hunt, Bennett and the Mullen Company. But the possibility should certainly not be ruled out. Hunt's clandestine dispatches from the White House to the CIA were, judging by CIA officer Ratliff's written statement about their destination and contents, obviously intended to help create psychological profiles of Americans. The intimate nature of Hunt's information, coupled with his secretive relationship to McCord and the bugging of the Columbia Plaza by McCord's employee, Lou Russell, suggests that the gossip issued at least in part from that bordello. CIA Director Helms's destruction of tapes and records pertaining to the CIA's "mind control experiments"—which included tape-recorded encounters between agency-supported prostitutes and their clients—was probably not unrelated to Watergate (as, indeed, the House Armed Services Committee suspected). Unfortunately, the destruction of those records makes it unlikely that the CIA's activities, at the Columbia Plaza and at the Mullen Company, will ever be completely understood.

What makes the matter even more difficult is the intraagency deception that is a hallmark of the affair. Clearly, that deception went deeper than the usual precautions of compartmentalization, deniability and need-to-know would have required. For example, even while Robert Bennett was deceiving the press to protect the Mullen Company's covert relationship to the CIA, the agency was itself deceiving Bennett. CIA memoranda reflect the agency's determination to sever its relationship to the Mullen Company while at the same time not wanting to be honest with Bennett about its reasons for wishing to do so. It was Hunt's job, and a sensitive one at that, to "negotiate" an end to the cover arrangement. But why would a *negotiation* have been necessary? Since Mullen's overseas offices existed almost entirely for the convenience of the agency, one would have thought that the CIA could have closed them at will.[30]

But matters were not so simple. According to Senator Baker's report to the Ervin committee, the Mullen Company's case officer, Martin Lukoskie, wrote in a memo to Richard Helms that the Watergate affair should not be used as an excuse for ending the company's relationship to the agency. (Obviously, someone had suggested this course of action.) According to Baker, Lukoskie's report

> contains mysterious reference to a "WH flap." The report states that if the Mullen cover is terminated, the Watergate could not be used as an excuse. It suggests that the Agency might have to level with Mullen about the "WH flap." Nonetheless, a July 24, 1972, contact report shows that the CIA convinced Robert Mullen of the need to withdraw its Far East cover through an "agreed upon scenario" which included a falsified Watergate publicity crisis. The Agency advises that the "WH flap" has reference to a [DELETION AT AGENCY REQUEST] that threatened to compromise Western Hemisphere operations, but has not explained sufficient reason to withhold such information from Mullen nor explained the significance of same to Watergate developments. This Agency explanation is clouded by conflicting evidence. The Assistant Deputy Director of Plans has testified that he is very familiar with the matter and that it had no unique effect on Mullen's cover. The Mullen case officer testified that the flap concerned cover. Bennett . . . thought the reference concerned a "White House flap". . . .[31]

There are any number of mysteries here. On the one hand, Helms and Lukoskie had given at least tacit approval to Bennett for a backdoor entry to the *Post*. So far as Bennett was concerned, the purpose of that liaison was to "kill off" any revelations of the Mullen Company's relationship to the CIA. On the other hand, *and at the same time*, Lukoskie and Helms were planning to take advantage of the opportunity that Watergate presented: a contrived publicity crisis to extricate the agency from its ties to the Mullen Company. And, indeed, the Mullen Company's Singapore office, Suite 306 in the Cathay Building, was closed precipitately in August 1972—just as Lukoskie and Helms had planned. The firm's employee, Arthur

---

[30]The Mullen Company's overseas offices were in Mexico City, Amsterdam, Stockholm and Singapore.
[31]Ervin committee, *Final Report*, pp. 1125–26.

H. Hochberg, simply "vanished" one afternoon and, according to
the *New York Times*, "has not been heard from since."[32] The decision to bring Hochberg in from the cold occurred more than a year
before the Mullen Company's ties to the CIA were revealed. Obviously, Watergate had nothing to do with that decision, however
much Lukoskie and Helms wished others to think that it did.

The real reason for terminating the Mullen Company cover was,
as CIA memoranda and reports make clear, the "WH flap." What
was it, and why was the agency so reluctant to "level" with Mullen
about it?

Questioned by Senate staffers, CIA representatives claimed that
"WH" stood for Western Hemisphere and that the "flap" concerned Philip Agee. A former CIA operative in the Western Hemisphere Division, Agee was engaged in writing an exposé of his CIA
career in Latin America. The exposé would "name names," including (it was supposed) that of the Robert R. Mullen Company (with
which Agee had had some contact in Mexico City).[33] Thus, the CIA
argued, it was necessary to terminate that cover before Agee could
blow it and, in doing so, endanger those under cover. If we are to
believe this, then it would appear that William Colby was referring
to Agee when he alluded, in his conversation with the Ervin committee's Fred Thompson, to CIA "defections" and KGB "infiltration" of the agency.

But that argument is contrived. Agee was one person, rather than
several. He had not defected that spring (if, indeed, he can be said
to have "defected" at all), and he was never a "high-level officer"
(as Colby's remarks would have suggested). He was a junior case
officer whose political views had swung to the Left after his retirement from the CIA in 1968. There was no reason for the CIA to
deceive Bennett or Mullen where Agee was concerned. If the CIA
believed that Agee was about to blow its relationship to the Mullen
Company, it need only have ordered its agents home and no harm
would have come to them. Instead, Agee became a convenient
excuse. Not only was he invoked to explain away the CIA's concern
about what was almost certainly a *White House* flap of some sort,
but he was also used as an excuse to terminate a battalion of employees, operations and covers that, for one reason or another, could

[32]Schanberg, "Employee of C.I.A. 'Cover' Quit Two Years Ago."
[33]The Mullen Company is mentioned in passing in Agee's book. See *Inside the Company: CIA
Diary* (New York: Stonehill Press, 1975), p. 552.

not otherwise have been put out to pasture so easily.[34]

Indeed, in the summer of 1972 Agee had a remarkable opportunity to shape the Watergate story, and failed to do so. Though he was then giving interviews to the press,[35] he failed to identify the Mullen Company as a CIA cover. Had he done so, the press would certainly have paid closer attention to the CIA's role in the scandal and questioned Howard Hunt's true allegiances. Instead, Bob Woodward, the *Post* and the press as a whole were left to struggle in the dark, never realizing that one of their principal sources on the story was a CIA disinformation agent.

[34]Agee's literary efforts were a "mixed curse" to the agency. While railing against its former case officer, the CIA used the impending book to conduct what was, in effect, a purge. Former CIA officer Joseph Burkholder Smith describes how he was deputed to assist "a [Ted] Shackley henchman . . . [in] the task of getting rid of the [Western Hemisphere] Division's [existing] operations and much of its officer staff. . . . I was disturbed to have to dismiss so many loyal men and upset to have the defenses [that] I kept putting up to try to salvage something of their old lives summarily dismissed by the Star Chamber conducting the purge in Washington. When Agee's book finally appeared, not one of the people I was ordered to fire was mentioned [in it]" (*Portrait of a Cold Warrior*, [New York: Putnam, 1976], pp. 2–3). In fact, this was just the tip of the iceberg. The purge extended to other divisions as well, with more than two thousand CIA employees being forced into retirement during the Watergate period. (The excuses ranged from Agee to budgets to unsatisfactory performance to a need to make room at the top for younger officers.) These "retirements," carried out under the successive auspices of CIA Directors Schlesinger and Colby, reduced the agency's size by almost 15 percent. The hostility this created was such that both directors were assigned extra bodyguards—the fear being that a newly "retired" employee might take it upon himself to "forcibly retire" his former boss. It has been suggested that this decimation of the agency's senior personnel was in fact an "administrative purge" undertaken in an effort to purify the CIA of any possible Soviet taint. In other words, more than two thousand people may have been let go in order to cleanse the agency of a single defector-in-place, whose identity could not be ascertained.

[35]Agee, *Inside the Company*, pp. 591–92.

19.
Throat

In considering the identity of Bob Woodward's most important and most secret source, "Deep Throat," it should be said at the very beginning that any conclusion must be speculative. Only Woodward and Deep Throat—if there is a Deep Throat—can be certain of the latter's identity. And if, as many of Woodward's colleagues in the Washington press corps believe, Throat is actually a composite of several sources, then the secret of their separate identities may never be known.

Still, it is possible to reach some conclusions based upon what we know about Woodward and what we are told about Throat. If, for example, Deep Throat is a public figure who served in the Nixon administration in a highly visible capacity, then only one person comes close to satisfying Woodward's description of his source. If, on the other hand, Throat is (or was) a relatively obscure bureaucrat, then the problem is more complex.

One's interest in the subject is more than idle curiosity. As the guiding light behind much of the *Post*'s Watergate reportage, Throat has a historic responsibility with respect to the Nixon administration's downfall. One would like to know who he is. The *Post*'s editors insist that they are only protecting a valuable source. They would have us believe that Throat is an altruist who seeks no personal gain and who wants to shun the tribulations that sometimes attend whistle-blowers. The suggestion, then, is that Throat is a patriotic civil servant who, while outraged by the administration's disregard of constitutional concerns, fears the retribution that has been meted out to other whistle-blowers. But, surely, this is a specious argument. Throat belongs in a category different from that of GSA employees and disaffected CIA officers who have protested cost-overruns and underestimates of enemy troop strengths. The whistle that he blew was heard 'round the world, and a grateful nation has offered to bestow its accolades upon him even as publishers dangle the lure of seven-figure advances for his story. Clearly, Deep Throat's anonymity has nothing to do with job security. It may be, therefore, that Throat remains anonymous because if he was identified our perception of him and of the *Post*'s Watergate reportage would change. That is, it may be that Throat's position within the Nixon administration was such that he would stand revealed as a Machiavellian figure moved more by his own ambitions than by any concern for fair play in national politics. In which case, Woodward and the *Post* would be seen as mere tools in a power struggle. So there is reason to be skeptical. While Woodward and Bernstein prefer to believe in Deep Throat's altruism, we should not trust their judgment on that matter: the *Post*'s reporters, after all, have an important stake in the selflessness of their source.

Two routes may be taken in an effort to identify Deep Throat. The first is a study of Woodward and Bernstein's *All the President's Men*. While Woodward's description of his source is deliberately vague, and while the circumstances of their meetings are intentionally obscured, analysis of the book will enable us to narrow the field of candidates to a single one—providing only that we may assume that Deep Throat was a prominent figure in the Nixon administration, because, of course, we can only compare the characteristics of those who are known to us: if Throat is someone of whom we have never heard, Woodward's description will not help us to identify him. It would then be necessary to examine Woodward's own background to learn where he might have met someone who, while perhaps unknown to the public, was in a position to know, and had the motive to reveal, so many of the Nixon administration's most embarrassing secrets.

For now, however, let us begin with the assumption that Throat was a famous man. Even if that assumption turns out to be incorrect, it will be helpful to review Woodward's contacts with his source, and what he had to say about him.

The first Watergate-related contact between Woodward and Deep Throat occurred on June 19, two days after the arrests. Woodward tells us that he telephoned "an old friend," a federal employee who sometimes helped him with needed information. His friend, Woodward adds, did not like getting calls at the office, and all he would say on this occasion was that the break-in story was about to "heat up." Later that same day Woodward again called his friend. On an off-the-record basis, the reporter was told that the FBI considered Howard Hunt to be a major suspect in the case.[1] That it was Deep Throat who passed this information to Woodward is stated explicitly in *All the President's Men.* [2]

The most important clue embedded in Woodward's account of this contact is, of course, the news that Throat was already an "old friend" when the Watergate affair began. Indeed, Woodward tells us that he and Throat had spent many evenings together, "long before Watergate," discussing power politics in the capital.[3] By itself, this information suggests that Throat's identity is more likely to be revealed by an examination of Woodward's background than by a content analysis of his book because, of course, at the tender age of twenty-nine years, Woodward cannot have been friends with many people holding important positions in the Nixon administration. Still, let's see what else can be learned about Throat from the pages of *All the President's Men.*

The conditions under which Woodward spoke to his source are interesting in their own right. Some of the conversations were "off the record," which meant that their contents could not appear in print. Other talks were held on the basis of "deep background," which is to say that the information could be used to inform a story or to generate leads but could not be cited directly. Moreover, Woodward tells us, he had promised Deep Throat that he would never reveal the man's position with the government, nor would he ever quote him, not even anonymously. Insofar as Watergate was concerned, Throat would be a guide: he would offer "perspective" and confirm leads that the *Post* had already developed, but he would not be expected to leak information of which the *Post* was unaware.[4] These are extraordinarily protective conditions, but what is most surprising about them is that they were cast to the winds so very quickly. Woodward did identify Throat to others—to Carl Bernstein, for example, and to Ben Bradlee. Throat did supply leads, as well as guidance and perspective, and he did come to be quoted anonymously in the *Post* (albeit not until November 1973). But most dramatically of all, Deep Throat is described in detail, quoted at

[1] Woodward and Bernstein, *All the President's Men,* pp. 23–25.
[2] Ibid., p. 72.
[3] Ibid., p. 130.
[4] Ibid., p. 71.

length, and made into a major character—literally a folk hero—in *All the President's Men*.

Clearly, something had changed between the time that Woodward first contacted Throat about Watergate—in June 1972—and a year later when Woodward and Bernstein sat down to write their first book.[5] What that change may have been is uncertain, but obviously Throat was emboldened—perhaps by the decline in Nixon's fortunes or by some increase in his own, or both.

As we will see, General Alexander Haig is that "prominent official" within the Nixon administration who most closely fits Woodward's description of his source. By late May 1973 General Haig had assumed the position that was formerly held by H. R. Haldeman, a onetime confidant of Haig's whom the general now referred to as "that criminal."[6] In effect, Haig was suddenly second in command at the White House, subordinate only to an increasingly incapacitated President Nixon. In that role, with the administration effectively purged through a string of enforced resignations, Haig exercised authority that was almost beyond challenge. If he was Deep Throat, the restrictive ground rules set down between himself and Woodward at the start of the affair may no longer have seemed necessary.

In *All the President's Men* we are told that Throat held an "extremely sensitive" job in the executive branch of government,[7] and that what he knew amounted to an assemblage of information "flowing in and out of many stations," including the White House, Justice Department, FBI and CRP.[8] We are told, also, that Throat hated inexactitude and the sort of superficial reports that one was likely to find in newspapers. "He could be rowdy, drink too much, [and] overreach," Woodward writes, adding that Throat's inability to keep his feelings hidden was a liability for someone in his job.[9] To Woodward, Throat seemed resigned and almost beaten down, as if he had been "worn out in too many battles."[10]

This last remark may give us pause. Alexander Haig is hardly the

---

[5] Although Woodward and Bernstein had signed a contract with Simon & Schuster in the fall of 1972, it was not until the summer of 1973 that they actually began work on the book that was eventually published.
[6] Roger Morris, *Haig: The General's Progress* (New York: Playboy Press, 1982), p. 123.
[7] Woodward and Bernstein, *All the President's Men*, p. 72.
[8] Ibid., p. 131.
[9] Ibid.
[10] Ibid., p. 130.

burnt-out case that Woodward appears to be describing. The context of the reporter's remark, however, suggests that it may have
been made not as a general observation but as a comment on
Throat's demeanor at a particular meeting. As for the rest, who
knows? It might be Haig, and it might not. Woodward's observations are subjective, and they are by no means always accurate.
Woodward is mistaken when he tells us, for example, that Throat
was forever careful to distinguish between fact and rumor, that he
always told less than he knew, and that he never told Woodward
anything that was incorrect.[11] Throat was wrong about a lot of
things, including his belief that Howard Hunt was briefly assigned
to help John Mitchell conduct an investigation of the events surrounding the break-in and arrests.[12] He was wrong, also, when he
asserted that the White House and the CRP had more than fifty
agents spying for them, mostly against their own supporters.[13] Yet
another mistake was his claim that there were four White House
intelligence groups, including the November Group, responsible
for undercover operations.[14] And as for Throat's allegation that
Mitchell and Colson were "behind" the Watergate operation, the
evidence simply does not not support it.[15]

It is not my intention, however, to deprecate Deep Throat or
ridicule the quality of his information. On the whole, he gave the
Post extraordinary guidance throughout the affair, and most of his
information was absolutely accurate. Still, the mistakes that he made
make it apparent that he was neither infallible nor omniscient.
There were sources that he did not have, and contrary to what
Woodward tells us, one of the sources that he seems to have lacked
was someone in the FBI. For example, one of the most critical and
newsworthy developments in the Watergate affair was Alfred Baldwin's blockbuster confession concerning the electronic eavesdropping that he had conducted, the earlier May break-in and much
more, but, like everyone else, Woodward and Bernstein did not
learn about Baldwin until the Democrats held a press conference on
the subject in September. Which is to say that insofar as Woodward
was concerned, *Deep Throat watched for nearly three months as his*

[11]Ibid., pp. 131, 72.
[12]Ibid., p. 132.
[13]Ibid., p. 131.
[14]Ibid., p. 133.
[15]Ibid., p. 244.

friend proceeded on the wrongheaded assumption that the Watergate arrests were the outcome of a failed attempt to place bugs inside the DNC. For Throat to have known about Baldwin and not to have mentioned the matter to Woodward would have been an unconscionable breach of faith. The *Post* reporters risked their careers with every article that they wrote, and much of what they wrote was falling on deaf ears, in part because the burglars were thought to have been ineffectual. Because the reporters were unaware that electronic eavesdropping had actually occurred, and that transcripts of intercepted conversations had been passed up the chain of command, implicating increasingly important officials in the administration, the *Post*'s efforts to break open the scandal acquired an element of desperation. Why, then, didn't Throat tell Woodward about Baldwin? The simplest explanation is best: he didn't know about him. Which is to say that some members of the Nixon administration can be ruled out as candidates for Deep Throat on the ground that they knew too much.

The FBI's top echelon and many of its agents can be eliminated from consideration, since it was they who first developed the lines of investigation leading to Baldwin. Their reports, including interviews with Baldwin, were disseminated throughout the bureau. Contrary to what Woodward says, therefore, Throat did not have sources in the FBI—or if he did, their reports to him were perfunctory at best. For the same reason that L. Patrick Gray, Mark Felt and other FBI officials can be forgotten, so also can we exclude from consideration those whose job it was to prosecute the burglars. Assistant U.S. Attorney Earl Silbert, Assistant Attorney General Henry Petersen and their aides had known about Alfred Baldwin for months before the Democrats gave their press conference. And to these noncandidates must be added those in the White House who were privy to information developed by the FBI. On an early recommendation of Gordon Liddy's, John Dean requested that FBI Director Patrick Gray provide him with copies of the bureau's air-tels and 302 reports containing every lead, instruction and interview having to do with the Watergate investigation.[16] The exact date of Dean's request to the bureau has not been established, but it is known that he began receiving the FBI's raw data prior to June

[16]Ervin committee *Hearings*, Book 9, pp. 3469–70, 3477–82, 3514–15, 3576–77, 3583, 3606; Dean, *Blind Ambition*, pp. 122, 131, 184, 387–88.

28, 1972, less than two weeks after the Watergate arrests. Moreover, as a part of White House efforts to contain the scandal, Dean began sharing the FBI's data with top administration officials and their assistants, including H. R. Haldeman, John Ehrlichman, Fred Fielding and others.

Whoever Deep Throat was, he had access to a mix of hard information and, considering the mistakes that he sometimes made, top-echelon gossip. Among others in the Nixon administration, this description applies to Alexander Haig. While he did not initially have any direct responsibility with respect to the investigation, his position in the executive branch was nevertheless one of unusual sensitivity that gave him access to vital information. From the very beginning of his tenure at the White House, long before Watergate, he had been given access to "every piece of intelligence" that went to the White House.[17] Not content with the administration's national security secrets, Haig was said to have become "Kissinger's man in Haldeman's office and Haldeman's man in Kissinger's office."[18] That is to say, he reported secretly to Haldeman about Kissinger, and secretly to Kissinger about Haldeman. Whether these descriptions of Haig's functions are compatible with Woodward's descriptions of Deep Throat is for the reader to decide. Certainly Haig's position was extremely sensitive (without being all-knowing), and it is fair to say that, like Throat, he had access to a great deal of hard information "flowing in and out of many stations." Even more specifically, Woodward tells us in the original manuscript of *All the President's Men* that Throat was "perhaps the only person in the government in a position to possibly understand the whole scheme, and not be a potential conspirator himself."[19] Could he have been writing about Haig? Possibly, but some would insist that Haig's responsibility for supervising the so-called Kissinger wiretaps—against NSC staffers, Defense officials and journalists—made him a part of the "scheme" and, at least potentially, part of a "conspiracy."

According to Woodward, Deep Throat was "an incurable gossip."[20] So, of course, was Haig. As Henry Kissinger's only staff

[17]Bob Woodward and Carl Bernstein, *The Final Days* (New York: Simon & Schuster, 1976), p. 209.
[18]Morris, *Haig*, p. 121.
[19]The quote here is from page 519 of the original manuscript. The description was deleted from the published book. A note in the margin of the manuscript suggests that the description comes "too close" to Deep Throat's identity.
[20]Woodward and Bernstein, *All the President's Men*, p. 131.

contact between the NSC and the White House, Haig was said to use gossip to ingratiate himself with every faction. Thus, he told Haldeman "intimate tidbits . . . about Kissinger—he's screwing this or that broad in New York," while at the same time referring to Nixon as "our drunk" and to Nixon's principal aides as "those shits." Also, Haig was said to joke viciously about the President's "limp wrist," and about his relationship with White House "intimate" Bebe Rebozo.[21] But if Haig and Deep Throat shared a predilection for gossip, they had other things in common as well. Like Throat, Haig smoked cigarettes and was partial to Scotch whisky. Like Throat, he detested superficiality, and his attitude toward the press seemed a mixture of contempt and patronization. So, too, as millions saw in the aftermath of President Ronald Reagan's wounding, Haig has a "tendency to overreach"—that is, like Throat, he has an unseemly enthusiasm for taking command and an apparent inability to hide his excitement at doing so. As Woodward commented about Throat, this was hardly an ideal characteristic for someone in his position.

Elsewhere in *All the President's Men*, we see Throat telling the reporter of the President's anger at developments, saying that Nixon had gone "wild, shouting and hollering. . . ."[22] How could Throat have known that unless he had been present at the scene, or learned of it from someone else who had? In either case, Haig remains a viable candidate.

There are other details, in and out of the reporters' book, that support the possibility that Haig was the one. He is, for example, well regarded by the *Post*, which applauded his appointment as White House chief of staff, calling him a man of "great intelligence and integrity." While this is by no means prima facie evidence, the *Post*'s editorial approval would seem to be a sine qua non for any viable candidate. More substantively, however, Haig was one of the few people at the White House who knew, in early November 1973, that there were "gaps" in the presidential tapes. According to Woodward, it was in the first week of that month that Throat told him about the gaps, hinting sharply that they might have been the result of deliberate erasures.[23] This information was passed to Carl Bernstein, who, Woodward tells us, got on the phone to his sources at the White House. Four of those

[21]Morris, *Haig*, p. 127.
[22]Woodward and Bernstein, *All the President's Men*, p. 269.
[23]Ibid., p. 333.

sources confirmed that there were gaps in the tapes.[24]

According to *Time* magazine, only a handful people in the White House were privy at this early date to the existence of the tape gaps. They were Richard Nixon, Rose Mary Woods, Alexander Haig, Charles Colson, Stephen Bull (Alexander Butterfield's assistant) and three of the President's attorneys: Fred Buzhardt, Leonard Garment and Samuel Powers.[25]

If *Time* is correct, and if Woodward and Bernstein have told the truth, then four of these eight must have been Bernstein's sources. Declaring Nixon and Woods "nonstarters," *Time* eliminated attorney Samuel Powers from consideration, saying that his tenure at the White House was too brief. Stephen Bull was then ruled out because he did not match Woodward's description of Throat. There, however, the magazine balked, unwilling to go any further. But of the four candidates with whom its readers were left, three could be eliminated at once. Colson, for example. The idea that Colson might be Deep Throat is as comical as it is sur-real. Not only had he planned to "shove it to the *Post*," but he would hardly have told Woodward—as Throat did—that he, Charles Colson, was the official to whom Howard Hunt was reporting about his undercover operations.[26] Colson, in any case, can be eliminated as a candidate for Throat on the grounds that his government career ended in the midst of the Watergate affair, whereas Woodward tells us that Throat continued in federal service for years afterward. This same reason rules out Leonard Garment, and as for Fred Buzhardt, he cannot have been Deep Throat because, according to Woodward, "If [Throat] were to die, I would feel obliged to reveal his identity."[27] Since Buzhardt is dead and we still do not know who Throat is, we must conclude that he is someone else.

Which is to say Haig, since only he is left among *Time*'s eight candidates. But who is to say that the magazine was correct when it asserted that only eight people knew of the tape gaps during the first week in November 1973? The White House was full of tremulous whispers in the fall of that year, and no one can say for certain just who knew what or when they learned it. Indeed, the

[24]Ibid.
[25]"Deep Throat: Narrowing the Field," *Time*, May 3, 1976, pp. 17–18.
[26]Woodward and Bernstein, *All the President's Men*, pp. 220–21.
[27]"Deep Throat: Narrowing the Field," May 3, 1976, p. 17.

elitist assumption that Deep Throat was a prominent Nixon appointee is unfounded and quite possibly incorrect. He might just as easily have been a military attaché, a White House liaison officer to one of the intelligence agencies, or even a member of that Secret Service contingent that maintained the presidential taping system.

But if Throat *was* a prominent person, then the evidence is overwhelming that he can only have been General Alexander Haig. If, however, we are able to show that Throat was not a prominent person, i.e., not Haig, then the identity of Woodward's source may only be discovered through an examination of the reporter's own past. Are there any reasons, then, for eliminating Haig from contention?

There are several. But whether they are conclusive is a decision that the reader will have to make for himself. For instance: Haig's role as a source for Woodward and Bernstein's second book, *The Final Days* is, while never admitted, transparent. Certain anecdotes in that book can only have come from him. On the surface, therefore, this would seem to support the idea that Haig is Deep Throat because, since he was a source for the second book, he may also have been a source for the first. But if this is so, why did Woodward go to such extravagant lengths to protect the identity of his source for the first book, while permitting Haig to be so easily identified as a source for the second? It doesn't make sense, and one is tempted to conclude that the sources are different people.

A second reason to doubt that Throat and Haig are one and the same has to do with a secret meeting that took place between the reporter and Throat at a working-class bar on the outskirts of Washington.[28] Surrounded by blue-collar workers, Woodward was apprehensive about seeing Throat in public, until Throat calmed him with the observation that neither Woodward's friends nor his own were likely to see them in a low-rent dive of the kind that they were in. The point is that Woodward and Deep Throat were concerned not that the *public* would recognize them, but that their colleagues might. While Haig was not yet as famous as he was about to become,[29] neither was he as faceless as Deep Throat appears to have

[28]Woodward and Bernstein, *All the President's Men*, pp. 268–69.
[29]The meeting seems to have occurred on February 25, 1973 (a Sunday), a few months before Haig was appointed Nixon's chief of staff.

been. Had Haig appeared in public with Woodward at that time, there was a real chance that both men would have been asked for autographs.

There are other reasons to doubt that Haig is Throat. It is difficult, for example, to imagine Haig skulking through the capital to predawn meetings with Woodward in an underground garage—the modus operandi that Throat preferred. Even more substantively, Haig lacked a motive to discredit Nixon. While he may be said to have benefited directly from the White House purges that followed on the heels of the *Post*'s revelations, Haig could never have predicted his own rise as a corollary to the administration's increasing debility.

Finally, Haig's candidacy has been objected to on the grounds that he cannot have been in Washington, meeting secretly with Woodward, at 2:00 A.M. on October 9, 1972.[30] That is the time and date that Woodward gives us of an underground rendezvous with Throat, and Haig is known to have been in Paris the previous day. The problem with this objection, however, is not merely that Kissinger and Haig sometimes deceived the public about their whereabouts—particularly on historic occasions.[31] The problem is that Woodward cannot always be trusted when it comes to his reports about the circumstances of his meetings with Deep Throat.

In *All the President's Men*, Woodward makes reference to fifteen conversations with Deep Throat during the Watergate period.[32] Of

[30]In fact, other objections have been raised to Haig's candidacy. Writing in the *New Republic* ("Ah, Watergate!" June 23, 1982), Watergate buff Ron Rosenbaum points out that Haig did not have access to grand jury "trivia" about Donald Segretti. But this should not rule out Haig as a candidate for Throat. Woodward himself tells us that Throat "would not talk specifically about Segretti's operation" (*All the President's Men*, p. 132). Leaving aside the fact that it is risky to say what Haig knew—or what Throat knew—or when they learned it, the *Post*'s sources on the subject of Segretti appear to have been Segretti himself and his friends. While Rosenbaum appears to have made a mistake about this, his article remains one of the best and most amusing that have been written in recent years. Moreover, the piece is an important one for having put to rest the red herring that it was Deep Throat who informed Woodward and the *Post* of the identity of George Wallace's would-be assassin. It was, in fact, the late Ken Clawson, a noncontender for Throat honors, who tipped off the *Post* about Arthur Bremer.
[31]October 8, 1972, was a historic occasion. It was on that day that the North Vietnamese finally accepted Henry Kissinger's peace plan.
[32]Monday, June 19, 1972 (two phone calls); Saturday, September 16, 1972 (phone call); Sunday, September 17, 1972 (phone call); Sunday, October 8, 1972 (phone call); Monday, October 9, 1972 (garage meeting); Saturday, October 21, 1972 (garage meeting); Friday, October 27, 1972 (garage meeting); late December 1972 (probable garage meeting); Thursday, January 25, 1973 (garage meeting); Monday, February 25, 1973 (meeting in bar); Monday, April 16, 1973 (phone call); Thursday, April 26, 1973 (phone call); Wednesday, May 16, 1973 (garage meeting); and a meeting, probably in a garage, during the first week in November 1973.

these, seven were telephone conversations, seven apparently took place in an underground garage, and one occurred in the working-class bar described earlier. In addition, an undetermined number of other meetings and telephone calls are implied by Woodward, but are never specifically described.

The first five of these contacts occurred during the summer and early fall of 1972, and all were by telephone. The last three calls were placed on weekends (after Throat warned Woodward not to call him at work), and we may deduce from this that the calls were probably made to Throat's home. But Deep Throat disdained the telephone. Accordingly, he and Woodward agreed to a signaling system by which one of them could inform the other of the need for a meeting. That system was then put into operation during the fall of 1972. In essence, the system reportedly required that Woodward move a flowerpot from one side of his balcony to another, thereby signaling the need for a meeting at a predetermined site (the underground garage) after midnight. If Deep Throat wished to initiate a meeting, Woodward would learn of that in his morning newspaper—that is, when he went down to the lobby to pick up his copy of the *New York Times,* he would find a circle drawn on page 20, and in that circle would be a clockface indicating the time of the proposed meeting.[33]

But none of this makes much sense. For Woodward and Throat to rely on the flowerpot as a signal, it would have been necessary for Throat to monitor the pot's position on Woodward's balcony, and to do so, moreover, on a daily basis. A clumsier system could not be imagined in view of the fact that the system is said to have been in use from at least October 19, 1972, until early November 1973. Which is to say that whoever Deep Throat was, he was obliged to look daily for the signal for more than a year, with a meeting resulting on the order of about once every two months. It may be argued, of course, that the signal may not have been inconvenient for Throat to monitor—that is, perhaps Deep Throat drove past Woodward's balcony each day on his way to work. In that case, he would only have had to glance out the window of his car. But no: when the signaling system was supposedly instituted, Woodward resided in a sixth-floor apartment on P Street, near Dupont Circle. That apartment, and its balcony, fronted on an interior courtyard

[33]Woodward and Bernstein, *All the President's Men,* p. 180.

removed from the street. It could only be seen by someone who took the trouble to enter the courtyard through an alleyway. For Throat to have monitored the position of the flowerpot while Woodward was living on P Street, he would have needed to park his car each morning in the vicinity of the reporter's apartment building—no mean feat in that congested neighborhood—walk through the alley and look up. To do this on a daily basis for any length of time would certainly have attracted attention, and it would also have represented an enormous waste of time. Even so, it is hard to understand how Throat could have seen anything less than a giant banyan growing on Woodward's balcony: the courtyard in question is small and the building rather tall. As a result, the balconies on the upper floors are eclipsed from view by the ones below, and one cannot see much more of the upper balconies than a portion of their undersides. No matter how much Throat craned his neck, a flowerpot simply would not have been visible.[34]

As with the flowerpot, so also with the supposed signal involving the *New York Times:* it is impossible. Woodward's P Street apartment building was a secure one. In the early morning hours, access to the building was inhibited by locked doors and a security guard. The guard, who stood behind a desk in the lobby of the building, received the tenants' copies of the *Times* each day, and he would hand them out to the tenants when they came down in the morning. Individual copies, in other words, were not delivered to the apartments of subscribers, and there does not seem to have been any moment when the newspapers were unwatched. How, then, could Throat have gotten to Woodward's copy of the *Times,* unobtrusively scribbling clockfaces on its inner pages?

There are other peculiarities in Woodward's account of his meetings with Deep Throat. He tells us, for example, that because it was impossible to find a taxi late at night in the neighborhood where he

[34]In the later stages of the affair, however, it would not have been so difficult for Woodward to use the flowerpot as a signal. This is because he moved from P Street in mid-November 1972, taking residence in a large apartment near the *Washington Post.* By then, though, there had already been three meetings in the underground garage, at least two of which were supposedly cued by the flowerpot. Still later, in January 1973, Woodward moved once again. This time he moved into a two-bedroom apartment on the top floor of a high rise in Washington's southwest quarter, quite near Fort McNair. There, Woodward actually had a balcony that faced the street, but by then he and Throat had already had at least four—and possibly five—of their seven meetings in the garage. (Still later, the peripatetic Woodward moved to a house on Edmunds Street, four doors from a house in which General Haig resided, and back-to-back with Ben Bradlee's house on Dexter Street.)

lived, he was forced to walk for miles to meet with his source. And yet, Dupont Circle is alive with taxis at every hour of the night. So, too, when Woodward subsequently changed apartments, moving to Washington's southwest quadrant, he was only a few blocks from one of the city's all-night cabstands.

These are not major inconsistencies, but they are important because they call into question the accuracy of Woodward's account of his relationship to Deep Throat and the circumstances of their meetings. If Woodward has not been candid about the signaling system that he used, then he may not have been truthful in his description of Throat or in his recollection of specific meetings (such as the one that is said to have occurred on October 9). Indeed, he may even have introduced a few red herrings: e.g., the seemingly gratuitous information that he, Woodward, stands five feet ten— this, immediately after telling us that he could not reach a note that Throat had left for him in the garage. Obviously, we are supposed to conclude that Throat is taller than five feet ten.[35]

So a content analysis of *All the President's Men*, while it helps us to eliminate many of the known candidates from consideration, will not permit us to eliminate every one. In the end, Alexander Haig's candidacy remains viable, however battered and improbable. (Can you actually *see* Haig sneaking into an underground garage at 2:00 A.M. to meet with a cub reporter?) While one cannot prove that Haig was Throat, neither can one prove that he was not.

Still, Haig does not *feel* like Deep Throat, and as suggested earlier, it is probably a mistake to assume that Throat was a public figure. Though Woodward certainly knew him, you and I may never have heard of him. For that reason, then, Woodward's own background is worth examining to learn where he might first have met someone as interesting as Deep Throat.

The son of a Republican judge, Robert Upshur Woodward was graduated from Yale University in 1965. Enlisting in the Navy, he served in succession aboard the USS *Wright* and the USS *Fox.* The former is one of two ships designated a National Emergency Command Post Afloat (NECPA), and Woodward became its communications watch officer.[36] The mission of the *Wright,* according to one

[35]Woodward and Bernstein, *All the President's Men*, p. 268.
[36]The USS *Northampton* is the second National Emergency Command Post Afloat.

of Woodward's former commanding officers, Rear Admiral Francis J. Fitzpatrick, was to "stand in readiness to embark the President and take him to sanctuary at sea in the event of national emergency. And, also, to provide him with the high level of command control communications capability required by the National Command Authority. [The President's] other options were to go to the airborne command post, or to other facilities that exist on shore." The *Wright*, in other words, was the President's aquatic bunker, and, as such, it received and processed the same intelligence that flows through the Situation Room at the White House. In the event of a "national emergency" (e.g., a nuclear war) there was to be no interruption in the flow of information to and from the President. As the communications watch officer aboard the *Wright*, Woodward had a high security clearance and access to many of the President's secrets.

His four-year hitch with the Navy came to an end in the first months of the Nixon administration, and he was free to return to civilian life. But he did not. While serving aboard the USS *Fox*, Woodward seems to have become a protégé of his commanding officer, Admiral Robert O. Welander. According to a Navy colleague of Woodward's, who asked not to be identified, it was at the urging of Welander—who had yet to be embarrassed by the Moorer-Radford affair—that Woodward extended his tour of duty for another year; his new assignment was to the Pentagon, where he came to serve as the communications duty officer for the Chief of Naval Operations. Admiral Welander was assigned to the same office, having just returned to Washington from his fellowship at the Council on Foreign Relations.

It was a fascinating assignment for someone so young. In his new position, Woodward presided over all communications traffic going to and from the CNO's office. This included top-secret communiqués from the White House, the CIA, the National Security Agency (NSA), the State Department, the Defense Intelligence Agency (DIA) and the NSC. On a shift basis, surrounded by the clatter of teletypes, cryptographic equipment and the hum of a Spectro-70 computer, Woodward supervised the encoding and decoding of all such traffic, maintained a journal of "highlights" for each day, and decided when, where, how and to whom each communication should be routed, and with what priority. He held, in other words, a position of strategic trust within the intelligence community; while others of much higher rank and longer service labored within the constraints of the "need to know" stricture, Woodward was in an oversight position vis-à-vis a broad spectrum of interagency intelligence operations.

Even under ordinary circumstances, the CNO's communications duty officer was well informed, to say the least. But the circumstances that prevailed during Woodward's tenure at the Pentagon were anything but ordinary. The Chief of Naval Operations at that time was Admiral Thomas Moorer; in effect, he was head of the United States Navy. As such, his domain included any matter that might touch upon America's military presence or capability at sea —which is to say that this same information was, necessarily, a part of Woodward's domain as well. But what made Moorer an even more powerful CNO than usual was his ability to get along well with two of the administration's most powerful figures, John Mitchell and Henry Kissinger. Because he was trusted by them, very little was kept from him, and the man through whom much of that information passed was Lieutenant Woodward.

The communiqués that Woodward handled included those that were transmitted on the top-secret SR-1 channel assigned to Task Force 157—the same channel to which, as we saw earlier, Moorer had given Kissinger access. What is uncertain, however, is whether this channel was being used by Kissinger during the time that Woodward processed its contents: the summer of 1969 until June of 1970. While Kissinger is known to have used the channel to make arrangements for his mid-1971 visit to Peking, it is unclear whether this was the first occasion on which he began to use the channel or, indeed, just when those first arrangements were made. Still, the Nixon administration's first year, coincident with Woodward's tour of duty at the Pentagon, was a critical one in terms of national security, and there were many secrets to which Woodward became privy. Besides Nixon's vision of a rapprochement with the People's Republic of China, efforts were under way to initiate secret negotiations with North Vietnam, and clandestine meetings were being held with the Soviets to prepare the way for SALT talks and, it was hoped, détente. Henry Kissinger's plate was full. So was Moorer's. And so, on a much lower level, was Woodward's.

In 1982 I asked Admiral Moorer if he remembered his former communications duty officer at the Pentagon. He did. Seated in his office at the Georgetown Institute for Strategic Studies, surrounded by photographs of combat planes and ships at sea, the admiral seemed to levitate in his chair and then exploded. "He should have been court-martialed," Moorer said. "I gave him a tongue-lashing. That book of his is nothing but fiction—pure fiction. He should have been prosecuted!" For writing *All the President's Men*? "No," Moorer said, "for the other stories. You don't just walk out of the Navy with classified information. There are debriefings, oaths. What he did was inexcusable. He should have been kicked out of the service!" Moorer confirmed that "the other stories" were those that Woodward had written about Task Force 157 and former CIA agent Edwin P. Wilson's relationship to it.[37] In Moorer's view, their publication was a breach of national security, and a breach, also, of the oaths that Woodward had taken.

Informed of Moorer's apoplexy, Woodward asked rhetorically, "How could he court-martial me, or kick me out of the service, if I was already [a civilian]?" Told that Moorer had presumably not meant to be taken literally but was only expressing his anger, Woodward denied that he had violated his security oath. Was it untrue, then, that TF-157's communications were among those that he had helped to monitor, decode and route through the Pentagon? The reporter declined to say. Asked specifically about SR-1, Woodward said that he had had access to more than a hundred communications channels and could hardly be expected to remember the designation of each one. No, SR-1 did not ring a bell. As for TF-157 itself, Woodward said that his articles about the unit, and about its agent, Ed Wilson, were based on information that he acquired while a reporter.

That may be true because, while in the Navy, Woodward became part of an elite group and, in doing so, tapped into an astonishing grapevine of sources in the military, on Capitol Hill, in the foreign-policy-making establishment and in the intelligence community. That is, during his year at the Pentagon, he was one of a handful of officers chosen by the Navy to brief the government's most important intelligence officials on events and operations around the world. On a rotational basis, these officers would arrive at the Pentagon at 2:30 A.M., review the day's traffic and prepare a summation, or narrative, of its most important elements. At 8:00 A.M., the officer whose turn it was would go to any of several locations, including

---

[37]Bob Woodward, "CIA Director Fires 2 for Aiding Ex-Agents," April 27, 1977; "Pentagon to Abolish Secret Spy Unit," May 18, 1977. Both articles were published on page one of the *Washington Post*.

the CIA, the National Security Agency and the White House. There he would present the Navy's views, sometimes briefing special committees, more often speaking to a single individual: to the director of the CIA or the NSA, for example, or to the President's National Security Adviser or his principal deputy.

The men selected for this assignment were the best that the Navy could find. They were Rhodes scholars in some cases, but in every case they were young, bright and articulate. Many of them seemed to have stepped out of a recruiting poster. They came from some of the best schools, and entrusted with so much responsibility so early, they seemed earmarked for success. And, in fact, among those (besides Woodward himself) who have held the briefing post, there are any number of men who have gone on to achieve unusual prominence in political affairs: Dr. William Bader, formerly chief of staff (under Senator William Fulbright) for the Senate Foreign Relations Committee, and currently an executive at the Stanford Research Institute; Senator Richard Lugar, a subcommittee chairman on both the Senate Foreign Relations and Intelligence committees; and Admiral Bobby Ray Inman, formerly director of the Office of Naval Intelligence, the National Security Agency and, more recently, deputy director of the CIA.

That these men tended to know many of their predecessors, as well as their successors, is unsurprising: continuity in the position is essential. Besides, as Dr. Bader said to me with a chuckle, "It's a club. An Old Boys' network. We rely on each other from time to time." In light of which, the possibility suggests itself that Deep Throat may be one of the men who had formerly held Woodward's elite position in the Navy, or he may be one of those whom Woodward briefed. Who were they? Woodward refuses to say, commenting that he does not wish to expose his sources. "Not necessarily Deep Throat," he told me. "Other sources." He will, however, deny one report. Told that he is alleged to have regularly briefed Alexander Haig when Haig was Kissinger's deputy on the National Security Council, Woodward says no. "Not to my knowledge, anyway—though he may have been part of some large group [that I briefed]. But if he was," Woodward adds, "I wasn't aware of it."

We will return to the question of Woodward's predecessors, and the identities of those he briefed. But first, let us see how he came to work for the *Post*. Leaving the Navy in August 1970, and now a member of the "Old Boys' network," Woodward was accepted for the fall term at Harvard Law School. That was, in its own right, a remarkable achievement, since American universities and colleges were glutted with applications at the time, and none more so than the prestigious schools of the Ivy League. Despite this, Woodward rejected Harvard Law in order to look for work as a newspaper reporter.

A surprising decision in most ways, it did not come as a shock to Woodward's friends. David Miller, for example, was an alumnus of Yale who was then an aide to John Mitchell, and he was well aware of Woodward's interest in journalism. In fact, it was as an indirect result of his friendship with Miller that, near the end of his hitch at the Pentagon, Woodward got to know *Wall Street Journal* reporter Jerry Landauer. The circumstances of that meeting are worth relating because they show Woodward in the curious role of source, rather than of reporter, and also for the questions that they raise about the existence of a diary.

The introduction to Landauer occurred as a consequence of a misunderstanding between Woodward and Miller. The misunderstanding concerned the Puerto Rican island of Culebra, a hot intelligence item at the time because the Navy had used the island for target practice for more than fifty years and hoped to keep doing so. The Culebrans wanted the bombing to stop, and the issue promised to impinge upon Puerto Rico's domestic politics. It was in this context, then, that Miller, on the basis of apparently erroneous information from Woodward, contacted the attorneys for Culebra. Acting upon the mistaken impression that these attorneys represented the government of Puerto Rico, Miller suggested that it would be in their supposed client's best interests if the attorneys would desist from urging a meeting between President Nixon and Puerto Rico's Luis Ferré. When Miller was belatedly told whom the lawyers actually represented and suddenly realized that he had given the game away, he asked Woodward to help him rectify the matter. Woodward agreed, and a series of meetings followed: at the Washington Hotel, the Golden Ox restaurant and, eventually, at Woodward's apartment on P Street. Richard Copaken, one of the lawyers representing the Culebrans, brought Landauer along to the apartment. He knew that Woodward was interested in journalism, and thought that Landauer might be interested in the story.[38] Copaken says that while at the apartment he was surprised to find

[38]He was. See Jerry Landauer, "Culebrans Fire Back: Islanders Seek to End Role as a Navy Target," *Wall Street Journal*, June 10, 1970, p. 1.

a handwritten diary in Woodward's bookcase, a diary that seemed
to concern his work at the Pentagon. Copaken recalled one of the
entries in particular. It had to do with the Navy's interest in Culebra,
which the diary described as a "redoubt."

"I remember the incident clearly," Copaken told me, "because I
didn't recognize the word 'redoubt.' I didn't know what it meant,
and I had to look it up in the dictionary." The diary is a surprise.
While it is true that, as a part of his work at the Pentagon, Woodward was responsible for keeping a daily digest of communications
highlights, this was not a document that was to be taken home and
read over cocktails. Asked if he had kept such a diary for his private
use, Woodward said that he had not. Neither had he taken home
from the Pentagon any documents that he was not supposed to have.
Copaken, he said, was mistaken.

Woodward's first job as a reporter was a two-week tryout with
the *Washington Post* immediately after his discharge from the Navy
in 1970. During that time he worked unusually hard, hammering out
seventeen stories. Never a fluent writer—indeed, his colleagues
joked that English was Woodward's second language—he saw each
of his articles go unpublished. He did not, therefore, get the job he
was seeking at the *Post*. But what he did get was a recommendation
to the editor of the *Montgomery County Sentinel*, Roger Farquahar.
While Woodward says that there was "no guarantee" that he would
one day work for the *Post*, it was understood that after a year's
experience in the suburbs, his reapplication would be given careful
consideration.[39]

According to Farquahar, he hired Woodward on the strength of
his Yale diploma ("I'm a sucker for prestigious degrees," he said),
and on the recommendation of Woodward's commanding officer in
the Navy. "It was the most glowing recommendation that I have
ever seen in my life," Farquahar says. Asked if he knew what Woodward's duties had been while in the Navy, Farquahar said that he
did not. "He was in naval intelligence—but he never talked about
it. It was classified. On the other hand, he'd always come to the office
and say things like 'Well, there's going to be a revolution down in
such-and-such banana republic in about ten days.' And by God,
there was. It was uncanny, and, obviously, he had access to some
very high places and sources of information downtown. I have a

[39]Woodward started work for the *Sentinel* on September 17, 1970. On September 14, 1971—
a Friday—he quit to go to work for the *Post*. His first article appeared in the *Post* on Monday
morning, September 17.

pretty good damn idea that Deep Throat is a Yale graduate or somebody in naval intelligence that Woodward got to know."

Exactly. Deep Throat is probably a spook—someone in the intelligence community—with sources in high places. Whether or not Woodward fudged the actual details and circumstances of his meetings with Throat, it is clear that he and his source relied upon some sort of "tradecraft" to meet covertly at odd hours in strange places, and that these meetings were arranged with the help of a secret signaling system. Precautions were taken by both men against physical and electronic surveillance, and the reporter and his source had even worked out a "dead drop" for leaving messages in the event that Throat missed a meeting. This is not to say, necessarily, that Deep Throat was a James Bond figure, but, certainly, he knew the ropes.

The realization that Throat might be a spook should not come as a complete surprise. As mentioned before, Woodward's circle of acquaintances prior to his Watergate success cannot have been especially large. While it is true that he may have met some influential people at Yale, and perhaps some others while toiling at the *Montgomery County Sentinel,* most of the important people he knew were those whom he had met while in the Navy. Deep Throat, therefore, was likely a part of the intelligence milieu associated with the office of the chief of naval operations—the same milieu, ironically, that was responsible for the Moorer-Radford affair.

In view of Woodward's obfuscation of his source, it is ultimately fruitless to speculate about Throat's identity, especially if we have reason to believe that he was not a prominent figure in the Nixon administration. Throat could be an obscure communications technician, feeding data to the President's emergency command posts, though that seems unlikely in view of the fact that so much of Throat's information was political trivia and gossip (not what one would expect a President to read while hunkered down inside Mount Weather). Or Throat could be a part of the Old Boys' network, in which case Admiral Bobby Ray Inman must be a leading candidate. A quintessential spook, Inman satisfies some of the most obvious criteria for any Deep Throat candidate: e.g., he was in Washington throughout the period that Woodward was secretly meeting with his source, and, at some point or other, he himself became a source of Woodward's.[40]

---

[40]Inman came to Washington in July 1971 from Japan, where he had been the intelligence officer to the commander of the Seventh Fleet. In that capacity, he must have signed many of the cables that Woodward read during his stint at the Pentagon. In Washington, Inman

What may be more important than Throat's actual identity, however, is the distinct possibility that by confiding in Woodward about
Watergate he was acting on behalf of—or with the approval of—his
superiors. That is to say, Throat may have been "carrying water"
for that part of the military which Admiral Zumwalt represented,
the part that was perhaps the most vigorously opposed to the Nixon
administration's "immorality" and foreign policy. Zumwalt himself
lends support to that idea when he writes: "Conscientious officials,
when they find that the direct channels through which they are
accustomed to transact their business have been blocked, inevitably
and properly seek other, circuitous ones that make it possible for
them to meet their responsibilities. At the same time, less conscientious officials respond to the intrigues in the parlor with below-stairs
intrigues of their own."[41] So it is that "luncheons prolong themselves, late evening bull sessions proliferate, telephone conversations
become portentous, photocopying machines hum day and night,
leaks appear in the press, Congressmen come into possession of
papers that were presumably under lock and key, and everyone
looks askance at his neighbor."[42]

---

was first assigned to the National War College at Fort McNair. After a year there he was
appointed in June 1972 to the post of executive assistant and senior aide to the vice chief of
naval operations. He remained at that job through all of 1973, and then began his astonishing
tour through the uppermost echelons of the national security establishment: director of the
Office of Naval Intelligence (1974–76), vice director of the Defense Intelligence Agency
(1976–77), director of the National Security Agency (1977–81) and deputy director of the CIA
(1981–82). It was in his capacity as head of ONI that Inman disbanded Task Force 157, after
which Woodward became the first reporter to write about the unit and its past operations.
So, too, even as Inman focused his attention (and the FBI's) on TF-157/CIA agent Ed Wilson,
it was Woodward who first wrote about the gunrunner. And when, in 1982, Inman decided
to resign his post at the CIA—a decision that led to considerable hand-wringing on Capitol
Hill—it was Bob Woodward who broke the story of his departure.
[41]Zumwalt, *On Watch*, p. xiii.
[42]Ibid.

20.
Legacy:
A Counterfeit History

"Early in April . . . the hand of the Lord was upon me . . . going nearer I saw a man whose face shone like bronze, standing beside the Temple gate, holding in his hand A MEASURING TAPE. . . . He said to me, 'Son . . . watch and listen and take to heart everything I show you, for you have been brought here so I can show you many things, and then you are to return to the people of Israel to tell them all you have seen. . . .'"[1]

In point of fact, it was not the hand of the Lord that rested upon James McCord in April 1973, and neither did this "hand" hold a measuring tape. It was, instead, the long arm of the law, and what it held was a grant of immunity in return for McCord's testimony against his former colleagues. Appearing before the Watergate grand jury on April 9 and 12, McCord told the assembled "Israelites" all that he had seen—and, it seems, a great deal that he assumed or imagined. He revealed, for example, that Dorothy Hunt was the bag-person for payments of hush money to the arrested men, and claimed that John Mitchell was the sinister force behind the whole affair; it was he, McCord insisted behind closed doors, who had identified the eavesdropping targets and received transcripts of same.

As questionable as his claims concerning Mitchell were, they were not, strictly speaking, news. On March 19 McCord had delivered a letter to Judge John Sirica, alleging that perjury had been committed and that pressure had been put upon the defendants to

[1]Ezekiel 40:30, quoted from *The Living Bible* in James McCord's *A Piece of Tape*.

maintain their silence. From that moment on, McCord had begun to cooperate with the prosecution, the FBI and the Ervin committee. It was, by every account, the *Apocalypse Now* phase of the Watergate affair, and if McCord, with his biblical incantations, seems to have gone overboard, he was not alone. Consider what had occurred in the course of the winter:

On December 8 a mistrial had been declared in the Ellsberg case even as Dorothy Hunt buckled her seat belt for a fatal landing in Chicago. On December 21 McCord had written a letter to his White House contact, Jack Caulfield, promising that if Richard Helms should be replaced as CIA director, "every tree in the forest will fall." That same day, McCord had met with his attorney, Gerald Alch, who suggested to his client that perhaps the CIA had somehow been involved in the affair.[2] That suggestion so unsettled McCord that, in effect, he began to function as a double agent within the defense team, reporting secretly by letter to the CIA's General Gaynor.

By January 1973 Helms had been replaced, and cries of "Timber!" could be heard everywhere. L. Patrick Gray had witlessly destroyed the most sensitive contents of Howard Hunt's safe, burning them over the Christmas vacation. John Dean acted similarly in mid-January, by shredding Hunt's operational diary. And as we have seen, prior to his departure for Tehran, Helms imposed a kind of magnetic amnesia upon the CIA's central taping system. These were trees that fell out of sight and, at the time, beyond anyone's hearing. It was not until February 7, by a vote of 77 to nil, that the Senate prepared the way for the Nixon administration's public deforestation by creating a select committee of four Democrats and three Republicans to investigate the Watergate affair. In March, Lou Russell successfully prevailed upon attorney Bud Fensterwald to represent McCord and, not incidentally, to provide his new client with some $40,000 toward bail.

Fensterwald's entry into the case came as a complete surprise to Alch, who, days afterward, was to be acrimoniously fired by McCord. According to Alch, he first met Fensterwald at a meeting

[2] A dispute exists between McCord and Alch concerning precisely what was said at this time and at other, related meetings. There seems no way to settle the issue today, but it is McCord's contention that Alch conspired to concoct a phony CIA defense using falsified evidence. Alch (convincingly, in my opinion) rejects that charge, insisting that he raised the possibility of CIA involvement because it seemed a logical avenue to pursue in McCord's defense.

with McCord on March 23. At that meeting Fensterwald turned to McCord, saying, "The reporters have been asking me whether or not you or I had ever had any past relationship. I told them that we had." McCord, according to Alch, "looked up with a surprised expression.

" 'Well, after all,' Fensterwald said, 'you have, in the past, submitted to me checks which were donations to the Committee for Investigation of the Assassination of the President.'[3] Mr. McCord smiled and said, 'Oh, yes, that's right.' "

In fact, McCord does not seem to have made any such "donations." As Fensterwald recalls, he sometimes converted to cash Lou Russell's payroll checks from McCord Associates. He did so, he says, as a favor to Russell, a sometime employee of Fensterwald's. This was necessary, according to the lawyer, because Russell did not himself have a bank account, and so had trouble cashing his checks from McCord. In the course of translating McCord's checks into cash on Russell's behalf, Fensterwald would deposit them in his own personal account or, on occasion, to an account belonging to the Committee to Investigate Assassinations. The practice involved an estimated six to ten checks, and had been current at the time of the Watergate arrests.

In the context of McCord's dramatic turnabout and whispers suggesting that Fensterwald was himself a deep-cover CIA agent,[4] the affair was at once complicated and controversial. No one could be certain precisely what the matter involved. On the one hand, it appeared that Russell, or McCord, was a "contributor" to the Committee to Investigate Assassinations—if true, an exotic interest for a Nixon security agent such as McCord. On the other hand, Fensterwald's explanation suggested that there had been an exchange of checks for the simple convenience of Lou Russell—that is to say, it was "a wash" without being "a laundry." In the climate of the time,

---

[3]Properly, the Committee to Investigate Assassinations, founded by Fensterwald in the wake of John F. Kennedy's murder. Fensterwald testified in executive session before the Ervin committee on October 1, 1973; his account of the McCord or Russell "donations" to the CtIA is contained in transcripts of that session.
[4]The allegations about Fensterwald are anything but proven and, indeed, seem to be based upon groundless suspicions that proceed from the fact that Fensterwald's private and professional lives reflect a consuming interest in matters involving the intelligence community. His friends, clients and sources include any number of spooks from any number of intelligence services. This, however, seems mostly to be a function of Fensterwald's commitment to unraveling the mysteries that surround the assassination of President Kennedy, his brother and Dr. Martin Luther King.

however, there were some who voiced the opinion that the check-cashing procedure meant that Russell was actually in the employ of Fensterwald while technically on the payroll of McCord and working at the Committee to Re-elect the President.

The Senate did its best to learn the truth, questioning both Alch and Fensterwald, but proved unable to resolve the matter. Indeed, Senate questioning served only to deepen the mystery. In its interrogation of Russell's patron, William Birely, the Senate inquired about Russell's financial condition. Despite the detective's full-time employment by McCord, and his occasional work for other clients, he appeared to have been in a state of virtual poverty until Birely's intervention after the Watergate arrests, whereupon, as we have seen, Russell's material condition improved by quantum leaps. In November 1972, three days after Nixon's election, Russell purchased more than $4,000 in stock of the Thurmont Bank, a bank in which Birely was then a director. Five months later, on March 23, 1973, Russell purchased an additional 274 shares in the Thurmont Bank, paying for them with a check in the amount of $20,745. A few days later, Russell sold those same shares at a profit of $2,445. The first transaction had been handled by Birely's son-in-law, and the second by Birely himself. Birely insisted that the transactions were entirely lawful, and perhaps they were. What was more to the point, however, was the question of Russell's sudden wealth—and the disappearance of that money upon his death. Senate investigators privately concluded that Russell had served as a "straw man" in the stock transactions and that the money had not in fact been his own. They were convinced that the matter was somehow connected to Russell's relationship with McCord, but no one could say just how. In the confusion, the investigators appear to have overlooked a startling coincidence: the improbable stock transaction, involving more than $20,000 that Russell plainly did not have, took place on March 23, 1973, the same day that James McCord's Watergate-busting letter to Judge Sirica was made public in open court.

The affair is made even more perplexing by an FBI interview to which the Ervin committee seems not to have had access.[5] This was an interview with Warren L. ("Bud") Love, vice-president of the First National Bank in Washington. The bank is located at 1701

[5] FBI serial 139-4089-744, interview of July 3, 1972, by FBI agents James R. Pledger and James W. Hoffman.

Pennsylvania Avenue, directly below the offices of the CRP. According to Love, he was well acquainted with both Fensterwald and McCord. He remembered his surprise at McCord's arrest, and at a comment that Russell made shortly afterward. "I guess you're wondering who 'the sixth man' was," Russell said. "Well, it wasn't me."

What is more relevant than this unsolicited remark by Russell, however, is the fact that, as Love told the FBI, he was in the habit of cashing checks made out to Russell on McCord's personal bank account. He did this, he said, because both men were known to him, worked in the same building as he did, and Russell seemed not to have a bank account of his own. Which raises the following questions: Why was Russell sometimes paid from McCord's personal checking account, and why did he cash his checks with Fensterwald when, as Love makes clear, he was able to cash them in the very building in which he worked?

That these issues were not resolved (or, in some cases, never raised) was due in large measure to Russell's sudden illness and untimely death. In the spring of 1973, minority staffers on the Ervin committee knew enough about the Russell connection to realize that he had played, and continued to play, an important if mysterious role in the affair. Accordingly, they determined to get to the bottom of it all, and, on May 9, placed Russell under subpoena. The Ervin committee sought his telephone records, work diaries, bank statements and other materials that, in the end, Russell was unwilling to submit. On May 11 the detective replied in writing to the committee, saying that he kept no diaries, had no bank account, made no long-distance calls (except to his daughter) and, in short, could not be of any help. Senate staffers were unsatisfied with the reply, but there was nothing that they could do. On the morning of May 18, shortly after the reply was received, Russell suffered a massive heart attack. Taken to Washington Adventist Hospital, he remained there until his release on June 20. The date of the heart attack is significant. On May 18, three hours after Russell had been wheeled into the hospital's intensive care ward, James McCord began his first day of public testimony before the Ervin committee. A coincidence? Apparently. Russell's life had been a drunken, whoring and brutish one, and it may well be that he was overdue for a coronary. But Russell thought otherwise. As he told his daughter shortly before his death, he believed that he had been poisoned, that someone had entered his apartment and "switched pills on me." In retrospect, that may seem "paranoid" of the private eye, but, after all, the stakes were very high: Russell had been involved in the June break-in; he had almost certainly planted false evidence at the DNC in September; and throughout the fall and winter he had been instrumental in McCord's defense, helping him to secure bail and to switch attorneys. That switch had not been of mere tactical value; it represented a strategic change. Alch saw the case as a criminal one, whereas Fensterwald saw it in political terms. According to Alch, Fensterwald's entry into the case was marked by the assertion "We're going after the President." Which, as it happened, is precisely what McCord did.

Lou Russell was not alone, however, in the belief that lives were at stake and that murder might soon be committed. Less than forty-eight hours before Russell's heart attack, in the late evening of May 16 and the early morning of May 17, Deep Throat warned Bob Woodward that "Everyone's life is in danger."[6] It was the last meeting that the two men would have for nearly six months, and it was a scary one with an apocalyptic note that left Woodward wholly unnerved. According to Deep Throat, Nixon had threatened John Dean with jail if he ever revealed unspecified "national security activities"—activities that may or may not have involved Hunt, Liddy and McCord. He said that Hunt was "blackmailing" the President, that Nixon had "fits of 'dangerous' depression," and that Liddy was prepared to commit suicide. He said that McCord's life had been threatened by Jack Caulfield, and that the CIA was carrying out electronic surveillance against certain individuals—Throat didn't say who the targets were, but the implication was that the *Post* reporters were among them. Recounting Throat's urgent message to Bernstein and Bradlee, Woodward said that "The covert activities involve the whole U.S. intelligence community and are incredible. Deep Throat refused to give specifics because it is against the law. *The cover-up had little to do with Watergate, but was mainly to protect the covert operations.*"[7] (Emphasis added.) This is unquestionably the most dramatic of all Deep Throat's revelations, and yet we can only wonder at its meaning. *Whose* covert operations, and what did Throat mean by "the whole intelligence community"? The CIA? Task Force 157, the FBI, Joint Chiefs, NSA, DIA? These were not questions that the *Post* was willing to raise. What Deep

[6]Woodward and Bernstein, *All the President's Men*, p. 317.
[7]Ibid., pp. 348–49.

Throat had to say, in virtually his last reported message to Woodward, flatly contradicted the thrust of both the Senate's investigation and the *Post*'s own reports. If anything, it hinted at the as yet
unrevealed Moorer-Radford affair, the alleged CIA defections mentioned in Charles Colson's notes, and the *Seven Days in May* story
to which both Pentagon investigator Donald Stewart and CIA agent
Robert Bennett alluded. It hinted, in short, at the clandestine crisis
underlying the whole of the Watergate affair. Neither Woodward
nor Bernstein was in a position to define that crisis, to break the
story, or to say how it impinged on Watergate. But, as we have seen,
the evidence is overwhelming that the retirements of Hunt and
McCord had been fabricated by the CIA. Hiring the Cubans under
false flags, they conducted domestic operations on behalf of the
CIA's Security Research Staff, using the White House as a deniable
cover in the event of the operation's exposure. That this was an
institutional commitment of the CIA, rather than some "runaway"
operation conducted by rogue agents, is plain. The support given
to Hunt, McCord and Liddy came from a broad array of agency
components: the Central Cover Staff (which helped to arrange
Hunt's work for Mullen Company), the Medical Services Staff
(which provided psychological profiles), the Technical Services
(Bang and Boom) Division (which provided disguises, clandestine
cameras, voice-alteration equipment, etc.), the Office of Security
(which provided safehouses for secret meetings with Hunt and
Liddy), the CIA's graphics section (which prepared the Gemstone
charts), the Clandestine Services Division (whose deputy director,
Thomas Karamessines, may well have been Hunt's case officer
throughout the operation), the CIA's White House liaison office
(which served as courier for regular pouches from Hunt to Helms
and the Medical Services Staff), the External Employment Assistance Branch (which recommended suitable retirees from the Covert
Action Staff to assist Hunt and McCord in their lock-picking and
eavesdropping activities), the Western Hemisphere Division (from
whose ranks Martinez was drawn), and the agency's executive staff
(General Cushman and Director Helms). How many other sections
of the CIA may have been involved, if any, is unknown, but, clearly,
the assistance was so broad and so deep that one can only conclude
that institutional sanction had been given. Secretly. "Unofficially."
But definitely.

The cover-up, as Throat told Woodward, was motivated by national security concerns as much as by partisan politics because, apparently, the covert operations of the White House and the CIA overlapped and, finally, collided. With the arrest of Phillip Bailley and the receipt by the White House of evidence of sexual misconduct within both its own precincts and the DNC, administration officials such as Magruder were no longer content with McCord's bowdlerized logs and tales of malfunctioning tape recorders and bugs. The DNC, with its lurid connection to the call-girl ring at the Columbia Plaza, was re-targeted—whether for positive- or counter-intelligence purposes is unknown. That the Columbia Plaza ring was itself either a CIA operation or the target of a CIA operation is strongly suggested by its list of political clients; its bugging by Lou Russell; the circumstances under which McCord and Hunt were barred from the Furbershaw apartment; the ring's congress with CIA and KCIA agents; the known operational methods of the Office of Security with respect to sexual blackmail; the obsession of General Gaynor, head of the Security Research Staff, with sexual deviance; the manner in which the Bailley affair was brought to a sudden, almost silent resolution; and Terpil's account of Ed Wilson's role in intelligence operations involving sexual blackmail and prominent political figures.

In effect, the snake had swallowed its tail: CIA agents working under cover of the CRP came to be targeted against their own operation by the very organization that unwittingly provided them with cover. All that the agents could do was to stall and, when all else failed, blow their own cover. Whereupon the White House, lacking deniability, attempted to cover up—with the result that it was soon buried.

It was, as Throat insisted to Woodward, a frightening and dangerous time. Quoting Ecclesiastes, McCord raved "for a king who is devoted to his country!"[8] and, citing Samuel, praised the devastation of "Moab" and the destruction of the forces of "Hadezer."[9] McCord was by no means alone in his petitions to heaven. Slurred prayers rose in a fog of alcohol from the Oval Office itself, and telegrams praying for deliverance of the country from its President, or for the President's deliverance from his countrymen, came pouring into Congress and the White House.

[8]McCord, *Piece of Tape.*
[9]Ibid.

It was in this atmosphere of heart attacks and prayer that Lou Russell emerged from Washington Adventist Hospital. He was obviously a very sick man—pale, drawn and tremulous. Believing himself to have been poisoned, he seems to have undergone a change of heart in more ways than one. While still employed by McCord, he accepted a retainer from his friend John Leon, who was at that time conducting a counterinvestigation for the Republicans. Leon was convinced that Watergate was a setup, that prostitution was at the heart of the affair, and that the Watergate arrests had taken place following a tip-off to the police; in other words, the June 17 burglary had been sabotaged from within, Leon believed, and he intended to prove it.

Integral to Leon's theory of the affair was Russell's relationship to the Ervin committee's chief investigator, Carmine Bellino, and the circumstances surrounding Russell's relocation to Silver Spring in the immediate aftermath of the Watergate arrests. In an investigative memorandum submitted to GOP lawyer Jerris Leonard, Leon described what he hoped to prove: that Russell, reporting to Bellino, had been a spy for the Democrats within the CRP, and that Russell had tipped off Bellino (and the police) to the June 17 break-in. The man who knew most about this was, of course, Leon's new employee, Lou Russell. But Russell was not to be of any help. On July 2, 1973, two weeks after his release from the hospital, Russell suffered a second heart attack, which proved fatal, and he was buried on the following day.

Well aware of Russell's conviction that he had been poisoned, Leon was shocked and dismayed by his friend's death. In Russell's absence, however, there was no obvious way to get at the truth of his involvement in the Watergate affair. It occurred to Leon, therefore, that pressure had to be brought on Bellino, and as it happened, Leon was ideally situated to do just that. Among other things, Leon was a convicted wiretapper who had worked for Bellino in John F. Kennedy's 1960 campaign for the presidency. That presidential campaign had been an unusually rambunctious one, and Leon claimed to know where the bodies were buried. In the week after Russell's death, therefore, Leon contacted others who had worked with him for Bellino during that campaign. With a notary at his side, he obtained affidavits from himself and several others. Leon, former rogue CIA officer John Frank and former congressional investigator Edward M. Jones described physical surveillances that they had conducted for Bellino during the 1960 campaign. Joseph Shimon, once an inspector for the Washington Police Department, told in a sworn statement how he had been approached by another Kennedy operative in an attempt to secure keys and cooperation from hotel security personnel in a plan to bug rooms at the Wardman Park Hotel, where important members of Nixon's entourage were staying. Leon's affidavit went on to describe how he used an eavesdropping device known as "the big ear" to pick up room conversations of a prominent GOP official, and quoted another private detective in the employ of Bellino to the effect that candidate Nixon had been bugged while rehearsing for the debates with candidate Kennedy.[10] These sensational allegations were provided by Leon to Republican attorneys on July 10, 1973, exactly a week after Russell's funeral. Immediately, attorney Jerris Leonard conferred with RNC Chairman George Bush. It appeared to both men that a way had been found to place the Watergate affair in a new perspective and, perhaps, to turn the tide. A statement was prepared and a press conference scheduled at which Leon was to be the star witness, or speaker. Before the press conference could be held, however, Leon suffered a heart attack on July 13, 1973, and died the same day.

Jerris Leonard remembers that news of Leon's death "came as a complete shock. It was . . . well, to be honest with you, it was frightening. It was only a week after Russell's death, or something like that, and it happened on the very eve of the press conference. We didn't know what was going on. We were scared." With the principal witness against Bellino no longer available, and with Russell dead as well, Nixon's last hope of diverting attention from Watergate—slim from the beginning—was laid to rest forever.[11]

On July 13, as John Leon was literally breathing his last, presidential appointments secretary Alexander Butterfield told astonished Senate investigators that the President had bugged himself for the

---

[10]The Republican official whom Leon claimed to have bugged was Albert B. Hermann. The private detective whom Leon claimed to be quoting was Oliver Angelone.

[11]The release of the affidavits concerning the 1960 campaign occurred on July 24, 1973, and created a small sensation. Twenty-two senators signed a petition calling for an investigation to determine Bellino's fitness to serve as chief investigator for the Ervin committee. On August 3, 1973, a special subcommittee was formed to study the allegations. On November 19 the findings of that subcommittee were printed in the Congressional Record (pp. S-20817–21). In essence, the subcommittee found that while physical surveillance had been carried out against the Republicans in 1960, electronic eavesdropping could not be proved. The evidence was contradictory, and the subcommittee found "no basis for discharging Mr. Bellino."

past several years. Tapes existed that might well resolve the conflicting testimony of witnesses before the Ervin committee and, even
more important, would help to clarify the President's own role in
the cover-up by documenting what he knew and when he knew it.

In the months that followed, the Nixon administration would
fight a legal battle to preserve the confidentiality of the tapes until,
on August 5, 1974, Nixon would be forced to make public transcripts
of three conversations between himself and H. R. Haldeman. Those
conversations had taken place on June 23, 1972, less than a week after
the Watergate arrests. Within hours of the tapes' release it was
obvious to all that the "smoking gun" had been found: the transcripts documented the President's complicity in a gross obstruction
of justice—they demonstrated his early knowledge of Hunt and
Liddy's involvement in the break-in as well as his efforts to bury the
affair, partly by instigating a spurious controversy between the FBI
and the CIA. The President was guilty, and three days later, on
August 8, 1974, he would resign.

To Nixon's supporters the release of the tapes was unforgivable.
It showed the President's weakness, his unwillingness to fight to the
end. Why had he not burned the tapes as soon as their existence had
been revealed? In retrospect, Nixon agrees that this is precisely what
he should have done. That he failed to do so was "an error in
judgment."

If that is what it was, then the error was not entirely, or even
mostly, of Nixon's own making. White House assistant Patrick
Buchanan had urged Nixon to destroy the tapes from the moment
that their existence had become known. But others on Nixon's staff,
principally Alexander Haig and Fred Buzhardt, counseled against
doing so and prevailed. In any event, the tapes were not the only
smoking gun in evidence at the time. In early June 1974 White
House Chief of Staff Alexander Haig had ordered the Army's Criminal Investigation Command (CIC) to make a study of the President's alleged ties to organized crime and also to the smuggling of
gold bullion to Vietnam. The results of that investigation, carried
out by the CIC's Russell Bintliff at the direction of Colonel Henry
Tufts, were submitted to Haig in late July 1974.

Whether Haig confronted Nixon with the CIC report, or
whether Haig informed Nixon's successor, Gerald Ford, of the
report and its contents, is unknown. Bintliff himself is convinced
that both events occurred, and that the President's resignation fol-

lowed as a consequence of his investigative findings. But Bintliff cannot prove that, and since Haig refuses to discuss the issue, the matter remains in doubt. Still, Ford's pardon of Nixon, enacted in the absence of any criminal charges, remains a disconcerting anomaly in American history. Indeed, it seems almost a contradiction in terms. For how does one forgive and forget what has not been committed or what remains unknown?

In the end we are left with only an approximation of a major episode in our own history. In these pages we have answered many questions about the Watergate affair, raised others, and come closer to understanding its hidden meaning. But questions remain, questions that are unlikely to be answered in the absence of congressional powers to compel sworn testimony and to gain access to materials that have, to date, remained secret. Whether a forum exists to hear such testimony is doubtful. The Congress is content with the established order, itself a function of the established history—however distorted the latter may be. Those who were damaged by the affair no longer have much heart for controversy—not, at least, for this controversy. As for the CIA, it remains truculent, a stone wall, while the former President himself seems to wish for nothing more than that the affair be put behind him. In the end, the ultimate victims of the scandal are those who did not play a direct role in it: the public. You and I.

Appendixes

I. Some Notes on Paisley

That John Paisley worked closely with the Plumbers through the CIA's Office of Security is established by the Plumbers' own internal memoranda (quoted in the text) and the recollection of Paisley's wife (or widow), Marianne. This does not mean, of course, that Paisley had anything to do with "Watergate" proper, much less that his death or disappearance was somehow related to the scandal. The Ervin committee's studious disregard of all leads suggesting a connection between Watergate and the CIA ensured that Paisley himself would remain a lacuna insofar as the scandal was concerned. Nevertheless, if only as an addendum, Paisley's life and death are worth discussing.

The last known communication between John Paisley and the living came on September 24, 1978, when he radioed to friends that he intended to stay out late, sailing aboard his sloop, the *Brillig*, on Chesapeake Bay. As an afterthought, he asked that lights be left on for him at the dock so that he might navigate safely home that night, which, in fact, he did not do.

A day passed before a crab boat found the 31-foot *Brillig* abandoned at sea. The Coast Guard was notified, and boarded the boat. In its cabin was found an attaché case containing numerous classified documents, including a notebook with the names and telephone numbers of CIA officers under cover in various parts of the world. The Coast Guard did not examine the notebook carefully, but had they done so, they would have found David Young's name and, beside it, his White House interdepartmental telephone number (103-6699) —that is to say, Young's telephone number at the time that he headed the Plumbers.

In light of the classified documents and other materials aboard the boat, the Coast Guard notified the CIA's Office of Security. OS officers went to the boat and, according to Maryland State Police responsible for investigating the matter, removed a number of materials that should properly have been considered "evidence." These materials included the classified documents found on the boat and radio equipment of a disputed nature; according to some who were present at the seizure, the radio equipment included a burst-transmitter capable of communicating by means of satellite with receiving stations worldwide. The Office of Security's agents then went to Paisley's Washington apartment (he was estranged from his wife), where the missing man's papers were rifled and various objects confiscated (among them, a camera, tape-recordings and a Rolodex).

Days later, Paisley himself was found floating in the bay, his bloodless body bloated with gas, ripped by fish, and constricted by two sets of diving belts cinched around his waist. According to the coroner who conducted the autopsy, death was caused by a gunshot wound behind the victim's left ear. While no determination could be made as to whether the death was a homicide or a suicide, there was good reason to suspect foul play. The diving belts, for example, seemed calculated to sink the body out of sight, and it was difficult to reconcile Paisley's hypothetical "suicide" with his request that the dock lights be left on for his return. The site of the wound, behind the victim's left ear, also militated against the suicide theory, since Paisley himself had been right-handed, and would presumably have fired the gun with his right into the right side of his head. Adding to the suspicion that murder had been committed was the fact that no blood, brain tissue, weapon or expended cartridge was found aboard the *Brillig*, which suggested that the victim had been killed in the water or perhaps murdered elsewhere and his body dumped at sea.

Other anomalies had to do with the physical appearance of the corpse itself. It was, for example, four inches shorter than Paisley's own height; its waist was four inches smaller, and its weight twenty-five pounds lighter than Paisley's own dimensions. The corpse had no hair on its body; there was no blood left to type; and neither fingerprint nor dental records were immediately available for comparison—an unusual circumstance in view of Paisley's employment by the CIA. Despite all this, however, the cadaver was somehow "positively identified" as John Paisley's, whereupon it was cremated at a CIA-approved funeral home. No members of the family were permitted to view the body, the state coroner expressing the opinion that their sensibilities would have been shocked by its grotesque appearance.

Only later was "Paisley's widow," Marianne, permitted to see photographs that had been taken at the autopsy—this upon her own insistence after she learned of the numerous discrepancies between the characteristics of the corpse and those of her husband. Examining the photos, she said that she was not satisfied that the body in question was her husband's. Like him, she had been a CIA employee, and she was angry at the agency's handling of the matter. Aside from the agency's preemptive strike on the contents of both the *Brillig* and her husband's apartment, she resented CIA efforts to depict her husband as a low-echelon employee whose career had been spent entirely on the overt side of the CIA. That was a part of the agency's peculiar efforts to deflect the press's attention away from the Paisley case, and Marianne Paisley knew that the agency was lying.

The affair dragged on for months as skeptics attacked the official verdict of suicide. And then, in June 1979, two men volunteered new information. They were Harry Lee Langley, owner of the marina where Paisley had serviced the *Brillig*, and Dr. George Weems. County coroner for more than twenty years, Weems had been Lou Russell's best friend and personal physician. He had figured in Russell's disregarded alibi for the night of the Watergate arrests, but otherwise seems to have played no role in the affair. According to Weems, he and Lee Langley had seen the body when the Coast Guard first brought it to shore. In their opinion, "foul play" was involved. Weems told reporters that the body had marks on its neck, suggesting that it had "been squeezed or had a rope around it. . . . They were the type of things you see when people are strangled." Langley agreed, saying that the marks were either "a helluva rope burn" or "the throat had been slashed, because a bad gash ran from ear to ear."

Washington attorney Bud Fensterwald, representing Marianne Paisley, pointed out that "There was no suicide note. I'm told that 95 percent of suicide cases have left a note." More tellingly, perhaps, James McCord's former attorney cited as evidence of homicide the absence of blood, brain tissue, weapon and spent cartridge aboard the *Brillig*. "Strapping on two sets of diving belts, jumping off the boat with gun in hand, and then shooting yourself in the water is, to be charitable about it, a weird way to commit suicide," Fensterwald said. Yet another anomaly in the case, which Fensterwald also pointed out, is the fact that the corpse had a nine-millimeter bullet in its brain. According to ballistics experts, a nine-millimeter handgun, fired into the head from less than three feet, will *inevitably* result in an exit wound. Which strongly suggested that Paisley had been shot by someone else, from a distance, since no exit wound existed.

If Paisley's supposed suicide was "weird," his life was almost as interesting. A career CIA officer, he'd retired in 1974. This retirement simply meant that he had undergone a change in status, becoming a $200-per-day CIA consultant while employed at Cooper's and Lybrand. This is a large accounting firm whose clients have included both Robert Vesco and Air America, the latter a CIA proprietary whose involvement in opium trafficking and gold-bullion smuggling would one day embarrass the agency.

Paisley's CIA "consultancy" seems to explain the fact that four years after his supposed retirement he remained in possession of up-to-the-minute classified documents of the most strategic kind. An expert on nuclear weapons, computer and satellite systems, he was from 1976 until his putative death the executive director of the so-called B Team. This was a task force of civilian experts on strategic defense matters whose input did much to shape America's negotiating position at the SALT talks. The responsibility of the B Team was to make estimates of Soviet military policies and capabilities that would then be compared with the CIA's own analyses (i.e., the analyses of the A Team). Paisley was liaison between the A and B teams. Defense intelligence sources indicate that the documents recovered from the *Brillig* suggest that he was working on the B Team's product shortly before his death.

This was hardly the "low-level analyst" or consultant on "routine administrative matters" that the CIA pretended he had been when it was first questioned by reporters about the death. In a letter to the then CIA director, Stansfield Turner, written in the wake of her husband's death or disappearance, Mrs. Paisley suggested that the affair's explanation might rest with her husband's relationship to Soviet defector Yuri Nosenko, because, she claimed, only nine days prior to the *Brillig*'s discovery in the Chesapeake Bay, CIA officer John Hart had testified before the House Assassinations Committee on the subject of Nosenko. Hart was one of the CIA's principal defenders of Nosenko and a champion of his bona fides, despite the fact that the defector had himself just admitted to the same committee that he had been lying for years. In her letter to Admiral Turner, Mrs. Paisley wrote: "You know that John Paisley was deeply involved in Nosenko's indescribable debriefing. It has crossed my mind and that of others, that my husband's fate might somehow be connected with the Nosenko case. John's death and/or disappearance coincided with Nosenko headlines in every newspaper and news broadcast nationwide. Katherine Hart or Len McCoy will tell you that I am not a fool."

Katherine Hart is John Hart's wife, and was formerly Mrs. Paisley's supervisor at the CIA. Like Hart, McCoy was a Nosenko champion, defending his bona fides against all odds, and had made the phony defector a consultant to the counterintelligence staff following the 1974 ouster of Angleton from the CIA. It was in the wake of that ouster, itself the culmination of a purge that saw more than a thousand CIA officers forced into retirement, that McCoy became the new research chief on the counterintelligence staff. In that capacity he had flown to Vienna in 1975 to be present at a meeting that ended in catastrophe: the disappearance, and presumed death, of Nicolai Shadrin, a Soviet defector and longtime U.S. resident who had been coerced into a double agent's role targeted at the Soviet Union. (Shadrin was to have met with the KGB in Vienna and, in particular, with a supposed defector-in-place, one "Igor." Shadrin's disappearance is as controversial as Paisley's, in part because the CIA seems to have duped not merely the KGB but Shadrin and the FBI as well. The affair is a complicated one, but, in essence, Shadrin was duped because he was not told that Igor was pretending to be a defector-in-place, and the FBI was duped because it was not told that the CIA had strong doubts about the legitimacy of Igor's supposed defection.)

According to the *New York Times:*

> Government sources said it is not possible to rule out the theory that the Paisley affair touches on the existence of a Soviet "mole"—a deep-cover Soviet agent planted inside the Agency—and the dead officer's knowledge thereof. . . . At first, the CIA claimed the documents in Mr. Paisley's possession were relatively unimportant papers classified "for internal use only." Later it acknowledged that Mr. Paisley had kept materials pertaining to the top secret comparative study of Soviet nuclear capabilities conducted in late 1977 by a CIA group and . . . "Team B." The CIA also admitted that Mr. Paisley had served as coordinator of "Team B." The agency . . . also was said to have initially misinformed the White House and the Senate [Intelligence] Committee concerning Mr. Paisley's actual importance during his formal CIA career and afterward. It was called an effort to portray Mr. Paisley as simply a CIA analyst while, in reality, he had participated in numerous top-level clandestine intelligence operations. Government sources said specifically that Mr. Paisley's documents were "over and above" the "Team B" papers that were also found aboard the sloop. They said that the CIA was unable or unwilling to explain to the Senate panel why Mr. Paisley had the documents for so long after his formal retirement as deputy chief of the Office of Strategic Research. Normally, the sources said, documents of this nature would never be removed from CIA headquarters in Langley, Va.[1]

Paisley's participation in Nosenko's "indescribable debriefing" is well documented. So, also, is Paisley's subsequent friendship with Nosenko, whose North Carolina residence Paisley visited often. By themselves, these facts are hardly astonishing, but what makes them interesting is, as it happens, James Angleton's vigorous denial of them. Under oath before the Senate, and over drinks with a member of Paisley's family, Angleton swore that he himself had never met Paisley, that Paisley had never participated in Nosenko's debriefing, and that it was somehow "unthinkable" that the two men should ever have met each other. Why, Angleton would not say.

These remarks of the former CIA counterintelligence chief were met with

[1]From a report of the *New York Times News Service*, published in the Baltimore *Sun*, January 26, 1979, p. A-6.

widespread skepticism. Bud Fensterwald, among others, pronounced it incredible that Angleton and Paisley, career CIA officers with counterintelligence responsibilities involving the Soviet Union, should never have met.

In questioning Angleton, however, one is left with the distinct impression that he is telling the truth as he knows it. For whatever reason, he seems never to have encountered Paisley, and as for Paisley's relationship to Nosenko, Angleton was in ignorance of it. And that bothers Angleton quite a bit because, after all, it was his business to know such things.

This, in itself, may be illuminating. It is Angleton's curse that after decades of toiling anonymously in the most secret precincts of the intelligence community, he has come to be seen as a legend. Reporters tend to regard him as the agency's gray eminence, and his knowledge of U.S. intelligence matters is generally presumed to border on omniscience. But, as we have seen, the intelligence community is anything but a monolith. It is, and always has been, a collection of feudal, and sometimes feuding, estates. Angleton, then, is but one of several barons in a kingdom of perpetual twilight, a land of illusions, doubts and constantly shifting ground. One ought not, therefore, rule out the possibility that Angleton is speaking the truth when he claims to be ignorant of important matters that should have been within his purview.

That there should be differences of opinion within the CIA is not surprising. That the counterintelligence staff should doubt the bona fides of a Soviet defector in whom the Office of Security (and the FBI) had confidence is a bit grim, but disagreements of that kind can be handled in such a way as to minimize the damage, regardless of who is right and who is wrong. If Angleton is telling the truth, however, and is in fact ignorant of matters that were at once vital and within the domain of his CIA responsibilities, then the situation is worse than anyone has imagined. On the basis of Angleton's statements, one can only conclude that the Office of Security (and, in particular, its Security Research Staff) undertook counterintelligence operations that not merely were concealed from Angleton's staff but were in fact based upon conclusions diametrically opposed to those that Angleton and his men had reached. If this conclusion is correct, then the Office of Security and the SRS would appear to have acted as a counterweight within the agency, neutralizing the efforts of the counterintelligence staff.

In this connection, U.S. intelligence sources have been quoted to the effect that John Paisley was himself a counterintelligence operative (as distinct from an analyst). According to these reports, he was approached by the KGB at one of the earliest rounds of the SALT talks. He is said to have reported this contact to his superiors (which "superiors" we are not told), who urged him to take the bait and serve the United States as a double agent, feeding disinformation to the Soviets. Which, we are told, Paisley then proceeded to do for perhaps twenty years, a period encompassing a wave of Soviet defections, from Michael Goleniewski to Yuri Nosenko, Nick Shadrin to "Igor." Angleton's denials of these reports about Paisley's labors on the counterintelligence continuum mean little. If he is telling the truth, then Paisley would appear to have been operating on the "blind side" of that continuum, the side on which Hunt and McCord also labored, the side that Angleton was never permitted to see.

There is a certain logic, then, to Paisley's appointment as liaison between the Office of Security and the Plumbers. Beyond that, however, one cannot go. The Ervin committee's indifference to Paisley's identity and activities, coupled with his subsequent death or disappearance, makes it unlikely that his role in the affair will ever be fully understood.

II. "If I Was a Jury, I'd Convict Me"

Among those who are skeptical of the Ervin committee's investigation of the Watergate affair, there is a school of thought that holds that some Washington police knew in advance that the June 16–17 break-in was about to occur. In particular, skeptics as politically disparate as H. R. Haldeman and Carl Oglesby point the finger of suspicion at arresting officer Carl Shoffler.

The evidence cited by Oglesby and others is circumstantial, but not inconsiderable; and further investigation will yield even more information tending to bolster their suspicions. For example: the skeptics point out that Shoffler, injured on duty some months before, was assigned to desk work on the evening of June 16. They note that his shift ended at 10:00 P.M., and yet he voluntarily undertook a second shift, jointing a plainclothes tactical unit cruising the streets in the early-morning hours. The skeptics' suspicions are further aggravated by the fact that, contrary to police procedure, it was junior officer Shoffler (rather than Sergeant Paul Leeper) who responded to the dispatcher's call for assistance at the Watergate. Finally, the skeptics' theory is augmented by the fact that when the dispatcher's call came, Shoffler and his fellow officers were parked only a block or two from the Watergate, as if they were awaiting the dispatcher's summons.

As evidence of a conspiracy involving Shoffler and the police, these facts are hardly conclusive. Further investigation, however, unearths even more reasons to wonder about Shoffler's role. For example, June 17 was Shoffler's birthday. The relevance of that coincidence has to do with the fact that Shoffler's wife and children had gone to Pennsylvania on the afternoon of June 16, intending to spend the weekend at Shoffler's parents' home. Shoffler himself was to join them on the seventeenth, driving up from Washington to celebrate his birthday with Mom and Dad, the wife and kids. Given the long ride in front of him, it seems odd that he chose to work a second shift on that particular night.

Suspicion of Shoffler can only be heightened when we learn that the police officer deliberately changed Watergate guard Frank Wills's statement to reflect a nonconspiratorial interpretation of events. As we have seen, Shoffler acknowledges his misquotation of the Watergate guard, saying that he changed Wills's statement because the timing "did not make sense." Which, indeed, it did not unless the break-in was sabotaged from within, in which case Wills's statement makes perfect sense.

Adding to the suspicions surrounding Shoffler is the fact that he is no ordinary cop. Prior to joining the police department in Washington, he had served for years at the Vint Hill Farm Station in Virginia. This is one of the NSA's most important domestic "listening posts." Staffed by personnel assigned to the Army Security Agency (ASA), Vint Hill Farm is thought to be responsible for intercepting communications traffic emanating from Washington's Embassy Row. By itself, this proves nothing, but it is ironic that the police officer responsible for making the most important IOC (Interception of Communications) bust in American history should himself have worked in the same area only a few years earlier.

Shoffler's work at Vint Hill Farm was mentioned in passing in the staff interviews of the Ervin committee. This occurred as the result of an allegation against Shoffler that was made by his former commanding officer at Vint Hill Farm, Captain Edmund Chung. According to Captain Chung, he had occasion to dine with Shoffler in the aftermath of the Watergate arrests. Chung claimed that Shoffler told him the arrests were the result of a tip-off, that Baldwin and Shoffler had been in contact with each other prior to the last break-in, and that if Shoffler ever made the whole story public, "his life wouldn't be worth a nickel."

Shoffler, however, denied making those statements that Chung attributed to him. According to Shoffler, Chung attempted to "bribe" him with a $50,000 "loan" on the condition that Shoffler "confess" to prior knowledge of the break-in. Chung, of course, categorically denied having made such an offer, and the truth of the matter is impossible to ascertain. Questioned by the Senate, Chung did not seem to have any special knowledge of Watergate (other than his recollection of the dinner conversation with Shoffler), and neither did he seem to have any partisan political interest—he was, it appeared, a very ordinary sort of person. On the other hand, it was Shoffler—and not Chung—who first went to the Senate to report the disputed conversation. Shoffler told the Senate that he thought Chung had attempted to bribe him, and suggested that perhaps Chung was a CIA agent. To some, however, this suggestion had the appearance of the pot calling the kettle black. Shoffler himself had assisted the CIA in the past, and was personally acquainted with General Paul Gaynor. In the end, the Senate was unable to reconcile the accounts of Shoffler and Chung, and neither was it able to decide which, if either, of them was lying. The incident was therefore codified and buried as a "misunderstanding," though no one could say just how two friends could "misunderstand" each other so thoroughly.

The mysteries surrounding Shoffler are peculiar in the extreme, and none more so than the allegations made by one of Shoffler's former informants, Robert "Butch" Merritt. A homosexual, Merritt was employed by the police and the FBI in spying on the New Left, a task that ultimately led to his infiltration of the Institute for Policy Studies (IPS), a bête noire of America's right wing. According to Merritt, Shoffler approached him sometime after June 16, 1972, and asked him to undertake a bizarre assignment. If we are to believe the disaffected informant, Shoffler told him to establish a homosexual relationship with Douglas Caddy, stating falsely that Caddy was gay and a supporter of Communist causes. In fact, Caddy was about as conservative as they come, and there was no reason to suspect that he was anything but heterosexual. Indeed, testimony as to the conservatism of his politics was received by the Senate during its 1978 questioning of Tong Sun Park, Caddy's former roommate at Georgetown University.

SEN. WEICKER: "Who is Douglas Caddy?"

TONG SUN PARK: "Douglas Caddy was . . . not only my roommate, but also treasurer of the class and, I believe, he was Executive Director of Young Americans for Freedom. . . . [H]e was someone that I spent a lot of time with. So when I came to Georgetown, my exposure to the American politics was first to the conservative movement."[2]

[2]*Korean Influence Inquiry, Executive Session Hearings before the Senate Select Committee on Ethics,* 95th Cong., 2d sess., March–April 1978, Vol. 1, p. 153.

Predictably, perhaps, Shoffler ridicules Merritt's accusation, calling it absurd. One can only agree with the police detective, and yet, where Merritt is concerned, there appears to have been more going on than met the eye. To begin with, Merritt's place of residence was above a pornography store at the corner of Columbia Road and Eighteenth Street. The proprietor of the store, whose tenant Merritt was, was a notorious Washington pimp named Buster Riggin. Riggin was credited by the police with having brokered the division-of-labor agreement (day shift/night shift) between Columbia Plaza madam Lil Lori and Helen Henderson; reportedly, Riggin split a 40 percent commission on each trick.[3]

In an apparent coincidence, *Washington Post* reporter Carl Bernstein was an acquaintance of Riggin's, and a sometime visitor to the pimp's porn parlor. Years later, word of Bernstein's friendship with Riggin would cause the *Washington Post* enough concern that the then metro editor Bob Woodward would assign *Post* reporter Tim Robinson to "investigate Bernstein's sex life."[4] That, at least was Robinson's understanding of the unpleasant task, which, he said, was predicated upon fears that Riggin might somehow have compromised Bernstein in the past. Robinson says that he hated the investigation. Nevertheless, he confirmed Bernstein's friendship with Riggin, and found that Riggin had made presents of pornographic material to the Watergate hero. Robinson could not determine, however, whether Bernstein was ever involved with prostitutes working for Riggin, and found no evidence that Bernstein had ever provided Riggin with police information in return for sexual materials or favors. Which is not to say that the investigation was a dead end. Aside from confirming Riggin's gifts to Bernstein, Robinson uncovered a matter of fact that he found tantalizing. This was that Bernstein was a participant in the frolics of an informally organized "social club" whose membership seemed to be dominated by CIA officers, their girlfriends and wives. Among others who participated in the club's affairs, Robinson said, was John Paisley, who at that time was the CIA's liaison with the Plumbers.[5]

All of which may be no more than a chain of coincidences, though Shoffler himself, considering the information, shakes his head and says, "If I was a jury, I'd convict me." Of what? "I don't know. Setting up Watergate, or something. Prior knowledge." Would the jury be right? "Hell no! I'm innocent."

And, really, in spite of all appearances, Shoffler would indeed seem to be

---

[3]February 8, 1971, report to Lieutenant George F. Richards, Prostitution and Perversion Branch of the Washington police department: "Subject: Intelligence information concerning call girl and prostitution activities of Walter R. Riggin."

[4]Asked about the investigation of his former colleague, Woodward said that he did not recall the matter. Certainly the idea for such an investigation had not originated with him, he emphasized, and he did not "assign" Robinson to cover the story. Perhaps, Woodward speculated, Robinson had come to him with a rumor or allegation of impropriety concerning Bernstein. In that case, he would have told Robinson to investigate the matter in the same way that he would investigate allegations against any other public figure, "but perhaps a little more intensively than usual because of Carl's relationship to the *Post*," Woodward added.

[5]Bernstein did not return this writer's calls, but according to Robinson, Bernstein told him that he does not recall having met Paisley at any of the group's functions. Still, the existence of a "swingles" club dominated by spooks fascinated Robinson. Among the allegations that the reporter investigated but was unable to verify was a rumor to the effect that the Fairfax County Police facilitated the group's parties by blocking off the street leading to the house in which the parties were held.

innocent of everything but making the Watergate arrests. We may doubt his explanation for working overtime on June 16 ("I just felt like it"), and we may question his proximity to the Watergate at the time of the police dispatcher's call. His intelligence background may cause us to wonder, and the allegations of Chung and Merritt may give us pause. We may shake our heads at his having changed Frank Wills's initial statement to the police, and we may be bothered by the news that Shoffler was once nicknamed Little Blick by his colleagues in the department.[6] *But what we simply cannot do is fit Shoffler into a conspiracy theory about the Watergate affair.* Because, of course, it would never have made sense to tip him off. He could not have responded to the scene of the crime unless and until the police dispatcher had first issued a call for investigation of the premises at the Watergate. Once this is understood, Shoffler is revealed as a much maligned cop, a lint trap for ultimately senseless suspicions. Someone, after all, had to be closest to the scene of the crime that night, and it is just as well that it was Shoffler. Similarly, Shoffler's decision to work a second shift is not so unusual, *especially* in view of the fact that his family had left that same day for Pennsylvania: with no one to go home to, he might just as well have stayed out with the boys—which is what he did. Finally, Shoffler's intelligence background has all the fragrance of a red herring: because of it, were Shoffler to attempt to play the role of a secret agent, he would stand out as obviously as a Stetson in Moscow.

III: Ehrlichman vs. Cushman

Virtually every book about the Watergate affair contains the flat assertion that John Ehrlichman telephoned General Robert E. Cushman, Jr., deputy director of the CIA, to request assistance for Howard Hunt. That most writers have reported this without ever questioning it, despite Ehrlichman's testimony that he did not make the call, is understandable. The evidence that the call was made is overwhelming, and yet a careful analysis of the circumstances surrounding the alleged call suggests that it would have been impossible for Ehrlichman to have made it. If this is true, then the evidence seems to have been fabricated.

The issue is not an unimportant one because it goes directly to the question of Hunt's continuing relationship to the CIA. If Ehrlichman did not request the CIA to help Hunt, then the likelihood is that the agency extended that assistance unilaterally—not out of the goodness of its heart, but because Hunt's operational activities were useful to it.

According to Ehrlichman, "My one and only view of Howard Hunt came on July 7, 1971, the day after Charles Colson hired him. Charles Colson and Mr. Hunt came to my office for a brief introductory meeting. We discussed Hunt's project, which was to be a review of the content of the Pentagon Papers to determine their authenticity and accuracy. As far as I then knew, that was what he would be doing for the White House. That same day, . . . I left for San Clemente. As of then, I knew of no reason for Hunt to have CIA aid."[7]

---

[6]Shoffler says that he received this sobriquet as a consequence of his interest in Captain Blick's files.

[7]Nedzi report, pp. 335–36.

Colson's testimony supports Ehrlichman's, but only in part. According to Colson, "Mr. Hunt was hired basically to do research into the Pentagon Papers . . . , to find out how complete the Papers were, to find out how accurate they were . . ."[8] Colson emphasizes that Hunt's hiring had nothing to do with the Special Investigations Unit—which did not yet formally exist —and that no undercover work was contemplated for him. Nevertheless, Colson says, there was need for liaison between Hunt and the CIA, and, he claims, he told Ehrlichman of that on July 7. "The need for contact with the CIA," he subsequently swore to Congress, "was immediate in that one of Mr. Hunt's first assignments was to interview Lt. Col. Lucien Conein, who had been a principal CIA operative during the period of the Diem coup [in Vietnam]."[9]

But Colson is clearly mistaken, as Hunt himself points out in his memoirs. Both Hunt and Conein had retired from the CIA (or so we are told), and neither man required (or sought) permission to speak with the other. Hunt, moreover, had known Conein for more than twenty years. When the time came for the interview to take place, on July 8, Hunt conducted it in the White House, and in doing so, he had no need to resort to the disguises and spy paraphernalia that would later constitute the CIA's assistance to him.

The need for that assistance, Hunt says, was anticipated in connection with his plans to interview Clifton DeMotte, a former employee of Robert Bennett's, who was thought to have information about the Chappaquiddick scandal that would prove embarrassing to Senator Edward Kennedy. Hunt wanted to conduct that interview in full disguise. Even more relevantly, however, Hunt is explicit in his memoirs about the fact that he did not tell Colson about DeMotte, and the need for the CIA's technical support, until *after* he had left John Ehrlichman's office on July 7. According to Hunt, he'd shaken hands with Ehrlichman, and then gone off to have his "hiring papers" processed. He was required to fill out the usual forms, to submit to fingerprinting and photographing by the Secret Service, and was finally issued a White House pass. He was then sent over to the old Executive Office Building, assigned an office and given a typewriter and a safe, both of which had to be moved in from somewhere else. Secret Service technicians then arrived to provide him with the safe's combination. It was not, Hunt writes, until "That afternoon [that] I told Colson about Clifton DeMotte. . . ."[10] By which time, John Ehrlichman had enplaned for California.

According to General Robert E. Cushman, Jr., however, Ehrlichman telephoned him on July 7 to request technical support for Howard Hunt. Cushman was then deputy director of the CIA, and knew Hunt rather well. The two men had shared offices at the CIA in the 1950s, and Hunt had worked with Cushman when the latter was military assistant to Vice-President Johnson during preparations for the Bay of Pigs invasion.

Cushman's certainty that it was Ehrlichman who telephoned him is subject to doubt. When the controversy first surfaced, Ehrlichman questioned Cushman about the matter, and the general told him that he was "actually uncertain who had called him . . . , or the date of the call, which he believed was right after the Fourth of July."[11] In two subsequent memos to Ehrlich-

[8]Ibid., p. 584.
[9]Ibid., p. 582.
[10]Hunt, *Undercover*, pp. 148–49.
[11]Nedzi report, p. 333.

man, General Cushman wrote that he could not remember who had phoned to ask for CIA assistance to Hunt, though he did seem to recall that it "was someone with whom I was acquainted, as opposed to a stranger."[12] Perhaps it was not Ehrlichman, the general suggested; perhaps it was John Dean or Charles Colson.

The general's subsequent conviction that it was, indeed, John Ehrlichman was due to the belated discovery of notes concerning a CIA staff meeting that had taken place on the morning of July 8 and the still later discovery of what purports to be a verbatim transcript of Ehrlichman's alleged call to Cushman.

The staff notes were of one of the meetings that are held in CIA headquarters each morning at 9:00 A.M. The meeting is attended by nine or ten of the agency's principal officers, who report to the director on "things of interest that had come up in their particular area during the preceding day."[13] According to former CIA Director James R. Schlesinger, the staff notes reflect Cushman's statement that John Ehrlichman had called to say that Howard Hunt had been appointed a White House security consultant.[14]

What is said to be a verbatim account of that telephone call was unearthed by Cushman's secretary (the same secretary who had found the staff notes). The discovery was made even as the Senate's Ervin committee was writing its *Final Report* in 1974. According to the notes, which were apparently made on a "dead-key extension," Ehrlichman told Cushman: "I want to alert you that an old acquaintance, Howard Hunt, has been asked by the President to do some special consultant work on security problems. He may be contacting you sometime in the future for some assistance. I wanted you to know that he was in fact doing some things for the President. He is a long-time acquaintance with the people here. He may want some help on computer runs and other things. You should consider he has pretty much carte blanche."[15]

There are serious problems with this testimony, however. To begin with, the "need" for CIA assistance did not come up, according to Hunt, until after his interview with Ehrlichman and, it seems, after Ehrlichman had left Washington for the Western White House. By the time that Ehrlichman arrived in California and settled in, Cushman would almost certainly not have been in his East Coast office at the CIA. How, then, could Ehrlichman have notified Cushman on July 7 of Hunt's "needs" when he did not know of them? The records of the Western White House indicate that Ehrlichman did not place any calls to the CIA during his stay there. Thus, if we are to believe that Ehrlichman somehow contacted Cushman on the seventh of July, we must also believe that Colson telephoned Ehrlichman that night to inform him of Hunt's request, and that Ehrlichman then called Cushman later that evening, using a private telephone, and reached the general at his home. But that is ludicrous: the scenario implies a sense of urgency that is belied by the fact that Hunt did not meet with the CIA for weeks—and, in any case, Cushman's secretary would hardly have been present to make the verbatim transcript that surfaced so belatedly and fortuitously.

We may wonder, then, whether the transcript was a fabrication. That

[12] Ibid., pp. 324, 334.
[13] Ibid., p. 23.
[14] Ibid., p. 2.
[15] Ervin Committee's *Final Report*, p. 16.

possibility is, of course, a disturbing one, but as the discovery of the September bug has shown, there is a precedent in the Watergate affair for the fabrication of false evidence for the purpose of protecting CIA operations.

As for the transcript of Ehrlichman's reputed call to Cushman, it seems odd of Ehrlichman—if it was Ehrlichman—to refer to Hunt as "an old acquaintance." Presumably, the reference is to Hunt's long-standing acquaintance with Cushman, but how was Ehrlichman to have known of that? He had just met Hunt, for the first and only time; in their conversation, which had been brief and formal, Hunt had minimized (to obfuscation) his continuing connections to the agency. And Ehrlichman's alleged instruction that Hunt should be given "pretty much carte blanche" seems at once more generous and less prudent of Ehrlichman than he is known to have been.

In the end, the question is probably impossible to resolve. John Ehrlichman's testimony, however, is to the point: "I don't stand or fall on whether that phone call is ultimately determined to have come from me. As I see it, there is no culpability in that, in and of itself. So all I can do is be as honest with you as I know how to be in saying I don't recall the call. And, as I say, abide."[16]

He is correct, of course. It makes no difference to Ehrlichman if Ehrlichman made the call because, after all, he was fully empowered to do so. One tends to believe him because, in the end, he has little or no stake in the matter. The CIA, on the other hand, is anything but a disinterested party. If the agency unilaterally assisted Hunt, then that is a fact that it would certainly wish to conceal—not merely because to have done so would have been in violation of its charter (surely the single most raped document in American archives), but also because of what it would suggest about the agency's relationship to Hunt's activities: i.e., that the agency was voluntarily behind them, and may actually have instigated them.

IV. BREAK-IN OPERATIONS

AUGUST 26, 1971
Target: office of Dr. Lewis J. Fielding, Daniel Ellsberg's psychiatrist.
Entry point: front doors to building and office.
Entry means: pretext and "tip" to cleaning lady.
Purpose: reconnaissance in preparation for later entry.
Participants: Hunt and Liddy.
Result: Two rolls of film exposed in Tessina and Minox cameras. Former allegedly did not work; latter yielded photos of building's exterior. Film developed by CIA.

SEPTEMBER 3, 1971
Target: office of Dr. Fielding.
Entry point: front doors to building and office.
Entry means: crowbar.
Purpose: to photograph Dr. Fielding's notes on Ellsberg.

[16]Nedzi report, pp. 358–59.

Participants: Barker, De Diego and Martinez. Hunt and Liddy remained outside.

Result: Polaroid snapshots of havoc wrought in office. Other results disputed. Fate of Minox film, and its contents, uncertain.

MAY 26, 1972

Target: offices of the Democratic National Committee (DNC).

Entry point: B-2 level doors leading to underground garage.

Entry means: via corridor leading from Continental Room to door at B-2.

Purpose: to install bugging devices and photograph DNC records.

Participants: Hunt and Gonzalez remained in Continental Room after banquet. McCord kept surveillance from Howard Johnson's across the street.

Result: operation aborted upon report from McCord that corridor was site of an alarm.

MAY 27, 1972

Target: DNC.

Entry point: lobby of Watergate office building.

Entry means: burglars signed security log on pretext of visiting Federal Reserve Board on eighth floor.

Purpose: to install bugging devices and photograph DNC records.

Participants: Sturgis, Gonzalez, Barker, Martinez, McCord, De Diego and Pico. Hunt and Liddy remain in Watergate Hotel room.

Result: operation aborted when locksmith was unable to pick lock to DNC.

MAY 27–28, 1972

Target: DNC.

Entry point: doors at B-2 level.

Entry means: McCord taped open B-2 doors after signing security log.

Purpose: to install bugging devices and photograph DNC records.

Participants: Sturgis, Gonzalez, Barker, Martinez and McCord.

Result: Bugs allegedly installed; some forty photos taken; film apparently switched by McCord.

JUNE 17, 1972

Target: DNC.

Entry point: doors at B-2 level.

Entry means: McCord taped open doors at B-2 and elsewhere; when tape was discovered by guard, Sturgis and Gonzalez retaped the same doors.

Purpose: to install room bug in O'Brien's office, photograph DNC documents, break into Ida Wells's desk drawers.

Participants: Barker, Sturgis, Martinez, Gonzalez and McCord. Hunt and Liddy remain in Watergate Hotel room.

Result: Watergate arrests.

V. CIA Documents

My secretary, Mrs. *19* ,[17] and I frequently speculated about the possible involvement of Howard Hunt and the Watergate affair and the possible involvement of the Agency. I was aware that Hunt had frequently transmitted sealed envelopes via our office to the Agency. We had receipts for those envelopes but were unaware of the contents. However, Mr. *20* who had temporarily occupied my post during the illness of my predecessor, *21* and had been on hand to "break in" my immediate predecessor, *22* (who held the post for 30 days), had told me that he had opened one of the packages one day to see what Hunt was sending to the Agency. He said that the envelope was addressed to *6* and appeared to contain "gossip" information about an unknown person—he assumed that it had something to do with a psychological study of that person. Mrs. *19* subsequently confirmed this information.

Shortly after my assignment at the Executive Office Building, a new telephone list was issued by the White House and it contained Hunt's name. The Watergate news broke and Hunt was involved. The White House recalled the phone listings without reason and reissued them—we noted that Hunt's name had been deleted. As the news of the Watergate and Hunt's involvement spread, we—at a date unknown—decided that it was not prudent nor necessary to retain the receipts for envelopes which we had transmitted from him to CIA and we destroyed these receipts.

Earlier this year information appeared in the press which discussed Hunt and psychological studies. Linking the above information with these news reports I became concerned that the Agency might become publicly involved in this publicity and that it would be an embarrassment which the Agency should be aware of and prepared for. I had no knowledge of whether or not Hunt had arranged with Mr. Helms or someone else in authority for *6* do make psychological studies or whether Hunt had prevailed upon *6* because of some past connection or whether or not *6* was doing this officially or "free lance." But I felt strongly that the Agency should be aware of this Hunt— *6* connection, in case it did not already know.

I called Dr. Schlessinger and said that I had a confidential matter to discuss with him and visited him one night about 6:30. (I do not recollect the time but Mr. *1* fixes it at *2 May*.) I said that I was aware of some information that was not first hand but which I had verified and that I felt it had implications which might embarass the Agency and therefore he should be aware of this information so that he could prepare for public involvement, in case he was not already aware of it. I related what I knew about envelopes from Hunt to the Agency and specifically about the transmittal of information to *6* . He seemed surprised and unaware of any such link. He asked me, "What shall I do with *6* ." I said (somewhat taken aback at this question) that I thought he should first talk to *6* and get his side of the story and that I found it

---

[17]At the request of the CIA, numbers were substituted for the names of many of its employees who are mentioned in the statement. The number 24, for example, appears at the end of the statement, and represents Ratliff's signature. In addition, there is a handwritten notation, apparently written by Ratliff, that appears at the end of paragraph one. It reads: "We were also aware that Hunt passed 'gossip' items to Mr. Helms."

hard to believe that an individual of the Agency would become involved in something like this without some approval from higher authority within the Agency, also, that I was sure that someone had compiled the facts about the Agency's involvement with Hunt and the Watergate and that it should be available somewhere in the Agency if he had not already seen it. He seemed dismayed and bewildered that something like this could have happened and that he did not know about it. I repeated that I was sure that it was a matter of record somewhere and that it simply may not have been brought to his attention. He thanked me for reporting this information.

The following day I had a call from Mr. **23**, Dr. Schlessinger's assistant and a former colleague on the NSC staff, asking for a review of what I had reported saying that Dr. Schlessinger was very upset and had asked him to look into this right away. He wanted to know if I had any more details. I subsequently remembered another tangent to this subject and stopped in his office later that day (which was 3 May according to Mr. **1** timetable) and related it to him. It was that Mrs. **19** recalled that one day Hunt had come to see **22**, and they had talked behind closed doors. After the talk **22** came out and remarked to her that he was amazed, shocked and bewildered by the things that Hunt told him he was doing. He scratched and shook his head, remarked what an interesting job Hunt had, but revealed none of the details of his conversation. The only specific item he mentioned was a film that Hunt was working on for educational TV which involved one of the Nixon daughters. (I confirmed with Mrs. **19** this date that this is her recollection of this event.) **23** said that my report to Dr. Schlessinger was the first that the latter had heard that the Agency was in any way involved and that the Agency and Dr. Schlessinger, in particular, owed me a debt of gratitude for coming forward with this information. I remarked again that I would be surprised if the Agency had not already compiled a report on Hunt's involvement with the Agency because I knew that Mr. Helms was probably aware of some of Hunt's activities and might have authorized the use of **6** and that because of his **23** and Schlessinger's newness on the job they simply had not seen this material or had reason to ask for it. He said that he intended to find out.

23 subsequently told me that **22** had been interviewed and said that he knew nothing of Hunt's activities. I suggested that **20** be interviewed because not only had he opened at least the one Hunt— **6** envelope, but he may have additional information to report from his personal talks with Hunt.

23 told me sometime later that Schlessinger was awarding a medal to General Walters for his role in the Watergate affair and remarked again that my report had triggered the revelation of the iceberg. We joked about how the Generals always get the medals!

I do not believe that the subject has come up again until this time.

24

MEMORANDUM FOR THE RECORD BY MARTIN LUKOSKIE

Subject: Meeting with Robert Foster Bennett and his Comments Concerning E. Howard Hunt, Douglas Caddy and the "Watergate Five" Incident

The writer met with Robert Foster Bennett, President of the Robert R. Mullen Co. at noon on 10 July in the Hot Shop Cafeteria on H St., N.W. near

16th St. at his request to be brought up to date on developments resulting from the "Watergate Five" incident.

Mr. Bennett said that when E. Howard Hunt was connected with the incident, reporters from the Washington Post and he thought the Washington Star tried to establish a "Seven Days in May" scenario with the Agency attempting to establish control over both the Republican and Democratic Parties so as to be able to take over the country. Mr. Bennett said he was able to convince them that course was nonsense. He asked them why they should want to ruin himself, his Company and other innocent persons because the Company has innocently hired Hunt following his retirement from CIA.

Mr. Bennett was aware that the original plan when Hunt was hired was for Hunt to become president of the Company after a few years. Instead, General Foods stated its wish to buy the Company whereupon Robert R. Mullen revealed that he had given an option for purchase to Mr. Bennett and that General Foods would need to negotiate with Bennett. Douglas Caddy had for some time occupied space in the Mullen Company office as the representative of General Foods which is one of Mullen's principal accounts. For a time, consideration was given to a partnership arrangement with Bennett, Hunt and General Foods. Caddy, however, became so impossible in his attitude that Mr. Mullen complained to General Foods, and asked that Caddy be given new instructions concerning cooperation with the Mullen Company or removed. General Foods responded that inasmuch as Caddy had failed to comply with its instructions, he would be discharged. Bennett said Bob Mullen obtained for Caddy his job with the law firm currently employing him. According to Bennett, Caddy is extremely conservative in politics and is to the "far far right".

Howard Hunt was not able financially to become a partner. He then asked Bennett to increase his $24,000 annual salary to $37,000 which he would be earning if he had remained with CIA. Mr. Bennett refused the salary increase and suggested that he would give Hunt 10% of the profits if Hunt would buy 10% of the firm and assume responsibility for 10% of the notes which Bennett had signed when purchasing the Company from Bob Mullen. Hunt, after consulting his attorney, turned down the proposal and with Bennett's approval discussed his situation with Bob Mullen who somewhat bluntly informed Hunt that Bennett's proposal was a fair one. Hunt complained to Bennett that Mullen had practically suggested that he leave the company. Mr. Bennett believes, that as a result, Hunt is disenchanted with Bob Mullen and "has no love for Bob".

About this time, Hunt established his White House contact and with Bennett's blessing became a consultant at the White House for $100.00 per day and was placed on a consultant basis also by Bennett at $125.00. When asked by the writer whether Hunt had obtained the White House position via Charles Colson, as reported in the press, Mr. Bennett indicated there was some other intercession. (I have a feeling that Bennett may have participated in this as he said he had suggested the Mullen per diem arrangement to secure the $24,000 income with another position to enable Hunt to earn the requested $37,000). Mr. Bennett complained that Hunt had taken advantage of the Company on the arrangement. Mr. Bennett said the substitution of the consultant basis for the salary basis was fortunate as he was able to show the Grand Jury that Hunt had not worked for the Mullen Company on the same dates when with the White House.

Mr. Bennett said that the mission of the "Watergate Five" was to rejuvenate the bugging apparatus in the Democratic National Headquarters in the Watergate. Hunt had told Bennett that "THEY" had obtained such "great stuff" from the bug before it failed to function that McCord et al were instructed to install new batteries, mikes, et cetera, to make it work again. Hunt never identified "THEY" to Bennett who suspected that the order might have originated with Colson on a "I don't want to know about it, but get it done" basis, or the money came from a "RIGHTIST" group Caddy being "far far right" and Hunt also "conservative and to the right".

Bennett said the White House did a complete investigation of Colson's association with Hunt and had to be satisfied that he was not involved with Hunt's escapade with the Watergate Five. Of course, said Bennett, Colson could be lying. Bennett said he knew from an absolutely reliable source that President Johnson in 1968 had instructed the FBI to "bug" Nixon Headquarters and other prominent Republicans and surmised that the Republicans were retaliating without the knowledge of President Nixon.

Bennett recalled that Hunt had a private phone in his Mullen Company office in the name of "E. Warren" which was one of his pen names. Hunt had instructed initially that none but he was to touch the phone. He later asked that Mr. Bennett's secretary answer if Hunt was away from his desk. She commented to Bennett that a news story revealed that one of Hunt's pen names was E. Warren, the name used for the private phone. Mr. Bennett said that the D.C. police believe that nine persons were involved in the Watergate incident. The four men, besides McCord, who were arrested had registered at the Watergate in May as well as on the date of the abortive bugging attempt. Actually nine men ate dinner together that night. Bennett suspects that Hunt was among them and mentioned in this regard the trip taken to Miami by Hunt.

Mr. Bennett stated that Hunt's wife was aware of Hunt's association with the group involved in the Watergate incident. She said she can understand why Mr. Bennett fired Hunt and why the Mullen Company clients would refuse to have any future association with Hunt. Bennett claimed that he doesn't know Hunt's whereabouts.

Mr. Bennett related that he has now established a "back door entry" to the Edward Bennett Williams law firm which is representing the Democratic Party in its suit for damages resulting from the Watergate incident. Mr. Bennett is prepared to go this route to kill off any revelation by Ed Williams of Agency association with the Mullen firm if such a development seems likely. He said that he would, of course, check with CIA before contacting Mr. Williams for this purpose.

Mr. Bennett presently believes there is little likelihood of exposure of our current cover arrangements. He did not even mention [deleted] and said only that [deleted] was shocked by Hunt's alleged participation in the Watergate plot. If the Republicans are established as part of the conspiracy, [deleted] said he would not vote for Nixon!!!

Bennett will be in Miami at the Democratic Convention from Monday evening, July 10, to Friday July 14. Bob Mullen will return from the Far East on Tuesday, July 11. I made no reference to any concern on our part beyond the effect of the Watergate incident or that we plan to meet with Mullen and Bennett to discuss termination of the covers. I told Bennett that I would suggest to Ed Naeher, (Mullen cleared accountant) that if necessary Mullen should call me or I would telephone Mullen at this residence. Bennett stated that to this knowledge unwitting company employees knew me only as "a friend of Mr. Mullen's".

MEMORANDUM FOR THE DEPUTY DIRECTOR FOR PLANS BY ERIC EISENSTADT

MARCH 1, 1973.
Subject: Current Time Magazine Investigation of Robert R. Mullen & Company
  Connection with the Watergate Incident
  1. Mr. Robert R. Mullen, president of Robert R. Mullen & Company, telephoned CCS on the morning of February 28 to advise us that Sandy Smith, a reporter from Time Magazine, was in the Mullen office late on February 27. Smith started off by saying that "a source in the Justice Department" had informed him that the company "is a front for CIA." Mr. Mullen denied the allegation stoutly, said the company clients are all legitimate and offered to let Smith inspect the company books. Mr. Mullen said that his intuition was that Smith was on a fishing expedition and really had nothing to substantiate his suspicions.
  2. Smith had many questions concerning Howard Hunt, such as how he secured Mullen employment and his salary. Mullen told him the company paid him a salary initially and later on a consultant basis when Hunt began to work for The Committee to Re-elect The President. Smith wondered about Hunt's source of income as there is no record in above Committee's records of payments to Hunt. Mullen informed Smith that one source of Hunt's income was a government pension which, according to Hunt, was sizeable.
  3. Mullen told Smith that Bob Bennett, partner of Mr. Mullen who was on a business trip to California, really knew most about Hunt's later period of Mullen employment. Mullen could not show Smith records concerning Hunt as they are in possession of the U.S. attorney.
  4. Bob Mullen again telephoned CCS at 1650 hours on February 28, 1973 as a follow up to his morning call, as reported above.
  5. Sandy Smith, the Time reporter, was in again in the late afternoon and told Mr. Mullen that he had just seen, through an FBI contact, a paper allegedly personally delivered by a high official of CIA to Mr. Pat Gray, Acting Director of the FBI, during the height of the Watergate flap and investigation of Howard Hunt last summer.
  6. It was evident that Smith at least knew of the existence of such a document, but Mr. Mullen could only guess that Smith had not seen it long enough to digest it, or it said so little that Smith is trying to develop more information.
  7. Mr. Mullen continued to deny being associated with the Agency in any way except for the Cuban Freedom Committee, which connection had been admitted by Bob Bennett in June to the news media and U.S. attorney. Smith told Mullen, whom he has known for years because of some association in New York, that he is now in his "corner," but would be most unhappy if he ascertains that Mullen is not leveling with him. Mullen does not trust Smith and is certain Smith will write up whatever he develops. Presumably Time would publish the article.
  8. Mullen would like to know what exactly we gave the FBI so that he can tell Smith what he already seemingly knows from our memorandum to the FBI, or at least know how to best cope with Smith. Mr. Mullen requested that our reply be given him during the evening of February 28.
  9. Attached is a copy of the June 21, 1972 Memorandum for the Acting Director of the FBI from the Office of Security concerning Robert R. Mullen Company. Possession of the contents of this memorandum by Mr Smith could

be very damaging to the Agency and the company. The last sentence of Paragraph 4 states "Mr. Hunt was aware of the [deleted] under Robert R. Mullen and Company." Paragraph 5 relates that Mullen Company employees have been witting of the company's ties with the Agency. Paragraph 7 states "In view of the extreme sensitivity of this information concerning the current use of Robert R. Mullen Company, it is requested that this report be tightly controlled and not be disseminated outside your Bureau."

10. Mr. [deleted] C/CCS and the CCS case officer for the Mullen Company, Mr. [deleted], discussed the above with Mr. William E. Colby and Mr. [deleted] at approximately 1800 hours on February 28. It was agreed that Mr. Colby would recommend to the DCI, Mr. Schlesinger, that Messrs. Mullen and Bennett be allowed to read the June 21, 1972 memorandum to the FBI and that they be asked to continue to deny any allegation of association with the Agency, and state in effect that there was no relationship, and if there were, it, of course, would not be admitted. Mr. Schlesinger did endorse the proposed course of action.

11. Messrs. [deleted] of CCS met with Messrs [deleted] at 0840 hours on March 1 to inform them of developments which endanger [deleted], who is [deleted]. It was decided that Mr. [deleted], would further discuss with Mr. Mullen and Mr. Bennett, who had returned to his office, the Smith visits, allow them to read the June 21 memorandum to the FBI and propose the immediate return of [deleted] to the United States and termination of the [deleted] arrangement, the last with the company as the [deleted] cover was terminated in August 1972.

12. Mr. [deleted] and Mr. Mullen met near the Watergate and proceeded to Mr. Mullen's apartment in The Watergate through a rear entrance to The Watergate. Mr. Bennett joined them shortly and both read the memorandum. It developed that Mr. Bennett had been present during the second meeting with Mr. Smith, Messrs. Bennett and Mullen both were of the opinion that Smith had not seen the memorandum. They suggested that he had only heard of its existence or had seen an FBI report which summarized the memorandum and said only that the company had provided cover for the Agency. They felt that if he had seen the memorandum, he would not have re-visited them or would have accused them on the rather specific information contained in the memorandum. They said they would continue to deny any association with the Agency other than the already acknowledged relationship with the Cuban Freedom Committee.

13. They related that they told Smith he was beating a dead horse and that the Washington Star, Washington Post and Los Angeles Times had already investigated and concluded that the Mullen Company was not involved in the Watergate affair or the allegation that the CIA had instigated the Watergate Affair. It was an intriguing theory which just died. Mr. Bennett said that he recently spent four hours in Los Angeles being interviewed by a Newsweek reporter and had convinced him that the Mullen Company was not involved with the Watergate Affair. Mr. Bennett rather proudly related that he is responsible for the article "Whispers about Colson" in the March 5 issue of Newsweek. Mr. Bennett does not believe the company will be bothered much more by the news media which is concluding that "the company is clean and has gotten a bum rap while the real culprits are getting scot free." Mr. Bennett said also that he has been feeding stories to Bob Woodward of the Washington Post with the understanding that there be no attribution to Bennett. Wood-

wood is suitably grateful for the fine stories and by-lines which he gets and protects Bennett (and the Mullen Company). Typical is the article "Hunt Tried to Recruit Agent to Probe Senator Kennedy's Life" on page A16 of the Saturday, February 10, 1973, Washington Post. Mr. Bennett mentioned the February 12, 1973 meeting among himself, Mullen and [deleted], when he stated his opinion that the Ervin Committee investigating the Watergate incident would not involve the company. He said that, if necessary, he could have his father, Senator Bennett of Utah, intercede with Senator Ervin. His conclusion then was that he could handle the Ervin Committee if the Agency can handle Howard Hunt.

14. Mr. Bennett reported that he is well acquainted with a Charlotte, N.C. attorney named McConnell to whom Senator Ervin offered the position of Chief Investigator of the Congressional Committee investigating the Watergate incident. Mr. McConnell, according to Bennett, declined the offer because he is a millionaire in his own right and doesn't need to put up with all the grief associated with such a position. Mr. Bennett said he asked McConnell to inform Senator Ervin that Mullen, Bennett and the company are 100 percent clean of any involvement in the Watergate. Bennett is certain that Senator Ervin has no desire for revelation of legitimate arrangements or to harm the Agency and would avoid questions concerning our overseas cover placements. Mr. McConnell subsequently told Bennett that he and Senator Ervin were the only passengers on a private plane recently and he discussed Bennett, et al., as requested by Bennett. Mr. McConnell believes Senator Ervin accepted his comments and will not attempt to further involve the Mullen Company people. Bennett believes he and his Agency affiliations will not be raised again. He has the Ervin Committee shut off and feels the Agency has the responsibility to persuade Howard Hunt to avoid revealing what he knows of the history of cover arrangements with the company. Bennett and Mullen further suggested that the Agency "plug the leak" in the FBI and/or Department of Justice.

15. At this time the Agency proposal to bring [deleted] back PCS prior to 10 March with the legend that [deleted] has become disenchanted with the company, does not like the change in ownership from Mullen to Bennett, and has several job proposals he wishes to pursue was then set forth. They said that on the contrary Bennett and [deleted] get along very well and [deleted] is deeply involved in a Bennett project described as the art fund which purchases and sells paintings and works of art. Bennett said that [deleted] and his wife persuaded him to permit them to invest personal funds in the project and that [deleted] is devoting considerable time to it. It would do Bennett and the company serious financial damage if [deleted] were not permitted to continue. It is especially important that he be at the Art Show in Denmark from 1 June to 15 June 1973.

16. They proposed that they request [deleted] to return next week for consultation. The company has lost the [deleted] account to which [deleted] devoted some time, and new accounts are being acquired. [Deleted] could be kept away from the D.C. area by immediately assigning him to prepare the SUMMA Summit Conference in late April in Las Vegas. Summa consists of the top executives of the Howard Hughes companies and is the successor in the Hughes empire to the Hughes Tool Company, which was sold. [Deleted] with his extensive overseas experience, might also be a speaker. The Summa Conference will be a "dry run" for similar conferences which the Mullen Com-

pany is planning to do in representative West Coast cities to acquaint top West Coast executives with matters of interest such as pending legislation, overseas competition and the like. Bennett believes that if May 1 passes without any serious compromise, then nothing will happen. [Deleted] could then handle the Art Show in Denmark from 1 June to 15 June and then to [deleted], or if we prefer to [deleted] where the company has business interests sufficient to support [deleted], Mr. Mullen also recalled our proposal of two years ago for Mullen and Bennett took the position that while it was easy to ascribe the opening and closing of the [deleted] office to an experiment, it would be difficult to explain closing in Europe where [deleted] presence as a vice-president "has been trumpeted" among their clients, business prospects and in their literature. It would hurt badly and cost lots of money to end this one.

17. [Deleted] broached the possibility of the company continuing [deleted] as a legitimate employee if the Agency should be unable to locate an appropriate assignment for him. Mullen said that [deleted] does not possess qualifications such as the ability to write, which are requisite in the public relations field, but is an excellent businessman. [Deleted] asked whether [deleted] might assist in servicing the Hughes account. Bennett responded that the Hughes account cannot stand further expenses and some new clients would need to be obtained to support the legitimate employment of [deleted]. The proposal was not rejected, but it was evident that the company prefers the current arrangement which is supported almost entirely by the Agency. Mullen and Bennett both like and admire [deleted] and might employ him if [deleted] employment with the Agency terminates. It was learned that [deleted] discussed with Mullen the possibility of [deleted] resigning from the Agency to accept legitimate Mullen Company employment if the company needs so warranted.

18. Concerning the employment of Howard Hunt in May 1970, Bennett said smugly that he wasn't responsible and Mullen wishes now that he had not hired him. He recalled that as head of the Marshall Plan some 25 years ago, he became acquainted with Hunt. [Deleted] Retirement Division, Office of Personnel, approached Mullen concerning the qualifications needed by Hunt for public relations work and possible leads for employment for Hunt who was retiring from the Agency. Mullen stated that [deleted] "twisted my arm pretty hard" and he hired Hunt. Mullen believed that DCI, Helms, wished him to employ Hunt, especially after receipt of a splendid letter of recommendation of Hunt from Mr. Helms who later personally expressed his appreciation to Mr. Mullen for hiring Hunt. Mr. Mullen said he honestly believed, as a result of the pressure exerted by [deleted] that the Agency wished him to resolve problems attendant to Hunt's retirement by hiring Hunt.

19. The meeting concluded with Bennett stating that if [deleted] cover employment with Mullen is terminated before the mid-June ending of the Art Show in Denmark, it will hurt Bennett badly and cost him lots of money. Both then commented that they were "not letting the Agency down. Don't you let us down."

Bibliography

Agee, Philip. *Inside the Company: CIA Diary.* New York: Stonehill Press, 1975.

Allen, Gary. *Nixon's Palace Guard.* Boston: Western Islands, 1971.

Anderson, Jack (with George Clifford). *The Anderson Papers.* New York: Ballantine, 1974.

Bamford, James. *The Puzzle Palace: A Report on America's Most Secret Agency.* New York: Houghton Mifflin, 1982.

Barlett, Donald L., and James B. Steele. *Empire: The Life, Legend, and Madness of Howard Hughes.* New York: Norton, 1979.

Bernstein, Carl, and Bob Woodward. *All the President's Men.* New York: Simon & Schuster, 1974.

Boettcher, Robert, and Gordon L. Freedman. *Gifts of Deceit: Sun Myung Moon, Tongsun Park and the Korean Scandal.* New York: Holt, Rinehart & Winston, 1980.

Chester, Lewis, Cal McCrystal, Stephen Aris, and William Shawcross. *Watergate: The Full Inside Story.* New York: Ballantine, 1973.

Colby, William, and Peter Forbath. *Honorable Men: My Life in the CIA.* New York: Simon & Schuster, 1978.

Dash, Samuel. *Chief Counsel: Inside the Ervin Committee.* New York: Random House, 1976.

Dean, John. *Blind Ambition: The White House Years.* New York: Simon & Schuster, 1976.

Donner, Frank J. *The Age of Surveillance: The Aims and Methods of America's Political Intelligence System.* New York: Knopf, 1980.

Downie, Leonard, Jr. *The New Muckrakers.* Washington, D.C.: New Republic Book Company, 1976.

Doyle, James. *Not Above the Law: The Battles of Watergate Prosecutors Cox and Jaworski.* New York: Morrow, 1977.

Drew, Elizabeth. *Washington Journal: The Events of 1973–1974.* New York: Random House, 1975.

Ehrlichman, John. *Witness to Power: The Nixon Years.* New York: Simon & Schuster, 1982.

Epstein, Edward Jay. *Agency of Fear: Opiates and Political Power in America.* New York: Putnam, 1977.

———. *Legend: The Secret World of Lee Harvey Oswald.* New York: McGraw-Hill, 1978.

Ervin, Sam J., Jr. *The Whole Truth: The Watergate Conspiracy.* New York: Random House, 1980.

Garrow, David J. *The FBI and Martin Luther King, Jr.* New York: Norton, 1981.

Garza, Hedda (compiler). *The Watergate Investigation Index: Senate Select Committee Hearings and Reports on Presidential Campaign Activities.* Wilmington, Del.: Scholarly Resources Inc., 1982.

Haldeman, H. R. (with Joseph DiMona). *The Ends of Power.* New York: Times Books, 1978.

Hersh, Seymour M. *The Price of Power: Kissinger in the Nixon White House.* New York: Summit, 1983.

Hinckle, Warren, and William W. Turner. *The Fish Is Red: The Story of the Secret War Against Castro.* New York: Harper & Row, 1981.

Hunt, E. Howard. *Undercover: Memoirs of an American Secret Agent.* New York: Putnam, 1974.

Hurt, Henry. *Shadrin: The Spy Who Never Came Back.* New York: McGraw-Hill, 1981.

Jaworski, Leon. *The Right and the Power: The Prosecution of Watergate.* New York: Reader's Digest Press, 1976.

Johnson, George. *Architects of Fear.* Los Angeles: Tarcher, 1983.

Kalb, Marvin, and Bernard Kalb. *Kissinger.* Boston: Little, Brown, 1974.

Liddy, G. Gordon. *Will: The Autobiography of G. Gordon Liddy.* New York: St. Martin's Press, 1980.

Lukas, J. Anthony. *Nightmare: The Underside of the Nixon Years.* New York: Viking Press, 1976.

Magruder, Jeb Stuart. *An American Life.* New York: Atheneum, 1974.

Mankiewicz, Frank. *Perfectly Clear: Nixon from Whittier to Watergate.* New York: Quadrangle, 1973.

Marks, John. *The Search for the Manchurian Candidate: The CIA and Mind Control.* New York: Times Books, 1979.

Martin, David C. *Wilderness of Mirrors.* New York: Harper & Row, 1980.

McCord, James W., Jr. *A Piece of Tape.* Rockville, Md.: Washington Media Services, Ltd. 1974.

McLendon, Winzola. *Martha: A Biography of Martha Mitchell.* New York: Random House, 1979.

Meyer, Cord. *Facing Reality.* New York: Harper & Row, 1980.

Morris, Roger. *Haig: The General's Progress.* New York: Playboy Press, 1982.

New York Times staff. *The Watergate Hearings: Break-in and Cover-up.* New York: Bantam, 1973.

———. *The White House Transcripts.* New York: Bantam, 1974.

Nixon, Richard M. *RN: The Memoirs of Richard Nixon* (Volume 2). New York: Grosset & Dunlap, 1978.

Oglesby, Carl. *The Yankee and Cowboy War.* Mission, Kans.: Sheed Andrews & McMeel, 1977.

Phillips, David Atlee. *The Night Watch.* New York: Atheneum, 1977.

Powers, Thomas. *The Man Who Kept the Secrets: Richard Helms and the CIA.* New York: Knopf, 1979.

President's Commission on CIA Activities Within the United States. *Report to the President by the Commission on CIA Activities Within the United States.* Washington: Government Printing Office, June 1975.

Schilling, Joan H. (indexer). *The Watergate Index* (to material reported in the *Washington Post,* June 1972–June 1973). Wooster, O.: Micro Photo Division of Bell & Howell, 1975.

Sirica, John J. *To Set the Record Straight: The Break-in, the Tapes, the Conspirators, the Pardon.* New York: Norton, 1979.

Smith, Joseph Burkholder. *Portrait of a Cold Warrior.* New York: Putnam, 1976.

Smith, Myron J., Jr. *Watergate: An Annotated Bibliography of Sources in English, 1972–1982*. Metuchen, N.J.: Scarecrow Press, 1983.

Smith, R. Harris. *OSS: The Secret History of America's First Central Intelligence Agency*. Berkeley: University of California Press, 1972.

Stans, Maurice H. *The Terrors of Justice*. New York: Everest House, 1978.

Sullivan, William (with Bill Brown). *The Bureau: My Thirty Years in Hoover's FBI*. New York: Norton, 1979.

Summers, Anthony. *Conspiracy*. New York: McGraw-Hill 1980.

Sussman, Barry. *The Great Coverup: Nixon and the Scandal of Watergate*. New York: Crowell, 1974.

Szulc, Tad. *Compulsive Spy: The Strange Career of E. Howard Hunt*. New York: Viking Press, 1974.

———. *The Illusion of Peace: A Diplomatic History of the Nixon Years*. New York: Viking Press, 1978.

Thompson, Fred D. *At That Point in Time: The Inside Story of the Senate Watergate Committee*. New York: Quadrangle, 1975.

U.S. Department of Justice. Watergate Special Prosecution Force. *Report*. Washington: Government Printing Office, 1975.

U.S. House of Representatives. Committee on Armed Services. *Inquiry into the Alleged Involvement of the Central Intelligence Agency in the Watergate and Ellsberg Matters, Hearings before the Special Subcommittee on Intelligence*. 94th Cong., 1st sess., 1974.

U.S. House of Representatives. Committee on Government Operations. *Inquiry into the Destruction of Former FBI Director J. Edgar Hoover's Files and FBI Record-keeping, Hearings of the Government Information and Individual Rights Subcommittee*. 94th Cong., 1st sess., 1975.

U.S. House of Representatives. Committee on the Judiciary. *Statement of Information, Hearings*. 93d Cong., 2d sess., 1974.

U.S. Senate. Committee on Armed Services. *Transmittal of Documents from the National Security Council to the Chairman of the Joint Chiefs of Staff, Hearings*. 93d Cong., 2d sess., 1974.

U.S. Senate. Committee on the Judiciary. *Hearings on the Nomination of Earl J. Silbert to be United States Attorney*. 93d Cong., 2d sess., 1974.

U.S. Senate. Select Committee on Ethics. *Korean Influence Inquiry, Executive Session Hearings*. 95th Cong., 2d sess., 1978.

U.S. Senate. Select Committee on Presidential Campaign Activities. *Hearings*. 93d Cong., 1st sess., May 1972–June 1974.

U.S. Senate. Select Committee to Study Governmental Operations with respect to Intelligence Activities. *Alleged Assassination Plots Involving Foreign Leaders*. An Interim Report. 94th Cong., 1st sess., 1975.

Varner, Roy, and Wayne Collier. *A Matter of Risk: The Incredible Inside Story of the CIA's Hughes Glomar Mission to Raise a Russian Submarine*. New York: Random House, 1979.

White, Theodore Harold. *Breach of Faith: The Fall of Richard Nixon*. New York: Atheneum, 1975.

Woodward, Bob, and Carl Bernstein. *The Final Days*. New York: Simon & Schuster, 1976.

Wyden, Peter. *Bay of Pigs*. New York: Simon & Schuster, 1979.

Zumwalt, Elmo R., Jr. *On Watch*. New York: Quadrangle, 1976.

Index